A GUIDE TO MASSACHUSETTS CEMETERIES

By David Allen Lambert

NEW ENGLAND HISTORIC GENEALOGICAL SOCIETY
2002

International Standard Book Number: 0-88082-134-5
Library of Congress Control Number: 2001098389

Published by
New England Historic Genealogical Society
101 Newbury Street
Boston, Massachusetts 02116-3007

Printed by Royal Palm Press Inc., Charlotte Harbor, Florida.

TABLE OF CONTENTS

iii

INTRODUCTION

Many historians and genealogists like myself have struggled to determine the last resting place of our Massachusetts ancestors. One of the biggest problems that faced this type of research was the absence of a list of all cemeteries that exist in individual communities, and the whereabouts of cemetery records or gravestone transcriptions. In 1987, while working on the reference staff at the Massachusetts State Archives, I started a database of all cemeteries in the Boston area. This database grew to all those in Suffolk counties, then eventually Middlesex and Norfolk counties. After joining the reference staff at the New England Historic Genealogical Society, I realized the demand for this data was great. I continued for the past eight years collecting data on cemeteries throughout the Commonwealth of Massachusetts. After exhausting all the sources I could obtain in Boston, I then proceeded to contact the city or town clerk, librarian or local historian for each community. In some cases a wealth of material would be known, and in some cases I knew more from my research than they did. If the town or city personnel did not respond, I personally called or visited the town hall, library or cemetery department.

After locating each cemetery in a given town, I recorded the following information: the year the cemetery was consecrated, or the date of the earliest burial, or tombstone, the street or neighborhood in the community in which the cemetery was situated, and the existence of a physical building that houses the records for each cemetery. In some cases this was a church parish office or synagogue office located offsite. I avoided listing any home phone numbers for cemetery caretakers. My rationale behind this decision was the possibility of a change of employment for the individual caretaker, the change of their telephone number, and the possibility of the caretaker having died. For each cemetery I have included the author and title of any published book or article on the gravestone transcriptions of that cemetery. I have also personally visited and identified all the manuscript and typescript sources on cemetery transcriptions at both NSDAR (National Society of Daughter's of the American Revolution, Washington, D.C.) and NEHGS (New England Historic Genealogical Society, Boston, Mass.). Both of these repositories have a wealth of transcriptions created in the early nineteenth century. In the case of a weathered, broken or vandalized gravestone, this transcription may serve as the only record of the inscription. In the official series of Massachusetts Vital Records to 1850 published in part by NEHGS, one will find references in some death records with an abbreviation G.R. This abbreviation stands for Gravestone Record, and I have noted for each cemetery the identity of most of these cemeteries. The telephone number and address for each town and city clerk, and in some cases the cemetery department for each community is listed.

ACKNOWLEDGEMENTS

First I would like to thank my family for their support during the long process in researching and writing this book. I would like to acknowledge the assistance of Gabrielle Stone my editor, and Marsha Hoffman Rising, CG, FASG for their superb editing of this volume. I also appreciate the assistance of Dr. Ralph J. Crandall and Gary Boyd Roberts at NEHGS for their encouragement during the research stages of this work, as well as the assistance of Eric Grundset, the Director of the National Society of Daughters of the American Revolution Library, Washington, D.C. for help in locating many volumes of transcribed typescripts in their collection. The fine work of Chad Leinaweaver at NEHGS, who identified many gravestone transcriptions within printed volumes at NEHGS, was a great asset to the project. I would also like to thank all my colleagues at NEHGS for their support and advice while undertaking this project. I am grateful to the numerous town and city clerks, librarians and cemetery office employees who took time to answer my questions. And finally, I would like to acknowledge the continued assistance from individuals who assisted on specific cities and towns:

Charles E. Altwein Jr. (Easton), Linda Skinner Austin (Bolton), Marilyn R. Benaski (Norton), Chuckie Blaney (Sherborn), John Brigham (Sutton), Margaret Carroll (Millville), Wilfred Crozier (Quincy), Ann Dzindolet (Whitinsville), Margaret Goss (Arlington), Beverly Hurney (Weymouth and Newton), Joy E. Ingham (Norton and Turner's Falls), Mary Pearl (Marshfield), Richard Andrew Pierce (Boston Catholic cemeteries), Karen Proctor (Pembroke), Ruth Q. Wellner (Westminster), and Martin J. Wyndam III (Berkley).

This is the first time a book has been compiled attempting to catalog and give manuscript and printed sources for every cemetery in the Commonwealth of Massachusetts. Knowing there are cemeteries that may have been missed in my research, and are unknown to town officials, I welcome all additions. Also, I welcome any documented changes to the data I have supplied on each cemetery. It is with these requests we can all be certain that the largest majority of cemeteries have been correctly identified, and can be updated in a later edition of this volume.

David Allen Lambert

KEY

NEHGS: Manuscript or Typescript at the New England Historic Genealogical Society, Boston, Massachusetts. The number in brackets following is the call number for the item.

NSDAR: Manuscript or Typescript at the National Society of Daughters of the American Revolution, Washington, D.C. The number in brackets following is the call number for the item.

[G.R.]: Gravestone Records published in one of series of Vital Records prior to 1850.

Any book title that is followed by a call number. such as [F74/S18/1905] can be found at the New England Historic Genealogical Society in Boston, Massachusetts, or may be available from their Circulating Library.

This book is in loving memory of my parents George R. and Joan L. Lambert who taught me to respect the past and to remember my ancestors. And further dedicated to all my ancestors that lie in unmarked graves in cemeteries in Massachusetts.

ABINGTON (1712)
created from Bridgewater
Town Hall, 500 Gliniewicz Way, Abington, Mass. 02351 Tel: (781)-982-2112.

Adams Street Burying Ground Site
Adams St., near the junction of Pearl and Birch Sts., North Abington
Burials removed to the Mt. Vernon Cemetery.
"... in pine grove west of track between Abington and North Abington."
+ [G.R. 16] Vital Records of Abington, Massachusetts to the year 1850 (1912).

Bicknell Family Tomb
Washington and Chapel Sts.

Cobb Family Burying Ground
near 759 Hancock St., West Abington
+ [G.R. 18] *Vital Records of Abington, Massachusetts to the year 1850* (1912).

Cushing Family Tomb
Bedford St. and North Ave., North Abington

Gould Family Burial Ground (aka) Indian Cemetery (1798)
59 Sylvan Ct., North Abington
+ NEHGS [MS70/ABI/1]

Hillside Cemetery (18th century)
Randolph St., Rte. 139

Hunt Family Tomb
Bedford St., North Abington

Island Grove Cemetery (aka) Centre Cemetery and French's Burying Ground
on the hill at Island Grove Park.

Mount Vernon Cemetery (ca. 1732)
between 43–49 Pearl St., near Island Pond Grove
Tel: (781)-871-9488
+ [G.R. 1] *Vital Records of Abington, Massachusetts to the year 1850* (1912).
+ NEHGS [MS70/ABI/3], and [Mss/A/352]

Old Church Burying Ground
behind 325 Summer St.
+ [G.R. 14] *Vital Records of Abington, Massachusetts to the year 1850* (1912).

Plain Cemetery
behind 780 Hancock St., West Abington
+ [G.R. 19] *Vital Records of Abington, Massachusetts to the year 1850* (1912).

Richards Family Burial Ground (1750)
Chestnut St.

Torrey Family Burying Ground
High and Green Sts.

West Abington Cemetery
Randolph St., near Norfolk and Plymouth County line, West Abington.
+ [G.R. 17] *Vital Records of Abington, Massachusetts to the year 1850* (1912).
+ NEHGS [MS70/WES/1]

ACTON (1735)
from Concord
Town Hall, 472 Main St., Acton, Mass. 01720, Tel: (978)-264-9615
Cemetery Department, 472 Main St., Acton, Mass 02120, Tel: (978)-264-9644.

Mount Hope Cemetery (1848)
Central St., West Acton
Tel: records at the Woodlawn Cemetery Office, (508)-264-9644

North Acton Cemetery (aka)
North Part Cemetery (1701)
Carlisle Rd.
Tel: Woodlawn Cemetery, Everett (508)-264-9644
+ NEHGS [Mss/A/303]
+ NSDAR [G.R.C./S1/v. 111]

Woodlawn Cemetery (1737)
104 Concord Rd.
Tel: (978)-264-9644

ACUSHNET (1860)
from Fairhaven
Town Hall, 122 Main St., Acushnet, Mass. 02743, Tel: (508)-998-0215. Acushnet Cemetery Association, 91 Main St., Acushnet, Mass., Tel: (508)-995-1888

Achushnet Cemetery (1711)
91 Main St.
Tel: (508)-995-1888
+ [G.R. 39] *Vital Records of Dartmouth, Massachusetts to the year 1850* (1929).
+ NEHGS [MS/ACU/1] and [Mss/SL/SOU/15].
+ NSDAR [G.R.C./S1/v.128]

Ancient Long Plain Cemetery (17th century)
south of 1142 Main St., near Congregational Church
+ NSDAR [G.R.C./S1/v. 167]
+ Charles M. Thatcher, *Old Cemeteries of Southeastern Massachusetts.* (Middleborough, Mass., Middleborough Public Library, 1995) [F63/T53/1995/also Loan]

Dr. Josiah Burnham Graveyard (1895)
off Main St.

Congregational Church Cemetery (1823)
Lunds Corner

+ Charles M. Thatcher, *Old Cemeteries of Southeastern Massachusetts.* (Middleborough, Mass., Middleborough Public Library, 1995) [F63/T53/1995/also Loan]

Friends Burying Ground (aka)
Old Quaker Cemetery (1756)
Wing Rd. and Main St.

Long Plain Quaker Cemetery
behind the Long Plain Friends Meeting House, 1341 Main St., Rte. 105.

New Long Plain Cemetery
next to the Ancient Long Plain Cemetery
+ Charles M. Thatcher, *Old Cemeteries of Southeastern Massachusetts.*(Middleborough, Mass., Middleborough Public Library, 1995) [F63/T53/1995/also Loan]

Peckham Cemetery (1842)
Peckham Rd.

Sherman Cemetery (1861)
Peckham Rd., near Acushnet Ave.

Tabor Cemetery
on both sides of Wing Rd.
+ NSDAR [G.R.C./S1/v. 175]

Queen Anne Cemetery (a section of the Acushnet Cemetery)
"private burying ground adjacent to the Acushnet Cemetery"
+ [G.R. 41] *Vital Records of Dartmouth, Massachusetts to the year 1850* (1929).

ADAMS (1778)
Town Hall, 8 Park St., Adams, Mass. 01220, Tel: (413)-743-8320

Barker Family Cemetery (1839)
near 101 Leonard St.

Bellevue Cemetery (1886)
65 Park St.

Bowens Corner Cemetery (1808)
behind 35 East Rd.

Cole Cemetery (1820)
West Rd.

Daniels Court Cemetery (1807)
Daniels Ct.

Maple Grove Cemetery (1800)
Maple St.

Elijah Sprague Cemetery (aka) Town Cemetery (1800)
McGrath Rd.

St. Stanislaus Kostka Catholic Cemetery (1914)
Rte. 116, Orchard St.
Tel: St. Stanislaus Rectory, 8810 East Hoosac St., (413)-743-4224

Benjamin Vaughn Gravestone (1795)
off Walling Rd.

AGAWAM (1855)
from West Springfield
Town Hall, 36 Main St., Agawam, Mass. 01001, Tel: (413)-786-0400

Agawam Center Cemetery (1795)
Main St.
+ [G.R. 6] *Vital Records of West Springfield, Massachusetts to the year 1850* (1944).
+ NEHGS [Mss/SL/WES/18], [Mss/SG/LIN/52], and [Mss/A/304].

Springfield Street Cemetery (1829)
173 Springfield St., Feeding Hills
Tel: (413)-789-2330
+ [G.R. 8] *Vital Records of West Springfield, Massachusetts to the year 1850* (1944).
+ NEHGS [Mss/SL/WES/18]

Ferre Family Cemetery
(burials moved to Center Cemetery)
Main St.
+ [G.R. 10] *Vital Records of West Springfield, Massachusetts to the year 1850* (1944).
+ NEHGS [Mss/SL/WES/18], and [Mss/A/304]

Maple Grove Cemetery (1818)
325 Southwick St.
+ [G.R. 11] *Vital Records of West Springfield, Massachusetts to the year 1850* (1944).
+ NEHGS [Mss/A/304] and [Mss/SL/WES/18].

Old Feeding Hills Cemetery (1758)
South Westfield St.
+ [G.R. 7] *Vital Records of West Springfield, Massachusetts to the year 1850* (1944).
+ NEHGS [Mss/SL/WES/18], and [Mss/A/304]

Old North Burying Ground–Federal Hill Cemetery (1736)
Cooper St.
+ [G.R. 5] *Vital Records of West Springfield, Massachusetts to the year 1850* (1944).
+ NEHGS [Mss/SL/WES/18], and [Mss/A/304]

Smith Cemetery (1814)
South Westfield St.
+ [G.R. 9] *Vital Records of West Springfield, Massachusetts to the year 1850* (1944).

ALFORD (1773)
from Great Barrington
Town Hall, 5 Alford Center Rd., Alford, Mass. 01230, Tel: (413)-528-4536

Alford Center Cemetery (aka) Cemetery # 2 (1804)
Main St., in the center of town
+ NEHGS [Mss/A/306]
+ NSDAR [G.R.C./S1/v. 51]

Andrews Cemetery (1799)
West Rd.
+ NEHGS [Mss/A/306]

Calkins Family Cemetery (1838)
off West Rd.
+ NEHGS [Mss/A/306]

Jacquins–Baker–Rue–Coliver Burial Ground (1760)
West Rd.
+ NEHGS [Mss/A/306]

Johns Cemetery (aka) East Road Cemetery (aka) Cemetery # 3 (1785)
East Rd.
+ NEHGS [Mss/A/306]
+ NSDAR [G.R.C./S1/v. 51]

Lester–Church Cemetery (1811)
Cross Rd.
+ NEHGS [Mss/A/306]

Osborn–Otis Cemetery (aka) Cemetery # 1
North Egremont Rd.
+ NEHGS [Mss/A/306]
+ NSDAR [G.R.C./S1/v. 51]

Pierson Cemetery (1812)
off Cross Rd.
+ NEHGS [Mss/A/306]

Willoughby Family Cemetery (1828)
West Rd.
+ NEHGS [Mss/A/306]

AMESBURY (1668)
from Salisbury
Town Hall, 62 Friend St., Amesbury, Mass. 01913, Tel: (978)-388-8100
Cemetery Department, 21 Water St., Amesbury, Mass. 01913

Bartlett Cemetery (1888)
Rte. 110, Main St. behind the Union Cemetery.

Colby Family Cemetery (ca. 1825)
Meadowbrook Rd.

Friends Quaker Cemetery
Haverhill Rd., located within the Union Cemetery [this section has no marked stones]

Golgatha Cemetery (1654)
Macy St. (Route 110)

Mount Prospect Cemetery (1811)
Elm St. near Monroe St.

Old Corner Cemetery (1772)
Elm St., opposite Congress St.

Salisbury Plains Cemetery (1718)
Monroe St.
+ NEHGS [MS/AME/1]

St. Joseph's Cemetery (1883)
at the junction of Haverhill Rd., Rte. 150 and Rte. 110 off Rte. 495
Tel: St. Joseph's Rectory, 6 Allen Ct., Amesbury, Mass. (978)-388-0160

Salisbury Point Cemetery (1788)
Clark's Road, between Main and Macy Sts. (Rte. 110)

Small Pox Cemetery (aka) Kimball Cemetery (18th century)
Town Forest off Kimball Rd.

Tuxbury Farm Cemetery (1837)
Kimball Rd. (Rte. 110)

Union Cemetery (1663)
Haverhill Rd. Rte. 110, off Rte. 495
+ NSDAR [G.R.C./S1/v.28] Inscription Index only.

AMHERST (1759)
from Hadley

Town Hall, 4 Boltwood Ave., Amherst, Mass. 01002, Tel: (413)-256-4035. Cemetery Depar., 486 S. Pleasant St., Amherst, Mass. 01807, (413)-256-4050

North Amherst Cemetery (1823)
East Pleasant St.
+ NEHGS [Corbin Collection]

South Amherst Cemetery (1818)
between South East and Middle Sts.
+ NEHGS [Corbin Collection]

West Cemetery (aka) Center Cemetery (1737)
Triangle St.
+ NEHGS [Corbin Collection]
+ NSDAR [G.R.C./1932/S1/v. 16]

Wildwood Cemetery
70 Strong St.
Tel: (413)-549-4649

ANDOVER (1646)
Town Hall, 36 Bartlett St., Andover, Mass. 01810, Tel: (978)-623-8259

Christ Church Cemetery
25 Central St., corner of School St.
+ [G.R. 4]*Vital Records of Andover, Massachusetts to the year 1850* (1912).

Cornelius Gould Family Cemetery (1847)
Gould Rd.
+ NEHGS [Mss/SL/AND/6]

Phillips Chapel Cemetery (19th century)
Phillips Academy, Chapel Ave.
+ [G.R. 5]*Vital Records of Andover, Massachusetts to the year 1850* (1912).

Sacred Heart Cemetery (1904)
Corbett Rd.

St. Augustine's Cemetery (1855)
Lupine Rd.
Tel: St. Augustine's Rectory, 43 Essex St., Andover (978)-475-0050

South Parish Church Cemetery (17th century)
rear of 41 Central St.
Tel: South Parish Rectory, 41 Central St., Andover (978)-475-0321
+ [G.R. 2]*Vital Records of Andover, Massachusetts to the year 1850* (1912).
+ NSDAR [G.R.C./S1/v. 28] Inscription Index only.

Spring Grove Cemetery (1840)
Abbot St. and Spring Grove Rd.

Temple Emanuel Cemetery
Mt. Vernon Street

West Parish Cemetery (1704)
behind the West Parish Church, 129 Reservation Rd.
Tel: West Parish Rectory, 129 Reservation Rd., Andover (978)-475-3902
+ [G.R. 3]*Vital Records of Andover, Massachusetts to the year 1850* (1912).

Woodbridge Family Graveyard (1820)
behind 89 Jenkins Rd.

AQUINNAH (1998)
from Gay Head

Town Hall. 65 State Rd., R.R. 1, Aquinnah, Mass. 02535, Tel: (508)-645-2306

Gay Head Cemetery
off State Rd.

Indian Burial Ground
Old South Rd.

South Side Cemetery

ARLINGTON (1807)
from Cambridge
Town Hall, 730 Massachusetts Ave.,
Arlington, Mass. 02476, Tel: (781)-316-
3071.

**First Parish Burying Ground
(1732)**
Pleasant St.
+ NEHGS [Mss/A/305]

Mount Pleasant Cemetery (1843)
70 Medford St.
Tel: (781)-641-5483

**Prince Hall Masonic Burying
Ground (1856)**
7 Gardner St., East Arlington

St. Paul's Cemetery
Broadway St.

ASHBURNHAM (1765)
Town Hall, 32 Main St., Ashburnham,
Mass. 01430, Tel: (978)-827-4102.

Ashburnham New Cemetery (1814)
School St.
+ [G.R. 4]*Vital Records of Ashburnham,
Massachusetts to the year 1850* (1909).
+ NEHGS [Mss/A/353], and
[MS70/ASH/1]

Fairbanks Family Cemetery (1840)
Main St.
+ [G.R. 2]*Vital Records of Ashburnham,
Massachusetts to the year 1850* (1909).
+ NEHGS [Mss/A/353], and
[MS70/ASH/1]

**Meeting House Hill Burial Ground
(1760)**
Hastings Rd.
+ [G.R. 1]*Vital Records of Ashburnham,
Massachusetts to the year 1850* (1909).
+ NEHGS [Mss/A/353], [MS70/ASH/1]

Russell–Burbank Cemetery (1858)
Russell Hill Rd.
+ [G.R. 3]*Vital Records of Ashburnham,
Massachusetts to the year 1850* (1909).
+ NEHGS [Mss/A/353]

**St. Denis Catholic Cemetery
(1820)**
Kelton Rd.
+ NEHGS [MS70/ASH/1]

ASHBY (1767)
from Ashburnham, Townsend
and Fitchburg
Town Hall, 895 Main St., Ashby, Mass.
01431, Tel: (978)-386-2424

**Ashby First Parish Universalist
Church Burial Ground (1775)**
Main St., behind the First Parish
Universalist Church
Tel: (978)-386-5660
+NEHGS [Mss/A/308], [Mss/A/309],
[Mss/A/310], [Mss/A/348], and
[MS70/ASH/13]
+ NSDAR [MASS/COUNTIES/
MIDDLESEX/ ASHBY/GRC/N.H.]

Glenwood Cemetery
Main St.

West Ground Cemetery (1806)
West Rd.
+ NEHGS [MS70/ASH/12], and
[Mss/A/308]

ASHFIELD (1765)

Town Hall, 412 Main St., Ashfield, Mass. 01330, Tel: (413)-628-4441

Baptist Corner Cemetery (1775)

March Rd.
+ [G.R. 7] *Vital Records of Ashfield, Massachusetts to the year 1850* (1942).
+ NEHGS [Corbin Collection]

Beldingville–Ellis Burying Ground (1760)

Beldingville Rd.
+ [G.R. 6] *Vital Records of Ashfield, Massachusetts to the year 1850* (1942).

Briar Hill Cemetery (1828)

West Rd.
+ [G.R. 5] *Vital Records of Ashfield, Massachusetts to the year 1850* (1942).

Edson Cemetery Site (1844)

Barnes Rd.

Guilford Graves Cemetery (1814)

Bird Hill Rd.

Steady Lane Cemetery (aka) Hill Cemetery (1813)

Norton Hill Rd.
+ [G.R. 4] *Vital Records of Ashfield, Massachusetts to the year 1850* (1942).

Northwest Ashfield Cemetery (1793)

Apple Valley Rd.
+ [G.R. 2] *Vital Records of Ashfield, Massachusetts to the year 1850* (1942).

Plain Cemetery (1767)

Baptist Corner Rd.
+ [G.R. 8] *Vital Records of Ashfield, Massachusetts to the year 1850* (1942).

South Ashfield Cemetery (1818)

Williamsburg Rd.
+ [G.R. 3] *Vital Records of Ashfield, Massachusetts to the year 1850* (1942).

Spruce Corner Cemetery (1792)

Spruce Corner Rd.
+ [G.R. 1] *Vital Records of Ashfield, Massachusetts to the year 1850* (1942).

Wait Cemetery (1824)

Brier Hill Rd.

ASHLAND (1846)
from Framingham, Hopkinton and Holliston

Town Hall, 101 Main St., Ashland, Mass. 01721, Tel: (508)-881-0101

Ashland Cemetery (aka) Main Street Cemetery (19th century)

behind the Congregational Church
+ NEHGS [MS70/ASH/46], [Mss/A/311], and [Mss/A/359]

Simpson–Jones Family Burying Ground (aka) Old Revolutionary Burying Ground (1725)

Union and Esty Sts., next to St. Cecelia's Church
+ NEHGS [Mss/CB/95], and [Mss/A/311]

Small Pox Cemetery (18th c.)

Concord St., behind Mindess Middle School

Wildwood Cemetery (19th c.)

Chestnut St.
+ NEHGS [MS70/ASH/46], [Mss/A/311], and [Mss/A/359]

ATHOL (1762)

Town Hall, 584 Main St., Athol, Mass. 01331, Tel: (978)-249-4551
Cemetery Department, 584 Main St., Athol, Mass. 01331, Tel: (978)-249-4542

Calvary Roman Catholic Cemetery (1867)
Vine St.
Tel: Catholic Diocese Cemetery Office,
260 Cambridge St., Worcester, Mass.
(508)-757-7415

Chestnut Hill Cemetery (1786)
Chestnut Hill Ave.
+ NEHGS [MS70/ATH/1], and
[Mss/A/312]

Cosy Corner Cemetery
Conant Rd.

Ellinwood Cemetery (aka) Pleasant Street Cemetery (1842)
Doe Valley Rd.

Fay Cemetery (1834)
Conant St.
+ [G.R. 5]*Vital Records of Athol,
Massachusetts to the year 1850* (1910).

First Settler's Cemetery (aka) Old Indian Cemetery (1741)
399 Hapgood St.

Gethsemene Roman Catholic Cemetery (1911)
Brookside Rd.
Tel: Catholic Diocese Cemetery Office,
260 Cambridge St., Worcester, Mass.
(508)-757-7415

Highland Cemetery (1843)
Hillside Terr., off Pleasant St.
+ [G.R. 1]*Vital Records of Athol,
Massachusetts to the year 1850* (1910).
+ NEHGS [MS70/ATH/1], and
[Mss/A/312]

Mount Pleasant Cemetery (1741)
141 Mount Pleasant St.
+ [G.R. 2]*Vital Records of Athol,
Massachusetts to the year 1850* (1910).
+ NEHGS [MS70/ATH/1], and
[Mss/A/312]

Old Pleasant Street Cemetery (1773)
98 Pleasant St.
+ [G.R. 4]*Vital Records of Athol,
Massachusetts to the year 1850* (1910).

Silver Lake Cemetery (1875)
345 Silver Lake St.
+ NEHGS [MS70/ATH/1], and
[Mss/A/312]

Stratton Cemetery (1840)
Adams Rd.
+ [G.R. 6]*Vital Records of Athol,
Massachusetts to the year 1850* (1910).

Town Swamp Cemetery
New Sherburne Rd.

ATTLEBOROUGH (1694)
from Rehoboth
City Hall, 77 Park St., Attleborough,
Mass. 02703, Tel: (508)-223-2222

Briggsville Burial Ground (aka) Conant Cemetery (aka) Oak Knoll Cemetery (1752)
Park St., Briggs Corner, Rte. 118
+ Susan F. Salisbury, *Southern
Massachusetts Cemetery Collection*, Volume 2
(Bowie, Md., Heritage Books, 1996)
[F63/S25/1995/also Loan]
+ NEHGS [MS70/ATT/2],
[MS70/ATT/4],[Mss/A/313], and
[Mss/A/344]

Coombs Family Burial Ground (1847)
Pike Ave., between Thayer Farm Rd. and
Sheridan Circle.

Dodge Island Cemetery (1836)
off South Main St., Rte. 152 behind the
Hillside Cemetery
+ [G.R. 14] *Vital Records of Attleborough,
Massachusetts to the year 1850* (1934).

+ NEHGS [F74/A89/C3/1928]
Typescript in Mss.

Follett Family Burying Ground (1815)

Pike Ave.
+ [G.R. 8] *Vital Records of Attleborough, Massachusetts to the year 1850* (1934).
+ NEHGS [F74/A89/C3/1928]
Typescript in Mss.

Hillside Cemetery (1743)

Rte. 152, South Main St.opposite
Thurber Ave., Dodgeville
+ [G.R. 12] *Vital Records of Attleborough, Massachusetts to the year 1850* (1934).
+ Susan F. Salisbury, *Southern Massachusetts Cemetery Collection*, Volume 2 (Bowie, Md., Heritage Books, 1996)
[F63/S25/1995/also Loan]
+ NEHGS [F74/A89/C3/1928]
Typescript in Mss.

Indian Burial Ground

North Main St., Rte. 152 north

Jewish Cemetery

South Main St., Rte. 152 south
Tel: Congregation Agudas Achim
Temple, North Main St., Attleboro
(508)-222-2243

Newell Cemetery (aka) South Attleboro Cemetery (1715)

1502 West St., Rte. 123, South Attleboro
Tel: (508)-761-9050
+ [G.R. 13] *Vital Records of Attleborough, Massachusetts to the year 1850* (1934).
+ Susan F. Salisbury, *Southern Massachusetts Cemetery Collection*, Volume 2 (Bowie, Md., Heritage Books, 1996)
[F63/S25/1995/also Loan]
+ NEHGS [MS70/SOU/50],
[MS70/SOU/775], [Mss/SL/SOU/1],
[MS70/ATT/1], and [Mss/A/358]

North Purchase Cemetery–Balcom Burial Ground (1900)

825 North Main St., Rte. 152 north,
opposite Toner Blvd.
+ Susan F. Salisbury, *Southern Massachusetts Cemetery Collection*, Volume 2 (Bowie, Md., Heritage Books, 1996)
[F63/S25/1995/also Loan]

Old Kirk Yard Cemetery (aka) Old Second Parish Church Cemetery (1736)

Park St., Rte. 123, behind the Second Congregational Church.
+ [G.R. 1] *Vital Records of Attleborough, Massachusetts to the year 1850* (1934).
+ Marion Williams Pearce Carter, *Tombstone records of Old Kirk Cemetery* (Attleboro, 1928)
[F74/A89/C33/1928/also Loan]
+ NEHGS [MS70/ATT/2],
[Mss/A/344], and [F74/A89/C33/1928]
Typescript in Mss.

Peck Family Burial Ground (aka) Simmons Cemetery (1723)

North Main St., Rte. 152, in woods
opposite Elizabeth St.
+ [G.R. 3] *Vital Records of Attleborough, Massachusetts to the year 1850* (1934).
+ NEHGS [F74/A89/C3/1928]
Typescript in Mss

St. John's Cemetery (19th c.)

165 West St.
Tel: (508)-222-9086

St. Mary's Cemetery

Attleborough Falls
+ [G.R. 16] *Vital Records of Attleborough, Massachusetts to the year 1850* (1934).

St. Stephen's Cemetery (19th c.)

683 South Main St., Rte. 152 south,
behind St. Stephen's Church.
Tel: (508)-222-0641

Soloman Cemetery (1836)
Soloman St., off Maple St.
+ [G.R. 8] *Vital Records of Attleborough,
Massachusetts to the year 1850* (1934).
+ Susan F. Salisbury, *Southern
Massachusetts Cemetery Collection,* Volume 2
(Bowie, Md., Heritage Books, 1996)
[F63/S25/1995/also Loan]

Thayer Family Burial Ground (1845)
Wilmarth St., between Thayer Farm Rd.
and Sheridan Cir.
+ [G.R. 15] *Vital Records of Attleborough,
Massachusetts to the year 1850* (1934).

Wilmarth–Titus Cemetery (1732)
Briggs Corner
+ [G.R. 7] *Vital Records of Attleborough,
Massachusetts to the year 1850* (1934).

Woodlawn Cemetery (1754)
825 North Main St., opposite West St.
Tel: (508)-222-3446
+ [G.R. 2] *Vital Records of Attleborough,
Massachusetts to the year 1850* (1934).
+ Susan F. Salisbury, *Southern
Massachusetts Cemetery Collection,* Volume 2
(Bowie, Md., Heritage Books, 1996)
[F63/S25/1995/also Loan]
+ NEHGS [MS70/ATT/2],
[Mss/A/313], [Mss/A/344]

General Cemetery Reference for Attleboro:
+ NSDAR : Elisabeth H. Phillips,
Attleboro Burying Grounds pre dating 1830.
(1980).

AUBURN (1778)
from Leicester and Worcester
Town Hall, 104 Central St., Auburn,
Mass. 01501, Tel: (508)-832-7701

Auburn Town Cemetery (aka) Hillside Cemetery (1846)
73 Central St. Tel: (508)-832-7819

Center Burial Ground (1777)
Central St., next to the First
Congregational Church
+ [G.R.]*Vital Records of Auburn,
Massachusetts to the year 1850* (1900).

Cudworth Family Burial Ground
Prospect St.

Jewish Cemetery
off Strafford St.

West Auburn Burial Ground (1811)
Southbridge St.
+ [G.R.]*Vital Records of Auburn,
Massachusetts to the year 1850* (1900).

AVON (1888)
from Stoughton
Town Hall, Buckley Center, 65 East
Main St., Avon, Mass. 02322, Tel: (508)-
588-0414

Avon Cemetery (aka) East Stoughton Cemetery (1747)
Memorial Drive

Curtis Family Cemetery (aka) Page Street Cemetery (1812)
Page St.
+ NEHGS [MS70/AVO/1], and
[Mss/A/314]

East Main Street Cemetery (aka) Lower Road Cemetery (1777)
East Main St.
+ NEHGS [MS70/AVO/1], and
[Mss/A/314]

St. Michaels' Cemetery (ca. 1850)
East Spring St.
Tel: St. Michael's Rectory, 87 North
Main St., Avon, (508)-586-7210

AYER (1871)
from Groton
Town Hall, One Main St., Ayer, Mass.
01432, Tel: (978)-772-8215

St. Mary's Cemetery (19th c.)
Bishop Rd. near Park St.
Tel: St. Mary's Rectory, 31 Shirley St.,
Ayer (978)-772-2414

Woodlawn Cemetery (19th c.)
Rte. 110 Harvard Rd.

BARNSTABLE (1638)
Town Hall, 367 Main Street, Hyannis,
Mass. 02601, Tel: (508)-790-6240

Beechwood Cemetery (1834)
corner of Rte. 28 and Main St., Centerville
+ Paul J. Bunnell, *Cemetery inscriptions of
the town of Barnstable, Massachusetts and its
villages.* (Bowie, Md., Heritage Consulting,
1992) [F74/B14/B87/1992/also Loan]

Centerville Ancient Cemetery (1707)
Phinney's Lane, Centerville
+ NSDAR [G.R.C./S1/v. 3] and
[G.R.C./1932/S1/v. 16].
+ Paul J. Bunnell, *Cemetery inscriptions of
the town of Barnstable, Massachusetts and its
villages.* (Bowie, Md., Heritage Consulting,
1992) [F74/B14/B87/1992/also Loan]

Cobb Hill East and West Cemetery (1718)
Rte. 6A, Mill Way Rd.
+ Paul J. Bunnell, *Cemetery inscriptions of
the town of Barnstable, Massachusetts and its
villages.* (Bowie, Md., Heritage Consulting,
1992) [F74/B14/B87/1992/also Loan]

Crocker Park Cemetery (1950s)
Church St.
+ Paul J. Bunnell, *Cemetery inscriptions of
the town of Barnstable, Massachusetts and its*
villages. (Bowie, Md., Heritage Consulting,
1992) [F74/B14/B87/1992/also Loan]

Cummaquid Cemetery (1846)
Mary Dunn Rd., East Barnstable
+ Paul J. Bunnell, *Cemetery inscriptions of
the town of Barnstable, Massachusetts and its
villages.* (Bowie, Md., Heritage Consulting,
1992) [F74/B14/B87/1992/also Loan]

East and West Hillside Cemetery (1750)
Old Mill Rd., Osterville
+ Paul J. Bunnell, *Cemetery inscriptions of
the town of Barnstable, Massachusetts and its
villages.* (Bowie, Md., Heritage Consulting,
1992) [F74/B14/B87/1992/also Loan]

First Baptist Church Cemetery (1802)
Main St.

Hyannis Ancient Cemetery
South St., Hyannis

Lothrop Hill Cemetery (1694)
Main St., Rte. 6A
+ Paul J. Bunnell, *Cemetery inscriptions of
the town of Barnstable, Massachusetts and its
villages.* (Bowie, Md., Heritage Consulting,
1992) [F74/B14/B87/1992/also Loan]

Marstons Mills Cemetery (1775)
Rte. 149, Marstons Mills
+ Paul J. Bunnell, *Cemetery inscriptions of
the town of Barnstable, Massachusetts and its
villages.* (Bowie, Md., Heritage Consulting,
1992) [F74/B14/B87/1992/also Loan]

Old and New Mosswood Cemetery (1819)
Putnam Ave., Cotuit
+ Paul J. Bunnell, *Cemetery inscriptions of
the town of Barnstable, Massachusetts and its
villages.* (Bowie, Md., Heritage Consulting,
1992) [F74/B14/B87/1992/also Loan]

Oak Grove Cemetery (1868)
near 15 Sea St., Hynannis
+ Paul J. Bunnell, *Cemetery inscriptions of the town of Barnstable, Massachusetts and its villages.* (Bowie, Md., Heritage Consulting, 1992) [F74/B14/B87/1992/also Loan]

Oak Neck Cemetery (1800)
Oak Neck Rd.
+ Paul J. Bunnell, *Cemetery inscriptions of the town of Barnstable, Massachusetts and its villages.* (Bowie, Md., Heritage Consulting, 1992) [F74/B14/B87/1992/also Loan]

Old West Barnstable Cemetery (1712)
corner Rte. 149 and 6A, West Barnstable
+ Paul J. Bunnell, *Cemetery inscriptions of the town of Barnstable, Massachusetts and its villages.* (Bowie, Md., Heritage Consulting, 1992) [F74/B14/B87/1992/also Loan]

St. Francis Xavier Catholic Cemetery (1929)
Pine St.
+ Paul J. Bunnell, *Cemetery inscriptions of the town of Barnstable, Massachusetts and its villages.* (Bowie, Md., Heritage Consulting, 1992) [F74/B14/B87/1992/also Loan]

St. Mary's Episcopal Church Memorial Garden
Rte. 6A

St. Patrick's Cemetery (1832)
Barn and Elm Sts.

Sandy Street Cemetery (1796)
Rte. 6A
+ Paul J. Bunnell, *Cemetery inscriptions of the town of Barnstable, Massachusetts and its villages.* (Bowie, Md., Heritage Consulting, 1992) [F74/B14/B87/1992/also Loan]

South Street Cemetery (aka) Paupers Cemetery (1737)
South St., Hyannis

+ Paul J. Bunnell, *Cemetery inscriptions of the town of Barnstable, Massachusetts and its villages.* (Bowie, Md., Heritage Consulting, 1992) [F74/B14/B87/1992/also Loan]

Universalist Cemetery (1826)
Elm St.

BARRE (1753)
from Rutland
Town Hall, 2 Exchange St., Barre, Mass. 01005, Tel: (978)-355-5003

Adams Yard Cemetery (1778)
South St., opposite Adams St.

Barnes–Parker–Barre Falls–School District #17 Cemetery (1810)
Coldbrook Rd., on the grounds of the US Army Corps of Engineers property.

Barre School District #4 Cemetery (1820)
Farrington Rd.

Barre School District #9 Cemetery (1790)
Phillipston Rd.
+ NEHGS [MS70/BAR/11]

Barre School District #10– Hathaway Burial Yard (1800)
Spring Hill Rd.

Bassett Yard Cemetery Site
Skelly and Baldwinville Rd., burials were removed.

Buckminster Burial Yard (aka) South Burial Grounds (1766)
South St.

Caldwell Cemetery (1746)
Fruitland Rd.

+ *Caldwell Burying Ground* (Barre, Mass.:
Gazette Print, 1914) [F74/B15/C355]
+ NEHGS [MS/BAR/10], and
[MS70/BAR/11].

**Coldbrook Cemetery (aka) Baptist
Church Cemetery (1847)**
Granger Rd., just off Rte. 122
+ NEHGS [MS70/BAR/11]

Glen Valley Cemetery (1864)
Valley Rd.

Hemenway Cemetery (1850)
Phillipston Rd.

**High Plains Cemetery (aka) Pratt
Burial Ground (1813)**
Peach St.

Jenkins Yard Cemetery (1807)
Sheldon Rd.
+ NEHGS [MS70/BAR/11]

Jane King Yard Cemetery (1836)
Silver Brook Rd.

Kendall Plains Burial Grounds (1811)
Old Coldbrook Rd., opposite second
entrance to Felton Field.
+ NEHGS [MS70/BAR/11]

Ezekiel Lee Tomb (1804)
off Old Hardwick Rd.

Lee Burial Yard (1819)
Wauwinet Rd.
+ NEHGS [MS70/BAR/11]

Lincoln Cemetery
Pleasant St., opposite Washburn Rd.

**Riverside Cemetery (aka) Harwood
Cemetery (1800)**
Covered Bridge Rd., off Granger Rd.

Prince Walker Burial Plot (1858)
off Hubbardston Rd.

St. Joseph's Cemetery (1900)
Valley Rd., Rte. 32 near the junction with
Rte. 122. Tel: St. Joseph's Rectory, 29
South St., Barre (978)-355-4463

White Family Burial Yard Site
Cole Rd.

BECKET (1765)
Town Hall, 557 Main St., Becket, Mass.
01223, Tel: (413)-623-8934

Becket Center Cemetery (1757)
55 Y.M.C.A. Rd., behind the First
CongregationalChurch

Gibbs Cemetery (1829)
off Tyringham Rd.

Harris Burial Ground (1797)
off Captain Whitney Rd.

North Cemetery (1854)
across from 2994 Main St.

West Becket Cemetery (1837)
Rte. 20 1/4 mile east of Route 8 South

Yokum Pond Cemetery (1802)
Tyne Rd.

BEDFORD (1729)
from Billerica and Concord
Town Hall, 10 Mudge Way, Bedford,
Mass. 01730, Tel (781)-275-0083
Cemetery Department, 314 Great Rd.,
Bedford, Mass. 01730, Tel: (781)-275-7605

Old Burying Ground (1650)
Springs Rd.

+ Mrs. W. Alden Burrell, *Ye olde burying ground, Bedford, Massachusetts*. (Lexington, 1945) [F74/B2/B9/1945]
+ *Gravestone Survey, Map and Data Bases of the Old Burying Ground, Bedford, Massachusetts*. (Bedford, Mass.: Bedford Historical Society, 1995) [F74/B2/B43/1995]
+ NEHGS [Mss/C/3013], and [F74/B2/B9/1945] Typescript in Mss
+ NSDAR [G.R.C./S1/v. 271] and [G.R.C./S1/v. 111]

Shawsheen Cemetery (1849)
Great Rd., near Shawsheen Rd.

BELCHERTOWN (1761)
Town Hall, 2 Jabish St., Belchertown, Mass. 01007, Tel: (413)-323-0400
Cemetery Department, 290 Jackson St., Belchertown, Mass. 01007, Tel: (413)-323-0415

Bacon Family Cemetery Site
Burials were removed to Quabbin Park Cemetery, Ware, Mass. 1938.
+ NEHGS [MS/70/WAR/15]

Belchertown State School Cemetery (1920)
30 State St.

Blue Meadow Cemetery
Burials were removed to Quabbin Park Cemetery, Ware, Mass. 1938.
+ NEHGS [MS/70/WAR/15]

Dark Corner Cemetery (1769)
Rural Rd.

Dwight Cemetery (1790)
Federal St.

Evergreen Cemetry (aka) West Hill Cemetery (1795)
Munsell St.
+ NEHGS [Corbin Collection]

Hill Crest Cemetery (aka) Sleeterville Cemetery (1807)
Bardwell and Pine Sts.
+ NEHGS [Corbin Collection]

Jenks Cemetery (1845)
South Liberty and South Sts.

Kimball Cemetery (1867)
Kimball St.

Lake Vale Cemetery (aka) Pond Hill Cemetery (aka) Metacomet Cemetery (1755)
Bay Rd.
+ NEHGS [Corbin Collection]

Liberty Cemetery
South St.

Mount Hope Cemetery
Park St.
+ NEHGS [Corbin Collection]

Pine Grove Cemetery
Turkey Hill Rd.

Rural Cemetery (aka) Coleman
Rural St.
+ NEHGS [Corbin Collection]

South Center Cemetery (1752)
Mill Valley Rd.
+ NEHGS [Corbin Collection]

BELLINGHAM (1719)
from Dedham, Mendon and Wrentham
Town Hall, 2 Mechanic St., Bellingham, Mass. 02019, Tel: (508)-966-5827

Center Cemetery (19th century)
Rte. 14–Mechanic St.
+ Susan F. Salisbury, *Southern Massachusetts Cemetery Collection*, Volume 1

(Bowie, Md., Heritage Books, 1995)
[F63/S25/1995/also Loan]
+ NEHGS [Mss/A/342]

Center Street Cemetery (18th c.)
Center St.
+ Susan F. Salisbury, *Southern Massachusetts Cemetery Collection*, Volume 1 (Bowie, Md., Heritage Books, 1995)
[F63/S25/1995/also Loan]
+ NEHGS [MS70/BEL/10]

North Bellingham Cemetery (1714)
Hartford Ave.

Oak Hill Cemetery (18th c.)
Rte. 126, Hartford Ave.
+ Susan F. Salisbury, *Southern Massachusetts Cemetery Collection*, Volume 1 (Bowie, Md., Heritage Books, 1995)
[F63/S25/1995/also Loan]

Precious Blood and St. John Baptist Cemetery (1956)
310 ½ Wrentham Rd.
Tel: (508)-883-6600

Rakeville Cemetery (1818)
Lake St.
+ Susan F. Salisbury, *Southern Massachusetts Cemetery Collection*, Volume 1 (Bowie, Md., Heritage Books, 1995)
[F63/S25/1995/also Loan]

Scammell Cemetery (1757)
Depot St.
+ Susan F. Salisbury, *Southern Massachusetts Cemetery Collection*, Volume 1 (Bowie, Md., Heritage Books, 1995)
[F63/S25/1995/also Loan]

Scott's Crossing Cemetery (aka) South Bellingham Cemetery (1732)
Center St., South Bellingham
+ NEHGS [Mss/A/342], [MS70/BEL/10], [Mss/A/316], and [MS70/BEL/11]

+ NSDAR [G.R.C./S1/v. 28]
Inscription Index only.

Ukrainian Cemetery
Center St.

Union Cemetery (1804)
Rte. 140, Mechanic St.
+ Susan F. Salisbury, *Southern Massachusetts Cemetery Collection*, Volume 1, 1995

Wilcox Cemetery
Lake St.

BELMONT (1859)
from Waltham, Watertown, and Cambridge
Town Hall, 455 Concord Ave., Belmont, Mass. 02478, Tel: (617)-489-8203

Belmont Cemetery (1859)
121 Grove St., Tel: (617)-489-8287

BERKLEY (1735)
from Dighton and Taunton
Town Hall, One North Main St., Berkley, Mass. 02779, Tel: (508)-822-3348.

Algerine Street Cemetery Site
Algerine St., south of Bryant St.
+ Gail E. Terry, *Berkley, Massachusetts Cemetery Inscriptions* (Bowie, Md., Heritage Books, 1997) [F74/B27/T47/1997]

Apps Hill Cemetery
Berkley St.
+ Gail E. Terry, *Berkley, Massachusetts Cemetery Inscriptions* (Bowie, Md., Heritage Books, 1997) [F74/B27/T47/1997]
+ NEHGS [Mss/SG/HOD/6/60]

Berkley Common Cemetery (1775)
North Main St.

+ Gail E. Terry, *Berkley, Massachusetts Cemetery Inscriptions* (Bowie, Md., Heritage Books, 1997) [F74/B27/T47/1997]
+ NEHGS [Mss/SG/LIN/5/23], [MS70/BER/4], [Mss/A/316], and [Mss/A/320]

Edward Bobbett Gravesite (1675)

Berkley St.
+ Gail E. Terry, *Berkley, Massachusetts Cemetery Inscriptions* (Bowie, Md., Heritage Books, 1997) [F74/B27/T47/1997]
+ NEHGS [Mss/SG/LIN/5/23]

Nathan G. Bowen Cemetery Site

Jerome and Pine Sts.
+ Gail E. Terry, *Berkley, Massachusetts Cemetery Inscriptions* (Bowie, Md., Heritage Books, 1997) [F74/B27/T47/1997]

Briggs Family Cemetery (1) and (2)

35 Briggs Ln.
+ Gail E. Terry, *Berkley, Massachusetts Cemetery Inscriptions* (Bowie, Md., Heritage Books, 1997) [F74/B27/T47/1997]

Nathan Briggs Gravesite (1760)

Green St.
+ Gail E. Terry, *Berkley, Massachusetts Cemetery Inscriptions* (Bowie, Md., Heritage Books, 1997) [F74/B27/T47/1997]
+ NEHGS [MS70/BER/1]

Bryant and Anthony Street Gravesite

corner of Bryant and Anthony Sts.
+ Gail E. Terry, *Berkley, Massachusetts Cemetery Inscriptions* (Bowie, Md., Heritage Books, 1997) [F74/B27/T47/1997]
+ NEHGS [MS70/BER/1]

Burt Family Cemetery (1802)

Plain St. East, near Seymour St. extension. Next to the Caswell–Clark Cemetery.
+ Gail E. Terry, *Berkley, Massachusetts Cemetery Inscriptions* (Bowie, Md., Heritage Books, 1997) [F74/B27/T47/1997]

Burt–Dillingham Family Cemetery Site

Berkley St., Burt's Corner
+ Gail E. Terry, *Berkley, Massachusetts Cemetery Inscriptions* (Bowie, Md., Heritage Books, 1997) [F74/B27/T47/1997]

Caswell–Clark Cemetery (1811)

Plain St. East, next to the Burt Family Cemetery.
+ Gail E. Terry, *Berkley, Massachusetts Cemetery Inscriptions* (Bowie, Md., Heritage Books, 1997) [F74/B27/T47/1997]
+ NEHGS [MS70/BER/17], and [Mss/A/322]

Dean Cemetery (1840)

Howland Rd., near Bay View Ave.
+ Gail E. Terry, *Berkley, Massachusetts Cemetery Inscriptions* (Bowie, Md., Heritage Books, 1997) [F74/B27/T47/1997]
+ NEHGS [MS70/BER/12], and [Mss/A/321]

Dean–Dillingham Cemetery (1707)

next to 150 Bay View Ave., Assonet Neck
+ NEHGS [Mss/SG/LIN/5/23], and [Mss/SG/HOD/6/60]

Dighton Rock Cemetery Site

on the grounds of the Dighton Rock State Park
+ Gail E. Terry, *Berkley, Massachusetts Cemetery Inscriptions* (Bowie, Md., Heritage Books, 1997) [F74/B27/T47/1997]

Fletcher Cemetery Site

(graves moved to Mayflower Cemetery, Taunton)
Padelford St.
+ Gail E. Terry, *Berkley, Massachusetts Cemetery Inscriptions* (Bowie, Md., Heritage Books, 1997) [F74/B27/T47/1997]

Fox Cemetery (aka) North Cemetery (1704)

Bay View Ave.
+ Gail E. Terry, *Berkley, Massachusetts Cemetery Inscriptions* (Bowie, Md., Heritage Books, 1997) [F74/B27/T47/1997]
+ NEHGS [MS70/BER/1], [MS70/BER/4], [Mss/SG/LIN/5/23], [Mss/A/317] and [Mss/A/319]

Haskins Cemetery Site

Bryant St., near the Freetown line.
+ Gail E. Terry, *Berkley, Massachusetts Cemetery Inscriptions* (Bowie, Md., Heritage Books, 1997) [F74/B27/T47/1997]

Haskins Cemetery (1853)

Church St., near Myricks St.
+ Gail E. Terry, *Berkley, Massachusetts Cemetery Inscriptions* (Bowie, Md., Heritage Books, 1997) [F74/B27/T47/1997]
+ Charles M. Thatcher, *Old Cemeteries of Southeastern Massachusetts.* (Middleborough, Mass., Middleborough Public Library, 1995) [F63/T53/1995/also Loan]

Hathaway Family Cemetery Site (1788)

Mill and Myricks St.
+ NEHGS [Mss/SG/LIN/5/23], and [Mss/SG/HOD/6/60]
+ Gail E. Terry, *Berkley, Massachusetts Cemetery Inscriptions* (Bowie, Md., Heritage Books, 1997) [F74/B27/T47/1997]

Lydia Jones Gravesite (1838)

Bayview Ave., north of Grinnell St.
+ Gail E. Terry, *Berkley, Massachusetts Cemetery Inscriptions* (Bowie, Md., Heritage Books, 1997) [F74/B27/T47/1997]

Norcutt Cemetery (1809)

Berkley St.
+ Gail E. Terry, *Berkley, Massachusetts Cemetery Inscriptions* (Bowie, Md., Heritage Books, 1997) [F74/B27/T47/1997]

North Main Street Cemetery Site (19th century)

North Main St., between Berkley Common and Berkley St.
+ Gail E. Terry, *Berkley, Massachusetts Cemetery Inscriptions* (Bowie, Md., Heritage Books, 1997) [F74/B27/T47/1997]

Paull Family Cemetery (1810)

Padelford St., near Hill St.
+ Gail E. Terry, *Berkley, Massachusetts Cemetery Inscriptions* (Bowie, Md., Heritage Books, 1997) [F74/B27/T47/1997]
+ NEHGS [Mss/A/318]

Phillips Cemetery

Bayview Ave., south of Grinnell St.
+ Gail E. Terry, *Berkley, Massachusetts Cemetery Inscriptions* (Bowie, Md., Heritage Books, 1997) [F74/B27/T47/1997]

Tew Cemetery (1815)

Bay Meadow Dr.
+ Gail E. Terry, *Berkley, Massachusetts Cemetery Inscriptions* (Bowie, Md., Heritage Books, 1997) [F74/B27/T47/1997]

Townsend Family Cemetery (1799)

Padelford St.
+ Gail E. Terry, *Berkley, Massachusetts Cemetery Inscriptions* (Bowie, Md., Heritage Books, 1997) [F74/B27/T47/1997]
+ NEHGS [Mss/A/318]

Webster Cemetery (1841)

across from 29 Algerine St.
+ Gail E. Terry, *Berkley, Massachusetts Cemetery Inscriptions* (Bowie, Md., Heritage Books, 1997) [F74/B27/T47/1997]
+ NEHGS [Mss/A/340], and [MS70/BER/17]

BERLIN (1784)
from Bolton and Marlborough
Town Hall, Woodward Ave.,
Berlin, Mass. 01503, Tel: (978)-838-2931

North Cemetery
across from 235 Highland St.

Old Burying Ground (1769)
Linden St., Berlin Center
+ Esther K. Whitcomb, *Inscriptions from burial grounds of the Nashaway towns: Lancaster, Harvard, Bolton, Leominster, Sterling, Berlin, West Boylston, and Hudson, Massachusetts.* (Bowie, Md: Heritage Books, 1989) [F74/L2/I57/1989/also Loan]

Wheeler Cemetery (1867)
Highland St.

South Cemetery (1857)
181 Pleasant St.
+ NEHGS [MS70/BER/52]

BERNARDSTON (1762)
Town Hall, 38 Church St., Bernardston, Mass. 01337, Tel: (413)-648-5400

Center Cemetery–New Cemetery (1826)
Depot St.
+ NEHGS [Corbin Collection]

Hessian Cemetery (19th century)
Eden Trail

Old Cemetery (aka) Village Cemetery (1757)
Meadow Rd.
+ NEHGS [Corbin Collection]

BEVERLY (1668)
from Salem
City Hall, 191 Cabot St., Beverly, Mass. 01915, Tel: (978)-921-6000

Beverly Farms Cemetery (1840)
Hart St.

Central Cemetery (19th century)
Dane and Hale Sts.

Dodges Row Cemetery (1704)
enter at 292 Dodge St.
+ [G.R. 2]*Vital Records of Beverly, Massachusetts to the year 1850* (1907).

North Beverly Cemetery (1770)
Cabot and Conant Sts.
+ [G.R. 3]*Vital Records of Beverly, Massachusetts to the year 1850* (1907).

Old Cemetery (1681)
Abbott St.
+ William C. Carlson, *The genealogical history of the Abbot Street Cemetery* (Salem, Mass: W.C. Carlson, 1998) [F74/B35/C37/1998]
+ [G.R. 1]*Vital Records of Beverly, Massachusetts to the year 1850* (1907).
+ NSDAR [G.R.C./S1/v.94]

St. Mary's Cemetery (20th c.)
114 Brimball Ave.

Second Parish Cemetery (1717)
Conant St., near Elderly Housing complex

BILLERICA (1655)
Town Hall, 365 Boston Rd., Billerica, Mass. 01821, Tel: (978)-671-0924. Cemetery Department, 130 Andover Rd., Billerica, Mass. 01821 Tel: (978)-671-0946

Old Corner Burying Ground (aka) North Cemetery (1706)
Pollard St. and Salem Rd.
+ [G.R. 3] *Vital Records of Billerica, Massachusetts to the year 1850* (1908).
+ NEHGS [Mss/A/347], [MS70/BIL/1], [Mss/SL/BIL/4], and [MS70/NOR/60]
+ NSDAR [G.R.C./S1/v. 283]

Fox Hill Cemetery (1856)
130 Andover Rd.
+ [G.R. 5] *Vital Records of Billerica, Massachusetts to the year 1850* (1908).
+ NEHGS [MS70/BIL/1]

Job Hill Family Cemetery (1828)
Nashua Rd. (Rte. 4) and Dudley Rd.
+ [G.R. 4] *Vital Records of Billerica, Massachusetts to the year 1850* (1908).
+ NEHGS [MS70/BIL/1], and [Mss/A/347]

North Burial Ground (1816)
Salem Rd., and Pollard St.
+ [G.R. 2] *Vital Records of Billerica, Massachusetts to the year 1850* (1908).
+ NEHGS [MS70/BAR/11]

Roger's Family Tomb (1803)
off High St., near Tewksbury town line.

Small Pox Burying Ground (18th c.)
off High Street

South Burying Ground (1663)
Concord Rd., between French St. and Middlesex Turnpike
+ NEHGS [Mss/A/347], and [MS70/BIL/1]

BLACKSTONE (1845)
from Mendon
Town Hall, Municipal Center, 15 St. Paul St., Blackstone, Mass. 01504, Tel: (508)-883-1500

Blackstone Cemetery (1725)
near Mendon St.
+ [G.R. 16] *Vital Records of Mendon, Massachusetts to the year 1850* (1920).
+ Susan F. Salisbury, *Southern Massachusetts Cemetery Collection*, Volume 1 (Bowie, Md., Heritage Books, 1995) [F63/S25/1995/also Loan]

Cass Cemetery
south of Lincoln St.
+ [G.R. 25] *Vital Records of Mendon, Massachusetts to the year 1850* (1920).

Cook's Cemetery (aka) Four Families Cemetery (1838)
in woods off Elm St.

Elm Street Cemetery (19th century)
Elm St., East Blackstone
+ [G.R. 24] *Vital Records of Mendon, Massachusetts to the year 1850* (1920).
+ Susan F. Salisbury, *Southern Massachusetts Cemetery Collection*, Volume 1 (Bowie, Md., Heritage Books, 1995) [F63/S25/1995/also Loan]

Gaskill Family Cemetery (1809)
106-108 Blackstone St.
+ [G.R. 18] *Vital Records of Mendon, Massachusetts to the year 1850* (1920).
+ Susan F. Salisbury, *Southern Massachusetts Cemetery Collection*, Volume 1 (Bowie, Md., Heritage Books, 1995) [F63/S25/1995/also Loan]

Pickering Cemetery (1750)
south of Farm St.

Polish National Catholic Church of Our Saviour Cemetery (1924)
Farm St., behind St. Charles Cemetery.
Tel: (508)-762-0220

Poor Farm Cemetery (1860)
247 Mendon St.

Quaker Meeting Cemetery (1799)
Elm St., on the grounds of the Friends
Meeting House.
+ [G.R. 23] *Vital Records of Mendon,*
Massachusetts to the year 1850 (1920).
+ NEHGS [MS70/MIL/762]

St. Charles Cemetery (1860)
Farm St.
+ Susan F. Salisbury, *Southern*
Massachusetts Cemetery Collection, Volume 1
(Bowie, Md., Heritage Books, 1995)
[F63/S25/1995/also Loan]

St. Charlotte's Cemetery
Gaskill and Farm Sts.
+ [G.R. 22] *Vital Records of Mendon,*
Massachusetts to the year 1850 (1920).

St. Michael's Ukrainian Orthodox
Cemetery (1914)
Farm St., behind St. Paul's Cemetery

St. Paul's Cemetery (1848)
North Main St.
Tel: St. Paul's Rectory, 48 St. Paul St.,
Blackstone, Ma 01504, (508)-883-6726
+ [G.R. 21] *Vital Records of Mendon,*
Massachusetts to the year 1850 (1920).
+ Susan F. Salisbury, *Southern*
Massachusetts Cemetery Collection, Volume 1
(Bowie, Md., Heritage Books, 1995)
[F63/S25/1995/also Loan]

Rev. Charles O'Reilly Gravesite
(1857)
48 St. Paul St., front of St. Paul's Church

St. Stanislaus Cemetery
Farm St., next to St.Charles Cemetery

Southwick Cemetery (1853)
338 Main St.

Verry Family Cemetery (1757)
180 Lincoln St.

+ [G.R. 17] *Vital Records of Mendon,*
Massachusetts to the year 1850 (1920).

BLANDFORD (1741)
Town Hall, 102 Main St., Blandford,
Mass. 01008, Tel: (413)-848-2782

Blandford Cemetery (1742)
Main St., Blandford Center
+ NEHGS [MS70/BLA/15], and
[Mss/A/323]

Hastings Family Cemetery (1829)
Sperry Rd.
+ NEHGS [MS70/BLA/15]

Hill Cemetery (aka) Centre
Cemetery (1741)
North St.
+ NEHGS [MS70/BLA/15],
[Mss/A/323], and [Corbin Collection]
+ NSDAR [G.R.C./S1/v. 52]

North Blandford Cemetery (18th
Century)
Blair Rd., North Blandford
+ NEHGS [Mss/A/323]

Old Sperry Road Cemetery
Sperry Rd.

Stannard Cemetery (1800)
Southwest Blandford
+ NEHGS [Mss/A/323]

Gilbert Tracy Gravesite (1833)
near North Blandford Cemetery
+ NEHGS [MS70/BLA/15]

Henry B. Wadham Gravesite (1812)
near Stage Rd.
+ NEHGS [MS70/BLA/15]

BOLTON (1738)
from Lancaster
Town Hall, 663 Main St., Bolton, Mass.
01740, Tel: (978)-779-2771

Friends Burial Ground (1845)
next to 295 Berlin Rd.
+ Esther K. Whitcomb, *Inscriptions from
burial grounds of the Nashaway towns: Lancaster, Harvard, Bolton, Leominster, Sterling,
Berlin, West Boylston, and Hudson, Massachusetts.* (Bowie, Md: Heritage Books, 1989)
[F74/L2/I57/1989/also Loan]
+ NEHGS [Mss/SL/BOL/8]

Eastwood Family Cemetery
+ NEHGS [Mss/SL/BOL/8]

Fry Burial Ground (1822)
across from 39 and 47 Berlin Rd.
+ Esther K. Whitcomb, *Inscriptions from
burial grounds of the Nashaway towns: Lancaster, Harvard, Bolton, Leominster, Sterling,
Berlin, West Boylston, and Hudson, Massachusetts.* (Bowie, Md: Heritage Books, 1989)
[F74/L2/I57/1989/also Loan]

Old South Burial Ground (1740)
South Bolton Rd.
+ Esther K. Whitcomb, *Inscriptions from
burial grounds of the Nashaway towns: Lancaster, Harvard, Bolton, Leominster, Sterling,
Berlin, West Boylston, and Hudson, Massachusetts.* (Bowie, Md: Heritage Books, 1989)
[F74/L2/I57/1989/also Loan]

Pan Cemetery (1823)
Main St. near Rte. 495 on ramp.
+ Esther K. Whitcomb, *Inscriptions from
burial grounds of the Nashaway towns: Lancaster, Harvard, Bolton, Leominster, Sterling,
Berlin, West Boylston, and Hudson, Massachusetts.* (Bowie, Md: Heritage Books, 1989)
[F74/L2/I57/1989/also Loan]
+ NEHGS [Mss/SL/BOL/8]

Small Pox Cemetery (1845)
Sugar Rd., near Rte. 495 Bridge in
Philips' Field.
+ Esther K. Whitcomb, *Inscriptions from
burial grounds of the Nashaway towns: Lancaster, Harvard, Bolton, Leominster, Sterling,
Berlin, West Boylston, and Hudson, Massachusetts.* (Bowie, Md: Heritage Books, 1989)
[F74/L2/I57/1989/also Loan]

West Cemetery (1822)
Green Rd., near Nashoba Regional High
School.
+ Esther K. Whitcomb, *Inscriptions from
burial grounds of the Nashaway towns: Lancaster, Harvard, Bolton, Leominster, Sterling,
Berlin, West Boylston, and Hudson, Massachusetts.* (Bowie, Md: Heritage Books, 1989)
[F74/L2/I57/1989/also Loan]
+ NEHGS [Mss/SL/BOL/8]

General Cemetery Reference for Bolton:
+ NSDAR [G.R.C./S1/v. 353]
Revolutionary War soldiers buried in
Bolton.

BOSTON (1630?)
City Hall, One City Hall Square, Boston,
Mass. Tel: (617)-635-4600
Cemetery Department, 355 Walkhill St.,
Mattapan, Mass. 02126,
Tel: (617)-635-7361

Abramson Cemetery
(a section of the Baker Street Jewish
Cemetery)

Adath-Jeshurun Cemetery (aka) Grove Street Cemetery (1881)
350 Grove St., West Roxbury
Tel: (617)-325-1984

Agudath Israel Cemetery
(a section of the Baker Street Jewish
Cemetery)

American Friendship Cemetery
(a section of the Baker Street Jewish Cemetery)

Association Chavey Sedeck Cemetery (1895)
(a section of the Adath-Jeshurun Cemetery-Grove Street Cemetery)

Association Sons of Jacob Cemetery (1890)
(a section of the Adath-Jeshurun Cemetery-Grove Street Cemetery)

Atereth Israel Cemetery
(a section of the Baker Street Jewish Cemetery)

Austro-Hungarian Association Cemetery (a section of the Adath-Jeshurun Cemetery-Grove Street Cemetery)

Baker Street Jewish Cemetery (1920s)
766 Baker St., West Roxbury
Tel: (617)-323-4066

Bennington Street Burying Ground (1819)
475 Bennington St., corner Swift St., East Boston
+ Boston Historic Burying Grounds Initiative, Inventories of some Boston Cemeteries (Boston, Mass.:, 1990)
[F73.61/H62/1990]

Beth Abraham Cemetery
(a section of the Adath-Jeshurun Cemetery-Grove Street Cemetery)

Beth Hatefila Anshi Wilcomere Cemetery
(a section of the Adath-Jeshurun Cemetery-Grove Street Cemetery)

Beth El Cemetery
(a section of the Baker Street Jewish Cemetery)

Boston Neck Burying Ground Site (18th century)
No reference to location is given. It is thought the cemetery was abandoned.
+ Robert J. Dunkle and Ann Smith Lainhart, Inscriptions and Records of the old cemeteries of Boston (Boston, Mass.: NEHGS, 2000)
REF/F73.25/D86/1999/also Loan]

Boston United Hand in Hand Cemetery (1875)
2659 Centre Street, West Roxbury

Boylston Lodge Memorial Park Cemetery (a section of the Baker Street Jewish Cemetery)

Bresna Cemetery (section of the Boston United Hand in Hand Cemetery)

Bunker Hill Cemetery (1807)
197 A Bunker Hill St., Charlestown
+ Boston Historic Burying Grounds Initiative, Inventories of some Boston Cemeteries (Boston, Mass.:, 1990)
[F73.61/H62/1990]
+ NEHGS [MS70/CHA/10]

Butrimantzy Cemetery (a section of the Baker Street Jewish Cemetery)

Castle Island Cemetery (1762)
South Boston
+ Edward Rowe Snow, The Islands of Boston Harbor, Their History and Romance 1626-1935. (Andover, Mass. 1935, The Andover Press), p. 121. [BN/120/S1]

Cedar Grove Cemetery (1867)
920 Adams St., Dorchester
Tel: (617)-825-1360

Central Burying Ground (aka) Boston Common Burying Ground (1756)

Tremont and Boylston Sts., Boston
Common
+ Robert J. Dunkle and Ann Smith
Lainhart, *Inscriptions and Records of the old
cemeteries of Boston* (Boston, Mass.:
NEHGS, 2000)
[REF/F73.25/D86/1999/also Loan]
+ *Gravestone Inscriptions and Records of Tomb
Burials in the Central Burying Ground Boston
Common and Inscriptions in the South Burying
Ground, Boston* (Salem, Mass., The Essex
Institute, 1917). [F73.61/C3/C6/1917]
+ Boston, City of, Parks and Recreation
Department, *Alphabetical Indexes to Boston
Burying Grounds.* (Boston, Mass.: 1984)
[F73.61/H58/1984]

Chevra Shaas Cemetery (a section of the Baker Street Jewish Cemetery)

Codman Burial Ground (1848)
69 Norfolk St. and Darling St.,
Dorchester
+ NEHGS [Mss/C/4049]
+ NSDAR [G.R.C./S1/v. 97]

Congregation Adas Yisroeil Cemetery

(a section of the Adath–Jeshurun
Cemetery–Grove Street Cemetery)

Congregation Anshe Sfard Cemetery (a section of the Baker Street Jewish Cemetery)

Congregation Anshey Dowig Cemetery

(a section of the Boston United Hand in
Hand Cemetery)

Congregation Beth Israel Cemetery (1876)

(a section of the Boston United Hand in
Hand Cemetery)

Congregation Chai Odom Cemetery

(a section of the Boston United Hand in
Hand Cemetery)

Congregation Chevra Thillim Cemetery (a section of the Boston United Hand in Hand Cemetery)

Congregation Sharei Sedeck Cemetery

(a section of the Boston United Hand in
Hand Cemetery)

Copp's Hill Burying Ground (aka) North Burying Ground (1660)

Charter and Hull Sts.
+ Robert J. Dunkle and Ann Smith
Lainhart, *Inscriptions and Records of the old
cemeteries of Boston* (Boston, Mass.:
NEHGS, 2000)
[REF/F73.25/D86/1999/ also Loan]
+ Thomas Bridgman, *Epitaphs from
Copp's Hill Burial Ground, Boston with
Notes.* (Boston, Mass.: James Munroe and
Co., 1851). [RB/F73.25/B8]
+ William H. Whitmore, The Graveyards
of Boston. First Volume, Copp's Hill
Epitaphs. (Albany, NY: Joel Musell,
1878) [F73.61/C7/W6/1878]
+ E. MacDonald, *Old Copp's Hill and
Burial Ground with Historical Sketches.*
(Boston, Mass.: E. MacDonald, 1882)
[BN/70/8/40] and [BN/70/8/5]
+ "Historical Sketch and matters
Appertaining to the Copps Hill Burial-
Ground," *Annual Report of the Cemetery
Department of the City of Boston for the Fiscal
Year 1900-1901* (Boston, Mass.: Munici-
pal Printing Office, 1901), p. 33-56.
[F73.61/B68/1900-1902]
+ John Norton, Historical Sketch of
Copp's Hill, Burying Ground and
Inscriptions and Quaint Epitaphs
(Boston, Mass.: 1912) [BN/70/8/5A]
+ Boston, City of, Parks and Recreation
Department, *Historic Burying Grounds*

Report and Inventory, Copp's Hill Burying Ground. (Boston, Mass.: 1986) [F73.61/H6/1986/v. 2]
+ Charles Chauncey Wells, *Boston's Copp's Hill Burying Ground Guide.* (Oak Park, Ill: Chauncey Park Press, 1998) [F73.61/B681/1998]
+ NEHGS [Mss/C/1040], [Mss/C/1041], [Mss/C/4067] and [Mss/SL/BOS/4a-4b]
+ NSDAR [MASS COUNTIES/ SUFFOLK/BOSTON/GRC-1938]

Crawford Street Synagogue Cemetery (a section of the Baker Street Jewish Cemetery)

Custom Tailors Cemetery
(a section of the Baker Street Jewish Cemetery)

David Vicur Cholim Cemetery (a section of the Baker Street Jewish Cemetery)

Deer Island Cemetery (17th century)
Deer Island, Boston Harbor
Native American and Immigrant Cemetery (no marked graves)
+ Edward Rowe Snow, *The Islands of Boston Harbor, Their History and Romance 1626-1935.* (Andover, Mass. 1935, The Andover Press), p. 284. [BN/120/S1]

Dorchester North Cemetery (1634)
595 Columbia Rd. and Stoughton St., Upham's Corner, Dorchester
+ Alfred Mudge, *The Sexton's Monitor and Dorchester Cemetery Memorial.* (Boston, Mass.: Alfred Mudge, 1838) [RB/F74/D5/D15/1838]
+ "Historical Sketch of The First Burying Place in Dorchester [Dorchester North Ground] including Town records, record of all tombs, all epitaphs now in ground and of many of those buried in the ground with no gravestones standing," *Annual Report of the Cemetery*

Department of the City of Boston for the Fiscal Year 1904-1905 (Boston, Mass: Municipal Printing Office, 1905), p. 37-266. [F73.61/B68/1904-1906]+ Boston, City of, Parks and Recreation Department, *Historic Burying Grounds Report and Inventory, Dorchester North Burying Ground.* (Boston, Mass.: 1986) [F73.61/H6/1986/v. 1]
+ NEHGS [MS/70/DOR/1]

Dorchester South Cemetery (aka) South Burying Ground (1771)
Dorchester Ave., near Codman St., Dorchester Lower Mills.
+ Boston Historic Burying Grounds Initiative, *Inventories of some Boston Cemeteries* (Boston, Mass.:, 1990) [F73.61/H62/1990]

Evergreen Cemetery (1848)
2060 Commonwealth Ave., Brighton
Tel: (617)-635-7359
+Published list of lot Owners
1900: *Annual Report of the Cemetery Department of the City of Boston for the Fiscal Year 1899-1900* (Boston, Mass.: Municipal Printing Office, 1900), p. 106-113. [F73.61/B68/1897-1900]
1901: *Annual Report of the Cemetery Department of the City of Boston for the Fiscal Year 1900-1901* (Boston, Mass.: Municipal Printing Office, 1901), p. 123-131 [F73.61/B68/1900-1902]
1902: *Annual Report of the Cemetery Department of the City of Boston for the Fiscal Year 1901-1902* (Boston, Mass.: Municipal Printing Office, 1901), p. 137-146 [F73.61/B68/1900-1902]
Fairview Cemetery (1892)
45 Fairview Ave., Hyde Park
Tel: (617)-635-7360

Forest Hills Cemetery (1848)
95 Forest Hills Ave., Jamaica Plain
Tel: (617)-524-0128
+ [G.R. 4]*Vital Records of Roxbury, Massachusetts to the year 1850* (1925).

+ *Catalogue of the Proprietors of Forest Hills Cemetery, 1900.* (Boston, Mass.: Rockway and Churchill Press, 1900) [F73.61/C38/1900]
+ Neil J. Savage, *The Rural Cemetery at Forest Hills in the city of Roxbury* (Boston, Mass.: 1981) [F73.61/F7/S38/1981]

Free Sons of Israel Cemetery
(a section of the Adath-Jeshurun Cemetery–Grove Street Cemetery)

Gethsemane Cemetery (1871)
670 Baker St., West Roxbury
Tel: (617)-325-0186

Governor's Island Cemetery Site (19th century)
"*Sometime before 1892 the graves of the soldiers at Fort Warren were transferred...*" "*Every grave was moved in 1908, this time to Deer Island.*" Edward Rowe Snow, *The Islands of Boston Harbor, Their History and Romance 1626-1935.* (Andover, Mass. 1935, The Andover Press), p. 192. [BN/120/S1]

Granary Burying Ground (1660)
83-115 Tremont St., across from Bromfield St.
+ Robert J. Dunkle and Ann Smith Lainhart, *Inscriptions and Records of the old cemeteries of Boston* (Boston, Mass.: NEHGS, 2000)[REF/F73.25/D86/1999/also Loan]
+ *A sketch of the origin and history of the Granary Burial Ground.* (Boston, Mass.: Municipal Printing Office, 1879) [BN/70/11/1]
+ "Historical Sketch and matters appertaining to the Granary Burial-Ground," *Annual Report of the Cemetery Department of the City of Boston for the Fiscal Year 1901-1902* (Boston, Mass.: Municipal Printing Office, 1902), p. 31-65. [F73.61/B68/1900-1902]
+ *Gravestone Inscriptions and Records of Tomb Burials in the Granary Burying Ground,*

Boston, Mass. (Salem, Mass.: The Essex Institute, 1918) [F73.61/G7/C6/1918]
+ Boston, City of, Parks and Recreation Department, *Alphabetical Indexes to Boston Burying Grounds.* (Boston, Mass.: 1984) [F73.61/H58/1984]

Arthur Greenfield and Sons Cemetery (a section of the Baker Street Jewish Cemetery)

Grove Street Cemetery
(see Adath–Jeshurun Cemetery)

Hawes Cemetery (aka) South Boston Cemetery (1816)
Emerson and East Fifth Sts., next to the Union Cemetery, South Boston.
+ Robert J. Dunkle and Ann Smith Lainhart, *Inscriptions and Records of the old cemeteries of Boston* (Boston, Mass.: NEHGS, 2000) [REF/F73.25/D86/1999/also Loan]
+ Boston Historic Burying Grounds Initiative, *Inventories of some Boston Cemeteries* (Boston, Mass.:, 1990) [F73.61/H62/1990]

Hebrew Home for the Aged Cemetery (a section of the Baker Street Jewish Cemetery)

Hebrew Progressive Cemetery
(a section of the Adath–Jeshurun Cemetery–Grove Street Cemetery)

Hebrew Volin Cemetery (a section of the Baker Street Jewish Cemetery)

Holyhood Cemetery
(see St. Joseph's Cemetery)

HRCA Memorial Park Cemetery
(a section of the Baker Street Jewish Cemetery)

**Independent Pride of Boston
Cemetery** (a section of the Baker Street
Jewish Cemetery)

**Independent Workmen's Circle
Cemetery** (a section of the Baker Street
Jewish Cemetery)

Jewish Benevolent Cemetery
(a section of the Adath–Jeshurun
Cemetery–Grove Street Cemetery)

Jewish Civil Servant Cemetery
(a section of the Adath–Jeshurun
Cemetery–Grove Street Cemetery)

Kaminker Cemetery (a section of
the Baker Street Jewish Cemetery)

Kehillath Jacob Cemetery (a section
of the Baker Street Jewish Cemetery)

**King's Chapel Burying Ground
(1630)**
Tremont and School Sts.
Tel: King's Chapel, 58 Tremont St.,
Boston, Mass. (617)-523-1749
+ Robert J. Dunkle and Ann Smith
Lainhart, *Inscriptions and Records of the old
cemeteries of Boston* (Boston, Mass.:
NEHGS, 2000)
[REF/F73.25/D86/1999/also Loan]
+ Thomas Bridgman, *Memorials of the
Dead in Boston, containing exact transcripts of
inscriptions on the sepulchral monuments in the
King's Chapel Burial Ground.* (Boston,
Mass.: Benjamin B. Mussey & Co., 1853)
[RB/F73.61/K5/B8]
+ "Historical Sketch of King's Chapel
Burying Ground," *Annual Report of the
Cemetery Department of the City of Boston for
the Fiscal Year 1902-1903* (Boston, Mass.:
Municipal Printing Office, 1901), p. 35-
82. [F73.61/B68/1902-1904]
+ Boston, City of, Parks and Recreation
Department, *Alphabetical Indexes to Boston
Burying Grounds.* (Boston, Mass.: 1984)
[F73.61/H58/1984]

King's Chapel interior tombs (1749)
58 Tremont and School Sts.
Tel: .(617)-523-1749
+ Robert J. Dunkle and Ann Smith
Lainhart, *Inscriptions and Records of the old
cemeteries of Boston* (Boston, Mass.:
NEHGS, 2000)
[REF/F73.25/D86/1999/also Loan]

**King Solomon Memorial Park
Cemetery**
(a section of the Boston United Hand in
Hand Cemetery)

Kovner Cemetery
(a section of the Baker Street Jewish
Cemetery)

Lawrence Avenue Cemetery
(a section of the Baker Street Jewish
Cemetery)

Lord Rothschild Cemetery
(a section of the Baker Street Jewish
Cemetery)

**Long Island Hospital Cemetery
(1893)**
Long Island, Boston Harbor, no marked
gravestones aside from numbered lot
stones.
+ Edward Rowe Snow, *The Islands of
Boston Harbor, Their History and Romance
1626-1935.* (Andover, Mass. 1935, The
Andover Press), p. 301. [BN/120/S1]

Market Street Cemetery (1762)
380 Market St., Brighton
In 1872 about 150 burials were removed
to the Evergreen Cemetery. (*Annual
Report of the Cemetery Department of the City
of Boston for the Fiscal Year 1897-98)* p. 9.
+ Boston Historic Burying Grounds
Initiative, *Inventories of some Boston
Cemeteries* (Boston, Mass.:, 1990)
[F73.61/H62/1990]

+ NEHGS [Mss/C/4048]
+ NSDAR [G.R.C./S1/v. 20] and
[G.R.C./S1/v. 48]
+ NSDAR [G.R.C./S1/v.28] Inscription
Index only.

Mishkan Teflla Cemetery (1876)
(section of the Boston United Hand in
Hand Cemetery)

Mohliver Cemetery (a section of the
Baker Street Jewish Cemetery)

Mount Benedict Catholic
Cemetery (1877)
409 Corey St., West Roxbury
Tel: (617)-323-8389

Mount Calvary Cemetery (1866)
366 Cummings Hwy., Roslindale
Tel: (617)-325-6830
+ Richard Andrew Pierce, *The Stones
Speak: Irish place names from inscriptions in
Boston's Mount Calvary Cemetery.* (Boston,
Mass.: NEHGS, 2000).

Mount Hope Cemetery (1851)
355 Walk Hill Street, Mattapan
Tel: (617)-635-7361
Lot Owners:
1900 : *Annual Report of the Cemetery
Department of the City of Boston for the Fiscal
Year 1899-1900* (Boston, Mass.:
Municipal Printing Office, 1900), p. 52-
104. [F73.61/B68/1897-1900]
1901: *Annual Report of the Cemetery
Department of the City of Boston for the Fiscal
Year 1900-1901* (Boston, Mass.:
Municipal Printing Office, 1901), p. 66-
121 [F73.61/B68/1900-1902]
1902: *Annual Report of the Cemetery
Department of the City of Boston for the Fiscal
Year 1901-1902* (Boston, Mass.:
Municipal Printing Office, 1902), p. 77-
135 [F73.61/B68/1900-1902]

Mount Lebanon Cemetery
(section of Baker Street Jewish Cemetery)

New Calvary Cemetery (1899)
800 Harvard St., near Walk Hill St., West
Roxbury
Tel: (617)-296-2339

New Palestine Cemetery
(section of the Baker Street Jewish
Cemetery)

Nix's Mate Island Site (1726)
Nix Mate Island, Boston Harbor.
This was used for the burial of some
pirates in the 18th century.
+ Edward Rowe Snow, *The Islands of
Boston Harbor, Their History and Romance
1626-1935.* (Andover, Mass. 1935, The
Andover Press), p. 337-8. [BN/120/S1]

Oak Lawn Cemetery (1989)
427 Cummins Highway, Roslindale
Tel: (617)-325-4490

Old North Church Tombs (aka)
Christ Church Tombs (1723)
193 Salem St., North End
Tel: Old North Church, 193 Salem St.,
Boston, Mass. (617)-523-6676

Olita Cemetery (a section of the
Baker Street Jewish Cemetery)

Ostro Marshoe Cemetery (a section
of the Baker Street Jewish Cemetery)

Park Street Church Tomb Site
One Park St.
Tel: (617)-523-3383
Tombs were in use between 1824-1861.
Some burials were transferred to the
Mount Auburn Cemetery, Cambridge in
1861.

Phipps Street Cemetery (1638)
Phipps St., Charlestown
+ Boston, City of, Parks and Recreation
Department, *Alphabetical Indexes to Boston*

Burying Grounds. (Boston, Mass.: 1984)
[F73.61/H58/1984]
+ NEHGS [Mss/A/338], [Mss/A/339],
[Mss/A/340], [Mss/A/354], and
[Mss/SL/CHA/3]

Polonnoe Cemetery (a section of the
Baker Street Jewish Cemetery)

Putusker Cemetery (a section of the
Baker Street Jewish Cemetery)

Quaker Burying Ground Site (1694)
Brattle St.
" *The Burying Ground had been undisturbed for
eleven years, when the remains of one hundred
and eleven bodies were exhumed and removed
thence to Lynn for re-interment, in July,
1826.* "
+ Robert J. Dunkle and Ann Smith
Lainhart, *Inscriptions and Records of the old
cemeteries of Boston* (Boston, Mass.:
NEHGS, 2000)
[REF/F73.25/D86/1999/also Loan]

Rainsford Island Cemetery (1749)
Rainsford Island Hospital, Rainsford
Island, Boston Harbor
+ Edward Rowe Snow, *The Islands of
Boston Harbor, Their History and Romance
1626-1935.* (Andover, Mass. 1935, The
Andover Press), p. 212-7. [BN/120/S1]

**Roxbury Eliot Burying Ground
(aka) Eustis Street Burying
Ground (1630)**
Washington and Eustis Sts., Roxbury,
Mass.
+ [G.R. 1] *Vital Records of Roxbury,
Massachusetts to the year 1850* (1925).
+ "Historical Sketch of The First Bury-
ing Place in Roxbury [Eustis Street Bury-
ing Ground] also inscriptions on all
gravestones and biographical notes and
record of the deaths and burials from
First Church Record and First Town
Records from 1630 to 1689," *Annual
Report of the Cemetery Department of the City*

of Boston for the Fiscal Year 1903-1904
(Boston, Mass.: Municipal Printing
Office, 1904), p. 39-148. [F73.61/B68/
1902-1904] and [MS/ROX/115].
+ Boston, City of, Parks and Recreation
Department, *Alphabetical Indexes to Boston
Burying Grounds.* (Boston, Mass.: 1984)
[F73.61/H58/1984]
+ NEHGS [MS70/ROX/1]

Roxbury Lodge Cemetery
(a section of the Baker Street Jewish
Cemetery)

St. Augustine's Cemetery (1819).
225 Dorchester St. and West Sixth St.,
South Boston
Tel: Archives of the Archdiocese of
Boston, 2121 Commonwealth Ave.,
Brighton, Mass. 02135, (617)-254-0100.
The Archdiocese Archives has
gravestone inscriptions starting in 1805;
Burial Records 1850-1859; Cemetery Lot
Sales 1840-1859.

**St. Francis DeSales Church
Cemetery (1830)**
Bunker Hill St., Charlestown
Tel: Archives of the Archdiocese of
Boston, 2121 Commonwealth Ave.,
Brighton, Mass. 02135, (617)-254-
0100.The Archdiocese Archives has
Burial Records 1833-1890; Cemetery Lot
Sales 1834-1849.

**St. Joseph's Cemetery Site (aka)
Tommy Rock Cemetery (1847)**
on the grounds of St. Joseph's Rectory,
Fenwick St., Roxbury
Cemetery was still in existence in 1873,
currently a playground. No record of the
removal of the burials has been determined.

St. Joseph's Cemetery (1852)
990 Lagrange St., West Roxbury
Tel:(617)-327-1010
Tel: Archives of the Archdiocese of
Boston, 2121 Commonwealth Ave.,

Brighton, Mass. 02135, (617)-254-0100.The Archdiocese Archives has burial records 1852-1868, and grave lot sales 1852-1868.

St. Mary's Cemetery (1867)
Grove and Washington St., West Roxbury

St. Mary's Cemetery (1851)
125 Bernard St., Dorchester
Tel: Mount Calvary Cemetery, (617)-325-6830

St. Matthews Episcopal Church Tomb Site (1819)
Broadway near E. Sts., South Boston
"*Tombs were built in the cellar of the church, and June 16, 1818, the Board of Health granted permission to use them for burial purposes.*"
+ John J. Toomley and Edward P.B. Rankin, History of South Boston (Boston 1901), p. 127.

St. Michael's Cemetery (1905)
227 Walk Hill St., near Canterbury St., Roslindale
Tel: (617)-524-1036

St. Paul's Cathedral Tomb Site (1823)
138 Tremont St.
Tel: (617)-482-5800
The Tombs were in use between 1823 and the late nineteenth century. Burials were removed in 1914, and some were removed to Mount Hope Cemetery, Mattapan.

Shari Jerusalem Cemetery
(a section of the Adath–Jeshurun Cemetery–Grove Street Cemetery)

Sons of Abraham Cemetery
(a section of the Baker Street Jewish Cemetery)

Sons of Benjamin Cemetery
(a section of the Adath–Jeshurun Cemetery–Grove Street Cemetery)

South End Cemetery (aka) Franklin Square Cemetery (1810)
Washington St., near East Newton St., South End
+ *Gravestone Inscriptions and Records of Tomb Burials in the Central Burying Ground Boston Common and Inscriptions in the South Burying Ground, Boston* (Salem, Mass.: 1917). [F73.61/C3/C6/1917]
+ Boston Historic Burying Grounds Initiative, *Inventories of some Boston Cemeteries* (Boston, Mass.:, 1990) [F73.61/H62/1990]

South Boston Tomb Site (1810)
West 7th and Dorchester Sts.
"*In 1810 fifteen tombs were built on the spot where now is located the Shurtleff school. But little mention is made of the burial place in the records, and it is supposed that it was used only a short time.*" John J. Toomley and Edward P.B. Rankin, History of South Boston (Boston 1901), p. 127.

Temple Emeth Memorial Park Cemetery
(a section of the Baker Street Jewish Cemetery)

Temple Ohabei Shalom Cemetery (1843)
Wordsworth and Homer Sts., East Boston

Thompson's Island Cemetery Site
Thompson's Island, Boston Harbor
Boston Death Record lists a Charles H. Austin who was buried there in 1842.

Tifareth Israel Cemetery
(a section of the Adath-Jeshurun Cemetery-Grove Street Cemetery)

Toll Gate Catholic Cemetery (1840)
Hyde Park Ave., near Walk Hill St., West Roxbury.

Old Trinity Church Tomb Site
Summer St.
There were tombs located in the old structure prior to the fire of 1872.

Union Cemetery (aka) Emerson Street Cemetery (1841)
East Fifth St., next to the Hawes Cemetery, South Boston
+ Robert J. Dunkle and Ann Smith Lainhart, *Inscriptions and Records of the old cemeteries of Boston* (Boston, Mass.: NEHGS, 2000)
[REF/F73.25/D86/1999/also Loan]
+ Boston Historic Burying Grounds Initiative, *Inventories of some Boston Cemeteries* (1990)

Vilno Cemetery
(a section of the Baker Street Jewish Cemetery)

Walter Street Cemetery (1711)
Walter St., Arnold Arboretum, West Roxbury
+ [G.R. 3] *Vital Records of Roxbury, Massachusetts to the year 1850* (1925).
+ Boston Historic Burying Grounds Initiative, *Inventories of some Boston Cemeteries* (Boston, Mass.:, 1990)
[F73.61/H62/1990]

Warren Burying Ground Site (aka) Kearsarge Avenue Burying Ground Site (1818)
Closed as a cemetery in 1883, converted to a playground in 1890. Most burials were removed to the Mount Hope and Forest Hills Cemetery.
+ [G.R. 1] *Vital Records of Roxbury, Massachusetts to the year 1850* (1925).
+ *Copy of Inscriptions upon the gravestones in the Kearsarge-Avenue Cemetery, Kearsage*

Avenue, Roxbury. Copied July, 1890, by Garbett & Wood, Surveyors. [Document 159–1890] (Boston, Mass.: Municipal Printing Office, 1890) [BN/70/15/1] and [MS/ROX/98]

Westerly Cemetery (aka) Centre Street Burial Ground (1683)
Centre St. near Lagrange St., Roxbury
+ [G.R. 2] *Vital Records of Roxbury, Massachusetts to the year 1850* (1925).
+ William B. Trask, "Inscriptions from the Burial Ground in West Roxbury, Mass."
NEHGR 7:331-2.
+ Luther M. Harris, "Inscriptions from the Burial Ground in West Roxbury, Mass. Being the whole number therein contained." *NEHGR* 10:20-4.
+ Boston Historic Burying Grounds Initiative, *Inventories of some Boston Cemeteries* (Boston, Mass.:, 1990) [F73.61/H62/1990]
+ NEHGS [F74/W59/M6], [Mss/3/W/23], [Mss/3/R/10], [Mss/3/W/19], and [Mss/C/4710].
+ NSDAR [G.R.C./S1/v.128] and [G.R.C./S1/v. 28] Inscription Index only.

Zviller Cemetery
(a section of the Baker Street Jewish Cemetery)

BOURNE (1884)
from Sandwich
Town Hall, 24 Pery Ave., Buzzards Bay, Mass. 02532, Tel: (508)-759-0613

Blackwell Cemetery
near 66 Sandwich Rd., Bourne. Most burials were moved to Oakland Grove Cemetery.

Bourne Family Cemetery
north of Main and Perry Sts., Buzzards
Bay

Cataumet Cemetery (ca. 1768)
County Rd., Catumet

Elijah Perry Grave (1814)
single grave at 388 County Rd..
Monument Beach.

Head of Bay Cemetery
Head of Bay Rd., Buzzards Bay.
+ NSDAR [G.R.C./S1/v.48]

**Herring Pond Wampanoag Indian
Cemetery (1849)**
Little Sandy Point Rd, in Plymouth and
Bourne

Indian Burial Hill
Herring Pond Rd., Bournedale

Massachusetts National Cemetery
Massachusetts Military Reservation
Tel: (508)-563-7113

Monument Beach Cemetery (1835)
County Rd., Monument Beach

Monument Neck Cemetery (1823)
Shore Rd.

Nightingale Cemetery (1847)
off Herring Pond Rd., behind 3 Palmer
Circle, Bournedale

Oakland Grove Cemetery (1866)
Shore Rd.

Old Bourne Cemetery (1740)
County Rd.

Packard Cemetery
off the beginning Head of Bay Rd., near
the junction of Wareham and Plymouth
town line.

Pocasset Cemetery
County Rd., Pocasset

Sagamore Cemetery (ca. 1804)
Ben Abbey and Sandwich Rds.,
Sagamore
+ NEHGS [MS70/SAG/5]

BOXBOROUGH (1783)
from Harvard and Stow
Town Hall, 29 Middle Rd., Boxborough,
Mass. 01719, Tel: (978)-263-1116

South Boxborough Cemetery (1769)
Burroughs Rd.
+ NSDAR [G.R.C./S1/v. 111]

BOXFORD (1694)
Town Hall, 28 Middleton Rd., Boxford,
Mass. 01921, Tel: (978)-887-0806

Ancient Graveyard (1693)
Main St. and Mill Run Rd.
+W.X, "The Oldest Burial Ground in
Boxford, Mass." *NEHGR* 15:20.
+ NEHGS [MS70/BOX/11]

Brookside Cemetery (1811)
Main St.

Harmony Cemetery (1717)
oppostie 144 Ipswich Rd., East Boxford
+ NEHGS [MS70/BOX/12], and
[Mss/A/324]

Killam–Curtis Cemetery (1807)
Endicott St., near Maconomet Regional
High School

Mount Vernon Cemetery (1702)
Mt. Vernon Rd.

Perkins Cemetery (1777)
Georgetown Rd.

Russell Cemetery (1750)
Bald Hill Rd.

Village Cemetery (1807)
Georgetown Rd., opposite a church

BOYLSTON (1786)
from Shrewsbury
Town Hall, 45 Main St., Boylston, Mass.
01505, Tel: (508)-869-2234
Cemetery Department, 599 Main St.,
Boylston, Mass. Tel: (508)-869-2261

**Boylston Old Burial Ground (aka)
Old Soldiers Graveyard (1745)**
Main St.

Pine Grove Cemetery (19th century)
Skar Hill Rd.

BRAINTREE (1640)
from Boston
Town Hall, 1 JFK Memorial Dr.,
Braintree, Mass. 02184, Tel: (781)-794-
8244

Blue Hill Cemetery (1893)
700 West Street
Tel: (781)-843-9000

Braintree First Burial Ground (1711)
off Plain St.
+ William S. Pattee, "Inscriptions from
the Burying Ground in Braintree,"
NEHGR 11:297-306, 12:39-41.
+ NEHGS [Mss/C/3239]

Dyer Hill Cemetery (1776)
Washington St., South Braintree
+ NEHGS [MS70/BRA/34],
[MS70/SOU/90], [Mss/SL/SOU/12],
and [Mss/A/345]

Elm Street Cemetery (1716)
Elm St.
+ NEHGS [MS70/BRA/34],
[MS70/BRA/31], [Mss/A/345], and
[Mss/A/325]

Lakeside Cemetery (1845)
Franklin St., South Braintree
+ NEHGS [MS70/BRA/34],
[Mss/A/345], and [MS70/SOU/71]

Plain Street Cemetery (1843)
Plain St.
+ NEHGS [MS70/BRA/34],
[Mss/A/345], [Mss/A/326], and
[MS70/BRA/32]

Pond Street Cemetery (1830)
Pond St., South Braintree
+ NEHGS [MS70/BRA/34],
[MS/BRA/132], and [Mss/A/345]

BREWSTER (1803)
from Harwich
Town Hall, 2198 Main St., Brewster,
Mass. 02631, Tel: (508)-896-4506

Brewster Cemetery (1819)
451 Lower Rd.
+ NEHGS [Mss/A/327],
[Mss/C/4629], and [MS70/BRE/5]
+ NSDAR [G.R.C./S1/v. 215]

Crosby Cemetery (1816)
Deer Park Rd., Nickerson State Park

Dillingham Cemetery (1716)
Stony Brook Rd., West Brewster
+ NEHGS [MS70/WES/80],
[Mss/A/330], and [MS70/BRE/9]
+ NSDAR [G.R.C./S1/v.261]

**Capt. David Eldredge Family
Cemetery (1836)**
two graves off Millstone Rd., Nickerson
State Park

First Parish Cemetery (1703)

Breakwater Rd., Rte. 6A
+ Charles E. Mayo, *Mortuary Record from the Gravestones in the Old Burial Ground in Brewster, Mass.* (Yarmouth, Mass.: Register Publishing Co., 1898) [F74/B64/M4/1898]
+ Charles E. Mayo, *Wellfleet, Truro, & Cape Cod Cemetery Inscriptions, Section - Five, from the gravestones in the Old Burial Ground in Brewster, Massachusetts, with biographical and genealogical notes.* (Wellfleet, Mass.: The Rich Family Assoc.) [F74/W39/R5/v. 5]
+ NEHGS [Mss/A/328], [Mss/A/329], [MS70/BRE/6], and [MS70/BRE/8]

Lincoln–Foster Cemetery (1827)

Long Pond Rd. Rte. 137

Pine Grove Cemetery (1833)

Foster and Old Cemetery Rd.

Red Top Cemetery (1818)

Red Top and Stony Brook Rds.
+ NEHGS [MS70/WES/80]

Sears Family Cemetery (1726)

off Main St., at Airline Rd. near Rte. 6A, West Brewster, near Dennis town line.
+ Burton Nathaniel Derrick, *Cemetery Inscriptions of Dennis.*(Bowie, Md., Heritage Books, 1993) [F74/D43/D47/1993]

BRIDGEWATER (1656)

Town Hall, 64 Central Sq., Bridgewater, Mass. 02324, Tel: (508)-697-0921

Auburn Street Cemetery (18th c.)

Auburn St.

Benson Town Cemetery (19th c.)

Curve St.
+ Charles M. Thatcher, *Old Cemeteries of Southeastern Massachusetts.* (Middleborough, Mass., Middleborough Public Library, 1995) [F63/T53/1995/also Loan]

Cemetery near Alden's Bridge (18th century)

+ Charles M. Thatcher, *Old Cemeteries of Southeastern Massachusetts.* (Middleborough, Mass., Middleborough Public Library, 1995) [F63/T53/1995/also Loan]

Cherry Street Burial Ground (aka) Harlow Cemetery (1826)

Cherry St., near the Taunton River, and Halifax townline.
+ [G.R. 3] *Vital Records of Bridgewater, Massachusetts to the year 1850* (1913).
+ Charles M. Thatcher, *Old Cemeteries of Southeastern Massachusetts.* (Middleborough, Mass., Middleborough Public Library, 1995) [F63/T53/1995/also Loan]
+ NEHGS [Mss/A/346], and [F72/P7/N2] Typescript in Mss
+ NSDAR [G.R.C./S1/v.108]

Conant Street Cemetery (1821)

Conant St.
+ [G.R. 4] *Vital Records of Bridgewater, Massachusetts to the year 1850* (1913).
+ Charles M. Thatcher, *Old Cemeteries of Southeastern Massachusetts.* (Middleborough, Mass., Middleborough Public Library, 1995) [F63/T53/1995/also Loan]
+ NEHGS [Mss/A/346]

First Parish Cemetery (aka) South Parish Cemetery (1716)

Summer and Plymouth Sts.
+ [G.R. 7] *Vital Records of Bridgewater, Massachusetts to the year 1850* (1913).
+ NEHGS [Mss/BRI/1]

Hillside Cemetery (1813)

Auburn St., near Curve St., Benson Town
+ [G.R. 5] *Vital Records of Bridgewater, Massachusetts to the year 1850* (1913).
+ NEHGS [Mss/A/346]

Japan Graveyard Cemetery (1766)
High and Plain Sts.
+ [G.R. 11] *Vital Records of Bridgewater, Massachusetts to the year 1850* (1913).
+ Charles M. Thatcher, *Old Cemeteries of Southeastern Massachusetts.*(Middleborough, Mass., Middleborough Public Library, 1995) [F63/T53/1995/also Loan]

Jennings Hill Cemetery (1750)
High St.

Mount Prospect Cemetery (1842)
Mount Prospect St.
+ [G.R. 1] *Vital Records of Bridgewater, Massachusetts to the year 1850* (1913).
+ Charles M. Thatcher, *Old Cemeteries of Southeastern Massachusetts.*(Middleborough, Mass., Middleborough Public Library, 1995) [F63/T53/1995/also Loan]
+ NEHGS [Mss/A/346], MS70/BRI/1]

Orange Street Cemetery
Orange and Walnut Sts.

Pine Street Cemetery (1833)
Pine St., ¾ mile from Lake Nippenicket
+ Charles M. Thatcher, *Old Cemeteries of Southeastern Massachusetts.*(Middleborough, Mass., Middleborough Public Library, 1995) [F63/T53/1995/also Loan]

Pratt Town Burial Ground (1828)
Walnut and Orange Sts.
+ [G.R. 2] *Vital Records of Bridgewater, Massachusetts to the year 1850* (1913).
+ Charles M. Thatcher, *Old Cemeteries of Southeastern Massachusetts.*(Middleborough, Mass., Middleborough Public Library, 1995) [F63/T53/1995/also Loan]
+ NEHGS [Mss/A/346]

Roman Catholic Cemetery (1867)
Center St., near Aldrich Rd., near Mount Prospect Cemetery

St. Thomas Aquinas Roman Catholic Burial Ground (1854)
103 Center St., behind St. Thomas Aquinas Church
Tel: (508)-697-9528

Scotland Burial Ground (1753)
Pleasant St.
+ [G.R. 6]*Vital Records of Bridgewater, Massachusetts to the year 1850* (1913).
+ Charles M. Thatcher, *Old Cemeteries of Southeastern Massachusetts.*(Middleborough, Mass., Middleborough Public Library, 1995) [F63/T53/1995/also Loan]
+ NEHGS [Mss/BRI/1], and [Mss/A/346]

Small Pox Cemetery (1785)
east side of Conant St.
+ [G.R. 13] *Vital Records of Bridgewater, Massachusetts to the year 1850* (1913).
+ Charles M. Thatcher, *Old Cemeteries of Southeastern Massachusetts.*(Middleborough, Mass., Middleborough Public Library, 1995) [F63/T53/1995/also Loan]

South Street Burial Ground (aka) Keith Cemetery (1756)
South St., near Titicut Bridge
+ [G.R. 9] *Vital Records of Bridgewater, Massachusetts to the year 1850* (1913).
+ Charles M. Thatcher, *Old Cemeteries of Southeastern Massachusetts.* (Middleborough, Mass., Middleborough Public Library, 1995) [F63/T53/1995/also Loan]

Titicut Cemetery (aka) Great Woods Graveyard (1793)
northwesterly side of Titcut St.

Trinity Episcopal Church Cemetery (1748)
north side of Main St., near Trinity Church., near West Bridgewater town line.
+ [G.R. 10] *Vital Records of Bridgewater, Massachusetts to the year 1850* (1913).

+ Charles M. Thatcher, *Old Cemeteries of Southeastern Massachusetts*.(Middleborough, Mass., Middleborough Public Library, 1995) [F63/T53/1995/also Loan]

Vernon Street Cemetery (aka) Alden Cemetery (1751)
Vernon and Cross Sts., Titicut
+ [G.R. 8] *Vital Records of Bridgewater, Massachusetts to the year 1850* (1913).
+ Charles M. Thatcher, *Old Cemeteries of Southeastern Massachusetts*.(Middleborough, Mass., Middleborough Public Library, 1995) [F63/T53/1995/also Loan]
+ Williams Latham, *Epitaphs in Old Bridgewater, Massachusetts* (Bridgewater, Mass.: Henry T. Pratt, 1882) [F74/B7/L3/also Loan]

BRIMFIELD (1714)
Town Hall, U.S. Rte. 20, Main St., Brimfield, Mass. 01010, Tel: (413)-245-4101

Brimfield Center Cemetery (1720)
Wales Rd., Rte. 90
+ NEHGS [Mss/SL/BRI/26b], and [Corbin Collection]

Little Alum Pond Cemetery (aka) Brownell Lot Cemetery(1817)
behind Little Alum Pond, near Seventh St., West Brimfield
+ NEHGS [Mss/SL/BRI/26b], and [Corbin Collection]

West Brimfield Cemetery (aka) Powers Cemetery (1815)
Dunhamton St. and West Brimfield Rd.
+ NEHGS [Mss/SL/BRI/26b], and [Corbin Collection]

BROCKTON (1821)
from Bridgewater
City Hall, 45 School St., Brockton, Mass. 02301, Tel: (508)-580-7114

Agudas Achim Cemetery
(*part of the Plymouth Rock Jewish Cemetery*)
Pearl St.
Congregation Agudas Achim, 144 Belmont Ave., Brockton, Tel: (508)-583-0717.

Ames Cemetery (1778)
Melrose Ave.
+ [G.R. 11] *Vital Records of Brockton, Massachusetts to the year 1850* (1911).
+ NEHGS [MS70/BRO/1], and [Mss/A/343]

Ashland Cemetery (aka) North End Cemetery (aka) East Ashland Cemetery (1681)
397 North Main St.
+ [G.R. 6] *Vital Records of Brockton, Massachusetts to the year 1850* (1911).
+ NEHGS [MS70/BRO/1], [Mss/SL/BRO/2], [Mss/A/343]

Beth Emunah Cemetery (part of the Plymouth Rock Jewish Cemetery)
Pearl St.

Calvary Cemetery (1890)
163 North Cary St.
Tel: St. Patrick's Rectory, 335 Main St., Brockton (508)-586-4840

Chevra Telium Cemetery (part of the Plymouth Rock Jewish Cemetery)
Pearl St.

Coweeset Cemetery (1792)
875 Pearl St., near Belmont St., Marshall's Corner
+ [G.R. 5] *Vital Records of Brockton, Massachusetts to the year 1850* (1911).

+ Charles M. Thatcher, *Old Cemeteries of Southeastern Massachusetts*. (Middleborough, Mass., Middleborough Public Library, 1995) [F63/T53/1995/also Loan] + NEHGS [Mss/A/343], and [MS70/BRO/1]

First Parish Cemetery (aka) Main Street Cemetery (1731)
759 Main St., near Grove and Shepard Sts.
+ [G.R.1] *Vital Records of Brockton, Massachusetts to the year 1850* (1911).

Leach Cemetery (1768)
823 Crescent St., near Quincy St.
+ [G.R. 3] *Vital Records of Brockton, Massachusetts to the year 1850* (1911).

Melrose Cemetery (1761)
88 North Pearl St., Brockton Heights
Tel: (508)-580-7833
+ [G.R. 8] *Vital Records of Brockton, Massachusetts to the year 1850* (1911).
+ Charles M. Thatcher, *Old Cemeteries of Southeastern Massachusetts*.(Middleborough, Mass., Middleborough Public Library, 1995) [F63/T53/1995/also Loan] + NEHGS [MS70/BRO/1], and [Mss/A/343]

Mulberry Street Cemetery Site (1820)
Mulberry St., all burial moved to Ashland and Melrose Cemeteries.
+ [G.R. 10] *Vital Records of Brockton, Massachusetts to the year 1850* (1911).
+ Charles M. Thatcher, *Old Cemeteries of Southeastern Massachusetts*.(Middleborough, Mass., Middleborough Public Library, 1995) [F63/T53/1995/also Loan] + NEHGS [MS70/BRO/1], and [Mss/A/343]

Pleasant Street Cemetery (aka) Thayer Cemetery (1814)
Pleasant St., across from Poole St.
+ [G.R. 9] *Vital Records of Brockton, Massachusetts to the year 1850* (1911).

+ Charles M. Thatcher, *Old Cemeteries of Southeastern Massachusetts*.(Middleborough, Mass., Middleborough Public Library, 1995) [F63/T53/1995/also Loan] + NEHGS [MS70/BRO/1], and [Mss/A/343]

Plymouth Rock Jewish Cemetery (1906)
Pearl St., across from Coweset Cemetery
+ NEHGS [Mss/A/343], and [MS70/BRO/1]

Snell Cemetery (aka) West Street Cemetery (aka) Old Cemetery (1747)
Forrest Ave. and Belmont St., west of Brockton Fairgrounds
+ [G.R. 4] *Vital Records of Brockton, Massachusetts to the year 1850* (1911).
+ Charles M. Thatcher, *Old Cemeteries of Southeastern Massachusetts*.(Middleborough, Mass., Middleborough Public Library, 1995) [F63/T53/1995/also Loan] + NEHGS [Mss/SL/BRO/2]

St. Patrick's Cemetery (1857)
340 Court St.
St. Patrick's Rectory, 335 Main St., Brockton, Tel: (508)-586-4840

Temple Israel Cemetery
(part of the Plymouth Rock Jewish Cemetery)
Pearl St.

Thompson Cemetery (aka) Summer Street Cemetery (1796)
699 Summer St., near Perkins Ave and Leyden St.
+ [G.R. 2] *Vital Records of Brockton, Massachusetts to the year 1850* (1911).
+ NEHGS [Mss/SL/BRO/2]

Union Cemetery (1790)
327 Centre St., and 75 Lyman St.
Tel : (508)-580-7833

+ [G.R.7] *Vital Records of Brockton, Massachusetts to the year 1850* (1911).
+ NEHGS [MS70/BRO/1], and [Mss/A/343]

BROOKFIELD (1673)
Town Hall, 6 Central St., Brookfield, Mass. 01506, Tel: (508)-867-8004

Brookfield Cemetery (1737)
Rte. 9, West Main St. and Boston Post Rd.
+ NEHGS [Mss/SL/BRO/12]

BROOKLINE (1705)
from Boston
Town Hall, 333 Washington St., Brookline, Mass. 02445, Tel: (617)-730-2010

First Parish Burying Ground–Walnut Street Cemetery (1717)
332 Walnut St., corner of Walnut and Chestnut Sts.
Tel: Walnut Hills Cemetery, (617)-730-2179
+ Harriet Alma Cummings, *Burials and inscriptions in the Walnut Street cemetery of Brookline.* (Brookline, Mass.: The Riverdale Press, 1920)
[F74/B9/C89/1920/also Loan]
+ NEHGS [Mss/A/331],[Mss/A/332], [MS70/BRO/21], and [MS70/BRO/23]

Holyhood Catholic Cemetery (1857)
587 Heath St., between Hammond and Hammond Pond Parkway
Tel: St. Joseph's Cemetery, West Roxbury, Mass. (617)-327-1010

Walnut Hills Cemetery (1875)
96 Grove St., Chestnut Hill, corner of Grove and Allandale Rds.
Tel: (617)-730-2179

BUCKLAND (1779)
from Charlemont
Town Hall, 17 State St., Buckland, Mass. 01338, Tel: (413)-625-8572

Buckland Baptist Cemetery (1850)
Charlemont Rd.

Buckland Center Cemetery (1777)
Upper St.

Old Cemetery (aka) Buckland Union Cemetery (1785)
Taylor St.

East Buckland Cemetery (aka) Cemetery Number 2 (1804)
East Buckland

First Buckland Cemetery (1849)
Buckland Rd.

Old Cemetery (aka) Buckland Union Cemetery, and Cemetery Number 3 (1785)
Taylor St.

Second East Buckland Cemetery (1849)
Old County Rd.

Upper City Cemetery (1841)
Old Apple Valley Rd.

Daniel Woodward Family Cemetery Site
"the site of the old Alfred Woodward place"
Fannie Shaw Kendrick, *The History of Buckland 1779-1935* (Buckland, Mass. 1937) p. 78

BURLINGTON (1799)
from Woburn
Town Hall, 29 Center St., Burlington, Mass. 01803, Tel: (781)-270-1660

Chestnut Hill Cemetery (1810)
Bedford St. and Terrace Hall Ave.

Old Burial Ground (aka) Precinct Burying Ground (1736)
Bedford and Center Sts.
+ NEHGS [Mss/A/333], [Mss/A/350], and [MS70/BUR/11]

Pine Haven Cemetery (1994)
Bedford St. and Laurel Ln.

CAMBRIDGE (1631)
City Hall, 795 Massachusetts Ave., Cambridge, Mass. 02139, Tel: (617)-349-4260
Cemetery Department, 76 Massachusetts Ave., Cambridge, Mass. Tel: (617)-340-4890.

Cambridge Catholic Cemetery (aka) St. John's Cemetery (aka) Rindge Avenue Cemetery
244 North Rindge Ave., North Cambridge Tel: (781)-729-1445
Tel: Archives of the Archdiocese of Boston, 2121 Commonwealth Ave., Brighton, Mass. 02135, (617)-254-0100.The Boston Archdiocese Archives has gravestone inscriptions starting in 1845-1877; Burial Records 1846-1877, and grave lot sales 1845-1881.

Cambridge Cemetery (1854)
76 Coolidge Ave.

Mount Auburn Cemetery (1831)
580 Mount Auburn St.
Tel: (617)-547-7105
+ A Catalogue of Proprietors in the Cemetery of Mount Auburn (Boston, Mass.: James Munroe and Co., 1855) [RB/F74/C1/M9/1855]
+ Foster W. Russell, *A Biographical Listing distinguished persons interred in Mount Auburn Cemetery, Cambridge, Massachusetts,*
1831-1952. (Cambridge, Mass: Proprietors of the Cemetery of Mount Auburn, 1953) [F74/C1/R87/1953]
+ NEHGS [Mss/A/351], [MS70/CAM/3], and [MS70/CAM/7] 2 vols.
+ NSDAR [G.R.C./S1/v. 78-79]

Old Burying Ground (aka) Christ Church Cemetery (1653)
1450 Massachusetts Ave., Harvard Square
+ William Thaddeus Harris, *Epitaphs from the Old Burying Ground in Cambridge.* (Cambridge, Mass.: John Owens, 1845) [F74/C1/H3/1845]
+ Elizabeth Farnum, *Christ Church Record of Graves in Old Burying Ground in Harvard Square, Cambridge.* [F74/C1/F37]
+ NEHGS [Mss/A/350], and [MS70/CAM/8]
+ NSDAR [G.R.C./S1/v. 152] and [G.R.C./1934/S1/v. 38]

CANTON (1797)
from Stoughton
Town Hall, 801 Washington St., Canton, Mass. 02021, Tel: (781)-821-5013

Burr Lane Indian Cemetery Site
off Burr Ln.

Canton Corner Cemetery (1716)
Washington St.
Tel: (781)-821-5040
+ NEHGS [Mss/A/334]

Chapman Street Punkapoag Indian Cemetery Site
off Chapman St.

Gridley Cemetery Site (aka) Smallpox Cemetery Site (1764)
Kinsley Pl., off Washington St.
+ NEHGS [Mss/A/334]

Knollwood Memorial Park (1898)
319 High Street
Tel: (781)-828-7218

Proprietors Cemetery (aka) Old English Cemetery (1742)
Washington St., near Rt. 138, Punkapoag
+ NEHGS [MS70/CAN/3], and
[Mss/A/334]

Punkapoag Village Indian Cemetery (17th century)
in woods off Indian Lane

St. Mary's Catholic Cemetery (1847)
Washington and Randolph Sts.
Tel: St. John's Rectory, 700 Washington
St., Canton, Mass. (781)-828-0090
Tel: Archives of the Archdiocese of
Boston, 2121 Commonwealth Ave.,
Brighton, Mass. 02135, (617)-254-
0100.The Boston Archdiocese Archives
has burial records 1864-1891.

CARLISLE (1780)
from Acton and Chelmsford
Town Hall, 66 Westford St., Carlisle,
Mass. 01741, Tel: (978)-369-6155

Central Burying Ground (1778)
Carlisle Center
+ NEHGS [Mss/A/335], [Mss/A/336],
[MS70/CAR/3], and [MS70/CAR/6]
+ NSDAR [G.R.C./S1/v. 262]

Green Cemetery (19th century)
Rte. 225, intersection of Chestnut St. and
Bedford Rd.

CARVER (1790)
from Plympton
Town Hall, 108 Main St., Carver, Mass.
02330, Tel: (508)-866-3403

Central Cemetery (1811)
Main St., Carver Cemetery
+ Charles M. Thatcher, *Old Cemeteries of
Southeastern Massachusetts*. (Middlebor-
ough, Mass., Middleborough Public
Library,1995) [F63/T53/1995/also Loan]

East Carver Cemetery (1770)
Rte. 44, East Carver
+ Charles M. Thatcher, *Old Cemeteries of
Southeastern Massachusetts*. (Middlebor-
ough, Mass., Middleborough Public
Library,1995) [F63/T53/1995/also Loan]

Lakenham Cemetery (aka) North Cemetery (1718)
Center and Main Sts., North Carver
+ Charles M. Thatcher, *Old Cemeteries of
Southeastern Massachusetts*. (Middleborough,
Mass., Middleborough Public Library,
1995) [F63/T53/1995/also Loan]

Our Lady of Lourdes Parish (1920)
Center St.

Union Cemetery (1777)
Main St., South Carver
+ Charles M. Thatcher, *Old Cemeteries of
Southeastern Massachusetts*.(Middleborough,
Mass., Middleborough Public Library,
1995) [F63/T53/1995/also Loan]

Wenham Road Cemetery (1770)
Plymouth St. and Wenham Rd., East Carver

CHARLEMONT (1765)
Town Hall, 157 Main St., Charlemont,
Mass. 01339, Tel: (413)-625-6157

East Charlemont Cemetery (1810)
Rte. 2
+ [G.R. 10] *Vital Records of Charlemont,
Massachusetts to the year 1850* (1917).
+ NEHGS [Mss/A/347]

Leavitt Cemetery (1818)
Rte. 2, Mohawk Trail
+ [G.R. 7] *Vital Records of Charlemont, Massachusetts to the year 1850* (1917).
+ NEHGS [Mss/A/347]

Old Burying Ground (1818)
located on the grounds of the New England Power Co.
+ [G.R. 1] *Vital Records of Charlemont, Massachusetts to the year 1850* (1917).
+ NEHGS [Mss/A/337], and [Corbin Collection]
+ NSDAR [G.R.C./S1/v. 348]

Old Colonial Burial Ground (1781)
Barrington Hill Rd.
+ [G.R. 9] *Vital Records of Charlemont, Massachusetts to the year 1850* (1917).
+ NEHGS [Mss/A/347]

Moses Rice Family Cemetery
"Old burying ground near the Charlemont railroad station"
+ [G.R. 4] *Vital Records of Charlemont, Massachusetts to the year 1850* (1917).
+ NEHGS [Mss/A/347]

Tea Street Cemetery (aka) Hawks Cemetery (1777)
Tea St.
+ [G.R. 2] *Vital Records of Charlemont, Massachusetts to the year 1850* (1917).
+ NEHGS [Mss/A/347]

Thayer–Williams Family Cemetery (1814)
"a private burying ground on the Tower place"
+ [G.R. 5] *Vital Records of Charlemont, Massachusetts to the year 1850* (1917).
+ NEHGS [Mss/A/337]

Village Cemetery (1797)
Main St., across from the town hall
+ [G.R. 3] *Vital Records of Charlemont, Massachusetts to the year 1850* (1917).
+ NEHGS [Mss/A/347]

Warner Cemetery (1802)
off Maxwell Rd.
+ [G.R. 6] *Vital Records of Charlemont, Massachusetts to the year 1850* (1917).
+ NEHGS [Mss/A/337]

Zoar Road Cemetery (1789)
Zoar Rd.
+ [G.R. 8] *Vital Records of Charlemont, Massachusetts to the year 1850* (1917).
+ NEHGS [Mss/A/347], and [Corbin Collection]

CHARLTON (1754)
from Oxford
Town Hall, 37 Main St., Charlton, Mass. 01507, Tel: (508)-248-2051

Bay Path Cemetery (aka) Charlton Centre Cemetery (1764)
Mugget Hill Rd. and Main St. Rte. 31

Capt. Jonathan Tucker Family Cemetery (1756)
Smith Rd.

Capt. Jesse Smith and Paupers' Cemetery (1800)
Stafford St.

Charlton City Union Cemetery (1841)
Rte. 20 and Rte. 169

Cranberry Meadow Yard Cemetery (1803)
Cranberry Meadow Rd.

Dresser Hill Public Cemetery (aka) Blood Cemetery (1745)
Baylies Rd.

Fitts Burial Yard Cemetery (1831)
Haggerty Rd.

Harvey–Dresser Yard Cemetery Site (1835)
Sandersdale Rd., burials removed in 1986 to Southbridge, Mass.

Harvlin Towne Yard Cemetery (1815)
City Depot Rd.

Hobbs Burial Place Cemetery Site (1817)
North Sturbridge Rd.

Indian Hill Cemetery Site
Stafford St.

Joseph Martin Family Yard Cemetery (1827)
30 Gale Rd.

McIntire Cemetery (19th century)
Horne Homestead Rd.

Mixter Burial Yard Cemetery (1816)
rear of 31 Colburn Rd.

North Side Cemetery (1813)
Cemetery Rd.

Putney Yard Cemetery (aka) Bearfoot–West Cemetery (1807)
Berry Corner Rd.

St. Lazarus Cemetery
Gould Rd.

Town Burying Yard (1815)
Depot Rd.

Union Cemetery
Rte. 20 and Rte. 169

Westridge Cemetery (1890)
Main St. and Westridge Rd.

Major Daniel William Family Burial Ground (1791)
opposite 17 Glen Shore Rd.

CHATHAM (1712)
Town Hall, 549 Main St., Chatham, Mass. 02633, Tel: (508)-945-5101
Cemetery Office, 549 Main St., Chatham, Mass. 02633, Tel: (508)-945-5117

Baptist Cemetery (1766)
Old Queen Anne Rd.
+ *The Mayflower Descendant* (19:50-1)
+ NEHGS [Mss/C/3014]

Bassett Family Cemetery (aka) Cockle Cove Road Cemetery (1847)
Cockle Cove Rd., and Songbird Ln.
+ NEHGS [MS70/SOU/131]

Bethel Cemetery (1780)
Rte. 28, Main St., South Chatham
+ NEHGS [MS70/SOU/20]

Crowell Gravesite
a gravestone in a field near the East Harwich town line.

Eldredge Family Cemetery (1818)
Mill Creek Rd., South Chatham
+ NEHGS [MS70/SOU/131]

Eldredge Family Cemetery (1826)
Rte. 28, off Bay View Rd., South Chatham

Eldredge (David) Cemetery (1840)
31 Juniper Ln., South Chatham
+ NEHGS [MS70/SOU/131]

Eldredge and Bassett Cemetery (1845)
Ridgevale Rd.

Lord (Doctor) Grave (1766)
in front of 252 Training Field Rd.

Methodist Cemetery
Crowell and Depot Rds., in front of
Seaside Cemetery

Seth Nickerson–Burgess Cemetery (1832)
off Barcliff Ave.

William Nickerson Cemetery (1689)
4 Ryders Cove, off Cod Ln.

Old North Queen Anne Cemetery (1742)
Queen Anne and George Ryder Rds.,
across from Old South Cemetery
+ NEHGS [MS70/CHA/71]

Old South Queen Anne Cemetery (1718)
Queen Anne and George Ryder Rds.,
across from Old North Cemetery
+ NEHGS [MS70/CHA/71]

Peoples Cemetery (aka) Universalist Cemetery (1786)
Crowell and Stepping Stones Rd.

Ryder, Doane, Berry, Smiths Cemetery (1766)
off Old Corners Rd., located in the
woods.

Sailors Cemetery (1846)
Main St., next to the Lighthouse.
The gravestones of over forty unknown
shipwrecked sailors.

Seaside Cemetery (1811)
Crowell and Depot Rds., behind
Methodist Cemetery.

Smith, Doane, Rider and Lord Family Cemetery (aka) Small Pox Burying Ground (1766)
Old Comers Rd.

Union Cemetery (1800)
Rte. 28 and Heritage Ln., behind the
Congregational Cemetery.

CHELMSFORD (1655)
Town Hall, 50 Billerica Rd., Chelmsford,
Mass. 01824, Tel: (978)-250-5205
Cemetery Department, 130 Billerica Rd.,
Chelmsford, Mass. 01824, Tel: (978)-
250-5245

Fairview Cemetery (1928)
Main St.

Forefathers' Cemetery (1690)
Westford St., and Littleton Rd.
+ NEHGS [Mss/A/349], and
[MS70/CHE/1]

Heart Pond Cemetery (1774)
Garrison and Parkerville Rds.
+ NEHGS [Mss/A/349]

Pine Ridge Cemetery (1888)
130 Billerica Rd.
Tel: (978)-250-5245

Riverside Cemetery (1841)
Middlesex St., North Chelmsford
+ NEHGS [Mss/A/349]

St. Joseph's Cemetery (1894)
96 Riverneck Rd., East Chelmsford
Tel : (978)-458-4851

Temple Beth El Cemetery
Stedman St.
Tel: Temple Beth El, 105 Princeton
Blvd., Lowell, Mass. 01851, (978)-453-
7744

West Chelmsford Cemetery (1852)
Cemetery Ln. and School St., West Chelmsford
+ NEHGS [Mss/A/349]

CHELSEA (1739)
from Boston
City Clerk, 500 Broadway St., Room 209, Chelsea, Mass. 02150, Tel: (617)-889-8226.

Garden Cemetery (1842)
Shawmut St.

CHESHIRE (1793)
from Adams, Lanesborough, New Ashford, and Windsor
Town Hall, 80 Church St., Cheshire, Mass. 01225, Tel: (413)-743-1690

Baptist Churchyard Cemetery (aka) Jenks Road Cemetery (1785)
Jenks Rd.
+ NEHGS [MS70/CHE/30], and [MS70/CHES]
+ NSDAR [G.R.C./S1/v. 346]

Burt Cemetery (1817)
Stewart White Rd.

Cheshire Cemetery (1790)
West Mountain Rd., both sides.

Coman-Whipple Cemetery (1813)
Ingalls Rd.

Notch Cemetery (1773)
off Windsor Rd.

Old North Cemetery (1775)
Rte. 8, North St. (formerly Main St.)
+ NSDAR [G.R.C./S1/v. 348]

Sand Mill Cemetery (1796)
off Fales Rd.

Stafford Hill Memorial Cemetery
off of Stafford Hill Rd.
+ NEHGS [Corbin Collection]

CHESTER (1765)
Town Hall, 15 Middlefield Rd., Chester, Mass. 01011, Tel: (413)-354-6603

Bell Cemetery (1831)
Lynes Rd., Chester Hill
+ [G.R. 10] *Vital Records of Chester, Massachusetts to the year 1850* (1911).
+ Francis H. O'Leary, *Gravestone inscriptions for Chester, Massachusetts.* (Agawam, Mass, 1983)
[F74/C56/O43/1983]
+ NEHGS [Mss/A/357]

Campbell Cemetery (1844)
Crane Rd.
+ Francis H. O'Leary, *Gravestone inscriptions for Chester, Massachusetts.* (Agawam, Mass, 1983)
[F74/C56/O43/1983]

Chester Center Cemetery (1769)
Skyline Trail
+ [G.R. 1] *Vital Records of Chester, Massachusetts to the year 1850* (1911).
+ Francis H. O'Leary, *Gravestone inscriptions for Chester, Massachusetts.* (Agawam, Mass, 1983)
[F74/C56/O43/1983]
+ NEHGS [Mss/A/357], and [MS70/CHE/40]

Dunbar Cemetery (1840)
Smithies Rd.
+ Francis H. O'Leary, *Gravestone inscriptions for Chester, Massachusetts.* (Agawam, Mass, 1983)
[F74/C56/O43/1983]

Eastman Cemetery (1837)
Bromley Rd.
+ Francis H. O'Leary, *Gravestone inscriptions for Chester, Massachusetts.* (Agawam, Mass, 1983) [F74/C56/O43/1983]

Fiske Cemetery (1830)
Bromley Rd., Littleville
+ [G.R. 8] *Vital Records of Chester, Massachusetts to the year 1850* (1911).
+ Francis H. O'Leary, *Gravestone inscriptions for Chester, Massachusetts.* (Agawam, Mass, 1983) [F74/C56/O43/1983]
+ NEHGS [Mss/A/357], and [MS70/CHE/40]

Huntington Street Cemetery
Rte. 20, Huntington St.
+ [G.R. 2] *Vital Records of Chester, Massachusetts to the year 1850* (1911).
+ Francis H. O'Leary, *Gravestone inscriptions for Chester, Massachusetts.* (Agawam, Mass, 1983) [F74/C56/O43/1983]
+ NEHGS [Mss/A/357], and [MS70/CHE/40]

Ingell Cemetery (1831)
Ingell Rd., Chester Hill
+ [G.R. 5] *Vital Records of Chester, Massachusetts to the year 1850* (1911).
+ Francis H. O'Leary, *Gravestone inscriptions for Chester, Massachusetts.* (Agawam, Mass, 1983) [F74/C56/O43/1983]

Kinne Brook Cemetery (1833)
Kinne Brook Rd., Littleville
+ [G.R. 14] *Vital Records of Chester, Massachusetts to the year 1850* (1911).
+ Francis H. O'Leary, *Gravestone inscriptions for Chester, Massachusetts.* (Agawam, Mass, 1983) [F74/C56/O43/1983]
+ NEHGS [Mss/A/357], and [MS70/CHE/40]

Littleville Cemetery
Littleville
+ [G.R. 4] *Vital Records of Chester, Massachusetts to the year 1850* (1911).
+ NEHGS [Mss/A/357], and [MS70/CHE/40]

Horatio Lyman Cemetery (1821)
Mica Mill Rd.
+ [G.R. 12] *Vital Records of Chester, Massachusetts to the year 1850* (1911).
+ Francis H. O'Leary, *Gravestone inscriptions for Chester, Massachusetts.* (Agawam, Mass, 1983) [F74/C56/O43/1983]

Moor Cemetery (1790)
near East River Rd., North Chester
+ [G.R. 9] *Vital Records of Chester, Massachusetts to the year 1850* (1911).
+ Francis H. O'Leary, *Gravestone inscriptions for Chester, Massachusetts.* (Agawam, Mass, 1983) [F74/C56/O43/1983]
+ NEHGS [Mss/A/357]

North Chester Cemetery (1803)
Bemis Rd., North Chester
+ [G.R. 6] *Vital Records of Chester, Massachusetts to the year 1850* (1911).
+ NEHGS [Mss/A/357], and [MS70/CHE/40]

Pine Hill Cemetery (1834)
Lee Rd.
+ [G.R. 3] *Vital Records of Chester, Massachusetts to the year 1850* (1911).
+ Francis H. O'Leary, *Gravestone inscriptions for Chester, Massachusetts.* (Agawam, Mass, 1983) [F74/C56/O43/1983]
+ NEHGS [Mss/A/357], and [MS70/CHE/40]

Quigley Family Cemetery Site
Quigley Hill
+ Francis H. O'Leary, *Gravestone inscriptions for Chester, Massachusetts.*

(Agawam, Mass, 1983)
[F74/C56/O43/1983]

Smith–Toogood Tomb (1869)
Maynard Hill Rd., near Chester center
+ [G.R. 13] *Vital Records of Chester,
Massachusetts to the year 1850* (1911).
+ Francis H. O'Leary, *Gravestone
inscriptions for Chester, Massachusetts.*
(Agawam, Mass, 1983)
[F74/C56/O43/1983]
+ NEHGS [Mss/A/357], and
[MS70/CHE/40]

Webster Cemetery (aka) R. L. Bromley Cemetery (1811)
Bromley and Higgins Rds.
+ [G.R. 11] *Vital Records of Chester,
Massachusetts to the year 1850* (1911).
+ Francis H. O'Leary, *Gravestone
inscriptions for Chester, Massachusetts.*
(Agawam, Mass, 1983)
[F74/C56/O43/1983]
+ NEHGS [Mss/A/357]

Wright Cemetery (aka) Round Hill Cemetery (1813)
Round Hill Rd.
+ [G.R. 7] *Vital Records of Chester,
Massachusetts to the year 1850* (1911).
+ Francis H. O'Leary, *Gravestone
inscriptions for Chester, Massachusetts.*
(Agawam, Mass, 1983)
[F74/C56/O43/1983]
+ NEHGS [Mss/A/357], and
[MS70/CHE/40

CHESTERFIELD (1762)
Town Hall, 422 Main Rd., Chesterfield,
Mass. 01012, Tel: (413)-296-4741

Center Cemetery (1764)
across from 30 North Rd.
+ NEHGS [MS70/CHE/50] and
[Corbin Collection]
+ NSDAR [G.R.C./S1/v. 182]

Ichabod Damon Cemetery (1850)
Fuller Rd.

Damon Cemetery (1844)
Cowper Rd., off of South St.
+ NEHGS [Corbin Collection]

First Highland Street Cemetery
South Worthington Rd.
+ NEHGS [Corbin Collection]
+ NSDAR [G.R.C./S1/v. 182]

Gate Cemetery (1808)
near 120 Ireland St.
+ NEHGS [Corbin Collection]

Huntington Hill Cemetery
Old Huntington Rd.
+ NEHGS [MS70/CHE/50]
+ NSDAR [G.R.C./S1/v. 182]

Ireland Street Cemetery (1843)
Ireland St.

Mount Cemetery (1796)
Mount Rd.
+ NEHGS [MS70/CHE/50]
+ NSDAR [G.R.C./S1/v. 182]

Mount Bowfat Cemetery (aka) East Cemetery (1820)
near 142 East St.
+ NEHGS [MS70/CHE/50] and
[Corbin Collection]
+ NSDAR [G.R.C./S1/v. 182]

Robinson Hollow Cemetery (1846)
South Worthington Rd.
+ NEHGS [MS70/CHE/50]
+ NSDAR [G.R.C./S1/v. 182]

Second Highland Street Cemetery
South Worthington St.
+ NSDAR [G.R.C./S1/v. 182]

Tilden Cemetery (aka) Corliss Cemetery (1837)
near 115 Indian Hollow Rd.

Torrey Cemetery (aka) Engram Cemetery (1838)
South St.
+ NEHGS [Corbin Collection]

Witherell Cemetery (1849)
Sweeney Rd.
+ NEHGS [Corbin Collection]

CHICOPEE (1848)
from Springfield
City Hall, 17 Springfield St., Chicopee, Mass. 01013, Tel: (413)-594-4711
Cemetery Department, 687 Front St., Chicopee, Mass. 01013, Tel: (413)-594-3481

Calvary Cemetery (1836)
Hampden St. near Marble Ave.
Tel: Holy Name Rectory, 33 South St., Chicopee, Ma 01013   (413)-592-0122

Chicopee Street Cemetery (1743)
228 Chicopee St.
+ NEHGS [Corbin Collection]

East Street Cemetery (1741)
70 East St.
+ NEHGS [MS70/CHI/11], and [MS70/CHI/5]
+ NSDAR [G.R.C./S1/v. 96]

Fairview Cemetery (1870)
Fairview Ave.

Maple Grove Cemetery (aka) Cabotville Cemetery (1836)
Auburn St.

Rodphey Sholom Cemetery
North S. Highway

St. Patrick's Cemetery (1872)
Fuller Rd.
Tel: St. Patrick's Rectory, 319 Broadway St., Chicopee, Mass. (413)-592-4178

St. Rose's Cemetery
Christopher St.
Tel: St. Rose's Rectory, Groton St., Chicopee, Mass., (413)-536-4558

St. Stanislaus Cemetery
800 Montgomery St.
Tel : (413)-532-8636

Sons of Zion Cemetery
New Ludlow Rd.

CHILMARK (1694)
Town Hall, 401 Middle Rd., Chilmark, Mass. 02535, Tel: (508)-645-2107

Abel's Hill Cemetery
319 South Rd., across from Chappaquoit Rd.

Hillman Cemetery
off Middle Rd.

Indian Cemetery
Sheriffs Meadow Conservation Land Cemetery, off Middle Rd

North Road Cemetery
located off North Rd.

Quitsa Lane Gravesite
(single grave)
Quitsa Ln.

South Road Cemetery
(single grave)
South Rd. near the Allen Farm

CLARKSBURG (1798)
Town Hall, 111 River Rd., Clarksburg,
Mass. 01247, Tel: (413)-663-8247

Beth Israel Cemetery (ca. 1900)
Walker St.

Clark Cemetery (1803)
Horrigan Rd.
+ NEHGS [MS70/CLA/1]

Clarksburg Cemetery (1829)
Henderson Rd.
+ NEHGS [MS70/CLA/1]

East Road Cemetery
East Road, near Stamford, Vt. town line.
+ NEHGS [MS70/CLA
+ NSDAR [G.R.C./S1/v. 436]

Gates Avenue Cemetery
Gates Ave.

West Road Cemetery (1841)
across from 53 West Rd.

CLINTON (1850)
from Lancaster
Town Hall, 242 Church St., Clinton,
Mass. 01510, Tel: (978)-365-4130

New Cemetery
(proposed and unnamed in 1999)
225 West Boylston St.

St. John's Cemetery (1847)
Burials moved to St. John's Cemetery,
Lancaster, Mass. in 1901 due to the con-
struction of the Wachusett Reservoir.

Woodlawn Cemetery (1837)
Woodlawn St.
Tel: (508)-365-4611

COHASSET (1770)
from Hingham
Town Hall, 41 Highland Ave., Cohasset,
Mass. 02025, Tel: (781)-383-4100
Cemetery Department, 91 Cedar St.,
Cohasset, Mass. 02025, Tel: (781)-383-
6709

Beechwood Cemetery (1734)
Beechwood St.
+ NEHGS [MS70/COH/1]

Cedar Street Cemetery (1760)
Cedar St.
+ NEHGS [MS70/COH/1]

Central Cemetery (1706)
North Main St.
+ NEHGS [MS70/COH/1]

**Capt. Nathaniel Nichols Gravesite
(1833)**
618 Jerusalem Rd.
+ NEHGS [MS70/COH/1] and
[Mss/3/H/20]

Green Gate Cemetery
off Jerusalem Rd, North Cohasset
+ NEHGS [MS70/COH/1]

Woodside Cemetery (1902)
30 North Main St.

COLRAIN (1761)
Town Hall, 55 Main Rd., Colrain, Mass.
01340, Tel: (413)-624-3454

Brick Cemetery
95 Shelburne Line Rd.
+ NEHGS [MS70/COL/16], and
[Mss/CB/108a]

Chandler Hill Cemetery (1745)
Greenfield and West Leyden Rds.
+ NEHGS [MS70/COL/10],
[MS70/COL/16], and [Mss/CB/108a]

Christian Hill Cemetery (1790's)
190-192 Ed Clark Rd.
+ NEHGS [MS70/COL/14], and
[Mss/CB/108a]

Farley Family Cemetery
in the woods of Catamount Hill
+ NEHGS [MS70/COL/12]

Fulton Family Cemetery
located in the woods near Halifax,
Vermont border
+ NEHGS [MS70/COL/14], and
[Mss/CB/108a]

North River Cemetery (1792)
102-104 Jacksonville Rd.
+ NEHGS [MS70/COL/13],
[MS70/COL/16], and [Mss/CB/108a]

**West Branch Cemetery (18th
Century)**
Adamsville and Foundry Village Rd.
+ NEHGS [MS70/COL/12],
[MS70/COL/16], [MS70/COL/18], and
[Mss/CB/108a]

**"Old Cemetery in Colrain near
Shelburne"**
+ [G.R. 7] *Vital Records of Shelburne,
Massachusetts to the year 1850* (1931).

CONCORD (1635)

Town Hall, 22 Monument Sq., Concord,
Mass. 01742, Tel: (978)-318-3080
Cemetery Department, 135 Keyes Rd.,
Concord, Mass 01742, Tel: (978)-369-
3778

**Gravesite of One British Soldier
(1775)**
across from 15 Monument St.

**Gravesite of Two British Soldiers
killed at Concord (1775)**
off Monument St., near North Bridge,
Concord River, Minute Man National
Park

New Hill Burying Ground (1823)
part of the Sleepy Hollow Cemetery
Rte. 62, Bedford St.
+ NSDAR [G.R.C./S1/v. 111]

Old Hill Burying Ground (1673)
Main St., Monument Square, Concord
Center
+ Donald E. Pusch, *An edited transcription
of the genealogical notes contained in 'The
Inscriptions from the Old Burying Ground in
Concord, Mass.' by George Tolman,1873.*
[Donald E. Pusch, 1977]
[F74/C8/T72/1977]
+ NEHGS [MS70/CON!]
+ NSDAR [G.R.C./S1/v. 57], and
[G.R.C./S1/v. 111]

St. Bernard's Cemetery (1864)
478 Bedford St.

Sleepy Hollow Cemetery (1855)
Rte. 62, Bedford St.
+ NSDAR [G.R.C./S1/v. 111]

Smallpox Cemetery (1792)
Barrett's Mill Rd.

Smallpox Cemetery (1792)
Fairhaven Rd.

Smallpox Cemetery (1792)
Main St.

South Burying Place (1697)
Main St. and Keyes Rd., Concord Center
+ NEHGS [MS70/CON/1] and
[MS70/CON/3]

CONWAY (1767)
from Deerfield
Town Hall, 32 Main St., Conway, Mass.
01341, Tel: (413)-369-4235

Charles Boyden Cemetery (1823)
off Eldridge Rd.
+ [G.R. 9] *Vital Records of Conway,*
Massachusetts to the year 1850 (1943).
+ NEHGS [MS70/CON/22] and
[Mss/SL/CON/20b].
+ NSDAR [G.R.C./S1/v. 308]

Boyden and Lee Cemetery
Roaring Brook Rd.
+ [G.R. 2] *Vital Records of Conway,*
Massachusetts to the year 1850 (1943).
+ NEHGS [MS70/CON/22] and
[Mss/SL/CON/20]
+ NSDAR [G.R.C./S1/v. 308]

Burnett Place Cemetery (1838)
off Rte. 116
+ [G.R. 7] *Vital Records of Conway,*
Massachusetts to the year 1850 (1943).
+ NEHGS [MS70/CON/22] and
[Mss/SL/CON/20b].
+ NSDAR [G.R.C./S1/v. 308]

Cricket Hill Cemetery (1790)
Cricket Hill Rd., off Whately Rd.
+ [G.R. 4] *Vital Records of Conway,*
Massachusetts to the year 1850 (1943).
+ NEHGS [MS70/CON/22] and
[Mss/SL/CON/20]
+ NSDAR [G.R.C./S1/v. 308]

Howland Cemetery (18th century)
Shelburne Falls Rd.
+ [G.R. 4] *Vital Records of Conway,*
Massachusetts to the year 1850 (1943).
+ NEHGS [MS70/CON/22] and
[Mss/SL/CON/20]
+ NSDAR [G.R.C./S1/v. 308]

Maynard Family Cemetery (1785)
Town Farm Rd.

+ [G.R. 9] *Vital Records of Conway,*
Massachusetts to the year 1850 (1943).
+ NEHGS [MS70/CON/22] and
[Mss/SL/CON/20b].
+ NSDAR [G.R.C./S1/v. 308]

North Shirkshire Cemetery
Wilder Hill Rd.
+ [G.R. 4] *Vital Records of Conway,*
Massachusetts to the year 1850 (1943).
+ NEHGS [MS70/CON/22]
+ NSDAR [G.R.C./S1/v. 308]

Pine Grove Cemetery (1845)
Reeds Bridge Rd.
+ [G.R. 3] *Vital Records of Conway,*
Massachusetts to the year 1850 (1943).
+ NEHGS [MS70/CON/22] and
[Mss/SL/CON/20]
+ NSDAR [G.R.C./S1/v. 308]

South Centre Cemetery (aka)
Pumpkin Hollow Cemetery (1772)
Maple St.
+ [G.R. 10] *Vital Records of Conway,*
Massachusetts to the year 1850 (1943).
+ NEHGS [MS70/CON/22] and
[Mss/SL/CON/20b].
+ NSDAR [G.R.C./S1/v. 308]

South Part Cemetery (aka) Allis
District Cemetery
South Part Rd., Allis District
+ [G.R. 5] *Vital Records of Conway,*
Massachusetts to the year 1850 (1943).
+ NEHGS [MS70/CON/22] and
[Mss/SL/CON/20b].
+ NSDAR [G.R.C./S1/v. 308]

Southwest Cemetery (aka) Poland
District Cemetery
East Guinea Rd., Poland District
+ [G.R. 6] *Vital Records of Conway,*
Massachusetts to the year 1850 (1943).
+ NEHGS [MS70/CON/22] and
[Mss/SL/CON/20b].
+ NSDAR [G.R.C./S1/v. 308]

CUMMINGTON (1779)

Town Hall, 33 Main St., Cummington, Mass. 01026, Tel: (413)-634-5354.

Bartlett Cemetery

Trouble St., (no surviving gravestones)
+ William W. Streeter, *The Vital Records of Cummington, Massachusetts 1762-1900* (1979).

Bryant Cemetery (1776)

Trow Rd.
+ William W. Streeter, *The Vital Records of Cummington, Massachusetts 1762-1900* (1979).
+ NEHGS [Corbin Collection]

Cobb Cemetery

Porter Hill Rd.
+ William W. Streeter, *The Vital Records of Cummington, Massachusetts 1762-1900* (1979).
+ NEHGS [Corbin Collection]

Dawes Cemetery (1773)

Potash Hill Rd.
+ William W. Streeter, *The Vital Records of Cummington, Massachusetts 1762-1900* (1979).
+ NEHGS [Corbin Collection]

Gurney Cemetery

Mount Rd.
+ William W. Streeter, *The Vital Records of Cummington, Massachusetts 1762-1900* (1979).

Harlow Cemetery (1778)

Harlow Rd.
+ NEHGS [Corbin Collection]

Mellor Cemetery

off Stage Rd.
+ William W. Streeter, *The Vital Records of Cummington, Massachusetts 1762-1900* (1979).

Plainfield Cemetery

West Hill Rd.
+ William W. Streeter, *The Vital Records of Cummington, Massachusetts 1762-1900* (1979).

Potash Hill Cemetery

Potash Hill Rd., no surviving gravestones
+ William W. Streeter, *The Vital Records of Cummington, Massachusetts 1762-1900* (1979).

Shaw Cemetery

Stage Rd.
+ William W. Streeter, *The Vital Records of Cummington, Massachusetts 1762-1900* (1979).
+ NSDAR [G.R.C./S1/v. 346]

Streeter Cemetery (1793)

Stage Rd.
+ William W. Streeter, *The Vital Records of Cummington, Massachusetts 1762-1900* (1979).
+ NEHGS [Corbin Collection]

William C. Stevens Cemetery

Main St.
+ William W. Streeter, *The Vital Records of Cummington, Massachusetts 1762-1900* (1979).

Talboy Family Cemetery

Swift River
+ William W. Streeter, *The Vital Records of Cummington, Massachusetts 1762-1900* (1979).

Village Cemetery (1823)

Main St.
+ William W. Streeter, *The Vital Records of Cummington, Massachusetts 1762-1900* (1979).

West Cummington Cemetery (1806)

Rte. 9
+ NEHGS [Mss/C/1080] and [Corbin Collection]
+ NSDAR [G.R.C./S1/v.94]

DALTON (1801)

Town Hall, 462 Main St., Dalton, Mass.
01226, Tel: (413)-634-6103
Dalton Cemetery Records
+ NEHGS [MS70/DAL/3]

Ashuelot Street Cemetery (1959)
Ashuelot St., off Park Ave., West Dalton.

East Main Street Cemetery (1780)
Main St., East Dalton
+ NEHGS [MS70/DAL/1] and
[MS70/DAL/5]
+ NSDAR [G.R.C./S1/v.94]

Fairview Cemetery (1884)
Curtis Ave., off Main St.

**Main Street Cemetery (aka) Old
South Burial Ground (1800)**
321 Main St.
Tel: (413)-684-6117

Roman Catholic Cemetery
+ NEHGS [MS70/DAL/1]

Smith Cemetery (1832)
off Notch Rd. on North Mountain.

DANA (1801)
from Greenwich, Hardwick and Petersham

This town was flooded in 1938 for the
Quabbin Reservoir. All burials in the
following cemeteries were removed to
Quabbin Park Cemetery, Ware, Mass.
1938
+ NEHGS [MS/70/WAR/15]

Brown's Family Cemetery Site
Dana Center Cemetery Site
Frank Demars Gravesite
Evergreen Cemetery Site
Hopkins Family Cemetery Site
Loomis Family Cemetery Site

Old North Cemetery Site
Pine Grove Cemetery Site
Richardson Cemetery Site
Stone Cemetey Site
Town Cemetery Site
Williams Cemetery Site

DANVERS (1752)
from Salem

Town Hall, One Sylvan St., Danvers,
Mass. 01923, Tel: (978)-777-0001

Ahbat Shalom
(a section of the Anshe Sfard of Lynn
Cemetery)

**Annunciation Cemetery (19th
century)**
near 163 Hobart St.

**Anshi Sfard of Lynn Cemetery (19th
century)**
Buxton Rd. off Andover St.

Buxton–Goodale Cemetery (1775)
20 Buxton Ln. off Andover St.

Chesed Shel Emeth
(a section of the Anshe Sfard of Lynn
Cemetery)

**Danvers State Hospital Cemetery
(19th century)**
Danvers State Hospital [no stones other
than numbered markers]

Endicott Family Cemetery (1723)
25 Clinton Ave.
+ [G.R. 3] *Vital Records of Salem,
Massachusetts to the year 1850* (1916).

Ezrath Israel of Malden
(a section of the Anshe Sfard of Lynn
Cemetery)

Farband Jewish National Workers Cemetery
(a section of the Anshe Sfard of Lynn Cemetery)

High Street Cemetery (1758)
Between 45 High and Gould Sts.

Holten Cemetery (1784)
131 Holten St.

Hutchinson Private Burial Ground (1808)
103 Newbury St.

Jewish Community Centre of Chelsea
(part of Anshe Sfard of Lynn Cemetery)

Leech Cemetery (1774)
128 Elliot St. across from Congress St.

Nichols Cemetery (18th century)
Spring St.

Rebecca Nurse Burying Ground (1692)
149 Pine St.
+ [G.R. 2]*Vital Records of Salem, Massachusetts to the year 1850* (1916).

Old Settlers Burying Ground (1791)
Pat Drive off Green St.

Pedricks Cemetery Site
off Locust St.; no stones

Porter Burying Ground
Rte. 35, Locust St. in a pasture near Connor's farm; field stone markers

Potter's Field–Pauper Cemetery (1870s)
off Adam St., next to St. Mary;'s Cemetery; no markers

Preston Cemetery (1774)
57 Preston St.

Prince Cemetery (1759)
rear of 7 Spring St.

Putnam Cemetery (1775)
485 Maple St., opposite Danvers State Hospital

Putnamville Cemetery (1811)
270 Locust St.

Roumanian American
(part of Anshe Sfard of Lynn Cemetery)

Russell Cemetery (1794)
Clinton Ave., next to Endicott Cemetery

Sons of Jacob of Salem
(part of Anshe Sfard of Lynn Cemetery)

St. Mary's Cemetery (1851)
Sylvan St. near Adams St.
Tel: Archives of the Archdiocese of Boston, 2121 Commonwealth Ave., Brighton, Mass. 02135, (617)-254-0100. The Boston Archdiocese Archives has burial records 1868-1967, and grave lot sales 1868-1946.

Swinerton Cemetery (1813)
38 Garden St.

Temple Emmanuel at Chelsea
(part of Anshe Sfard of Lynn Cemetery)

Temple Emmanuel at Marblehead
(part of Anshe Sfard of Lynn Cemetery)

Temple Sinai
(part of Anshe Sfard of Lynn Cemetery)

Wadsworth Burying Ground (1682)
18 Summer St.
+ [G.R. 4]*Vital Records of Salem, Massachusetts to the year 1850* (1916).

Walnut Grove Cemetery (1844)
30 Sylvan St.
Tel: (978)-774-1024
+ "Walnut Grove Cemetery", *Danvers Historical Society, Historical Collections*, 31 (1943) 6-14.

Xaverian Brothers Cemetery (1886)
St. John's Preparatory School Grounds, Spring St.

General Cemetery Reference for Danvers:
+ Samuel P. Fowler, "Danvers Inscriptions" *NEHGR* 8:73-74.

DARTMOUTH (1652)
Town Hall, 400 Slocum Rd., Dartmouth, Mass. 02747, Tel: (508)-999-0700

Akin Family Cemetery (1801)
Anthony and Akin Sts.
+ Judith N. Lund, *Burials and Burial Places in the Town of Dartmouth, Massachusetts*. (Dartmouth, Mass.: Dartmouth Cemetery Commission, 1997) [F74/D25/L86/1997]

Allens Neck Friends Cemetery (aka) Bald Hill Meeting House Cemetery (1826)
739 Horseneck Rd.
+ [G.R. 36] *Vital Records of Dartmouth, Massachusetts to the year 1850* (1929).
+ Judith N. Lund, *Burials and Burial Places in the Town of Dartmouth, Massachusetts*. (Dartmouth, Mass.: Dartmouth Cemetery Commission, 1997) [F74/D25/L86/1997]

Alms House Cemetery Site
(all burials removed to the South Dartmouth Cemetery)
400 Slocum Rd.

Job Almy Family Cemetery (1774)
1194 Horseneck Rd., Quansett Farm
+ [G.R. 24] *Vital Records of Dartmouth, Massachusetts to the year 1850* (1929).
+ Judith N. Lund, *Burials and Burial Places in the Town of Dartmouth, Massachusetts*. (Dartmouth, Mass.: Dartmouth Cemetery Commission, 1997) [F74/D25/L86/1997]
+ NEHGS [Mss/SL/SOU/15]

Almy–Briggs–Sanford Family Cemetery (1833)
next to 10 Crocker St.
+ [G.R. 40] *Vital Records of Dartmouth, Massachusetts to the year 1850* (1929).
+ Judith N. Lund, *Burials and Burial Places in the Town of Dartmouth, Massachusetts*. (Dartmouth, Mass.: Dartmouth Cemetery Commission, 1997) [F74/D25/L86/1997]

Apponegansett Friends Meeting House Burial Ground (1706)
Russells Mills Rd.
+ [G.R. 34] *Vital Records of Dartmouth, Massachusetts to the year 1850* (1929).

Arrowhead Lane Cemetery
behind 50 Arrowhead Ln.

Ashley Family Cemetery (1815)
behind 710 High Hill Rd., North Dartmouth
+ [G.R. 12] *Vital Records of New Bedford, Massachusetts to the year 1850* (1932).
+ Judith N. Lund, *Burials and Burial Places in the Town of Dartmouth, Massachusetts*. (Dartmouth, Mass.: Dartmouth Cemetery Commission, 1997) [F74/D25/L86/1997]

Ashley Family Cemetery (1822)
near 346 High Hill Rd.
+ [G.R. 13] *Vital Records of New Bedford, Massachusetts to the year 1850* (1932).

Baker Cemetery (1819)
next to 132 Horseneck Rd.
+ Judith N. Lund, *Burials and Burial Places in the Town of Dartmouth, Massachusetts.*
(Dartmouth, Mass.: Dartmouth Cemetery Commission, 1997)
[F74/D25/L86/1997]

Barker Family Cemetery
(no stones)
Manchester Lane
+ Judith N. Lund, *Burials and Burial Places in the Town of Dartmouth, Massachusetts.*
(Dartmouth, Mass.: Dartmouth Cemetery Commission, 1997)
[F74/D25/L86/1997]

Bliss Family Cemetery
(all burials removed to South Dartmouth Cemetery)
567 Dartmouth St., South Dartmouth
+ Judith N. Lund, *Burials and Burial Places in the Town of Dartmouth, Massachusetts.*
(Dartmouth, Mass.: Dartmouth Cemetery Commission, 1997)
[F74/D25/L86/1997]

Briggs Family Cemetery
located at Nonquitt Golf Course

Briggs–O'Kelley Family Cemetery
near 177 Gulf Rd.

Brightman Family Cemetery (1840)
across from 445 Division Rd.
+ [G.R. 25] *Vital Records of Dartmouth, Massachusetts to the year 1850* (1929).
+ Judith N. Lund, *Burials and Burial Places in the Town of Dartmouth, Massachusetts.*
(Dartmouth, Mass.: Dartmouth Cemetery Commission, 1997)
[F74/D25/L86/1997]
+ NEHGS [Mss/SL/SOU/15]

British Soldiers Burial Ground (1725)
behind 143 Mishaum Point Rd.

+ Judith N. Lund, *Burials and Burial Places in the Town of Dartmouth, Massachusetts.*
(Dartmouth, Mass.: Dartmouth Cemetery Commission, 1997)
[F74/D25/L86/1997]

Bussell–Gidley Family Cemetery (1847)
near 776 Fisher Rd.
+ [G.R. 28] *Vital Records of Dartmouth, Massachusetts to the year 1850* (1929).
+ Judith N. Lund, *Burials and Burial Places in the Town of Dartmouth, Massachusetts.*
(Dartmouth, Mass.: Dartmouth Cemetery Commission, 1997)
[F74/D25/L86/1997]

Cedar Ridge Cemetery (aka) Pierce–Lewis Cemetery (1852)
554 Rock o' Dundee Rd., Dartmouth
+ [G.R. 33] *Vital Records of Dartmouth, Massachusetts to the year 1850* (1929).
+ Judith N. Lund, *Burials and Burial Places in the Town of Dartmouth, Massachusetts.*
(Dartmouth, Mass.: Dartmouth Cemetery Commission, 1997)
[F74/D25/L86/1997]

Chace Family Cemetery (1846)
across from 879 Old Fall River Rd.
+ [G.R. 9] *Vital Records of Dartmouth, Massachusetts to the year 1850* (1929).
+ Judith N. Lund, *Burials and Burial Places in the Town of Dartmouth, Massachusetts.*
(Dartmouth, Mass.: Dartmouth Cemetery Commission, 1997)
[F74/D25/L86/1997]

Chace–Millard Family Cemetery (1846)
across from 879 Old Fall River Rd.
+ [G.R. 8] *Vital Records of Dartmouth, Massachusetts to the year 1850* (1929).
+ Judith N. Lund, *Burials and Burial Places in the Town of Dartmouth, Massachusetts.*
(Dartmouth, Mass.: Dartmouth Cemetery Commission, 1997)
[F74/D25/L86/1997]

John Collins Cemetery (1834)
North Hixville Rd.
+ [G.R. 3] *Vital Records of Dartmouth, Massachusetts to the year 1850* (1929).
+ Judith N. Lund, *Burials and Burial Places in the Town of Dartmouth, Massachusetts.* (Dartmouth, Mass.: Dartmouth Cemetery Commission, 1997)
[F74/D25/L86/1997]

Thomas Collins Family Cemetery (1836)
near 1407 North Hixville Rd.
+ Judith N. Lund, *Burials and Burial Places in the Town of Dartmouth, Massachusetts.* (Dartmouth, Mass.: Dartmouth Cemetery Commission, 1997)
[F74/D25/L86/1997]

Cornell Family Cemetery (1839)
behind 172 Mishaum Point Rd.
+ [G.R. 20] *Vital Records of Dartmouth, Massachusetts to the year 1850* (1929).
+ Judith N. Lund, *Burials and Burial Places in the Town of Dartmouth, Massachusetts.* (Dartmouth, Mass.: Dartmouth Cemetery Commission, 1997)
[F74/D25/L86/1997]
+ NEHGS [Mss/SL/SOU/15]

Crapo Family Cemetery (1831)
near 31 Bakerville Rd., South Dartmouth
+ [G.R. 27] *Vital Records of Dartmouth, Massachusetts to the year 1850* (1929).
+ Judith N. Lund, *Burials and Burial Places in the Town of Dartmouth, Massachusetts.* (Dartmouth, Mass.: Dartmouth Cemetery Commission, 1997)
[F74/D25/L86/1997]
+ NEHGS [Mss/SL/SOU/15]

Cross Road Cemetery
(no marked stones)
near 239 Cross Rd.

Cuffe Family Cemetery
(no marked stones)
Fisher and Old Westport Rd.

+ Judith N. Lund, *Burials and Burial Places in the Town of Dartmouth, Massachusetts.* (Dartmouth, Mass.: Dartmouth Cemetery Commission, 1997)
[F74/D25/L86/1997]

Joseph Davis Burial Ground (1792)
near 110 Faunce Corner Rd.
+ [G.R. 13] *Vital Records of Dartmouth, Massachusetts to the year 1850* (1929).

DeMoranville Family Cemetery (1898)
DeMoranville Ln.
+ Judith N. Lund, *Burials and Burial Places in the Town of Dartmouth, Massachusetts.* (Dartmouth, Mass.: Dartmouth Cemetery Commission, 1997)
[F74/D25/L86/1997]

Ralph Earl Family Cemetery (1718)
behind 288 Russells Mills Rd.
+ [G.R. 23] *Vital Records of Dartmouth, Massachusetts to the year 1850* (1929).
+ Judith N. Lund, *Burials and Burial Places in the Town of Dartmouth, Massachusetts.* (Dartmouth, Mass.: Dartmouth Cemetery Commission, 1997)
[F74/D25/L86/1997]

Evergreen Cemetery (aka) Russell Family Burial Ground (1846)
across from 600 Old Fall River Rd.
+ [G.R. 10] *Vital Records of Dartmouth, Massachusetts to the year 1850* (1929).
+ Judith N. Lund, *Burials and Burial Places in the Town of Dartmouth, Massachusetts.* (Dartmouth, Mass.: Dartmouth Cemetery Commission, 1997)
[F74/D25/L86/1997]

Faunce–Snell–Ashley Cemetery (1838)
near 636 Faunce Corner Rd.. North Dartmouth
+ [G.R. 5] *Vital Records of Dartmouth, Massachusetts to the year 1850* (1929).

+ Judith N. Lund, *Burials and Burial Places in the Town of Dartmouth, Massachusetts.* (Dartmouth, Mass.: Dartmouth Cemetery Commission, 1997) [F74/D25/L86/1997]

Flag Swamp Road Cemetery
near 30 Flag Swamp Rd.
+ Judith N. Lund, *Burials and Burial Places in the Town of Dartmouth, Massachusetts.* (Dartmouth, Mass.: Dartmouth Cemetery Commission, 1997) [F74/D25/L86/1997]

Friends Burial Ground (1851)
Chase and Old Westport Rd.
+ [G.R. 14] *Vital Records of Dartmouth, Massachusetts to the year 1850* (1929).

Samuel Gidley Family Cemetery (1861)
behind 687 Fisher Rd.

Great Rock Cemetery (aka) High Rock Cemetery (1844)
behind 1143 Fisher Rd.
+ [G.R. 31] *Vital Records of Dartmouth, Massachusetts to the year 1850* (1929).
+ Judith N. Lund, *Burials and Burial Places in the Town of Dartmouth, Massachusetts.* (Dartmouth, Mass.: Dartmouth Cemetery Commission, 1997) [F74/D25/L86/1997]

Hathaway Family Cemetery (1798)
near 26 Dean St., North Dartmouth
+ [G.R. 4] *Vital Records of Dartmouth, Massachusetts to the year 1850* (1929).
+ Judith N. Lund, *Burials and Burial Places in the Town of Dartmouth, Massachusetts.* (Dartmouth, Mass.: Dartmouth Cemetery Commission, 1997) [F74/D25/L86/1997]

Hathaway Family Cemetery (1866)
near 1216 North Hixville Rd
+ Judith N. Lund, *Burials and Burial Places in the Town of Dartmouth, Massachusetts.*

(Dartmouth, Mass.: Dartmouth Cemetery Commission, 1997) [F74/D25/L86/1997]

Hixville Christian Church Cemetery (1767)
1182 North Hixville Rd., North Dartmouth
+ [G.R. 11] *Vital Records of Dartmouth, Massachusetts to the year 1850* (1929).

Horseneck Road Cemetery
(no marked stones)
near 133 Horseneck Rd.
+ Judith N. Lund, *Burials and Burial Places in the Town of Dartmouth, Massachusetts.* (Dartmouth, Mass.: Dartmouth Cemetery Commission, 1997) [F74/D25/L86/1997]

Joseph Howland Family Cemetery (1839)
(burials removed to Padanaram Cemetery)
site 307 Smith Neck Rd.
+ [G.R. 19] *Vital Records of Dartmouth, Massachusetts to the year 1850* (1929).
+ NEHGS [Mss/SL/SOU/15]

Nathaniel Howland Cemetery (1804)
between 3 and 5 Salt Creek Rd., South Dartmouth
+ [G.R. 18] *Vital Records of Dartmouth, Massachusetts to the year 1850* (1929).
+ Judith N. Lund, *Burials and Burial Places in the Town of Dartmouth, Massachusetts.* (Dartmouth, Mass.: Dartmouth Cemetery Commission, 1997) [F74/D25/L86/1997]

Indian Cemetery (aka) Vieira Farm Cemetery
Jordan and Barney's Joy Rds.
+ Judith N. Lund, *Burials and Burial Places in the Town of Dartmouth, Massachusetts.* (Dartmouth, Mass.: Dartmouth

Cemetery Commission, 1997)
[F74/D25/L86/1997]

Susan Lamb Gravesite (1843)
between 405 and 411 Old Westport Rd.
+ [G.R. 15] *Vital Records of Dartmouth,
Massachusetts to the year 1850* (1929).
+ Judith N. Lund, *Burials and Burial Places
in the Town of Dartmouth, Massachusetts.*
(Dartmouth, Mass.: Dartmouth
Cemetery Commission, 1997)
[F74/D25/L86/1997]

Elijah Macomber Gravesite
Fisher and Gidleytown Rds., no stones
+ Judith N. Lund, *Burials and Burial Places
in the Town of Dartmouth, Massachusetts.*
(Dartmouth, Mass.: Dartmouth
Cemetery Commission, 1997)
[F74/D25/L86/1997]

Susan Macomber Gravesite (1848)
behind 589 Fisher Rd.
+ Judith N. Lund, *Burials and Burial Places
in the Town of Dartmouth, Massachusetts.*
(Dartmouth, Mass.: Dartmouth
Cemetery Commission, 1997)
[F74/D25/L86/1997]
+ NEHGS [Mss/SL/SOU/15]

Methodist Church Cemetery (1832)
behind 272 Russells Mills Rd., South
Dartmouth
+ [G.R. 38] *Vital Records of Dartmouth,
Massachusetts to the year 1850* (1929).
+ Judith N. Lund, *Burials and Burial Places
in the Town of Dartmouth, Massachusetts.*
(Dartmouth, Mass.: Dartmouth
Cemetery Commission, 1997)
[F74/D25/L86/1997]

Mosher Family Cemetery (1854)
next to 26 Division Rd.
+ [G.R. 29 *Vital Records of Dartmouth,
Massachusetts to the year 1850* (1929).
+ Judith N. Lund, *Burials and Burial Places
in the Town of Dartmouth, Massachusetts.*
(Dartmouth, Mass.: Dartmouth

Cemetery Commission, 1997)
[F74/D25/L86/1997]
+ NEHGS [Mss/SL/SOU/15]

Newtown Burial Ground (1778)
Old Faunce Corner Rd.
+ [G.R. 12] *Vital Records of Dartmouth,
Massachusetts to the year 1850* (1929).

Old Fall River Road Cemetery
(no marked stones)
site behind 910 Old Fall River Rd.
+ Judith N. Lund, *Burials and Burial Places
in the Town of Dartmouth, Massachusetts.*
(Dartmouth, Mass.: Dartmouth
Cemetery Commission, 1997)
[F74/D25/L86/1997]

Old Faunce Corner Road Cemetery
(no marked stones)
next to the Newtown Cemetery
+ Judith N. Lund, *Burials and Burial Places
in the Town of Dartmouth, Massachusetts.*
(Dartmouth, Mass.: Dartmouth
Cemetery Commission, 1997)
[F74/D25/L86/1997]

Padanaram Cemetery (1764)
Elm St., between Bush St. and Memorial
Dr., South Dartmouth
+ [G.R. 1] *Vital Records of Dartmouth,
Massachusetts to the year 1850* (1929).

Pine Grove Island Cemetery(1825)
near 161 Pine Island Rd., North
Dartmouth
+ [G.R. 2] *Vital Records of Dartmouth,
Massachusetts to the year 1850* (1929).

Lemuel Reed Family Cemetery (1849)
near 645 Reed Rd.
+ Judith N. Lund, *Burials and Burial Places
in the Town of Dartmouth, Massachusetts.*
(Dartmouth, Mass.: Dartmouth
Cemetery Commission, 1997)
[F74/D25/L86/1997]

Reed Family Cemetery (1852)
323 Highland Ave.
+ Judith N. Lund, *Burials and Burial Places in the Town of Dartmouth, Massachusetts.* (Dartmouth, Mass.: Dartmouth Cemetery Commission, 1997)
[F74/D25/L86/1997]

Reed Family Cemetery (1836)
Melissa Lynn Dr. at Deerfield Ln.
+ Judith N. Lund, *Burials and Burial Places in the Town of Dartmouth, Massachusetts.* (Dartmouth, Mass.: Dartmouth Cemetery Commission, 1997)
[F74/D25/L86/1997]

Reed Family Cemetery (1868)
451 Highland Ave.
+ Judith N. Lund, *Burials and Burial Places in the Town of Dartmouth, Massachusetts.* (Dartmouth, Mass.: Dartmouth Cemetery Commission, 1997)
[F74/D25/L86/1997]

Reed Road Cemetery
(no marked stones)
site at 1077 Reed Rd.
+ Judith N. Lund, *Burials and Burial Places in the Town of Dartmouth, Massachusetts.* (Dartmouth, Mass.: Dartmouth Cemetery Commission, 1997)
[F74/D25/L86/1997]

Reynolds-Teachman Cemetery (1846)
behind 555 Fisher Rd.
+ Judith N. Lund, *Burials and Burial Places in the Town of Dartmouth, Massachusetts.* (Dartmouth, Mass.: Dartmouth Cemetery Commission, 1997)
[F74/D25/L86/1997]

Rock O'Dundee Road Cemetery
(no gravestones)
site behind 297 Rock O'Dundee Rd.
+ Judith N. Lund, *Burials and Burial Places in the Town of Dartmouth, Massachusetts.* (Dartmouth, Mass.: Dartmouth Cemetery Commission, 1997)
[F74/D25/L86/1997]

Rogers Family Cemetery (1840)
near 856 Faunce Corner Rd., North Dartmouth
+ Judith N. Lund, *Burials and Burial Places in the Town of Dartmouth, Massachusetts.* (Dartmouth, Mass.: Dartmouth Cemetery Commission, 1997)
[F74/D25/L86/1997]

Joseph Russell's Orchard Cemetery Site
site on Elm St.
+ Judith N. Lund, *Burials and Burial Places in the Town of Dartmouth, Massachusetts.* (Dartmouth, Mass.: Dartmouth Cemetery Commission, 1997)
[F74/D25/L86/1997]

Russell's Mills Road Cemetery (1845)
behind 1168 Russell Mills Rd.
+ [G.R. 17] *Vital Records of Dartmouth, Massachusetts to the year 1850* (1929).
+ NEHGS [Mss/SL/SOU/15]

Ryder Family Cemetery (1818)
across from 486-512 Hixville Rd.
+ Judith N. Lund, *Burials and Burial Places in the Town of Dartmouth, Massachusetts.* (Dartmouth, Mass.: Dartmouth Cemetery Commission, 1997)
[F74/D25/L86/1997]

Sabins Family Cemetery (1830)
near 801 Hixville Rd., North Dartmouth
+ [G.R. 6] *Vital Records of Dartmouth, Massachusetts to the year 1850* (1929).
+ Judith N. Lund, *Burials and Burial Places in the Town of Dartmouth, Massachusetts.* (Dartmouth, Mass.: Dartmouth Cemetery Commission, 1997)
[F74/D25/L86/1997]

St. Aidan's Chapel Memorial Garden (1928)

185 Smith Neck Rd.
+ Judith N. Lund, *Burials and Burial Places in the Town of Dartmouth, Massachusetts.* (Dartmouth, Mass.: Dartmouth Cemetery Commission, 1997) [F74/D25/L86/1997]

Arabia Sampson Burial Ground Site (1860)

(burials removed to Pine Island Cemetery)
Collins Corner Rd.
+ Judith N. Lund, *Burials and Burial Places in the Town of Dartmouth, Massachusetts.* (Dartmouth, Mass.: Dartmouth Cemetery Commission, 1997) [F74/D25/L86/1997]

Sherman Family Cemetery (1763)

near 55 Bakerville Rd., South Dartmouth
+ [G.R. 26] *Vital Records of Dartmouth, Massachusetts to the year 1850* (1929).
+ Judith N. Lund, *Burials and Burial Places in the Town of Dartmouth, Massachusetts.* (Dartmouth, Mass.: Dartmouth Cemetery Commission, 1997) [F74/D25/L86/1997]
+ NEHGS [Mss/SL/SOU/15]

Sherman Family Cemetery

near 118 Division Rd.
+ Judith N. Lund, *Burials and Burial Places in the Town of Dartmouth, Massachusetts.* (Dartmouth, Mass.: Dartmouth Cemetery Commission, 1997) [F74/D25/L86/1997]

Slave Burial Ground Site

(site destroyed)
site Tucker Rd. and Allen St.

Sambo Slocum Cemetery

(no marked stones)
next to 171 Gaffney Rd.

Slocum Family Cemetery (1834)

across from 114 Barney's Joy Rd.

+ [G.R. 35] *Vital Records of Dartmouth, Massachusetts to the year 1850* (1929).
+ Judith N. Lund, *Burials and Burial Places in the Town of Dartmouth, Massachusetts.* (Dartmouth, Mass.: Dartmouth Cemetery Commission, 1997) [F74/D25/L86/1997]

Smith Family Cemetery (1692)

between 145 and 213 Little River Rd.
+ [G.R. 22] *Vital Records of Dartmouth, Massachusetts to the year 1850* (1929).
+ Judith N. Lund, *Burials and Burial Places in the Town of Dartmouth, Massachusetts.* (Dartmouth, Mass.: Dartmouth Cemetery Commission, 1997) [F74/D25/L86/1997]

Smith Family Cemetery (1849)

Smith Neck and Rock o' Dundee Rd., at Salters Point, South Dartmouth
+ [G.R. 37] *Vital Records of Dartmouth, Massachusetts to the year 1850* (1929).
+ Judith N. Lund, *Burials and Burial Places in the Town of Dartmouth, Massachusetts.* (Dartmouth, Mass.: Dartmouth Cemetery Commission, 1997) [F74/D25/L86/1997]
+ NEHGS [Mss/SL/SOU/15]

Christopher Smith Family Cemetery (1880)

near 820 Potomska Rd
+ Judith N. Lund, *Burials and Burial Places in the Town of Dartmouth, Massachusetts.* (Dartmouth, Mass.: Dartmouth Cemetery Commission, 1997) [F74/D25/L86/1997]

Smith Neck Friends Burial Ground (1843)

594 Smith Neck Rd.
+ [G.R. 37] *Vital Records of Dartmouth, Massachusetts to the year 1850* (1929).

Smith–Burdick Cemetery Site (1840)

Potomska Rd.

+ [G.R. 32] *Vital Records of Dartmouth, Massachusetts to the year 1850* (1929).

Sol E Mar Hospital Cemetery Site (1960)

site was located on Spinnaker Ln., South Dartmouth
Burials removed to Sacred Heart Cemetery, New Bedford, Mass.
+ Judith N. Lund, *Burials and Burial Places in the Town of Dartmouth, Massachusetts.* (Dartmouth, Mass.: Dartmouth Cemetery Commission, 1997)
[F74/D25/L86/1997]

Waldo Farm Cemetery

Waldo Farm Property, Horseneck Rd.

Weaver Family Cemetery (1831)

near 309 Lucy Little Rd.
+ [G.R. 16] *Vital Records of Dartmouth, Massachusetts to the year 1850* (1929).

Weeks Family Cemetery (1833)

behind 143 Bakerville Rd.
+ [G.R. 30] *Vital Records of Dartmouth, Massachusetts to the year 1850* (1929).
+ Judith N. Lund, *Burials and Burial Places in the Town of Dartmouth, Massachusetts.* (Dartmouth, Mass.: Dartmouth Cemetery Commission, 1997)
[F74/D25/L86/1997]
+ NEHGS [Mss/SL/SOU/15]

Nellie Weeks Cemetery

behind 441 Elm St., South Dartmouth

Whalon–King Cemetery (1856)

near 21 Highland Ave.
+ Judith N. Lund, *Burials and Burial Places in the Town of Dartmouth, Massachusetts.* (Dartmouth, Mass.: Dartmouth Cemetery Commission, 1997)
[F74/D25/L86/1997]

Wilber Family Cemetery (1843)

across from 879 Old Fall River Rd.

+ [G.R. 7] *Vital Records of Dartmouth, Massachusetts to the year 1850* (1929).
+ Judith N. Lund, *Burials and Burial Places in the Town of Dartmouth, Massachusetts.* (Dartmouth, Mass.: Dartmouth Cemetery Commission, 1997)
[F74/D25/L86/1997]

Wilbur Family Cemetery (1825)

near 1157 Tucker Rd.
+ Judith N. Lund, *Burials and Burial Places in the Town of Dartmouth, Massachusetts.* (Dartmouth, Mass.: Dartmouth Cemetery Commission, 1997)
[F74/D25/L86/1997]

DEDHAM (1636)

Town Hall, 26 Bryant St., Dedham, Mass. 02027, Tel: (781)-326-1638
Cemetery Department, 86 Brookdale Ave., Dedham, Mass. Tel: (781)-326-1177

Brookdale Cemetery (1890)

86 Brookdale Ave.
Tel: (781)-326-1177

Old Village Cemetery (1640)

Village Ave.
Carlos Slafter, *Epitaphs in the Old Burial Place, Dedham, Mass.* (Bowie, Md: Heritage Books, 1986)
[F74/D3/S53/1986]
+ NEHGS [MS70/DED/1]

DEERFIELD (1677)

Town Hall, 8 Conway St., South Deerfield, Mass. 01373, Tel: (413)-665-2130

Cemetery off Albany Road

near Clackdale Farm Orchard

Deerfield Village Old Burying Ground (1702)

Albany Rd.
+ [G.R. 1] *Vital Records of Deerfield, Massachusetts to the year 1850* (1920).
+ C.A. Baker, *Epitaphs in the Old Burying Ground at Deerfield, Ma.* (Deerfield, Mass.: Pocumtick Valley Memorial Association, 1924) [F74/D4/B3]
+ NSDAR [G.R.C./S1/v. 16]

East Deerfield Cemetery

River Rd.
+ [G.R. 12] *Vital Records of Deerfield, Massachusetts to the year 1850* (1920).

Hawks Cemetery

off Upper Rd., West Deerfield, near Shelburne town line.
+ [G.R. 6] *Vital Records of Deerfield, Massachusetts to the year 1850* (1920).

Holy Name of Jesus Cemetery (1929)

West and Porter Sts., South Deerfield
Tel: Holy Name of Jesus Parish, (413)-665-2129

Howes Orchard Cemetery

off Upper Road, West Deerfield

Laurel Hill Cemetery

Pine Nook Rd., Old Deerfield
+ [G.R. 2] *Vital Records of Deerfield, Massachusetts to the year 1850* (1920).

Mill River Cemetery

Lee and Stillwater Sts., South Deerfield
+ [G.R. 7] *Vital Records of Deerfield, Massachusetts to the year 1850* (1920).

Old Cemetery

Sugarloaf St., South Deerfield
+ [G.R. 8] *Vital Records of Deerfield, Massachusetts to the year 1850* (1920).

Pine Nook–Gunn Family Burial Ground (1811)

River Rd.
+ [G.R. 11] *Vital Records of Deerfield, Massachusetts to the year 1850* (1920).

River Road Notch Cemetery

River Road Notch, located one mile from Rte. 116 on the left hand side.

St. Stanislaus Cemetery

Borne Ave. and Thayer St.

Savage Farm Cemetery

Lower Road, West Deerfield

South Deerfield–Brookside Cemetery (1898)

South Main St.
+ [G.R. 9] *Vital Records of Deerfield, Massachusetts to the year 1850* (1920).
+ NSDAR [G.R.C./1932/S1/v. 16]

Stebbins Cemetery (1808)

South Deerfield, near the Connecticut River
+ [G.R. 10] *Vital Records of Deerfield, Massachusetts to the year 1850* (1920).
+ NEHGS [Corbin Collection]
+ NSDAR [G.R.C./S1/v. 48]

West Deerfield Cemetery

off Upper Rd.
+ [G.R. 5] *Vital Records of Deerfield, Massachusetts to the year 1850* (1920).
+ NSDAR [G.R.C./S1/v. 48]

"Old cemetery in pasture near boathouse on Connecticut River"

+ [G.R. 13] *Vital Records of Deerfield, Massachusetts to the year 1850* (1920).

DENNIS (1793)
from Yarmouth

Town Hall, 485 Main St., South Dennis, Mass. 02660, Tel: (508)-760-6115

Ancient Cemetery (18th century)
behind Town Offices on Main St., South
Dennis
+ *The Mayflower Descendant* (11:11-15)
+ NEHGS [MS70/DEN/8]

Baker Family Cemetery (1853)
near Swan River Rd., West Dennis

Dennis Village Cemetery (1794)
Old Bass River Rd., Rte. 6A
+ Burton Nathaniel Derrick, *Cemetery
Inscriptions of Dennis.*(Bowie, Md.,
Heritage Books, 1993)
[F74/D43/D47/1993]

Gravesite of a child who died from smallpox
corner of Setucket and Airline Sts.

Hall Family Cemetery (1696)
Whig St.
+ Burton Nathaniel Derrick, *Cemetery
Inscriptions of Dennis.*(Bowie, Md.,
Heritage Books, 1993)
[F74/D43/D47/1993]
+ NEHGS [MS70/DEN/1]
+ NSDAR [G.R.C./S1/v. 48] and
[G.R.C./S1/v. 425]

Howes Family Cemetery (1650)
New Boston Rd
+ *NEHGR* 100:320-323
+ NEHGS [MS70/DEN/5]
+ NSDAR [G.R.C./S1/v. 80] and
[G.R.C./S1/v.98] Inscription Index only.

Indian Cemetery
Rte. 6A, on shores of Scargo Lake [no
markers]
+ Burton Nathaniel Derrick, *Cemetery
Inscriptions of Dennis.*(Bowie, Md.,
Heritage Books, 1993)
[F74/D43/D47/1993]
+ NSDAR [G.R.C./S1/v. 80]

Oak Ridge Cemetery (1970)
Rte. 134

Paddock Family Cemetery (1707)
off Rte. 6A
+ Burton Nathaniel Derrick, *Cemetery
Inscriptions of Dennis.*(Bowie, Md.,
Heritage Books, 1993)
[F74/D43/D47/1993]
+ NEHGS [MS70/DEN/2]

Quaker Cemetery (1720)
Mayfair Rd.
+ Burton Nathaniel Derrick, *Cemetery
Inscriptions of Dennis.*(Bowie, Md.,
Heritage Books, 1993)
[F74/D43/D47/1993]

Quivet Cemetery (1823)
South St., East Dennis
+ Burton Nathaniel Derrick, *Cemetery
Inscriptions of Dennis.*(Bowie, Md.,
Heritage Books, 1993)
[F74/D43/D47/1993]
+ NEHGS [MS70/DEN/5]
+ NSDAR [G.R.C./S1/v. 80]

South Dennis Congregational Church Cemetery (1796)
Old Main St. and Old Bass River Rd.,
South Dennis.
+ Burton Nathaniel Derrick, *Cemetery
Inscriptions of Dennis.*(Bowie, Md.,
Heritage Books, 1993)
[F74/D43/D47/1993]

Swan Lake Cemetery (1847)
Depot St., Dennisport
+ Burton Nathaniel Derrick, *Cemetery
Inscriptions of Dennis.*(Bowie, Md.,
Heritage Books, 1993)
[F74/D43/D47/1993]

West Dennis Cemetery (1823)
Fisk and Pond Sts.
+ Burton Nathaniel Derrick, *Cemetery
Inscriptions of Dennis.*(Bowie, Md.,

Heritage Books, 1993)
[F74/D43/D47/1993]
+ NEHGS [Mss/C/4450]

Wixon Family Cemetery (aka) Smallpox Cemetery (1849)
east of Summer St., Dennisport

Werden-Worden-Homer Cemetery (1639)
off Rte. 6A
+ Burton Nathaniel Derrick, *Cemetery Inscriptions of Dennis.*(Bowie, Md., Heritage Books, 1993)
[F74/D43/D47/1993]

DIGHTON (1712)
Town Hall, 979 Somerset Ave., Dighton, Mass. 02715, Tel: (508)-669-5411

Baptist Church Cemetery (aka) Community Church Cemetery (1805)
Main St.
+ NEHGS [Mss/SG/LIN/5/23], and [Mss/SG/HOD/6/60]

Briggs Burial Ground (1832)
Forest St.
+ NEHGS [MS70/NOR/171]
+ Susan F. Salisbury, *Southern Massachusetts Cemetery Collection* - Volume 2 (Bowie, Md., Heritage Books, 1996) [F63/S25/1995/also Loan]

Briggs Burial Ground (1857)
Williams St.

Briggs-Edson Burial Ground (1810)
Williams St.

Briggs-Trafton Burial Ground (1796)
Pine St.
+ NEHGS [MS70/DIG/3]

Center Street Cemetery (1756)
West of Rte. 138, Center St.
+ Mrs. Wendell B. Presbrey, *Inscriptions from Eight Cemeteries in Bristol, County, Massachusetts.* (---, Massachusetts D.A.R., 1987) [F72/B8/I57/1987]
+ NEHGS [MS70/DIG/1] and [MS70/DIG/3]
+ NSDAR [G.R.C./S2/v. 1] and [G.R.C./S1/v. 433]

Dighton Center Burial Ground
Main St.

Elm Street Cemetery
Elm and Brook Sts.
+ NEHGS [MS70/DIG/3]

Gooding-Standish Burial Ground (1712)
Center St., near Somerset Ave.
+ NEHGS [MS70/DIG/3], and [Mss/SG/LIN/5/23]

Hathaway Cemetery (1837)
Elm St.

Horton-Talbot Burial Ground (1785)
Horton St.

Jones Burial Ground (1808)
Williams St.
+ NEHGS [MS70/DIG/3]

Lewis Street Cemetery (1805)
Lewis St.

Manchester Burial Ground (1802)
Williams St.
+ NEHGS [MS70/DIG/3]

Mount Pleasant Burial Ground (1712)
Elm St.

Perry Burial Ground (1808)
County St.

Phillips and Simmons Cemetery (1804)
Mains St., near Williams St.

Peter Pitts Burial Ground (1775)
Smith St.

Pratt–Cole Burial Ground (1812)
Elm St.

Reed Burial Ground (1803)
Wheeler St.
+ NEHGS [Mss/SG/LIN/5/23]

Riverside Burial Ground (1839)
Riverside Ave.

Oliver Perry Simmons Burial Ground (1816)
Elm St.

Smith–Bowen Burial Ground (1851)
Smith St.

Smith Street Cemetery (1817)
Smith St.

Anthony Snell Burial Ground
Hart St.

John Snell Burial Ground (1792)
Elm St.

Silas Talbot–Perry Burial Ground (1793)
Hart St.

Town Cemetery (1713)
Elm St.

Townsend–Walker Burial Ground (1808)
Middle St.

Unitarian Church Cemetery (1754)
Elm St.
+ NEHGS [Mss/SG/HOD/6/60]

Dr. Thomas Ware–Church Cemetery (1797)
Main St.

Walker Burial Ground (1815)
Williams St.
+ Susan F. Salisbury, *Southern Massachusetts Cemetery Collection*, Volume 2 (Bowie, Md., Heritage Books, 1996) [F63/S25/1995/also Loan]

Walker Burial Ground (1849)
Walker St.

Walker–Wheeler Burial Ground (1819)
Williams St.
+ Susan F. Salisbury, *Southern Massachusetts Cemetery Collection*, Volume 2 (Bowie, Md., Heritage Books, 1996) [F63/S25/1995/also Loan]

West Dighton Congregational Church Burial Ground (1775)
Wellington St.
+ NEHGS [Mss/SG/LIN/5/23], and [Mss/SG/HOD/6/60]
+ Susan F. Salisbury, *Southern Massachusetts Cemetery Collection*, Volume 2 (Bowie, Md., Heritage Books, 1996) [F63/S25/1995/also Loan]

Williams–Baker Burial Ground (1775)
Maple St.

Williams Burial Ground (1772)
Williams St.

DOUGLAS (1746)
Town Hall, 29 Depot St., Douglas, Mass. 01516, Tel: (508)-476-4000

Baker Cemetery (1865)
South St.

Buffum Cemetery (1820)
Maple St.

Coopertown Road Cemetery
Cooperstown Rd.

Douglas Center Cemetery (1746)
Rte. 16, Main St.
+ Susan F. Salisbury, *Southern Massachu-setts Cemetery Collection*, Volume 1 (Bowie, Md., Heritage Books, 1995)
[F63/S25/1995/also Loan]

Evergreen Cemetery (1818)
West St., East Douglas
+ Susan F. Salisbury, *Southern Massachu-setts Cemetery Collection*, Volume 1 (Bowie, Md., Heritage Books, 1995)
[F63/S25/1995/also Loan]

Parker Street Cemetery (1795)
Parker St.

Pine Grove Cemetery (1812)
Cemetery St.

Quaker Cemetery (1806)
Pine St.

St. Dennis Cemetery (1866)
Manchaug St.
Tel: St. Dennis Rectory, Manchaug St., Douglas, Mass. (508)-476-2002

South Douglas Cemetery (1820)
South St.
+ Susan F. Salisbury, *Southern Massachu-setts Cemetery Collection*, Volume 1 (Bowie, Md., Heritage Books, 1995)
[F63/S25/1995/also Loan]

Stockwell–King Cemetery (1846)
Northwest Main St.
+ Susan F. Salisbury, *Southern Massachusetts Cemetery Collection* - Volume 1 (Bowie, Md., Heritage Books, 1995)
[F63/S25/1995/also Loan]

Thayer Cemetery
Locust St.

Walker–Aldrich Cemetery (1819)
Yew St.

DOVER (1784)
from Dedham
Town Hall, 5 Springdale Ave., Dover, Mass. 02030, Tel: (508)-785-1719

Highland Cemetery (1729)
54 Center St.

St. Dunstan's Church Memorial Garden (1998)
18 Springdale Ave.

DRACUT (1702)
Town Hall, 62 Arlington St., Dracut, Mass. 01826, Tel: (978)-453-0951

East Dracut Cemetery (aka) Bailey Cemetery
Broadway St.
+ [G.R. 6] *Vital Records of Dracut, Massachusetts to the year 1850* (1907).
New Boston Cemetery
Hildreth St.
+ [G.R. 5] *Vital Records of Dracut, Massachusetts to the year 1850* (1907).

Garrison House Burial Ground
+ [G.R. 4] *Vital Records of Dracut, Massachusetts to the year 1850* (1907).

Oakland Cemetery (1811)
1463 Mammoth Rd.
+ [G.R. 11] *Vital Records of Dracut, Massachusetts to the year 1850* (1907).

Richardson Cemetery (aka) New East Dracut Cemetery
Broadway St., behind the Bailey Cemetery

+ [G.R. 7] *Vital Records of Dracut, Massachusetts to the year 1850* (1907).

Varnum Cemetery
Parker Rd.
+ [G.R. 10] *Vital Records of Dracut, Massachusetts to the year 1850* (1907).

DUDLEY (1732)
from Oxford
Town Hall, 40 Schofield Ave., Dudley, Mass. 01571, Tel: (508)-949-8004

Calvary Cemetery (1863)
Oxford Ave.
Tel: Catholic Diocese Cemetery Office, 260 Cambridge St., Worcester, Mass. (508)-757-7415

Corbin Cemetery (1765)
Corbin Rd.

Curtis Cemetery
near West Dudley
+ [G.S. 5] *Vital Records of Dudley, Massachusetts to the year 1850* (1908).
+ NEHGS [Mss/SL/DUD/5]

Holy Trinity Cemetery (1919)
New Boston Rd.

Marsh Road Burying Ground (1812)
Henry Marsh Rd., near Oxford line.
+ [G.S. 3] *Vital Records of Dudley, Massachusetts to the year 1850* (1908).
+ NEHGS [Mss/SL/DUD/5]

Northwest Cemetery (1788)
Durfee Rd.

New Cemetery
Dudley Center
+ [G.S. 2] *Vital Records of Dudley, Massachusetts to the year 1850* (1908).
+ NEHGS [Mss/SL/DUD/5]

Old Cemetery
Dudley Center
+ [G.S. 1] *Vital Records of Dudley, Massachusetts to the year 1850* (1908).
+ NEHGS [Mss/SL/DUD/5] and [Mss/C/2009]

Perry Family Cemetery (1829)
Carpenter Rd.
+ [G.S. 6] *Vital Records of Dudley, Massachusetts to the year 1850* (1908).
+ NEHGS [Mss/SL/DUD/5]

Polish National Cemetery
Main St., Dudley Hill

Quinebaug Cemetery
+ [G.S. 8] *Vital Records of Dudley, Massachusetts to the year 1850* (1908).
+ NEHGS [Mss/SL/DUD/5]

Ramshorn Road Cemetery (aka) Willard Cemetery (1825)
Ramshorn Rd.
+ [G.S. 4] *Vital Records of Dudley, Massachusetts to the year 1850* (1908).
+ NEHGS [Mss/SL/DUD/5]

Village Cemetery (1775)
Dudley Center Rd.

Old Gore Cemetery
+ [G.S. 9] *Vital Records of Dudley, Massachusetts to the year 1850* (1908).
+ NEHGS [Mss/SL/DUD/5]

DUNSTABLE (1673)
Town Hall, 511 Main St., Dunstable, Mass. 01827, Tel: (978)-649-4514

Blood Cemetery (1821)
corner of Hollis and River Sts.
+ [G.R. 4] *Vital Records of Dunstable, Massachusetts to the year 1850* (1913).

Central Burial Ground (1754)
426 Main St., near Westford Sts.
+ [G.R. 8] *Vital Records of Dunstable,*
Massachusetts to the year 1850 (1913).

Meetinghouse Hill Cemetery (1754)
186 Main St.
+ [G.R. 1] *Vital Records of Dunstable,*
Massachusetts to the year 1850 (1913).
+ NEHGS [Mss/C/3261]
+ NSDAR [G.R.C./S1/v.94]

Rideout Family Cemetery (1844)
near 291 Fletcher St.

Swallow Cemetery (1766)
Brook St.
+ [G.R. 3] *Vital Records of Dunstable,*
Massachusetts to the year 1850 (1913).

DUXBURY (1637)
Town Hall, 878 Tremont St., Duxbury,
Mass. 02332, Tel: (781)-934-1131
Cemetery Department, 774 Tremont St.,
Duxbury, Mass., Tel: (781)-934-5261

Ashdod Cemetery (1811)
Keene St.
+ [G.R. 4] *Vital Records of Duxbury,*
Massachusetts to the year 1850 (1911).
+ Charles M. Thatcher, *Old Cemeteries of*
Southeastern Massachusetts.(Middleborough,
Mass., Middleborough Public Library,
1995) [F63/T53/1995/also Loan]

Crooked Lane Cemetery (18th century)
Crooked Ln., North Duxbury
+ Charles M. Thatcher, *Old Cemeteries of*
Southeastern Massachusetts.(Middleborough,
Mass., Middleborough Public Library,
1995) [F63/T53/1995/also Loan]

Dingley Cemetery
West St.

+ [G.R. 2] *Vital Records of Duxbury,*
Massachusetts to the year 1850 (1911).

Mayflower Cemetery (aka) Unitarian Church Cemetery, and Duxbury Crematory (1788)
774 Tremont St.
Tel: (617)-934-5261
+ Charles M. Thatcher, *Old Cemeteries of*
Southeastern Massachusetts.(Middleborough,
Mass., Middleborough Public Library,
1995) [F63/T53/1995/also Loan]

Old Burying Ground (aka) Standish Cemetery, South Duxbury Cemetery (17th Century)
Chestnut St., South Duxbury
+ [G.R. 1] *Vital Records of Duxbury,*
Massachusetts to the year 1850 (1911).
+ Charles M. Thatcher, *Old Cemeteries of*
Southeastern Massachusetts.(Middleborough,
Mass., Middleborough Public Library,
1995) [F63/T53/1995/also Loan]

Orthodox Church Cemetery
rear of Orthodox Church, Washington
St., South Duxbury

Site of First Church Cemetery
Chestnut St., next to Old Burying
Ground [many graves not marked]
+ Charles M. Thatcher, *Old Cemeteries of*
Southeastern Massachusetts.(Middleborough,
Mass., Middleborough Public Library,
1995) [F63/T53/1995/also Loan]

Walker Cemetery
Valley and Franklin Sts.

"Large Cemetery"
+ [G.R. 3] *Vital Records of Duxbury,*
Massachusetts to the year 1850 (1911).

"Large Cemetery"
+ [G.R. 5] *Vital Records of Duxbury, Mass-*
achusetts to the year 1850 (1911).

EAST BRIDGEWATER (1823)
from Bridgewater
Town Hall, 175 Central St., East Bridgewater, Mass. 02333, Tel: (508)-378-1606

Beaver Cemetery (1842)
Summer St.
+ [G.R. 6] *Vital Records of East Bridgewater, Massachusetts to the year 1850* (1917).

Central Cemetery (1848)
Central St., off of Hobart St.
+ [G.R. 5] *Vital Records of East Bridgewater, Massachusetts to the year 1850* (1917).

Hudson–Briggs Family Tomb Site (1819)
site was located on the south side of Plymouth Rd.
+ [G.R. 2] *Vital Records of East Bridgewater, Massachusetts to the year 1850* (1917).

Joppa Cemetery (1847)
East St., Elmwood
+ [G.R. 8] *Vital Records of East Bridgewater, Massachusetts to the year 1850* (1917).
+ Charles M. Thatcher, *Old Cemeteries of Southeastern Massachusetts.*(Middleborough, Mass., Middleborough Public Library, 1995) [F63/T53/1995/also Loan]

Northville Cemetery
Oak St.
+ [G.R. 9] *Vital Records of East Bridgewater, Massachusetts to the year 1850* (1917).

Old Graveyard (1703)
Central St., next to Central Cemetery
+ [G.R. 1] *Vital Records of East Bridgewater, Massachusetts to the year 1850* (1917).
+ Charles M. Thatcher, *Old Cemeteries of Southeastern Massachusetts.*(Middleborough, Mass., Middleborough Public Library, 1995) [F63/T53/1995/also Loan]

Osborn Cemetery Site
Pond St., near Roberts Pond

Small Pox Cemetery (aka) Hill Cemetery
off West St., Elmwood

Thayer-Fish Family Cemetery (1818)
off West Union St., near the West Bridgewater town line.
+ [G.R. 3] *Vital Records of East Bridgewater, Massachusetts to the year 1850* (1917).
+ Charles M. Thatcher, *Old Cemeteries of Southeastern Massachusetts.*(Middleborough, Mass., Middleborough Public Library, 1995) [F63/T53/1995/also Loan]

Union Cemetery (1842)
Pleasant St.
+ [G.R. 7 *Vital Records of East Bridgewater, Massachusetts to the year 1850* (1917).

Whitman Family Cemetery (1816)
Harvard St.
+ [G.R. 4] *Vital Records of East Bridgewater, Massachusetts to the year 1850* (1917).
+ Charles M. Thatcher, *Old Cemeteries of Southeastern Massachusetts.*(Middleborough, Mass., Middleborough Public Library, 1995) [F63/T53/1995/also Loan]

EAST BROOKFIELD (1920)
from Brookfield
Town Hall, 101 Depot Sq., East Brookfield, Mass. 01515, Tel: (508)-867-6769

Adams Family Cemetery I (18th century)
Draper Rd.

Adams Family Cemetery II Site (18th century)
Draper Rd., site demolished

Evergreen Cemetery (1740)
off Main St.

Podunk Cemetery (1820)
Podunk Rd.

EAST LONGMEADOW (1894)
from Longmeadow
Town Hall, 60 Center Sq., East Longmeadow, Mass. 01028, Tel: (413)-525-5400

Baptist Village Cemetery (1783)
Hampden Rd. and Parker St.

Billings Hill Cemetery (1803)
Prospect St. and Pease Rd.

Brookside Cemetery (1803)
Porter Rd.

Greenlawn Cemetery (1817)
Calendar Ave. and Pleasant St.

EASTHAM (1646)
Town Hall, 2500 State Hwy., Eastham, Mass. 02642, Tel: (508)-240-5900

Bridge Road Burying Ground (1754)
Bridge Rd.
+ Eastham Historical Society, *Cove Burying Ground, 1660-1770: Bridge Road Cemetery, 1754-1886: a survey conducted in the bicentennial year 1976 at Eastham.* (Eastham, 1976) [F74/E2/C68/1976/also Loan]
+ NSDAR [Mass./Counties/Barnstable/Eastham/Cov]

Congregational and Soldiers Cemetery (1813)
Rte. 6

+ Margaret H. Weiler, *Cemetery Inscriptions: Congregational and Soldiers Cemetery, Evergreen Cemetery, Eastham, Mass.* (Eastham, Mass.: Eastham Historical Society, 1987) [F74/E2/C45/1987]

Evergreen Cemetery (1806)
Rte. 6
+ Margaret H. Weiler, *Cemetery Inscriptions: Congregational and Soldiers Cemetery, Evergreen Cemetery, Eastham, Mass.* (Eastham, Mass.: Eastham Historical Society, 1987) [F74/E2/C45/1987]

Old Cove Cemetery (1660)
Rte. 6
+ *Cove Burying Ground, 1660-1770: Bridge Road Cemetery, 1754-1886 : a survey conducted in the bicentennial year 1976 at Eastham.* (Eastham, Mass.: Eastham Historical Society, 1976) [F74/E2/C68/1976/also Loan]
+ NSDAR [Mass./Counties/Barnstable/Eastham/Cov]

EASTHAMPTON (1785)
from Northampton
Town Hall, 43 Main St., Easthampton, Mass. 01027, Tel: (413)-529-1460

Brookside Cemetery
43 Williston Ave.

East Street Cemetery (1775)
Janes Ln. and Everett St.
+ NEHGS [Corbin Collection]

Main Street Cemetery (1765)
Main St.
+ NEHGS [Corbin Collection]

St. Brigid's Cemetery (1884)
91 Everett St.

Tel: Immaculate Conception Rectory, 33 Adams St., Easthampton, Mass. (413)-527-9778

St. Stanislaus Cemetery
Mayher St.
Tel: Sacred Heart Rectory, (413)-527-9036

EASTON (1725)
from Norton
Town Hall, 136 Elm St., North Easton, Mass. 02356, Tel: (508)-230-3335

Almshouse Cemetery (1845)
rear of 34 Rachael Cir.

Center Street Cemetery (1803)
next to 367 Center St.
+ NEHGS [Mss/SG/HOD/6/60], and [Mss/SG/LIN/5/23]
+ NSDAR [G.R.C./S1/v. 375],

Apolls Clark Cemetery (1832)
Summer St.

Elijah Copeland Graveyard (1817)
Bay Rd. opposite Beaver Dam

Dr. Edward Dean Cemetery (1756)
opposite 23 Highland St.

William Dean Cemetery (1815)
opposite 144 Rockland St.

Cynthia Drake Cemetery (1714)
Church St., north side
+ NEHGS [Mss/SG/LIN/5/23]

George Fergusson Burying Ground (1764)
Picker Ln.

Furnace Village Cemetery (1752)
opposite 69 South St.
+ NEHGS [Mss/SG/HOD/6/60], and [Mss/SG/LIN/5/23]

Capt. Elisha Harvey Gravesite (1775)
in the parking lot of the Easton Fitness Center, Old Colony/YMCA

Elijah Howard Cemetery (1775)
opposite 123 Prospect St.

Nehemiah Howard Cemetery (1818)
next to 252 Turnpike St.

Oliver Howard Cemetery (1803)
across from 25 Short St.

Immaculate Conception Cemetery (1857)
opposite 100 Canton St.

Thomas Keith Cemetery (1812)
beyond 297 Bay Rd.

Isaac Lothrop Cemetery (1796)
opposite 395 Purchase St.

Thomas Manley Cemetery (1736)
rear of 112-118 Lincoln St.

Asa Newcomb Cemetery (1827)
Red Mill Rd.

Old Bay Road Cemetery (1772)
opposite 159 Bay Rd.

Old Burying Ground (1705)
Church St., south side

Perez Packard Cemetery (1878)
opposite 190 Lincoln St.

Silas Phillips Cemetery (1842)
opposite 214 Depot St.

Pine Grove Cemetery (1796)
227 Foundry St.
+ NSDAR [G.R.C./S1/v. 375]

Seth Pratt Cemetery (1801)
Washington St, Rte. 138 across from the
South Easton Cemetery, South Easton
+ NSDAR [G.R.C./S1/v. 48]

Macey Record Cemetery (1834)
opposite 82 Chestnut St.

John Selee Cemetery (1836)
opposite 18 Mill St.
Short Cemetery (1809)
Lyman Wheelock Rd.
+ NSDAR [G.R.C./S1/v. 363]

South Easton Cemetery (1851)
opposite 490 Washington St., Rte. 138

Stonehill College Cemetery (1950)
Stonehill College, Washington St.
entrance, Rte. 138

Village Cemetery (1877)
15 Main St., rear of the Unity Church,
North Easton
Tel: (508)-238-6778

Washington Street Cemetery (1796)
opposite 198 Washington St., Rte. 138

George Wilbur Cemetery (1807)
Borderland State Park, near Massapoag Ave.

Lt. John Williams Cemetery (1739)
Prospect St., south side

Col. John Williams Cemetery (1797)
Prospect St., north side

Jedediah Willis Cemetery (1820)
opposite 120 Bay Rd.

EDGARTOWN (1671)
Town Hall, 70 Main St., Edgartown,
Mass. 02539, Tel: (508)-627-6110

Belain Cemetery
Chappaquiddick Island
+ [G.R. 6] *Vital Records of Edgartown,
Massachusetts to the year 1850* (1906).
+ NEHGS [Mss/3/E/5]

Cottage City Cemetery
+ [G.R. 7] *Vital Records of Edgartown,
Massachusetts to the year 1850* (1906).

Farm Neck Cemetery
Cottage City
+ [G.R. 8] *Vital Records of Edgartown,
Massachusetts to the year 1850* (1906).

First Cemetery
Chappaquiddick Island
+ [G.R. 5] *Vital Records of Edgartown,
Massachusetts to the year 1850* (1906).
+ NEHGS [Mss/3/E/5]

Indian Cemetery
Chappaquiddick Island
+ [G.R. 4] *Vital Records of Edgartown,
Massachusetts to the year 1850* (1906).
+ NEHGS [Mss/3/E/5]

**Old Burying Ground (aka) Tower
Hill and Burial Hill Cemetery**
+ [G.R. 1] *Vital Records of Edgartown,
Massachusetts to the year 1850* (1906).

Pease's Point Way Cemetery
Pease's Point Way
+ [G.R. 2] *Vital Records of Edgartown,
Massachusetts to the year 1850* (1906).

Gravestone private grounds
+ [G.R. 3] *Vital Records of Edgartown,
Massachusetts to the year 1850* (1906).

**Graves near Old House Pond,
Cottage City**
+ [G.R. 9] *Vital Records of Edgartown,
Massachusetts to the year 1850* (1906).

EGREMONT (1760)

Town Hall, 171 Egremont Plain Rd.,
Egremont, Mass. 01258, Tel: (413)-528-0182

Hillside Cemetery (1986)
Rte. 71, North Egremont

Hollenbeck Cemetery (1828)
Rte. 71, near Baldwin Hill East Rd.

Mount Everett Cemetery (1810)
Rte. 23, behind the South Egremont
Public Library
+ NEHGS [Mss/A/243].
+ NSDAR [G.R.C./S1/v. 192]

Old Cemetery
Rte. 71, North Egremont

Race Cemetery (1818)
off Blunt Rd., North Egremont
+NEHGS [Mss/A/243]

Riverside Cemetery (1776)
Rte. 71, North Egremont Village
+ NEHGS [MS70/EGR/10]
+ NSDAR [G.R.C./S1/v. 192]

Town House Hill Cemetery (1732)
Town House Hill Rd. near Phillips Rd.,
South Egremont
+ NEHGS [Mss/A/243] and
[MS70/EGR/10]
+ NSDAR [G.R.C./S1/v. 192]

Tuller Cemetery (1778)
Sheffield Rd., South Egremont
+NEHGS [Mss/A/243], and
[MS70/EGR/10]
+ NSDAR [G.R.C./S1/v. 192]

ENFIELD (1816)
from Belchertown and Greenwich

This town was flooded in 1938 for the
Quabbin Reservoir. All burials in the
following cemeteries were removed to
Quabbin Park Cemetery, Ware, Mass.
1938
+ NEHGS [MS/70/WAR/15]

Cemetery Hill Cemetery Site
Church Cemetery Site
Packardsville Cemetery Site (1787)
Howe Family Cemetery Site
**Ludlow Manufacturing Association
Cemetery Site**
**Packardsville Church Cemetery Site
(1859)**
Wilder Family Cemetery Site
Woodlawn Cemetery Site

ERVING (1838)

Town Hall, 12 East Main St., Erving,
Mass. 01344, Tel: (978)-544-2765

Erving Center Cemetery (1814)
Mountain Rd.

Holton Cemetery (1815)
Main St.

ESSEX (1819)
from Ipswich

Town Hall, 30 Martin St., Essex, Mass.
01929, Tel: (978)-767-7111
Cemetery Office, 144 Centennial St.,
Essex, Mass. 01929

Essex Burial Ground (1680)
Main St., next to Essex Shipbuilding
Museum.
+ [G.R. 4] *Vital Records of Ipswich,
Massachusetts to the year 1850* (1910).

Spring Street Cemetery (1824)
Spring St.
+ [G.R. 6] *Vital Records of Ipswich,
Massachusetts to the year 1850* (1910).
+ NEHGS [MS70/ESS/1]

EVERETT (1870)
from Malden
City Hall, 484 Broadway St., Everett,
Mass. 02149, Tel: (617)-389-2100

Ahavas Achim Anshe Sfard
(a section of the Fuller Street Jewish
Cemetery)

B'nai Israel of Beachmont Cemetery
(a section of the Fuller Street Jewish
Cemetery)

Bessarabian
(a section of the Fuller Street Jewish
Cemetery)

**Fuller Street Jewish Cemetery (aka)
Beth Israel Jewish Cemetery (1920)**
232 Fuller Street
Tel: (617)-387-3980

Birsen
(a section of the Fuller Street Jewish
Cemetery)

Chevra Chai Odom
(a section of the Fuller Street Jewish
Cemetery)

**Chevra Thilim of Malden, Boston
and Chelsea** (a section of the Fuller
Street Jewish Cemetery)

Dorchester Hebrew Helping Hand
(a section of the Fuller Street Jewish
Cemetery)

Fuller Street Jewish Cemetery
Fuller St.

Glenwood Cemetery (1890)
Washington Ave.
Tel: (617)-394-2380

Greenview Memorial Park
(a section of the Fuller Street Jewish
Cemetery)

Guard of Moses
(a section of the Fuller Street Jewish
Cemetery)

Jewish Deed Holders
(a section of the Fuller Street Jewish
Cemetery)

Knights of Zaslav
(a section of the Fuller Street Jewish
Cemetery)

Liberty Progressive
(a section of the Fuller Street Jewish
Cemetery)

Linas Hazdeck # 1
(a section of the Fuller Street Jewish
Cemetery)

Mishna of Chelsea
(a section of the Fuller Street Jewish
Cemetery)

Montefiore
(a section of the Fuller Street Jewish
Cemetery)

Poali Zedeck
(a section of the Fuller Street Jewish
Cemetery)

Rabbi Isaac Eichonon Cemetery
(a section of the Fuller Street Jewish
Cemetery)

Sudlikov Cemetery
(a section of the Fuller Street Jewish
Cemetery)

Tifereth Israel of Everett
(a section of the Fuller Street Jewish
Cemetery)

Tifereth Israel of Revere
(a section of the Fuller Street Jewish
Cemetery)

Tifereth Israel of Winthrop
(a section of the Fuller Street Jewish
Cemetery)

**Woodlawn Cemetery and
Crematory (1852)**
302 Elm St.
Tel: (617)-387-0800

FAIRHAVEN (1812)
from New Bedford
Town Hall, 40 Center St., Fairhaven,
Mass. 02719, Tel: (508)-979-4025

Delano Family Cemetery
Wilbur's Point

Indian Cemetery
Wigwam Beach

**Nasketucket Cemetery (18th
century)**
Hutleston Ave., off Rte. 6

Riverside Cemetery (1850)
274 Main St.

Shaw Burying Ground
at the Mattapoisett town line.

Woodside Cemetery
380 Main St.
+ NSDAR [G.R.C./S1/v. 50]

FALL RIVER (1803)
from Freetown, Mass. and
Tiverton, Rhode Island
City Hall, One Government Ctr., Fall
River, Mass. 02722, Tel: (508)-324-2102

Agudath Achim Jewish Cemetery
(a section of the Beth El Jewish
Cemetery)

Beth El Jewish Cemetery
4561North Main St.
Tel: Temple Beth El, 385 High St., Fall
River, Mass. (508)-674-3529

North Burial Ground (1810)
1360 North Main St.

Notre Dame Cemetery (1883)
1540 Stafford Rd., next to Our Lady of
Light Cemetery.
Tel: (508)-675-2495

Oak Grove Cemetery (1822)
765 Prospect St.
Tel: (508)-324-2750

Our Lady of Light Cemetery
576 Newhall St., next to the Notre Dame
Cemetery
Tel: (508)-675-2495

St. John's Cemetery (1858)
258 Brightman St.
Tel: St. Patrick's Cemetery,(508)-679-
2535

St. Mary's Cemetery (1840)
Amity St.
Tel: St. Patrick's Cemetery, (508)-679-
2535

St. Patrick's Cemetery (1876)
2233 Robeson St.
Tel: (508)-679-2535

Valentine Cemetery
North Main St.
+ NEHGS [MS70/FAL/10]

General Cemetery Reference for Fall River:
+ Ebenezer W. Peirce, "Inscriptions from Freetown, Mass" *NEHGR* 10:53-54.
".. in the division of Freetown in 1803, this lot of land fell within the limits of Troy, now Fall River".

FALMOUTH (1694)
Town Hall, 59 Town Hall Sq., Falmouth, Mass. 02541, Tel: (508)-548-7611

Bayview Cemetery (1849)
Main St., Waquoit
+ [G.R. 6] *Vital Records of Falmouth, Massachusetts to the year 1850* (1976).

Church of the Messiah Episcopal Churchyard (1788)
22 Church St., next to the Church of the Messiah Woods Hole
Tel: Church of the Messiah Rectory, 22 Church St., Falmouth, Mass. (508)-548-2145
+ *The Village Cemetery and the Churchyard, Church of the Messiah Woods Hole, Mass. Known Burials, from 1788-1968.*

Crowell Family Cemetery (1848)
across from 856 Main St., Rte. 28A, West Falmouth
+ NEHGS [MS70/FAL/45], [MS70/WES/181] and [Mss/3/W/31]
+ NSDAR [G.R.C./S1/v. 48]

Davisville Cemetery (1845)
Davisville Rd., off Pasnecoy Ln.
+ [G.R. 10] *Vital Records of Falmouth, Massachusetts to the year 1850* (1976).

East End Cemetery (1796)
Hatchville Rd., Hatchville
+ [G.R. 3] *Vital Records of Falmouth, Massachusetts to the year 1850* (1976).
+ NEHGS [MS70/FAL/40]

Falmouth Jewish Cemetery (1994)
7 Hatchville Rd., next to the Falmouth Jewish Congregation Temple.
Tel: Falmouth Jewish Congregation, 7 Hatchville Rd., Falmouth, Mass. (508)-540-8094

Friends Cemetery (1688)
Rte. 28A, West Falmouth
+ [G.R. 5] *Vital Records of Falmouth, Massachusetts to the year 1850* (1976).
+ NEHGS [F74/F3/R6/1954]
Typescript in Mss
+ NSDAR [G.R.C./S1/v.345]

Indian Burying Ground Site
behind the North Falmouth Public Library

Methodist Society Burial Ground (1809)
between 704 and 744 East Main St., East Falmouth
+ [G.R. 9] *Vital Records of Falmouth, Massachusetts to the year 1850* (1976).

North Falmouth Cemetery (1804)
Main Rd. behind the Congregational Church
+ [G.R. 7] *Vital Records of Falmouth, Massachusetts to the year 1850* (1976).

Oak Grove Cemetery (1808)
Palmer Ave.
Tel: (508)-548-7510
+ [G.R. 8] *Vital Records of Falmouth, Massachusetts to the year 1850* (1976).

Old Burying Ground (1705)
off Mill Rd.
+ [G.R. 1] *Vital Records of Falmouth, Massachusetts to the year 1850* (1976).
+ *Transcriptions of the Old Burying Ground, Falmouth, Mass. from the Falmouth Enterprise, 1903-1904.*
[F74/F3/O43/1903-04]
+ NEHGS [MS70/FAL/40]
+ NSDAR [G.R.C./S1/v. 399]

Old Friends Cemetery (1689)
off Blacksmith Shop Rd., West
Falmouth [no stones]
+ Mrs. J. Clifford Ross, *Memorandum of
graves in Friends Burial Ground, West
Falmouth, Massachusetts* (Boston, 1954)
[F74/F3/R6/1954]

**Robinson Family Cemetery (aka)
Sady's Lane and Ennsbrook Road
Cemetery (1801)**
86 Sady Ln., East Falmouth
+ [G.R. 12] *Vital Records of Falmouth,
Massachusetts to the year 1850* (1976).

**St. Anthony's Cemetery (20th
century)**
off Acapesket Rd. behind St. Anthony's
Church
Tel: St. Anthony's Rectory, 167 East
Falmouth Highway,(508)-548-0108

**St. Joseph's and St. Patrick's
Cemetery (19th century)**
Gifford St.
Tel: St. Joseph's Rectory, 33 Millfield St.
Woods Hole, (508)-548-0990;

Village Cemetery (1788)
Church St., Woods Hole
+ [G.R. 2] *Vital Records of Falmouth,
Massachusetts to the year 1850* (1976).

Waqoit Cemetery (1849)
Rte. 28, Main St., Waqoit
+ NSDAR [G.R.C./S1/v. 48]

**Private cemetery, south of East
Falmouth Highway, East Falmouth**
+ [G.R. 11] *Vital Records of Falmouth,
Massachusetts to the year 1850* (1976).

FITCHBURG (1764)
from Lunenburg
City Hall, 718 Main St., Fitchburg, Mass.
01420, Tel: (978)-345-9594

Agudas Achim Jewish Cemetery
Rollstone Rd.

Alpine Hill Cemetery
Alpine Rd.
+ NSDAR [G.R.C./S1/v. 81]

Deane Hill Cemetery (1791)
Caswell Rd., off Ashburnham Rd.
+ NSDAR [G.R.C./S1/v. 81], and
[G.R.C./S1/v. 354]

Forest Hill Cemetery (1856)
115 Mt. Elam Rd., off of Electric Ave.
Tel: (978)-345-9578
+ NSDAR [G.R.C./S1/v. 170], and
[G.R.C./S1/v. 207]

Hartwell Cemetery
Scott's Rock Rd.
+ NSDAR [G.R.C./S1/v. 81]

Laurel Hill Cemetery (1873)
167 Laurel St., off of Rollstone St.
+ NSDAR [G.R.C./S1/v. 119]

**St. Bernard's Church Cemetery
(1858)**
St. Bernard St.
Tel: St. Bernard's Rectory, 45 Harvard
St., Fitchburg, Mass. (978)-342-4820
+ NSDAR [G.R.C./S1/v. 81]

St. Joseph's Cemetery
486 Clarendon St.
Tel: St. Joseph's Rectory, 46 Woodland
St., (978)-345-7997

South Street Cemetery (1766)
South St.
+ NEHGS [MS70/FIT/1] and
[MS/FIT/34]
+ NSDAR [G.R.C./S1/v. 81]

West Street Cemetery (1801)
West St., off of Main St.
+ NSDAR [G.R.C./S1/v. 81]

FLORIDA (1805)
Town Hall, 20 South St., Drury, Mass.
01343, Tel: (413)-664-6685

Bradley Cemetery (1826)
Stryker Rd.

Burnett Cemetery (1813)
South County Rd.

Center Cemetery (1821)
North County and Olson Rds.

Nathan Drury Burial Ground (1840)
Church Rd.

Monroe Road Cemetery (1815)
Monroe Rd.

Old Florida Center Cemetery (1846)
Church Rd.

Torrey Cemetery (1820)
South St.

Martin Tower Cemetery (1813)
Bliss Rd.

Whitcomb Cemetery (1813)
Whitcomb Hill Rd.

FOXBOROUGH (1778)
from Stoughton, Walpole, and Wrentham
Town Hall, 40 South St., Foxborough,
Mass. 02035, Tel: (508)-543-1208

Foxboro State Hospital Cemetery (1893)
across from 21 Cross St.

Boyden Burial Ground (1756)
across from 281 Cocasset St., near
Cannon Forge Dr., East Foxborough

+ [G.R. 5] *Vital Records of Foxborough,
Massachusetts to the year 1850* (1911).
+ NEHGS [MS70/FOX/1]

Centre Burial Ground (1773)
40 South St., on the grounds of the
Foxborough Museum, Foxborough
Center.
Tel: (508)-543-1248
+ [G.R. 1] *Vital Records of Foxborough,
Massachusetts to the year 1850* (1911).
+ NEHGS [MS70/FOX/1]

Clapp Family Burial Ground [no gravestones] (1827)
between 102 and 106 Beach St.
+ [G.R. 8] *Vital Records of Foxborough,
Massachusetts to the year 1850* (1911).
+ NEHGS [MS70/FOX/1]

Gethsemane Cemetery
across from 63 Mill St.

Hodges Burial Ground (1781)
between 105 and 109 East St., East
Foxborough
+ [G.R. 4] *Vital Records of Foxborough,
Massachusetts to the year 1850* (1911).
+ NEHGS [MS70/FOX/1]

Payson–Morse Family Cemetery (1761)
between 57 and 61 Chestnut St., across
from Kersey Rd.
+ [G.R. 2] *Vital Records of Foxborough,
Massachusetts to the year 1850* (1911).
+ NEHGS [MS70/FOX/1]

Quaker Hill Cemetery (aka) Sherman Burying Ground (1817)
Green St. and Faxon Rd.
+ [G.R. 6] *Vital Records of Foxborough,
Massachusetts to the year 1850* (1911).
+ NEHGS [MS70/FOX/1]

Rock Hill Cemetery (1853)
South and Union Sts.
Tel: (508)-543-8560
+ NEHGS [MS70/FOX/1] (G.R. 9)

St. Mary's Cemetery (19th century)
across from 108 Mechanic St., near
Chestnut St.
Tel: St. Mary's Rectory, 83 Central St.,
(508)-543-7726

Wading River Cemetery (1772)
across from 11 Cedar St., South
Foxborough
+ [G.R. 3] *Vital Records of Foxborough,
Massachusetts to the year 1850* (1911).
+ NEHGS [MS70/FOX/1]

Hepzibah Wilber Gravesite (1858)
Spring St., grave was moved to a family
plot at the Rock Hill Cemetery ca. 1972.
+ [G.R. 7] *Vital Records of Foxborough,
Massachusetts to the year 1850* (1911).
+ NEHGS [MS70/FOX/1]

FRAMINGHAM (1675)
Town Hall, 150 Concord St.,
Framingham, Mass. 01702, Tel: (508)-
620-4863
Cemetery Department, 475 Union Ave.,
Framingham, Mass. 01702

Church Hill Cemetery (aka) Old Burial Ground (1704)
Main St., near Union Ave.
+ NEHGS [MS70/FRA/1] and
[MS70/FRA/2]

Edgell Grove Cemetery (1848)
53 Grove St.
Tel: (508)-872-3801
+ NEHGS [MS70/FRA/3]

Edwards Cemetery (1838)
Edwards St., Saxonville, near Edwards
Congregational Church
+ NEHGS [MS70/FRA/2]

Indian Burying Ground (aka) Old Field Site
Framingham Common

Old South Cemetery (aka) South Burying Ground (1824)
Winthrop St., across from St. Tarcisius
Cemetery
+ NEHGS [MS70/FRA/2]

St. George's Cemetery (1856)
Cherry St.
Tel: St. George's Rectory, 71 School St.,
Framingham, Mass. (508)-877-5130
Tel: Archives of the Archdiocese of
Boston, 2121 Commonwealth Ave.,
Brighton, Mass. 02135, (617)-254-
0100.The Boston Archdiocese Archives
has grave lot sales from 1857.

St. Stephen's Cemetery (1887)
Fenwick St., Saxonville
Tel: (508)-881-1062

St. Tarcisius Cemetery (1899)
Winthrop St., across from the Old South
Cemetery
Tel: St. Tarcius Rectory, 562 Waverly St.,
Framingham, Mass. 01702 (508)-872-
9053

FRANKLIN (1778)
from Wrentham
Town Hall, 150 Emmons St., Franklin,
Mass. 02038, Tel: (508)-520-4900
Franklin Cemetery Association, 23
Forest St., Franklin, Ma 02038-2501 Tel:
(508)-541-8400

City Mills Cemetery (1740)
Green St.
+ Susan F. Salisbury, *Southern
Massachusetts Cemetery Collection* - Volume
2 (Bowie, Md., Heritage Books, 1996)
[F63/S25/1995/also Loan]
+ NEHGS [Mss/C/2463]

+ NSDAR [MASS COUNTIES/
NORFOLK/ FRANKLIN/DOW]

St. Mary's Cemetery
Beaver St., West Central
Tel: St. Mary's Rectory, 1 Church Sq.,
Franklin, Mass. 02038, (508)-528-0020.
Union Street Burying Ground (1725)
West Central and Union Sts.
+ Susan F. Salisbury, *Southern Massachu-
setts Cemetery Collection*, Volume 2 (Bowie,
Md., Heritage Books, 1996)
[F63/S25/1995/also Loan]

FREETOWN (1683)
Town Hall, 3 North Main St., Freetown,
Mass. 02702, Tel: (508)-644-2203

James Emerson Ashley Family Cemetery (1856)
Gurney Rd.,
+ Charles M. Thatcher, *Old Cemeteries of
Southeastern Massachusetts*. (Middleborough,
Mass., Middleborough Public
Library,1995) [F63/T53/1995/also Loan]

Assonet Burial Grounds
South Main St.
+ Mrs. Wendell B. Presbrey, *Inscriptions
from Eight Cemeteries in Bristol, County,
Massachusetts*. (---, Massachusetts D.A.R.,
1987) [F72/B8/I57/1987]+ NEHGS
[MS70/FRE/10]
+ NSDAR [G.R.C./S2/v. 1]

Assonet Cemetery #1
Howland Rd.

Assonet Cemetery #2
High St.

Dr. Bradford Braley Cemetery (1834)
Braley Rd.
+ Charles M. Thatcher, *Old Cemeteries of
Southeastern Massachusetts*. (Middleborough,
Mass., Middleborough Public Library,
1995) [F63/T53/1995/also Loan]

Braley's Station Cemetery (1841)
Chipaway Rd.
+ Charles M. Thatcher, *Old Cemeteries of
Southeastern Massachusetts*. (Middlebor-
ough, Mass., Middleborough Public
Library, 1995) [F63/T53/1995/also Loan]

Paul M. Burns Family Cemetery (1885)
Burns Ln.

Chace–Cummings Family Cemetery (1849)
15 Chase Rd.
+ Charles M. Thatcher, *Old Cemeteries of
Southeastern Massachusetts*.
(Middleborough, Mass., Middleborough
Public Library, 1995)
[F63/T53/1995/also Loan]

Crapo Cemetery (1789)
Bullock Rd.

Levi Dean Family Cemetery
North Main St.
+ NEHGS [Mss/3/F/11]

Josiah DeMoranville Family Cemetery (1840)
Chace Rd.

East Freetown Cemetery
Chace Rd.
+ Charles M. Thatcher, *Old Cemeteries of
Southeastern Massachusetts*. (Middlebor-
ough, Mass., Middleborough Public
Library, 1995) [F63/T53/1995/also Loan]

Evans Family Cemetery
Narrows Rd.

Evans Family Cemetery
Highland Ridge Rd.

Friends Cemetery (1783)
Friend St.
+ NEHGS [Mss/3/F/12]

Hathaway Family Cemetery (1750)
South Main St.
+ NEHGS [MS70/FRE/10]
Morton Cemetery (1809)
Middleboro Rd.

Nichols Family Cemetery
Pleasant St.

Paine Family Cemetery
South Main St.

Payne Family Cemetery
Mill St.

Payne Family Cemetery
High St.

Pierce and Morton Cemetery (18th century)
+ Charles M. Thatcher, *Old Cemeteries of Southeastern Massachusetts*. (Middleborough, Mass., Middleborough Public Library, 1995) [F63/T53/1995/also Loan]

Pittsley Cemetery (1834)
Middleboro Rd.
+ Charles M. Thatcher, *Old Cemeteries of Southeastern Massachusetts*. (Middleborough, Mass., Middleborough Public Library, 1995) [F63/T53/1995/also Loan]

Richmond Cemetery (1799)
Richmond Rd.
+ Charles M. Thatcher, *Old Cemeteries of Southeastern Massachusetts*. (Middleborough, Mass., Middleborough Public Library, 1995) [F63/T53/1995/also Loan]

Rousevell Cemetery (1740)
County Rd.

Spooner Family Cemetery (after 1850)
East Freetown

+ Charles M. Thatcher, *Old Cemeteries of Southeastern Massachusetts*. (Middleborough, Mass., Middleborough Public Library, 1995) [F63/T53/1995/also Loan]

Nathan Spooner Family Cemetery (1818)
Chace Rd.

Terry Family Cemetery (1785)
South Main St.
+ NEHGS [MS70/FRE/10]

Tisdale Family Cemetery (1795)
Jeffrey Ln.

White Cemetery (1803)
Long Plain Rd.
+ NSDAR [G.R.C./S2/v. 1]
+ Charles M. Thatcher, *Old Cemeteries of Southeastern Massachusetts*.(Middleborough, Mass., Middleborough Public Library, 1995) [F63/T53/1995/also Loan]

White Cemetery (1816)
off Rte. 18, Keene Rd., East Freetown
+ Mrs. Wendell B. Presbrey, *Inscriptions from Eight Cemeteries in Bristol, County, Massachusetts*. (---, Massachusetts D.A.R., 1987) [F72/B8/I57/1987]

Winslow Family Cemetery (1786)
Locust St.

Witherell Family Cemetery
Locust St.

GARDNER (1785)
from Ashburnham, Templeton, Westminster, and Winchendon
City Hall, 95 Pleasant St., Gardner, Mass. 01440, Tel: (978)-630-4008

Crystal Lake Cemetery (1858)
Park St.

Green Bower Cemetery (1849)
Winter St.

Notre Dame Cemetery (19th century)
West St.
Tel: Holy Rosary Church Office, 135 Nichols St., Gardner (978)-632-0253

Old Burying Ground (1780)
Green St.
+ NEHGS [MS70/GAR/1]
+ NSDAR [G.R.C./S1/v. 5]

St. John's Cemetery
West St.
Tel: Sacred Heart Church Office, 166 Cross St., Gardner (978)-632-0237

St. Joseph's Cemetery (1850)
West St.
Tel: St. Joseph's Church Office, 358 Pleasant St., Gardner (978)-632-0375
+ NEHGS [Vertical File/F74/G2/ M32/1988] (selected stones)

Wildwood Cemetery
West St.

GEORGETOWN (1838)
from Rowley
Town Hall, One Library St., Georgetown, Mass. 01833, Tel: (978)-352-5711

Harmony Cemetery (1831)
Central St.

South Byfield Cemetery
Warren St.

Union Cemetery (1732)
East Main St.
+ [G.R. 2] *Vital Records of Rowley, Massachusetts to the year 1850* (1928).

GILL (1793)
from Greenfield
Town Hall, 325 Main St., Gill, Mass. 01376, Tel: (413)-863-8103

Gill Center Cemetery (19th century)
Main Rd., ½ mile north of Gill Center.

North Gill Cemetery
Main Rd., ½ mile north of Rte. 2.

Riverside Cemetery
Main Rd.

West Gill Cemetery (19th century)
Hoe Shop Rd., off West Gill Rd.

GLOUCESTER (1642)
City Clerk, 9 Dale Ave., Gloucester, Mass. 01930, Tel: (978)-281-9720

Bay View Cemetery (aka) Third Parish Cemetery (1728)
903-919 Washington St.
+ [G.R. 2] *Vital Records of Gloucester, Massachusetts to the year 1850* (1924).

Beechbrook Cemetery (1878)
397-401 Essex Ave.

Bray Cemetery (ca. 1820)
near 381 Essex Ave., Rte. 133

Bridge Street Cemetery
Bridge St.
+ [G.R. 1] *Vital Records of Gloucester, Massachusetts to the year 1850* (1924).

Calvary Roman Catholic Cemetery (ca. 1890s)
151 Eastern Ave.

Cherry Hill Cemetery (1843)
13-19 Marsh St.

+ [G.R. 11] *Vital Records of Gloucester, Massachusetts to the year 1850* (1924).
Clark's Cemetery (ca. 1840's)
rear of 122 Cenetennial Ave., rear of the First Parish Cemetery

Cove Hill Cemetery (aka) Old Lanesville Cemetery (1729)
off a lane at 1052 Washington St.

First Parish Cemetery (1640)
122 Centennial Ave., in front of Clark Cemetery

High Street Cemetery
High St.
+ [G.R. 13] *Vital Records of Gloucester, Massachusetts to the year 1850* (1924).

Langsford Street Cemetery (1830)
32-34 Langsford St.

Dolliver Memorial Cemetery (1996)
13-15 Lincoln St., off of Essex Ave.

Magnolia Point Cemetery (1826)
61 Magnolia Ave., Magnolia

Mount Adnah Cemetery (ca. 1826)
107 Leonard St. off Washington St.
+ [G.R. 9] *Vital Records of Gloucester, Massachusetts to the year 1850* (1924).

Mount Jacob Cemetery (1913)
near 493 Essex Ave.

Mount Pleasant Cemetery (19th century)
25 Mt. Pleasant Ave., East Gloucester
+ [G.R. 10] *Vital Records of Gloucester, Massachusetts to the year 1850* (1924).

Oak Grove Cemetery (1855)
177 Washington St.
+ [G.R. 5] *Vital Records of Gloucester, Massachusetts to the year 1850* (1924).

Oak Hill Catholic Cemetery
45 Poplar St., corner of Cherry St.

Proctor Family Cemetery (1827)
499 Essex Ave., next to the West Gloucester Trinitarian Congregational Church

Prospect Street Unitarian Cemetery (1737)
16-22 Prospect St., opposite Church St.

Seaside Cemetery (1877)
88-94 Langsford St.
+ [G.R. 3] *Vital Records of Gloucester, Massachusetts to the year 1850* (1924).

Second Parish Cemetery (1716)
Thompson St., West Gloucester

Sumner Street Cemetery (1817)
42 Sumner St., West Gloucester, off of Essex Ave.
+ [G.R. 6] *Vital Records of Gloucester, Massachusetts to the year 1850* (1924).
+ NEHGS [Mss/3/W/22]
+ NSDAR [G.R.C./1932/S1/v. 16]

Universalist Yard Cemetery (aka) Pine Hill Cemetery (ca. 1805)
rear 25 Church St.
+ [G.R. 12] *Vital Records of Gloucester, Massachusetts to the year 1850* (1924).

Washington Cemetery (1839)
108 Western Ave.
+ [G.R. 8] *Vital Records of Gloucester, Massachusetts to the year 1850* (1924).

Wesleyan Cemetery (1865)
15 Wesley St. near Wheeler St., Riverdale
+ [G.R. 7] *Vital Records of Gloucester, Massachusetts to the year 1850* (1924).

Ancient Cemetery, West Gloucester
+ [G.R. 3] *Vital Records of Gloucester, Massachusetts to the year 1850* (1924).

GOSHEN (1781)
from Chesterfield
Town Hall, 42 Main St., Goshen, Mass.
01032, Tel: (413)-268-8236

Goshen Center Cemetery (1774)
Goshen Center
+ Hiram Barbus, *History of the Town of Goshen* (Boston, Mass. 1881) p. 119.
+ NEHGS [MS70/FRE/10] and [Corbin Collection]
+ NSDAR [G.R.C./S1/v. 219]

Old Williamsburg Road Cemetery (aka) Rogers-Butler-Bassett Family Cemetery (1788)
off Rte. 9
+ NEHGS [Corbin Collection]
+ NSDAR [G.R.C./S1/v. 48]

GOSNOLD (1864)
from Chilmark
Town Hall, 28 Tower Hill Rd.,
Cuttyhunk, Mass. 02713, Tel: (508)-990-7408

Town of Gosnold Cemetery
1 Cemetery Rd.
+ NEHGS [MS70/GOS/11]

GRAFTON (1735)
Town Hall, 30 Providence Rd., Grafton,
Mass. 01519, Tel: (508)-839-4722

Fairview Cemetery (1849)
Providence Rd.
+ Susan F. Salisbury, *Southern Massachusetts Cemetery Collection*, Volume 1 (Bowie, Md., Heritage Books, 1995) [F63/S25/1995/also Loan]

Farnumsville Cemetery (1812)
316 Providence Rd.
+ NEHGS [MS70/GRA/1]

Indian Burying Ground (1664)
Providence Rd.

Old Burying Ground and Indian Cemetery (1731)
Rte. 122, Oak St.
+ Rita F. Martin, *The Oak St. Burying Ground.* (Grafton, Mass.: Grafton Historical Commission, 1993) [F74/G7/O53/1993]
+ Susan F. Salisbury, *Southern Massachusetts Cemetery Collection*, Volume 1 (Bowie, Md., Heritage Books, 1995) [F63/S25/1995/also Loan]
+ NEHGS [MS70/GRA/1]

Pine Grove Cemetery (1846)
18 Waterville St., Rte. 30
+ Susan F. Salisbury, *Southern Massachusetts Cemetery Collection* - Volume 1 (Bowie, Md., Heritage Books, 1995) [F63/S25/1995/also Loan]

Riverside Cemetery (1850)
Millbury St.

St. Philips Cemetery (1862)
Millbury St.
Tel: (508)-839-3325

GRANBY (1768)
from South Hadley
Town Hall, 250 State St., Granby, Mass.
01033, Tel: (413)-467-7178

North Granby Cemetery (aka) Bachelor Street Cemetery (1764)
Bachelor St.
+ NEHGS [MS70/GRA/11], and [Corbin Collection]
+ NSDAR [G.R.C./S1/v. 260]

West End Cemetery (1769)
Kellogg and West Sts., off Rte. 202
+ NEHGS [Corbin Collection]

GRANVILLE (1754)

Town Hall, 707 Main Rd., Granville, Mass. 01034, Tel: (413)-357-8585

Blandford Road Cemetery (aka) Northeast, Woodlawn and Old Westfield Cemetery (1816)
Blandford Rd.
+ [G.R. 3] *Vital Records of Granville, Massachusetts to the year 1850* (1914).

Dickson Cemetery
all burials moved to the Granville Cemetery.
+ [G.R. 3] *Vital Records of Granville, Massachusetts to the year 1850* (1914).

Granville Cemetery (aka) Southeast, Silver Street Cemetery (1808)
Silver St.
+ [G.R. 2] *Vital Records of Granville, Massachusetts to the year 1850* (1914).

Main Road Cemetery (1742)
Main Rd.

North Cemetery Cemetery
Granville Center
+ [G.R. 3] *Vital Records of Granville, Massachusetts to the year 1850* (1914).

Searl Burial Plot Site (1864)
Searles Rd. (all burials removed to the West Granville Cemetery)

West Cemetery (1750)
West Granville
+ [G.R. 1]*Vital Records of Granville, Massachusetts to the year 1850* (1914).

West Granville Cemetery (1770)
Main Rd.
+ [G.R. 6 *Vital Records of Granville, Massachusetts to the year 1850* (1914).

GREAT BARRINGTON (1761)
from Sheffield

Town Hall, 334 Main St., Great Barrington, Mass., Tel: (413)-528-3140 Cemetery Department, 90 Stockbridge Rd., Great Barrington, Mass., Tel: (413)-528-1800

Ava Sholom Jewish Cemetery (20th century)
Blue Hill Rd.

Elmwood Cemetery (1888)
Blue Hill Rd.
+ NSDAR [G.R.C./S1/v. 140]

Greenlawn Cemetery (1837)
Van Deusenville Rd. and Oak St.
+ NSDAR [G.R.C./S1/v. 140]

Mahaiwe Cemetery (aka) South Burial Ground (1730)
Silver and South Main Sts.
+ Cynthia Tryon Hoogs,*Cemetery Inscriptions in Great Barrington, Massachusetts* (Great Barrington, 1987) [F74/G8/H6/1987]
+ L. Hasbrouck Vonsahler, "Inscriptions at Great Barrington, Mass." *NEHGR* 53:396-399; vol. 54 (1900) 69-70.
+ NSDAR [G.R.C./S1/v. 105]

Pelton Brook Cemetery (1767)
Rte. 183, Park Sq., behind the Van Deusen Cemetery.
+ Cynthia Tryon Hoogs,*Cemetery Inscriptions in Great Barrington, Massachusetts* (Great Barrington, 1987) [F74/G8/H6/1987]

Perry Cemetery Site (1845)
located within the Beartown State Forest

St. Bridget's Cemetery
VanDeusenville Rd.
Tel: (413)-274-3443

St. Peter's Cemetery
Stockbridge Rd.
Tel: St. Peter's, 16 Russell St., Great
Barrington, Mass., (413)-528-1157

Stimson Cemetery Site (1791)
off Stoney Brook Rd. in the Beartown
State Forest

Stoney Brook Road Cemetery (aka) Muddy Brook Cemetery (1792)
Stoney Brook Rd.
+ Mary E. and Emma Lee Watson,
"Inscriptions in the Muddy Brook
Cemetery, Great Barrington, Mass."
NEHGR 76:174-8.
+ NEHGS [MS/GRE/95], and [Corbin
Collection]

Van Deusen Cemetery (1789)
Division St. and Rte. 183, next to the
Pelton Brook Cemetery
+ NSDAR [G.R.C./S1/v. 105]

John Van Deusen Burial Plot (1792)
Alford Rd.

Water Street Cemetery (1747)
East and State Sts.
+ Cynthia Tryon Hoogs, *Cemetery Inscriptions in Great Barrington, Massachusetts*
(Great Barrington, 1987)
[F74/G8/H6/1987]
+ NSDAR [G.R.C./S1/v. 105]

GREENFIELD (1753)
from Deerfield
Town Hall, 14 Court Sq., Greenfield,
Mass. 01301, Tel: (413)-772-1555

Baptist Cemetery (19th century)
North Wisdom
+ [G.R. 4] *Vital Records of Deerfield,
Massachusetts to the year 1850* (1920).

Calvary Cemetery (1877)
Wisdom Way
Tel: Blessed Sacrement Church, 182
High St., Greenfield, Mass. (413)-773-3311
+ [G.R. 9] *Vital Records of Greenfield,
Massachusetts to the year 1850* (1915).

Country Farms (aka) Larrabee Cemetery (1794)
at the end of Health Camp Rd.

Federal Street (aka) Village Cemetery (1803)
187 Federal St.
+ [G.R. 1] *Vital Records of Greenfield,
Massachusetts to the year 1850* (1915).
+ NSDAR [G.R.C./S1/v. 28]
Inscription Index only.

Green River Cemetery (1851)
56 Wisdom Way
+ [G.R. 7] *Vital Records of Greenfield,
Massachusetts to the year 1850* (1915).

Greenfield Village Burial Ground (1803)
187 Federal St.
+ NEHGS [Mss/C/2021]

Hebrew Cemetery (1924)
Log Plain Rd. East
Tel: Temple Israel, 27 Pierce St.,
Greenfield, Mass. (413)-773-5884

High Street Cemetery (1768)
11 Silver St.
+ [G.R. 4] *Vital Records of Greenfield,
Massachusetts to the year 1850* (1915).
+ NSDAR [G.R.C./S1/v. 28]
Inscription Index only.

Long Plain Cemetery (aka) Sage Cemetery (1802)
1037 Bernardston Rd.
+ [G.R. 3] *Vital Records of Greenfield,
Massachusetts to the year 1850* (1915).

+ NSDAR [G.R.C./S1/v. 28]
Inscription Index only.

Lower Meadows Cemetery (1793)
213 Colrain Rd.
+ [G.R. 6] *Vital Records of Greenfield,
Massachusetts to the year 1850* (1915).
+ NSDAR [G.R.C./S1/v. 28]
Inscription Index only.

Master Dolorosa Cemetery (1923)
Wisdom Way
Tel: Sacred Heart Rectory, 75 Prospect
St., Greenfield, Ma (413)-772-6377

North Meadows Cemetery (1820)
Upper Colrain Rd.

North Wisdom Cemetery
+ [G.R. 3] *Vital Records of Deerfield,
Massachusetts to the year 1850* (1920).
+ NEHGS [F74/G85/D2] Typescript in
Mss
+ NSDAR [G.R.C./S1/v. 299]

Old Burial Yard Cemetery Site
(1753)
location on Miles St., burials were moved
to the Federal Street and Green River
Cemeteries.

Old Catholic Cemetery (1857)
Petty Plain Rd.
+ [G.R. 8] *Vital Records of Greenfield,
Massachusetts to the year 1850* (1915).

Our Lady of Sorrows Cemetery
(1877)
Wisdom Way

Sage Cemetery (aka) Bernardston
Road Cemetery (1802)
1037 Bernardston Rd.
+ [G.R. 2] *Vital Records of Greenfield,
Massachusetts to the year 1850* (1915).

South Meadows Cemetery (1793)
213 Colrain Rd.
+ NSDAR [G.R.C./S1/v. 16]
Revolutionary War soldier burials only.

Upper Meadows Cemetery (1821)
711 Colrain Rd.
+ [G.R. 5] *Vital Records of Greenfield,
Massachusetts to the year 1850* (1915).
+ NSDAR [G.R.C./S1/v. 28]
Inscription Index only.

GREENWICH (1754)
This town was flooded in 1938 for the
Quabbin Reservoir.

Greenwich Cemetery Site
Burials in this cemetery were removed to
Quabbin Park Cemetery, Ware,
Massachusetts 1938
+ NEHGS [MS/70/WAR/15]

GROTON (1655)
Town Hall, 173 Main St., Groton, Mass.
01450, Tel: (978)-448-1100

Groton Cemetery (1847)
Chicopee Row.

Old Burying Ground (1704)
Hollis St.
+ Samuel A. Green, *Epitaphs from the old
burying ground in Groton, Massachusetts.*
(Boston, Mass.: Little & Brown & Co.,
1878) [F74/G9/G74/also Loan]

GROVELAND (1850)
from Bradford
Town Hall, 183 Main St., Groveland,
Mass. 01834, Tel: (978)-469-5005

Colonial Cemetery (1777)
School St. opposite Elmer S. Bagnall
School

Riverview Cemetery (1727)
Main St., Rte. 113
+ Louis A. Woodbury, *Inscriptions from the Old Cemetery in Groveland, Mass.* (Groveland, Mass.: L.A. Woodbury, 1895) [F74/G95/W66/1895]
+ NEHGS [MS70/BRA/1]

HADLEY (1661)
Town Hall, 100 Middle St., Hadley, Mass. 01035, Tel: (413)-584-1590

Hockanum Cemetery (1767)
Rte. 47, Hockanum Rd.
+ NEHGS [Mss/SL/HAD/4] and[Corbin Collection]

Holy Rosary Cemetery (1920)
Huntington Rd.

North Hadley Cemetery (1790)
Rte. 47, River Dr.
+ NEHGS [Mss/SL/HAD/4] and [Corbin Collection].

Old Hadley Cemetery (1661)
Cemetery Rd.
+ NEHGS [Mss/SL/HAD/4] and.[Corbin Collection]
+ NSDAR [G.R.C./S1/v.94] Revolutionary War soldiers only.

Plainville Cemetery (1803)
Mount Warner Rd.
+ NEHGS [Mss/SL/HAD/4] and[Corbin Collection]

Russellville Cemetery (1809)
Rte. 47, River Dr.
+ NEHGS [Mss/SL/HAD/4] and [Corbin Collection]

St. Brigid's Cemetery (1871)
North Maple St.
Tel: St. Brigid's Rectory, 122 N. Pleasant St., Amherst, Mass., (413)-256-6181
+ NEHGS [Mss/SL/HAD/4]

HALIFAX (1734)
from Middleborough, Pembroke, and Plympton
Town Hall, 499 Plymouth St., Halifax, Mass. 02338,Tel: (781)-293-7970.
Cemetery Department, 60 Hemlock Ln., Halifax, Mass 02338, Tel: (781)-293-1760

Central Cemetery (1830)
499 Plymouth St. and Hemlock Ln.

Drew Family Plot (1807)
570 Thompson St.
+ Charles M. Thatcher, *Old Cemeteries of Southeastern Massachusetts.* (Middleborough, Mass., Middleborough Public Library,1995) [F63/T53/1995/also Loan]

Perkins Lot (1811)
Wood St.
+ Charles M. Thatcher, *Old Cemeteries of Southeastern Massachusetts.* (Middleborough, Mass., Middleborough Public Library, 1995) [F63/T53/1995/also Loan]

Sturtevant Cemetery Pond (aka) Monponsett Pond–East Cemetery (1728)
Plymouth St.
+ Charles M. Thatcher, *Old Cemeteries of Southeastern Massachusetts.* (Middleborough, Mass., Middleborough Public Library, 1995) [F63/T53/1995/also Loan]

Thomson Cemetery (1734)
541-575 Thompson St.
+ Charles M. Thatcher, *Old Cemeteries of Southeastern Massachusetts.* (Middleborough, Mass., Middleborough Public Library,1995) [F63/T53/1995/also Loan]

HAMILTON (1793)
from Ipswich
Town Hall, 577 Bay Rd., Hamilton,
Mass. 01936, Tel: (978)-468-5570
Cemetery Department, P.O. Box 429,
Hamilton, Mass. (978)-468-5580

Hamilton Cemetery (1707)
Bay Rd. Rte. 1A, across from Cutler Rd.
+ [G.R. 5] *Vital Records of Ipswich,
Massachusetts to the year 1850* (1910).

HAMPDEN (1878)
from Wilbraham
Town Hall, 625 Main St., Hampden,
Mass. 01036, Tel: (413)-566-3214

Old Hampden Cemetery (1755)
Chapin Rd.
+ Beryle C. Doten, *The Old Cemetery.*
(Hampden, Mass.: The Historical Society
of the Town of Hampden, 1978)
[F74/H18/D6]
+ NEHGS [Corbin Collection]

Prospect Hill Cemetery
Scantic Rd., next to St. Mary's Cemetery
+ Beryle C. Doten, *Prospect Hill Cemetery
and St. Mary's Cemetery* (Hampden, Mass.:
The Historical Society of the Town of
Hampden, 1978) [F74/H18/D6/1984]

St. Mary's Cemetery
Scantic Rd., next to Prospect Hill
Cemetery
Tel: St. Mary's Rectory, 27 Somers Rd.,
Hampden, Mass. 01036, (413)-566-8843
+ Beryle C. Doten, *Prospect Hill Cemetery
and St. Mary's Cemetery* (Hampden, Mass.:
The Historical Society of the Town of
Hampden, 1978) [F74/H18/D6/1984]

HANCOCK (1726)
Town Hall, 3650 Hancock Rd.,
Hancock, Mass. 01237, Tel: (413)-738-
5225

Bates Memorial Cemetery (1825)
south side on Rte. 20, at the top pf
Lebanon Mountain Rd.

Beach Cemetery (1802)
Rte. 43 near the Williamstown Line
[single stone]

Clothier Cemetery (1784)
Rte. 43, near Hancock School
+ NEHGS [Corbin Collection]

Noah Ely Cemetery (1772)
Rte. 43, next to Hancock Fire Station.
+ NEHGS [Corbin Collection]

Gardner Cemetery # 1 (1775)
Hancok Rd., Rte. 43
+ NEHGS [Mss/SL/HAN/5] and
[Corbin Collection]

Gardner Cemetery # 2 (1801)
Rte. 43
+ NEHGS [Mss/SL/HAN/5] and
[Corbin Collection]

Hadsell Cemetery (1793)
off Estes Terrace, across from Hancock
Baptist Church.

Mary Harris Cemetery (1802)
+ NEHGS [Mss/SL/HAN/5]

Haykes Cemetery (1796)
off Clark Rd., next to Town Cemetery

Jenks Cemetery (1813)
Rte. 43, across from Hancock School.

Maynard Farm Cemetery
+ NEHGS [Mss/SL/HAN/5] and
[Corbin Collection]

James Reynolds Cemetery (1802)
+ NEHGS [Mss/SL/HAN/5]

Shaker Village Cemetery (1804)
Lebanon Mountain Rd., at the Hancock
Shaker Village

Smith and Smalley Burial Ground (1816)
Brick Mountain Rd., Hancock

Southworth-Vaughn Cemetery (1791)
Main St. and Village Rd.
+ NEHGS [Corbin Collection]

Townsend Cemetery (1776)
Rte. 43
+ NEHGS [Mss/SL/HAN/5] and
[Corbin Collection]

Village Cemetery (1788)
Rte. 43, next to Town Hall.
+ NEHGS [Corbin Collection]

Wells Family Cemetery (1791)
+ NEHGS [Mss/SL/HAN/5] and
[Corbin Collection]

Whitman's Tomb (1857)
Potter Mountain Rd.

HANOVER (1727)
from Abington and Scituate
Town Hall, 550 Hanover St., Hanover,
Mass. 02339, Tel: (781)-826-2691

Assinippi Cemetery (1789)
at Assinippi
+ Charles M. Thatcher, *Old Cemeteries of
Southeastern Massachusetts*. (Middleborough,
Mass., Middleborough Public Library,
1995) [F63/T53/1995/also Loan]

Darling Cemetery (1829)
959 Circuit St.

Hanover Center Cemetery (1727)
Silver and Main Sts.
+ Charles M. Thatcher, *Old Cemeteries of
Southeastern Massachusetts*. (Middleborough,
Mass., Middleborough Public Library,
1995) [F63/T53/1995/also Loan]
+ Lloyd Vernon Briggs, *History and
Records of the First Congregational Church,
Hanover, Mass. 1727-1865, and Inscriptions
from the headstones and tombs in the cemetery at
Centre Hanover, Mass.* (Boston, Mass.:
Wallace Spooner, 1895)
[F74/H2/B81/1895]

**Hatch Family Cemetery (18th
Century)**
site west of Center St., ploughed up in
the 19th century.

Hobart Cemetery (1793)
near East Bridgewater Line
+ Charles M. Thatcher, *Old Cemeteries of
Southeastern Massachusetts*. (Middleborough,
Mass., Middleborough Public Library,
1995) [F63/T53/1995/also Loan]

Union Cemetery (1794)
Webster St.

HANSON (1820)
from Pembroke
Town Hall, 542 Liberty St., Hanson,
Mass. 02341, Tel: (781)-293-2772

Fern Hill Cemetery (aka) Gravely
Hill Cemetery (1745)
High St.
+ Charles M. Thatcher, *Old Cemeteries of
Southeastern Massachusetts*. (Middleborough,
Mass., Middleborough Public Library,
1995) [F63/T53/1995/also Loan]
+ [G.R. 1] *Vital Records of Hanson,
Massachusetts to the year 1850* (1911).

Hobart Family Burying Ground
Crystal Spring Farm, off Main and
Franklin Sts., near East Bridgewater
town line.
+ [G.R. 2] *Vital Records of Gloucester,
Massachusetts to the year 1850* (1924).
+ Charles M. Thatcher, *Old Cemeteries of
Southeastern Massachusetts.*(Middleborough,
Mass., Middleborough Public
Library,1995) [F63/T53/1995/also Loan]

Howland Family Burying Ground (19th century)
off Indian Head St.

Munroe Family Burying Ground
off Main St., South Hanson
+ [G.R. 3] *Vital Records of Gloucester,
Massachusetts to the year 1850* (1924).
+ Charles M. Thatcher, *Old Cemeteries of
Southeastern Massachusetts.* (Middleborough, Mass., Middleborough Public
Library,1995) [F63/T53/1995/also Loan]

Old Cemetery (1776)
off Grove Street, near Pembroke and
Halifax town line.
+ Charles M. Thatcher, *Old Cemeteries of
Southeastern Massachusetts.* (Middleborough,
Mass., Middleborough Public Library,
1995) [F63/T53/1995/also Loan]

Stetson Family Burying Ground
off Monponsett St.

John Thomas Family Tomb
Main St.
+ [G.R. 4] *Vital Records of Gloucester,
Massachusetts to the year 1850* (1924).

HARDWICK (1739)
Town Hall, 307 Main St., Gilbertville,
Mass. 01031, Tel: (413)-477-6700

Hardwick Baptist Cemetery (1803)
Collins Rd.

Hardwick Center Cemetery (1817)
Petersham Rd.

Hardwick Old Burying Ground (1749)
Common St.

St. Aloysius Cemetery (1897)
Church St., Gilbertville

HARVARD (1732)
from Groton, Lancaster and Stow
Town Hall, 13 Ayer Rd., Harvard, Mass.
01451, Tel: (978)-456-4100

Bellevue Cemetery (1891)
opposite from 130 Still River Rd.
+ NEHGS [MS70/HAR/30]
+ NSDAR [G.R.C./S1/v. 111]

Fort Devens Cemetery (1817)
Patton Rd.

Harvard Center Cemetery (1734)
Massachusetts Ave., near the Bromfield
School
+ Esther K. Whitcomb, *Inscriptions from
burial grounds of the Nashaway towns : Lancaster, Harvard, Bolton, Leominster, Sterling,
Berlin, West Boylston, and Hudson, Massachusetts.* (Bowie, Md: Heritage Books,
1989) [F74/L2/I57/1989/also Loan]
+ Henry S. Nourse, *History of the Town of
Harvard, Massachusetts. 1732-1893.*
(Harvard, Mass., 1894)
[F74/N29/1894/also Loan] p. 481-497.
+ NSDAR [G.R.C./S1/v. 111]

Park-Munroe Tomb (1808) (aka) Old Mill District
+ NEHGS [MS70/HAR/30]

Purgess Cemetery
"farm of Lester Brown"
+ NEHGS [MS70/HAR/30]

Shaker Cemetery (1792)
after 123 South Shaker Rd.
+ Esther K. Whitcomb, *Inscriptions from burial grounds of the Nashaway towns : Lancaster, Harvard, Bolton, Leominster, Sterling, Berlin, West Boylston, and Hudson, Massachusetts.* (Bowie, Md: Heritage Books, 1989) [F74/L2/I57/1989/also Loan]
+ Henry S. Nourse, *History of the Town of Harvard, Massachusetts. 1732-1893.* (Harvard, Mass., 1894) [F74/N29/1894/also Loan] p. 497.
+ NSDAR [G.R.C./S1/v. 111]

Capt. Benjamin Stewart Gravesite (1775)
"west of the old almshouse"
+ NEHGS [MS70/HAR/30]

Whitney Family Cemetery
land of Daniel Sheehan
+ NEHGS [MS70/HAR/30]

Whitney Cemetery
behind the Baptist Church.
+ NEHGS [MS70/HAR/30]

HARWICH (1694)
Town Hall, 732 Main St., Harwich, Mass. 02645, Tel: (508)-430-7516.
Cemetery Department, 273 Queen Avenue Rd., Harwich, Mass., Tel: (508)-430-7549.

Banks Street Burial Ground
Banks St., no stones

Baptist Church Cemetery (1816)
Depot St. and Rte. 28, West Harwich
+ Burton Nathaniel Derrick, *Cemetery Inscriptions of Dennis.*(Bowie, Md., Heritage Books, 1993) [F74/D43/D47/1993]
+ NEHGS [MS70/HAR/46]

Chase Family Cemetery
Depot St., no stones

Christ Church Episcopal Church Cremation Garden
behind the Christ Church Episcopal Church on Rte. 28, Harwichport

East Harwich Methodist Cemetery
Church St., East Harwich
+ *The Mayflower Descendant* (19:157-8, 21:49-52)
+ NEHGS [F74/E23/H6] Typescript in Mss

End of the Pond Cemetery (1825)
Spruce St.

Evergreen Cemetery (1807)
corner of Cemetery Ave. and Rte. 137

First Congregational Church Cemetery (1748)
Rte. 124 and Main St., Harwich Center
+ NEHGS [MS70/HAR/45]

First Methodist Cemetery (ca. 1758)
Queen Anne Rd.

Hawks Nest Pond Cemetery (1826)
off Spruce Rd., East Harwich

Holy Trinity Catholic Cemetery (1869)
Rte. 124, Pleasant Lake Ave.
Tel: Holy Trinity Rectory, Earle Rd., West Harwich, Mass. (508)-432-4000

Island Pond Cemetery (1778)
off Main St. at end of Island Pond Rd.
+ *The Mayflower Descendant* (13:2-3)
+ NEHGS [MS70/HAR/40]

Kelley Street Cemetery (1834)
off Kelley St.

Kildee Hill Cemetery
cemetery existed nearby Kildee Hill

Mount Pleasant Cemetery (1850)
90 Forest St., located between South and
Forest Sts., Harwichport
Tel: (508)-430-7531
+ NEHGS [MS70/HAR/51]

North Harwich Cemetery (1792)
corner North Main and Depot Sts.
+ *The Mayflower Descendant* (13:158-162)

Pine Grove Cemetery (1813)
Pine Grove St., West Harwich

**South Harwich Cemetery (aka)
Methodist Churchyard Cemetery
(1829)**
Old Chatham Rd., South Harwich
+ NEHGS [MS70/HAR/250]

Harding Ryder Gravesite
Rte. 39, near the water tower

Smith Family Cemetery (1834)
Bell's Neck Rd.

South Harwich Cemetery (1829)
Chatham Rd.

**Samuel Tripp Family Cemetery
(1832)**
Harwich

Union Cemetery (ca. 1811)
Harwich St. and Queen Anne Rd., next
to the Harwich United Methodist
Church.

**Mehitable Wixon–Chase Family
Cemetery (1832)**
off Lothrop Ave., Harwich

HATFIELD (1670)
from Hadley
Town Hall, 59 Main St., Hatfield, Mass.
01038, Tel: (413)-247-0492

Bradstreet Cemetery
Depot Rd.

Calvary Cemetery (1900)
Bridge St.
Tel: Holy Trinity Rectory, 73 Main St.,
Hatfield, Mass. (413)-247-3133

**First Burying Ground (aka) Hill
Burying Ground (1668)**
Elm St.
+ NEHGS [MS70/HAT/15], and
[Corbin Collection].

Main Street Cemetery (1772)
41 Main St.
+ NEHGS [MS70/HAT/15], and
[Corbin Collection]

North Hatfield Cemetery (1844)
West St.

Polish National Cemetery
Elm Court
Tel: St. Valentine's Rectory,
Northampton (413)-584-0133

West Hatfield Cemetery (1848)
West St.
+ NEHGS [MS70/HAT/15], and
[Corbin Collection].
+ NSDAR [G.R.C./S1/v. 425]

Westbrook Cemetery (1846)
+ NEHGS [MS70/HAT/15]

HAVERHILL (1641)
City Hall, 4 Summer St., Haverhill, Mass.
01830, Tel: (978)-374-2312

**Ancient West Parish Cemetery (aka)
Carleton Street Cemetery (1740)**
Carleton St., off Broadway and Lowell
Ave.
+ NEHGS [MS70/HAV/6]
+ NSDAR [G.R.C./S1/v. 324]

Bradford Burial Ground (1665)
273 Salem St., Bradford
+ NEHGS [Mss/C/3395]

Children of Israel Cemetery (1893)
Middle Rd.

Elmwood Cemetery (1846)
96 Salem St.
Tel: (978)-374-8901

Greenwood Cemetery (1785)
beyond 600 East Broadway St.

City Central Cemetery (19th century)
342 Hilldale Ave.

Hilldale Cemetery (1859)
337 Hilldale Ave.

Hillside Cemetery (1830)
859 Broadway St., across from the West Congregational Church.

Linwood Cemetery and Crematory (1845)
Mill St.
Tel: (978)-374-4191

Lithuanian Cemetery (1921)
Montvale St., Bradford

Maplewood North Parish Cemetery (1734)
North Main St.

Pentucket Cemetery (1668)
Water St., Rte. 97, near Mill St.
+ NSDAR [G.R.C./S1/v. 300]

St. James Catholic Cemetery (1852)
Primrose St.

St. Joseph Catholic Cemetery (1904)
Hilldale Ave.

St. Patrick's Catholic Cemetery (1904)
North Broadway St.

Walnut Cemetery (1748)
Kenoza St. and Middle Rd.

West Parish Cemetery (1786)
Broadway St., Rte. 97
+ NEHGS [MS70/HAV/2]
+ NSDAR [G.R.C./S1/v. 191]

Whittier Family Burial Ground (1696)
Whittier Road, off Amesbury Rd.

HAWLEY (1792)
Town Hall, 8 Pudding Hollow Rd., Hawley, Mass. 01339, Tel: (413)-339-5518

Bozrah Cemetery (1794)
Bozrah Rd.
+ NEHGS [MS/HAW/3] and [Corbin Collection]

Brynn Cemetery (1867)
Stetson Rd.

Doane Cemetery (1789)
Forget Rd.
+ NEHGS [MS/HAW/3] and [Corbin Collection]

East Hawley Cemetery (1815)
Ashfield Rd.
+ NEHGS [MS/HAW/3] and [Corbin Collection]

Pudding Hollow Cemetery (1794)
Pudding Hollow Rd.
+ NEHGS [MS/HAW/3] and [Corbin Collection]

South Hawley Cemetery (1826)
Hallockville Rd.

+ NEHGS [MS/HAW/3] and [Corbin Collection]

West Hawley Cemetery (1820)
West Hill Rd.
+ NEHGS [MS/HAW/3] and [Corbin Collection]

HEATH (1785)
from Charlemont
Town Hall, One East Main St., Heath, Mass. 01346, Tel: (413)-337-4934.

Center Cemetery (1789)
Colrain Stage and Hosmer West Rds.
+ *Heath Gravestone Records.*(Heath, Mass.: Heath Historical Society, 1990)
[F74/H57/H43/1990]
+ NEHGS [MS70/HEA/1] (G.R. 4)
+ NSDAR [G.R.C./S1/v. 359] and [G.R.C./S1/v. 48]

Maple Grove Cemetery
(a section of the North Cemetery)

North Cemetery (1821)
Brunelle and Sadoga Rds.
+ *Heath Gravestone Records.*(Heath, Mass.: Heath Historical Society, 1990)
[F74/H57/H43/1990]
+ NEHGS [MS70/HEA/1] (G.R. 1), and [MS70/COL/16]
+ NSDAR [G.R.C./S1/v. 359] and [G.R.C./S1/v. 48]

Anna Norton Gravesite (1747)
(gravestone is now in the Heath Historical Society)
burial site on Hosmer Rd. East, at the site of Fort Shirley
+ *Heath Gravestone Records.*(Heath, Mass.: Heath Historical Society, 1990)
[F74/H57/H43/1990]
+ NEHGS [MS70/HEA/1] (G.R. 3)

South Cemetery (1777)
South Rd., South Heath
+ *Heath Gravestone Records.*(Heath, Mass.: Heath Historical Society, 1990)
[F74/H57/H43/1990]
+ NEHGS [MS70/HEA/1] (G.R. 2)
+ NSDAR [G.R.C./S1/v. 359] and [G.R.C./S1/v. 48]

HINGHAM (1635)
Town Hall, 210 Central St., Hingham, Mass. 02043, Tel: (781)-741-1410

Barnes and Stoddard Cemetery (1820)
Weir St., near Rockland St.
+ NEHGS [Mss/3/H/20]

Fort Hill Street Cemetery (1751)
Fort Hill St., West Hingham
+ NEHGS [MS70/HIN/7]

High Street Cemetery (1688)
High St.
+ NEHGS [MS70/HIN/5]

Hingham Center Cemetery (1684)
Main St.
Tel: (781)-749-1048
+ NEHGS [MS70/HIN/6], [MS70/HIN/8], and [Corbin Collection].

Liberty Plain Cemetery (1739)
996 South Main St., South Hingham
+ NEHGS [MS70/SOU/260]

Old Ship Cemetery (1672)
12 South Ln.

St. Paul's Cemetery (1859)
Hersey St.
Tel: St. Paul's Rectory, 147 North St., Hingham, (781)-749-0587

HINSDALE (1804)
from Dalton
Town Hall, Maple St., Hinsdale, Mass.
01235, Tel: (413)-655-2301

Cady Family Cemetery (1835)
Old Windsor Rd.
+ NEHGS [MS70/HIN/25]

Chessman Cemetery (aka) Spring District Cemetery (1813)
Rte. 8, South Hinsdale
+ NEHGS [MS70/HIN/25]

Eames Cemetery (1791)
Fassell Rd.
+ NEHGS [MS70/HIN/25]

Hinsdale Center Cemetery (1781)
Maple St.
+ NEHGS [MS70/HIN/25]

Redway–Mory Cemetery (1835)
New Windsor Rd.
+ NEHGS [MS70/HIN/25]

St. Patrick's Roman Catholic Cemetery (1865)
Old Dalton Rd., on Dalton town line
Tel: St. Patrick's Rectory, 43 Church St.,
Hinsdale, Mass. (413)-655-2208

South Cemetery (1824)
Rte. 8

Hinsdale Inscriptions 1790-1863
(Rollin H. Cooke Collection)
F72/B5/B473 (roll 1) microfilm
available at N.E.H.G.S.

HOLBROOK (1872)
from Randolph
Town Hall, 50 North Franklin St.,
Holbrook, Mass. 02343, Tel: (781)-767-4314

Union Cemetery (1754)
199 Union St.
+ NEHGS [MS70/HOL/1],
[MS70/HOL/4], [Mss/A/345], and
[MS70/BRA/34]

Wendell Cemetery (1815)
1030 South Franklin St.
+ NEHGS [MS70/HOL/6],
[Mss/A/345], and [MS70/BRA/34]

HOLDEN (1741)
from Worcester
Town Hall, 1196 Main St., Holden,
Mass. 01520, Tel: (508)-829-0265

Gove Cemetery (1854)
Main St.

Old Burying Ground (1742)
Main and Resevoir Sts.
+ NSDAR [G.R.C./S1/v. 82]

Park Avenue Burying Ground (1826)
Main St. and Park Ave.

St. Mary's Cemetery (1867)
1304 Main St.
Tel: St. Mary's Rectory, 114 Princeton
St., Holden, Mass. (508)-829-4508

HOLLAND (1783)
from South Brimfield
Town Hall, 27 Sturbridge Rd., Holland,
Mass. 01521, Tel: (413)-245-7108

Holland Cemetery (1763)
+ NEHGS [Mss/C/4013]
"an acre of land a burying ground, north of John Bishop's land." Rev. Martin Lovering,
History of the Town of Holland, Massachusetts.
(Rutland, Vt. 1915) p. 104-5.

Munger–Marcy Burying Ground (1802)
Needham Hill
+ Rev. Martin Lovering, History of the Town of Holland, Massachusetts." (Rutland, Vt. 1915) p. 105-6.

Sholes Family Burying Ground
on the town line with Union, Conn.
+ Rev. Martin Lovering, History of the Town of Holland, Massachusetts." (Rutland, Vt. 1915) p. 105-6.

HOLLISTON (1724)
from Sherborn
Town Hall, 703 Washington St., Holliston, Mass. 01746, Tel: (508)-429-0601

Braggville Cemetery (1772)
Rockland St.
+ [G.R. 5] *Vital Records of Holliston, Massachusetts to the year 1850* (1908).
+ Susan F. Salisbury, *Southern Massachusetts Cemetery Collection*, Volume 2 (Bowie, Md., Heritage Books, 1996) [F63/S25/1995/also Loan]
+ NEHGS [MS70/HOL/33]
+ NSDAR [G.R.C./S1/v. 409]

Central Cemetery (1724)
Washington St.
+ [G.R. 1] *Vital Records of Holliston, Massachusetts to the year 1850* (1908).
+ Susan F. Salisbury, *Southern Massachusetts Cemetery Collection*, Volume 2 (Bowie, Md., Heritage Books, 1996) [F63/S25/1995/also Loan]
+ NEHGS [MS70/HOL/33]

East Holliston Cemetery (1800)
Washington St.
+ [G.R. 2] *Vital Records of Holliston, Massachusetts to the year 1850* (1908).
+ NEHGS [MS70/HOL/33]
+ NSDAR [G.R.C./S1/v. 409]

Lake Grove Cemetery (1859)
Highland St.
+ [G.R. 7] *Vital Records of Holliston, Massachusetts to the year 1850* (1908).
+ Susan F. Salisbury, *Southern Massachusetts Cemetery Collection*, Volume 2 (Bowie, Md., Heritage Books, 1996) [F63/S25/1995/also Loan]
+ NEHGS [MS70/HOL/31] and [MS70/HOL/32]

North Holliston Cemetery (aka) Old Indian Cemetery (1800)
Cedar St.
+ [G.R. 3] *Vital Records of Holliston, Massachusetts to the year 1850* (1908).
+ Susan F. Salisbury, *Southern Massachusetts Cemetery Collection*, Volume 2 (Bowie, Md., Heritage Books, 1996) [F63/S25/1995/also Loan]
+ NEHGS [MS70/HOL/32] and [MS70/HOL/33]
+ NSDAR [G.R.C./S1/v. 409]

Old South Cemetery (aka) Hoppin River Cemetery
Washington St.
+ [G.R. 4] *Vital Records of Holliston, Massachusetts to the year 1850* (1908).
+ Susan F. Salisbury, *Southern Massachusetts Cemetery Collection*, Volume 2 (Bowie, Md., Heritage Books, 1996) [F63/S25/1995/also Loan]
+ NEHGS [MS70/HOL/33]
+ NSDAR [G.R.C./S1/v. 409]

St. Mary's Cemetery
Central and Fiske Sts.
Tel: St. Mary's Rectory, 8 Church St., Holliston, Mass. (508)-429-4427

West End Cemetery (1800)
Gorwin Dr.
+ [G.R. 6] *Vital Records of Holliston, Massachusetts to the year 1850* (1908).
+ Susan F. Salisbury, *Southern Massachusetts Cemetery Collection*, Volume 2 (Bowie,

Md., Heritage Books, 1996)
[F63/S25/1995/also Loan]
+ NEHGS [MS70/HOL/33]
+ NSDAR [G.R.C./S1/v. 409]

HOLYOKE (1850)
from West Springfield
City Hall, 536 Dwight St., Holyoke,
Mass. 01040, Tel: (413)-534-2166

Calvary Cemetery (1882)
2166 Northampton St.
Tel: Gate of Heaven Cemetery, (413)-
733-0659
+ [G.R. 16] *Vital Records of West Springfield, Massachusetts to the year 1850* (1944).
+ NEHGS [Mss/SL/WES/18]

Elmwood Cemetery (aka) Baptist
Village Cemetery (1755)
2190 Northampton St.
+ [G.R. 13] *Vital Records of West Spring-
field, Massachusetts to the year 1850* (1944).
+ NEHGS [Mss/SL/WES/18]
+ NSDAR [G.R.C./S1/v. 433] and
[G.R.C./1932/S1/v. 16]

Forestdale Cemetery (1862)
304 Cabot St.
Tel: (413)-534-7894
+ [G.R. 15] *Vital Records of West Spring-
field, Massachusetts to the year 1850* (1944).
+ NEHGS [Mss/SL/WES/18]
+ NSDAR [G.R.C./S1/v. 433]

Rock Valley Cemetery (1771)
Rock Valley Rd., West Holyoke
+ [G.R. 14] *Vital Records of West Spring-
field, Massachusetts to the year 1850* (1944).
+ NEHGS [MS70/HOL/40] and
[Corbin Collection]
+ NSDAR [G.R.C./S1/v. 433]

St. Jerome Cemetery (1864)
125 St. Jerome Ave.
Tel: (413)-532-6381

+ [G.R. 17] *Vital Records of West Springfield, Massachusetts to the year 1850* (1944).
+ NEHGS [Mss/SL/WES/18]

Smith's Ferry Cemetery (1824)
Rte 5, Northampton Hwy.
+ NEHGS [Corbin Collection]
+ NSDAR [G.R.C./S1/v. 433]

HOPEDALE (1886)
from Milford
Town Hall, 78 Hopedale St., Hopedale,
Mass. 01747, Tel: (508)-634-2211

Hopedale Village Cemetery (1847)
Hope St.
+ Susan F. Salisbury, *Southern Massa-
chusetts Cemetery Collection,* Volume 1
(Bowie, Md., Heritage Books, 1995))
[F63/S25/1995/also Loan]

South Hopedale Cemetery
Plain St.
+ Susan F. Salisbury, *Southern
Massachusetts Cemetery Collection,* Volume 1
(Bowie, Md., Heritage Books, 1995))
[F63/S25/1995/also Loan]
+ NEHGS [MS70/HOP/3]

HOPKINTON (1715)
Town Hall, 18 Main St., Hopkinton,
Mass. 01748, Tel: (508)-497-9710

Bear Hill Cemetery (1670)
Pond St.
+ [G.R. 2] *Vital Records of Hopkinton,
Massachusetts to the year 1850* (1911).
+ NEHGS [Mss/CB/95]

Church Cemetery (aka) Old Church
Yard Cemetery (1725)
Main St.
Tel: Congregational Church Rectory, 146
Main St., Hopkinton, Mass. Tel: (508)-
435-9581

+ NEHGS [MS70/HOP/16], and
[MS70/HOP/18]
+ NSDAR [G.R.C./S1/v. 409]

East Hopkinton Cemetery (1813)
Clinton St.
+ [G.R. 1] *Vital Records of Hopkinton,
Massachusetts to the year 1850* (1911).
+ NEHGS [MS70/HOP/16],
[MS70/HOP/15], and [Mss/CB/95]

**Evergreen Cemetery (aka)
Woodville Cemetery (1805)**
Wood St., Rte. 135
+ [G.R. 4] *Vital Records of Hopkinton,
Massachusetts to the year 1850* (1907).
+ NEHGS [MS70/HOP/16] and
[Mss/CB/95]

Hayden Rowe Cemetery (1813)
Granite St. and Hayden Rowe
+ [G.R. 3] *Vital Records of Hopkinton,
Massachusetts to the year 1850* (1911).
+ NEHGS [Mss/CB/95]

Mount Auburn Cemetery (1793)
Mayhew and Mount Auburn Sts.
+ [G.R. 6] *Vital Records of Hopkinton,
Massachusetts to the year 1850* (1907).
+ NEHGS [MS70/HOP/15]

St. John's Catholic Cemetery (1851)
Wilson St.
Tel: St. John the Evangelist Rectory, 20
Church St., Hopkinton, Mass. (508)-435-
3313

St. John's Cemetery (1855)
Mayhew and Mount Auburn Sts.
Tel: (508)-435-3313

**St. Paul's Cemetery (aka) Tombs
and Valentine Cemetery (1799)**
East Main St.
Tel: St. Paul's Episcopal Rectory, 61
Wood St., Hopkinton, Mass. (508)-435-
4536

+ [G.R. 5] *Vital Records of Hopkinton,
Massachusetts to the year 1850* (1907).
+ NEHGS [MS70/HOP/16] and
[Mss/CB/95]

HUBBARDSTON (1767)
from Rutland
Town Hall, 7 Main St., Hubbardston,
Mass. 01452, Tel: (978)-928-5244

Brookside Cemetery (1938)
Worcester Rd., Rte. 68
+ Central Massachusetts Genealogical
Society, *Cemetery Inscriptions of Hubbard-
ston, Mass.*, (Westminster, Mass.:
C.M.G.S., 1999) [F74/H8/C46/1999]

Catholic Burying Ground (1856)
Mile Rd.

Clark Cemetery (1820)
New Westminster Rd.
+ Central Massachusetts Genealogical
Society, *Cemetery Inscriptions of Hubbard-
ston, Mass.*, (Westminster, Mass.:
C.M.G.S., 1999) [F74/H8/C46/1999]
+ [G.S. 8] *Vital Records of Hubbardston,
Massachusetts to the year 1850* (1907).
+ NEHGS [Mss/SL/HUB/2]

**East–Nicholsville–Dexter Cemetery
(1796)**
New Westminster Rd.

Evergreen Cemetery (1995)
Rte. 68, next to Rural Glen Cemetery
+ Central Massachusetts Genealogical
Society, *Cemetery Inscriptions of Hubbard-
ston, Mass.*, (Westminster, Mass.:
C.M.G.S., 1999) [F74/H8/C46/1999]

**Forest Hill Cemetery (aka)
Hastings Cemetery (1819)**
Williamsville Rd. and Hale Rd. Ext.
+ [G.S. 4] *Vital Records of Hubbardston,
Massachusetts to the year 1850* (1907).

+ Central Massachusetts Genealogical Society, *Cemetery Inscriptions of Hubbardston, Mass.*, (Westminster, Mass.: C.M.G.S., 1999) [F74/H8/C46/1999] + NEHGS [Mss/SL/HUB/2] and [Mss/SL/HUB/2a-c]

Greenwood Cemetery (1839)
off Old Westminster Rd.
+ [G.S. 7] *Vital Records of Hubbardston, Massachusetts to the year 1850* (1907).
+ Central Massachusetts Genealogical Society, *Cemetery Inscriptions of Hubbardston, Mass.*, (Westminster, Mass.: C.M.G.S., 1999) [F74/H8/C46/1999] + NEHGS [Mss/SL/HUB/2] and [Mss/SL/HUB/2a-c]

Harty Cemetery (1855)
Mile Rd.
+ Central Massachusetts Genealogical Society, *Cemetery Inscriptions of Hubbardston, Mass.*, (Westminster, Mass.: C.M.G.S., 1999) [F74/H8/C46/1999]

Hemenway Cemetery (1850)
road to Phillipston
+ NSDAR [G.R.C./S1/v. 354]

Lovewell-Nightingale Cemetery (1823)
Rte. 68, Gardner Rd.
+ [G.S. 5] *Vital Records of Hubbardston, Massachusetts to the year 1850* (1907).
+ Central Massachusetts Genealogical Society, *Cemetery Inscriptions of Hubbardston, Mass.*, (Westminster, Mass.: C.M.G.S., 1999) [F74/H8/C46/1999]

Parish Cemetery (aka) Hubbardston Center Cemetery (1772)
Rte. 68, Hubbardston Center, behind the Federated Church.
+ [G.S. 1] *Vital Records of Hubbardston, Massachusetts to the year 1850* (1907).
+ Central Massachusetts Genealogical Society, *Cemetery Inscriptions of Hubbard-*

ston, Mass., (Westminster, Mass.: C.M.G.S., 1999) [F74/H8/C46/1999]
+ NEHGS [Mss/SL/HUB/2]

Pine Grove Cemetery (1811)
24 Barre Rd.
+ [G.S. 3] *Vital Records of Hubbardston, Massachusetts to the year 1850* (1907).
+ Central Massachusetts Genealogical Society, *Cemetery Inscriptions of Hubbardston, Mass.*, (Westminster, Mass.: C.M.G.S., 1999) [F74/H8/C46/1999]
+ NEHGS [Mss/SL/HUB/2] and [Mss/SL/HUB/2a-c]

Flag-Underwood Cemetery (aka) Route 62 Cemetery (1849)
Rte. 62 , Old Boston Turnpike
+ NEHGS [Mss/SL/HUB/2]
+ Central Massachusetts Genealogical Society, *Cemetery Inscriptions of Hubbardston, Mass.*, (Westminster, Mass.: C.M.G.S., 1999) [F74/H8/C46/1999]

Rural Glen Cemetery (1795)
Rte. 68, Worcester Rd., next to the Evergreen Cemetery
+ [G.S. 2] *Vital Records of Hubbardston, Massachusetts to the year 1850* (1907).
+ Central Massachusetts Genealogical Society, *Cemetery Inscriptions of Hubbardston, Mass.*, (Westminster, Mass.: C.M.G.S., 1999) [F74/H8/C46/1999]
+ NEHGS [Mss/SL/HUB/2]

Warren Cemetery (1821)
South Cove Rd., near Rte. 68
+ Central Massachusetts Genealogical Society, *Cemetery Inscriptions of Hubbardston, Mass.*, (Westminster, Mass.: C.M.G.S., 1999) [F74/H8/C46/1999]

Cemetery near Sawyer's Pond
+ [G.S. 6] *Vital Records of Hubbardston, Massachusetts to the year 1850* (1907).

HUDSON (1866)
from Marlborough and Stow
Town Hall, 78 Main St., Hudson, Mass. 01749, Tel: (978)-568-9615

Forestvale Cemetery (1885)
between 135-177 Broad St.

Main Street Cemetery (1814)
between 404-410 Main St.
+ Esther K. Whitcomb, *Inscriptions from burial grounds of the Nashaway towns : Lancaster, Harvard, Bolton, Leominster, Sterling, Berlin, West Boylston, and Hudson, Massachusetts.* (Bowie, Md: Heritage Books, 1989) [F74/L2/I57/1989/also Loan]
+ NEHGS [MS70/HUD/1]

Pauper's Burying Ground (1822)
565 Main St.
+ Esther K. Whitcomb, *Inscriptions from burial grounds of the Nashaway towns : Lancaster, Harvard, Bolton, Leominster, Sterling, Berlin, West Boylston, and Hudson, Massachusetts.* (Bowie, Md: Heritage Books, 1989) [F74/L2/I57/1989/also Loan]
+ Edward L. Bell, *Historical archaeology at the Hudson Poor Farm Cemetery* (Boston, Mass.: Massachusetts Historical Commision, 1993) [F74/H82/B45/1993] [F74/H82/B45/1993]

St. Michael's Cemetery (1874)
Cox St., near Zina Rd.
+ Esther K. Whitcomb, *Inscriptions from burial grounds of the Nashaway towns : Lancaster, Harvard, Bolton, Leominster, Sterling, Berlin, West Boylston, and Hudson, Massachusetts.* (1989) [F74/L2/I57/1989/also Loan]

HULL (1644)
Town Hall, 253 Atlantic Ave., Hull, Mass. 02045, Tel: (781)-925-2262

Hull Cemetery (1710)
Spring St.

HUNTINGTON (1773)
Town Hall, 24 Russell Rd., Huntington, Mass. 01050, Tel: (413)-667-3260

Goss Hill Cemetery (aka) Ellis Cemetery (1805)
Goss Hill Rd., neart Kimball Rd.
+ NEHGS [Corbin Collection]

Norwich Bridge Cemetery (aka) Knightsville Cemetery (1783)
Littleville Rd.
+ NEHGS [Corbin Collection]

Norwich Hill Cemetery (1771)
County Rd., near Rte. 66
+ NEHGS [MS70/HUN/1], and [Corbin Collection]
+ NSDAR [G.R.C./S1/v. 48]

St. Thomas Aquinas Roman Catholic Cemetery (1893)
Rte. 20, Russell Rd.
Tel: St. Thomas Aquinas Rectory, East Main St., Huntington 01050 (413)-667-3350

IPSWICH (1634)
Town Hall, 30 South Main St., Ipswich, Mass. 01938, Tel: (978)-356-6600

Cowles Memorial Cemetery
Town Farm Rd.

Highland Cemetery (18th century)
Town Farm Rd.

Highland Annex–Old Greek Cemetery (19th century)
Fowlers Lane, off Town Farm Rd.

Locust Grove Cemetery (18th century)
Locust St. and Town Farm Rd.

New Highland Cemetery (1940's)
Town Farm Rd.

New Linebrook Cemetery (1864)
Linebrook Rd., off Rte. 1

Nourse Family Cemetery (1772)
Rte. 133, near Bay Side Nursery
+ [G.R. 3] *Vital Records of Ipswich, Massachusetts to the year 1850* (1910).

Old Linebrook Cemetery (1725)
Linebrook Rd., off Rte. 1. Next to New Linebrook Cemetery.

Old North Cemetery (1634)
High St., near Lords Sq.
+ [G.R. 1] *Vital Records of Ipswich, Massachusetts to the year 1850* (1910).

Sisters of Notre Dame Cemetery (1964)
Sisters of Notre Dame Convent, Jeffreys Neck Rd.

Old South Cemetery (18th century)
County St. Rte. 1A, near Davis Sq.
+ [G.R. 2] *Vital Records of Ipswich, Massachusetts to the year 1850* (1910).

General Cemetery Reference for Ipswich:
+ C.W. Smith, "Ipswich Burying-Ground Insriptions" *NEHGR* 7:79-80.

KINGSTON (1726)
from Plymouth
Town Hall, 23 Green St., Kingston, Mass. 02364, Tel: (781)-585-0502

Evergreen Cemetery (1854)
Evergreen St.

+ [G.R. 2] *Vital Records of Kingston, Massachusetts to the year 1850* (1911).
+ NEHGS [MS70/KIN/1]
Old Burying Ground (1717)
221 Main St.
+ [G.R. 1] *Vital Records of Kingston, Massachusetts to the year 1850* (1911).
+ Charles M. Thatcher, *Old Cemeteries of Southeastern Massachusetts*. (Middleborough, Mass., Middleborough Public Library, 1995) [F63/T53/1995/also Loan]
+ NEHGS [MS70/KIN/1]

Our Lady of Divine Providence Cemetery (1962)
Bishop's Highway
Tel: Sisters of Divine Providence Convent, 363 Bishop's Highway, Kingston (781)-585-7707

St. Joseph's Cemetery
off Elm St.
Tel: St. Joe's Rectory, 272 Main St., Kingston, Mass. (781)-585-6372

LAKEVILLE (1853)
from Middleborough
Town Hall, 346 Bedford St., Lakeville, Mass. 02347, Tel: (508)-946-8814

Ammon–Booth Cemetery (1778)
opposite Race Course Rd.
+ Charles M. Thatcher, *Old Cemeteries of Southeastern Massachusetts*. (Middleborough, Mass., Middleborough Public Library, 1995) [F63/T53/1995/also Loan]

Booth Cemetery (1823)
across from Hafford Cemetery
177 County Rd.
+ Charles M. Thatcher, *Old Cemeteries of Southeastern Massachusetts*. (Middleborough, Mass., Middleborough Public Library, 1995) [F63/T53/1995/also Loan]

Briggs Cemetery (1785)
Howland Rd.
+ Charles M. Thatcher, *Old Cemeteries of Southeastern Massachusetts*. (Middleborough, Mass., Middleborough Public Library, 1995) [F63/T53/1995/also Loan]

Brooman Square Cemetery
Winslow Neighborhood
+ Charles M. Thatcher, *Old Cemeteries of Southeastern Massachusetts*. (Middleborough, Mass., Middleborough Public Library, 1995) [F63/T53/1995/also Loan]

Canaedy Corner Cemetery (1818)
County Rd., across from Race Course Rd.
+ Charles M. Thatcher, *Old Cemeteries of Southeastern Massachusetts*. (Middleborough, Mass., Middleborough Public Library, 1995) [F63/T53/1995/also Loan]

Enoch Davis Cemetery (1840)
County Rd, between Parris Hill and Canedy's Corner

Douglass Yard Cemetery (1793)
off Mulain Hill Rd.

Graves on edge of Cranberry Pond
Bettys Neck
+ Charles M. Thatcher, *Old Cemeteries of Southeastern Massachusetts*. (Middleborough, Mass., Middleborough Public Library, 1995) [F63/T53/1995/also Loan]

Hafford Cemetery (1799)
177 County St., across from the Booth Cemetery.
+ Charles M. Thatcher, *Old Cemeteries of Southeastern Massachusetts*. (Middleborough, Mass., Middleborough Public Library, 1995) [F63/T53/1995/also Loan]

Haskins–Reed Cemetery (1819)
Rhode Island Rd.
+ Charles M. Thatcher, *Old Cemeteries of Southeastern Massachusetts*. (Middleborough, Mass., Middleborough Public Library, 1995) [F63/T53/1995/also Loan]

Hill Cemetery
Stetson Rd.

Howland Cemetery (1824)
Howland Rd.

Indian Cemetery–Squeen Family (1799)
on east bank of Little Quittacus Pond and Bedford St.
+ Charles M. Thatcher, *Old Cemeteries of Southeastern Massachusetts*. (Middleborough, Mass., Middleborough Public Library, 1995) [F63/T53/1995/also Loan]

Indian Shore Cemetery
Betty's Neck Rd., off of Bedford St.

Keith Cemetery
County Rd., south of Pierce Ave.

Lang Cemetery (1741)
Lang St., off of County St.

Ichabod Leonard Grave; Smallpox (1842)
County Rd., at telephone pole # 117
+ Charles M. Thatcher, *Old Cemeteries of Southeastern Massachusetts*. (Middleborough, Mass., Middleborough Public Library, 1995) [F63/T53/1995/also Loan]

Malbone Cemetery (19th century)
Malbone St., near Pierce Ave.

McCulley Cemetery near Mullain Hill (1787)
Highland Rd.
+ Charles M. Thatcher, *Old Cemeteries of Southeastern Massachusetts*. (Middleborough, Mass., Middleborough Public Library, 1995) [F63/T53/1995/also Loan]

Mullain Hill Cemetery (1843)
Highland Rd., across from Mullein Hill Rd.
+ Charles M. Thatcher, *Old Cemeteries of Southeastern Massachusetts*. (Middleborough,

Mass., Middleborough Public Library, 1995) [F63/T53/1995/also Loan]

New Bedford Road Cemetery (1820)
New Bedford Rd.
+ Charles M. Thatcher, *Old Cemeteries of Southeastern Massachusetts*. (Middleborough, Mass., Middleborough Public Library, 1995) [F63/T53/1995/also Loan]

North Lakeville Cemetery
Taunton St.

Parris Hill Cemetery (1778)
+ Charles M. Thatcher, *Old Cemeteries of Southeastern Massachusetts*. (Middleborough, Mass., Middleborough Public Library, 1995) [F63/T53/1995/also Loan]

Pauper Cemetery
off Race Course Rd.

Silas Pickens Cemetery (1830)
Pickens St., near Elders Pond
+ Charles M. Thatcher, *Old Cemeteries of Southeastern Massachusetts*.(Middleborough, Mass., Middleborough Public Library, 1995) [F63/T53/1995/also Loan]

Zattu Pickens Cemetery (1840)
Pickens St., near Precinct St. *"back on hill back from road"*
+ Charles M. Thatcher, *Old Cemeteries of Southeastern Massachusetts*.(Middleborough, Mass., Middleborough Public Library, 1995) [F63/T53/1995/also Loan]

Pierce and Allen Cemetery (1755)
Adams Ln. off of Rte. 79, close to Berkley, Mass
+ Charles M. Thatcher, *Old Cemeteries of Southeastern Massachusetts*.(Middleborough, Mass., Middleborough Public Library, 1995) [F63/T53/1995/also Loan]

Pond Cemetery (aka) Old Nelson Cemetery (1724)
Bedford St.

+ Charles M. Thatcher, *Old Cemeteries of Southeastern Massachusetts*.(Middleborough, Mass., Middleborough Public Library, 1995) [F63/T53/1995/also Loan]

Precinct Cemetery (1785)
near 185 Rhode Island Rd.

Race Course Road Cemetery (1784)
Race Course Rd., in woods at telephone pole #9.

Ramsdell-Robbins Family Cemetery (1775)
off Race Course Rd.
+ Charles M. Thatcher, *Old Cemeteries of Southeastern Massachusetts*.(Middleborough, Mass., Middleborough Public Library, 1995) [F63/T53/1995/also Loan]

Richmond Cemetery
Taunton Rd. and Cross St.

Sampson Cemetery (1885)
Bedford St.

Small Pox Cemetery
off County

Staples Cemetery
Myricks Rd.
no stones
+ Charles M. Thatcher, *Old Cemeteries of Southeastern Massachusetts*.(Middleborough, Mass., Middleborough Public Library, 1995) [F63/T53/1995/also Loan]

Strowbridge Cemetery (1833)
Kingman St.

Thompson's Hill Cemetery (1714)
east of Rhode Island Rd. and Precinct St.
+ Charles M. Thatcher, *Old Cemeteries of Southeastern Massachusetts*.(Middleborough, Mass., Middleborough Public Library, 1995) [F63/T53/1995/also Loan]
+ NEHGS [Mss/SG/HOD/6/60]

Wampanoag Royal Cemetery
Bedford St., Betty's Neck
+ Charles M. Thatcher, *Old Cemeteries of Southeastern Massachusetts*.(Middleborough, Mass., Middleborough Public Library, 1995) [F63/T53/1995/also Loan]

Ward Cemetery (1790)
near 45 Crooked Ln.

Cemetery on the Hill, Back of Elbridge Cushmans
+ Charles M. Thatcher, *Old Cemeteries of Southeastern Massachusetts*. (Middleborough, Mass., Middleborough Public Library, 1995) [F63/T53/1995/also Loan]

Cemetery betweeen McFall Hill and Mullain Hill
+ Charles M. Thatcher, *Old Cemeteries of Southeastern Massachusetts*. (Middleborough, Mass., Middleborough Public Library, 1995) [F63/T53/1995/also Loan]

Cemetery near Howland Station in the woods (1787)
+ Charles M. Thatcher, *Old Cemeteries of Southeastern Massachusetts*. (Middleborough, Mass., Middleborough Public Library, 1995) [F63/T53/1995/also Loan]

Cemetery near Quittacus Pond (1785)
New Bedford Rd.
+ Charles M. Thatcher, *Old Cemeteries of Southeastern Massachusetts*. (Middleborough, Mass., Middleborough Public Library, 1995) [F63/T53/1995/also Loan]

Cemetery near Town Hall (1845)
perhaps the Bump Family
+ Charles M. Thatcher, *Old Cemeteries of Southeastern Massachusetts*. (Middleborough, Mass., Middleborough Public Library, 1995) [F63/T53/1995/also Loan]

Graves at the back of Elisha Cudworth land of African American and Native Americans [field stone markers]
+ Charles M. Thatcher, *Old Cemeteries of Southeastern Massachusetts*. (Middleborough, Mass., Middleborough Public Library, 1995) [F63/T53/1995/also Loan]

LANCASTER (1653)
Town Hall, 695 Main St., Lancaster, Mass. 01523, Tel: (978)-368-1528

Center Cemetery
Lancaseter Center

Eastwood Cemetery (1842)
Old Common Rd.
+ NEHGS [Mss/SL/BOL/8]
+ NSDAR [G.R.C./S1/v. 106]

Middle Cemetery (1798)
Main St.
+ *Birth, Marriage and Death Register, Church Records and Epitaphs of Lancaster* (1890), p. 420.
+ Esther K. Whitcomb, *Inscriptions from burial grounds of the Nashaway towns : Lancaster, Harvard, Bolton, Leominster, Sterling, Berlin, West Boylston, and Hudson, Massachusetts*. (Bowie, Md: Heritage Books, 1989) [F74/L2/I57/1989/also Loan]
+ NEHGS [MS70/LAN/1]
+ NSDAR [G.R.C./S1/v. 106]

North Burial Ground (1805)
Old Turnpike Rd.
+ *Birth, Marriage and Death Register, Church Records and Epitaphs of Lancaster* (1890), p. 446.
+ Esther K. Whitcomb, *Inscriptions from burial grounds of the Nashaway towns : Lancaster, Harvard, Bolton, Leominster, Sterling,*

Berlin, West Boylston, and Hudson, Massachusetts. (Bowie, Md: Heritage Books, 1989) [F74/L2/I57/1989/also Loan] + NSDAR [G.R.C./S1/v. 106]

North Village Cemetery (1791)
Otis St.
+ *Birth, Marriage and Death Register, Church Records and Epitaphs of Lancaster* (1890), p. 449.
+ Esther K. Whitcomb, *Inscriptions from burial grounds of the Nashaway towns : Lancaster, Harvard, Bolton, Leominster, Sterling, Berlin, West Boylston, and Hudson, Massachusetts.* (Bowie, Md: Heritage Books, 1989) [F74/L2/I57/1989/also Loan]
+ NEHGS [MS70/LAN/1]
+ NSDAR [G.R.C./S1/v. 106]

Old Settlers Burial Field (1674)
Main St.
+ *Birth, Marriage and Death Register, Church Records and Epitaphs of Lancaster* (1890) [p. 398].
+ Esther K. Whitcomb, *Inscriptions from burial grounds of the Nashaway towns : Lancaster, Harvard, Bolton, Leominster, Sterling, Berlin, West Boylston, and Hudson, Massachusetts.* (Bowie, Md: Heritage Books, 1989) [F74/L2/I57/1989/also Loan]
+ NSDAR [G.R.C./S1/v. 106]

Old Common Burial Ground (1667)
Old Common Rd.
+ *Birth, Marriage and Death Register, Church Records and Epitaphs of Lancaster (1890), p. 408*
+ Esther K. Whitcomb, *Inscriptions from burial grounds of the Nashaway towns : Lancaster, Harvard, Bolton, Leominster, Sterling, Berlin, West Boylston, and Hudson, Massachusetts.* (Bowie, Md: Heritage Books, 1989) [F74/L2/I57/1989/also Loan]
+ NEHGS [MS70/LAN/1]
+ NSDAR [G.R.C./S1/v. 106]

St. John's Cemetery (1901)
Parker Rd.,

Cemetery was founded in 1847; graves were all moved from Clinton in 1901.
Tel: (978)-368-8816

Shirley Shaker Cemetery (1792)
Shirley Rd.
+ [G.R. 3] *Vital Records of Shirley, Massachusetts to the year 1850* (1918).
+ *Birth, Marriage and Death Register, Church Records and Epitaphs of Lancaster* (1890), p. 445.
+ Esther K. Whitcomb, *Inscriptions from burial grounds of the Nashaway towns : Lancaster, Harvard, Bolton, Leominster, Sterling, Berlin, West Boylston, and Hudson, Massachusetts.* (Bowie, Md: Heritage Books, 1989) [F74/L2/I57/1989/also Loan]
+ NEHGS [MS70/LAN/1]

LANESBOROUGH (1765)
Town Hall, 83 North Main St., Lanesborough, Mass. 01237, Tel: (413)-442-1351

Center Cemetery (aka) Lower Cemetery (1769)
South Main St.
+ NEHGS [MS70/LAN/10], and [Corbin Collection]
+ NSDAR [G.R.C./S1/v. 348]

Churchill–Barker Family Cemetery (1812)
Potter Mountain Rd.

Pettibone Cemetery (1809)
Old Cheshire Rd.

Riverside Cemetery (1847)
Bailey Rd.

Talcott Cemetery (1775
Rte. 7
+ NEHGS [MS70/LAN/10], and [Corbin Collection]
+ NSDAR [G.R.C./S1/v. 348]

LAWRENCE (1847)
from Andover and Methuen
City Hall, 200 Common St., Lawrence,
Mass. 01840, Tel: (978)-794-5803
Cemetery Department, 170 May St.,
Lawrence (978)-794-5876

Bellevue Cemetery (1847)
96 May St.
Tel: (978)-794-5876
+ [G.R. 1] *Vital Records of Lawrence,*
Massachusetts to the year 1850 (1926).
+ NEHGS [MS70/LAW/10 (A-C)] 4
vols.

Essex County Lodge IOBA
Cemetery–Sons of Israel (1940)
125 Beacon St., near the Tifereth Anshai
Shard Cemetery

St. Mary Immaculate Conception
Cemetery (1847)
29 Barker St.
Tel: (978)-682-8181

Temple Emmanuel Cemetery (1941)
Mt. Vernon St.

United Lebanese Cemetery (1907)
250 Hampshire St.
Tel: (978)-683-5416

LEE (1777)
from Great Barrington
Town Hall, 32 Main St., Lee, Mass.
01238, Tel: (413)-243-5505
Cemetery Department, 32 Main St., Lee,
Mass 01238, Tel: (413)-243-5520

Elwell Cemetery (18th century)
site of the burial for two individuals who
drowned located
between Lower and Upper Goose
Ponds; marked with field stones.

Fairmount Cemetery (1773)
Maple and Greylock Sts.
+ NEHGS [Mss/SL/LEE/4]

South Lee Cemetery (1780)
Meadow St.
+ NEHGS [Mss/SL/LEE/4]

St. Mary's Cemetery (1859)
Spring St., off West Park St.
Tel: St. Mary's Rectory, 40 Academy St.,
Lee,(413)-243-0275
+ Dorvil Miller Wilcox, *Vital records of*
Lee, Massachusetts, 1777-1801, from the
records of the town, Congregational church and
inscriptions in the early burial grounds. (Lee,
1899} [F74/L5/L6/1899/also Loan]

LEICESTER (1714)
Town Hall, 3 Washburn Sq., Leicester,
Mass. 01525, Tel: (508)-892-7070
Cemetery Department, 59 Peter Salem
Rd., Leicester, Mass., Tel: (508)-892-
7021

Cherry Valley Cemetery (1810)
10 Towtaid Rd.
+ NEHGS [Mss/SL/TIS/3]

Eliot Hill Burying Ground (aka)
Shaw Burying Ground (1747)
Marshall St., North Leicester
+ NEHGS [Mss/SL/TIS/3] and
[MS70/LEI/1]

Greenville Baptist Cemetery (1736)
next to 680 Pleasant St., Rochdale
+ NEHGS [MS70/LEI/10] and
[Mss/SL/TIS/3]

Ruth Paine's Gravesite (1778)
near Shaw Pond
+ NSDAR [G.R.C./S1/v. 156]

David Pearson Family Gravesite (1743)
+ NSDAR [G.R.C./S1/v. 156]

Pine Grove Cemetery (1842)
125 Pine St.
+ NEHGS [Mss/SL/TIS/3]
+ NSDAR [G.R.C./S1/v. 156]

Quaker Cemetery (1737)
15 Earle St., Manville
+ NEHGS [MS70/LEI/10] and
[Mss/SL/TIS/3]

Rawson Brook Cemetery (1735)
1190 Main St.
+ NEHGS [Mss/SL/TIS/3]

St. Joseph's Cemetery
90 Waite St.
Tel: St. Joseph and St. Pius Church
Rectory, 759 Main St., Leicester (508)-
892-7407

Small Pox Cemetery (1760)
Watson St.
Sons of Jacob Holy Society (Chevra
Kadisha) Cemetery
Cemetery Rd.

Southgate Family Cemetery (1798)
Rawson St., near Spencer town line.
+ NEHGS [Mss/SL/TIS/3]
+ NSDAR [G.R.C./S1/v. 156]

David Lynde Cemetery
+ NEHGS [MS70/LEI/5]

General Cemetery Reference for
Leicester:
+ NSDAR [G.R.C./S1/v.98] Inscription
Index for Leicester

LENOX (1767)
Town Hall, 6 Walker St., Lenox, Mass.
01240, Tel: (413)-637-5506

Cemetery Department, 6 Walker St.,
Lenox, Mass. 01240, Tel: (413)-637-5525

Church on the Hill Cemetery (1771)
Main St., next to the Congregational
Church

Mountain View Cemetery (ca. 1940s)
Housatonic St., across from Pine Knoll
Rd.

New Lenox Cemetery (1779)
New Lenox Rd., New Lenox
+ NEHGS [MS70/NEW/51]
+ NSDAR [G.R.C./S1/v.94]

St. Anne's Roman Catholic Cemetery (1908)
off Housatonic St., near Lenox center.
Tel: St. Anne's Rectory, 134 Main St.,
Lenox, (413)-637-0157

LEOMINSTER (1740)
from Lancaster
City Clerk, 25 West St., Leominster,
Mass., Tel: (978)-534-7536

Day Street Cemetery Site
(no gravestones)
Main and Day Sts.

Evergreen Cemetery (1842)
357 Main St.
Tel: (978)-534-7583
+ Esther K. Whitcomb, *Inscriptions from
burial grounds of the Nashaway towns : Lancaster, Harvard, Bolton, Leominster, Sterling,
Berlin, West Boylston, and Hudson, Massachusetts.* (Bowie, Md: Heritage Books,
1989) [F74/L2/I57/1989/also Loan]

Pine Grove Cemetery (1741)
Rte. 13 Main St., near North Main and
Mill Sts.

+ Esther K. Whitcomb, *Inscriptions from burial grounds of the Nashaway towns : Lancaster, Harvard, Bolton, Leominster, Sterling, Berlin, West Boylston, and Hudson, Massachusetts.* (Bowie, Md: Heritage Books, 1989) [F74/L2/I57/1989/also Loan]

St. Cecilia's Cemetery (1907)
St. Cecilia St.
Tel: St. Cecilia's Rectory, 168 Mechanic St., Leominster, Mass. (978)-537-6541
+ Esther K. Whitcomb, *Inscriptions from burial grounds of the Nashaway towns : Lancaster, Harvard, Bolton, Leominster, Sterling, Berlin, West Boylston, and Hudson, Massachusetts.* (Bowie, Md: Heritage Books, 1989) [F74/L2/I57/1989/also Loan]

St. Leo's Cemetery (1873)
360 Lancaster St.
Tel: St. Leo's Rectory, 108 Main St., Leominster, Mass. (978)-537-7257
+ Esther K. Whitcomb, *Inscriptions from burial grounds of the Nashaway towns : Lancaster, Harvard, Bolton, Leominster, Sterling, Berlin, West Boylston, and Hudson, Massachusetts.* (Bowie, Md: Heritage Books, 1989) [F74/L2/I57/1989/also Loan]

LEVERETT (1774)
from Sunderland
Town Hall, 9 Montague Rd., Leverett, Mass. 01054

Crocker Farm Cemetery Site
burials removed to Sunderland in 1908
+ NSDAR [G.R.C./S1/v. 346]

East Leverett Cemetery (1811)
Cemetery Rd., East Leverett
+ NEHGS [Corbin Collection]

Jackson Hill Road Cemetery (1870)
Jackson Hill Rd.
+ NEHGS [Corbin Collection]

Leverett Center Cemetery (aka) North Cemetery (1780)
Montague Rd.
+ NEHGS [Corbin Collection]

Long Plain Cemetery (1787)
Long Plain Rd., near the Amherst town line.

Marvel Cemetery (1800)
Jackson Hill Rd.
+ NEHGS [Corbin Collection]

Moor's Corner Cemetery (1810)
Rattlesnake Gutter Rd.
+ NEHGS [Corbin Collection]

Mount Hope Cemetery (1852)
Chestnut Hill Rd.
+ NEHGS [Corbin Collection]

Mount Toby Cemetery (1824)
Long Plain Rd., Rte. 63
+ NEHGS [MS70/LEV/3], and [Corbin Collection]

Plain View Cemetery (1875)
North Leverett Rd.
+ NEHGS [Corbin Collection]

Skerry Road Cemetery (aka) Gardner–Briggs Cemetery (19th century)
Skerry Rd.
+ Esther K. Whitcomb, *Inscriptions from burial grounds of the Nashaway towns : Lancaster, Harvard, Bolton, Leominster, Sterling, Berlin, West Boylston, and Hudson, Massachusetts.* (1989) [F74/L2/I57/1989/also Loan]

Abandoned Cemetery
located in Southwest Leverett
+ NEHGS [Mss/3/L/23]

Cemetery near Toby Road
+ NEHGS [MS70/LEV/3]

LEXINGTON (1713)
from Cambridge
Town Hall, 625 Massachusetts Ave., Lexington, Mass. 02420, Tel: (781)-862-0500.

Lexington Common Tomb
Massachusetts Ave., Lexington Common, next to the Revolutionary War Monument. Tomb for seven soldiers killed on Lexington Green April 19, 1775.

Munroe Cemetery (1831)
Massachusetts Ave.

Old Burying Ground (1690)
Harrington Rd
+ Francis H. Brown, *A copy of Epitaphs on the Old Burying-Grounds of Lexington, Massachusetts.* (Lexington, Mass.: The Lexington Historical Society, 1905) [F74/L67/B8/1905]
+ NEHGS [MS70/LEX/1]

Robbins Cemetery (1792)
Massachusetts Ave.
+ NEHGS [MS70/LEX/1]

Westview Cemetery (1921)
Bedford St., near Bedford town line.
Tel: (781)-861-2717

LEYDEN (1784)
from Bernardston
Town Hall, 16 West Leyden Rd., Leyden, Mass. 01337, Tel: (413)-774-7769

Beaver Meadow Cemetery (1791)
Brattleboro Rd.
+ Arthur D. Fiske, *Cemetery Records of Leyden, Franklin Co., Mass. to 1875.* (Seattle, 1964).
+ NEHGS [Corbin Collection]

Daniel Bliss Cemetery (1800)
Old County Rd.

East Hill Cemetery (1815)
East Hill Rd.
+ NEHGS [Corbin Collection]

Farm Cemetery (1800)
Greenfield Rd.
+ Arthur D. Fiske, *Cemetery Records of Leyden, Franklin Co., Mass. to 1875.* (Seattle, 1964).

Hessian Cemetery (aka) Eudy Family Cemetery (1815)
"on the road leading southward from Leyden"
+ William Tyler Arms, *History of Leyden,* (Orange, Mass. 1959) p. 74

Charles Packer Cemetery (1814)
Old County Rd.

South Leyden Cemetery (1797)
Old County Rd.
+ Arthur D. Fiske, *Cemetery Records of Leyden, Franklin Co., Mass. to 1875.* (Seattle, 1964).
+ NEHGS [Corbin Collection]

Stedman Family Cemetery (1789)
+ William Tyler Arms, *History of Leyden,* (Orange, Mass. 1959) p. 204

West Leyden Cemetery (1792)
West Leyden Rd.
+ NEHGS [Corbin Collection]

LINCOLN (1754)
from Concord and Lexington
Town Hall, 11 Lincoln Ctr., Lincoln, Mass. 01773, Tel: (781)-259-2607

Abor Vitae Cemetery (aka) Triangle Cemetery (1837)
Lexington and Trapelo Rds.

+ Edith Biggs, Town of Lincoln Town Report for 1927, "Inscriptions copied from the tomb stones, in the original town cemetery and the second town cemetery". [MS70/LIN/2]
+ [G.R. 2] *Vital Records of Lowell, Massachusetts to the year 1850* (1930).
+ NEHGS [MS70/LIN/1] and [MS70/LIN/4]

Center Cemetery (aka) Old Training Field Cemetery (1756)
Bedford St.
+ NEHGS [MS70/LIN/6]

Lincoln Road Cemetery (1884)
Lexington Rd., "*New Cemetery*"
+ [G.R. 3] *Vital Records of Lowell, Massachusetts to the year 1850* (1930).

Precinct Burial Ground (aka) Old Lincoln Cemetery (1747)
Lexington Rd.
+ Edith Biggs, Town of Lincoln Town Report for 1927, "Inscriptions copied from the tomb stones, in the original town cemetery and the second town cemetery". [MS70/LIN/2]
+ [G.R. 1] *Vital Records of Lincoln, Massachusetts to the year 1850* (1908).
+ NEHGS [MS70/LIN/1] and [MS70/LIN/5]
+ NSDAR [G.R.C./S1/v. 247]

Town Hill Cemetery (aka) Meeting House Burial Ground
Bedford Rd., behind Bemis Hall

LITTLETON (1715)
Town Hall, 37 Shattuck St., Littleton, Mass. 01460, Tel: (978)-952-2314

Old Burial Ground (aka) Littleton Common Cemetery (1721)
King and West Sts., Littleton Common
+ NSDAR [G.R.C./S1/v. 111]

Site of the Nashoba Cemetery (aka) Powers Burying Ground (1676)
Great Rd., The cemetery was plowed under prior to 1721. A bronze plaque about 1300 feet east of the site, marks where the cemetery was located.

Westlawn Cemetery (1801)
7 New Estate Rd.

LONGMEADOW (1783)
from Springfield
Town Hall, 20 Williams St., Longmeadow, Mass. 01106, Tel: (413)-567-1066

Longmeadow Cemetery (1675)
across from 20 Williams St.
+ NEHGS [MS70/LON/2]
+ NSDAR [G.R.C./S1/v. 83

LOWELL (1826)
from Chelmsford
City Hall, 375 Merrimack St., Lowell, Mass. 01852, Tel: (978)-970-4160
Cemetery Department, 1375 Gorham St., Lowell, Mass., Tel: (978)-970-3323

Clark Road Cemetery (1708)
Clark Rd.
+ NEHGS [MS70/TEW/2]
+ NSDAR [G.R.C./S1/v. 221]

Coburn–Pierce Burial Ground (1780)
Pawtucket Blvd.

Edson Cemetery (1848)
1375 Gorham St.
Tel: (978)-970-3323
+ [G.R. 4] *Vital Records of Lowell, Massachusetts to the year 1850* (1930).

Hamblett Cemetery (1713)
Jordan St.

Hildreth Family Cemetery (1740)
280 Hildreth St.
+ [G.R. 8] *Vital Records of Dracut,
Massachusetts to the year 1850* (1907).

Holy Trinity Cemetery (1927)
Boston Rd.
Tel: Holy Trinity Rectory, 340 High St.,
Lowell (978)-452-2564

Lowell Cemetery (1841)
1020 Lawrence St.
Tel: (978)-454-5191
+ [G.R. 5] *Vital Records of Lowell,
Massachusetts to the year 1850* (1930).
+ *Forty-fifth Annual report of the trustees of
the Lowell Cemetery.* (Lowell, Mass.:
Morning Mall, 1887) [MS/LOW/49]

Old English Cemetery
Gorham St.
+ [G.R. 1] *Vital Records of Lowell,
Massachusetts to the year 1850* (1930).
+ NEHGS [MS70/LOW/1]
+ NSDAR [G.R.C./S1/v. 221]

Old Ground Cemetery Site (aka) Clay Pit Cemetery Site
off Varnum Ave.
+ [G.R. 1] *Vital Records of Dracut,
Massachusetts to the year 1850* (1907).

Pawtucketville Burying Ground (1796)
Mammoth Rd., Pawtucketville
+ [G.R. 3] *Vital Records of Dracut,
Massachusetts to the year 1850* (1907).
+ NSDAR [G.R.C./S1/v. 221]

School Street Cemetery (1720)
464 School St.
+ [G.R. 3] *Vital Records of Lowell,
Massachusetts to the year 1850* (1930).
+ NEHGS [Mss/A/349]
+ NSDAR [G.R.C./S1/v. 221]

St. Patrick's Cemetery (1825)
1259 Gorham St.
Tel: (978)-458-8464
+ [G.R. 2] *Vital Records of Lowell,
Massachusetts to the year 1850* (1930).

Westlawn Cemetery I (1899)
Boston Rd., behind Edson Street
Cemetery

Westlawn Cemetery II (1993)
Boston Rd. and Swan St.

Woodbine Cemetery (1785)
West Meadow Rd.
+ [G.R. 2] *Vital Records of Dracut,
Massachusetts to the year 1850* (1907).
+ NSDAR [G.R.C./S1/v. 221]

LUDLOW (1774)
from Springfield
Town Hall, 488 Chapin St., Ludlow,
Mass. 01056, Tel: (413)-583-5610.
Cemetery Department, 198 Sportsmen's
Rd., Ludlow, Mass. 01056, Tel: (413)-
583-5625

East Yard Cemetery (aka) Ould Burying Ground, and Red Bridge Cemetery (1807)
Poole St., near Belchertown line.
+ NEHGS [MS70/LUD/8], and
[Corbin Collection]
+ NSDAR [G.R.C./S1/v.128]

Fuller Cemetery (aka) North Cemetery, and Old Ludlow Center Cemetery (1786)
Center St., Ludlow Center
+ NEHGS [Corbin Collection]

Island Pond Cemetery (1811)
Center St., across from Chapin Pond.
+ NEHGS [Corbin Collection]

Jenksville (aka) Village Cemetery Site (1811)
all burials moved to Island Pond Cemetery in 1902.

Benjamin Sikes Cemetery (1772)
west side of Munsing St., between Lyon and Church Sts.
+ NEHGS [Corbin Collection]

LUNENBURG (1728)
from Dorchester and Woburn
Town Hall, 17 Main St., Lunenburg, Mass. 01462, Tel: (978)-582-4130
Cemetery Department, P.O. Box 135, Lunenburg, Mass. 01462, Tel: (978)-582-4163

Fish Street Cemetery (19th c.)
Fish and Lincoln Sts.

North Cemetery (1770)
Holman and High St.

South Cemetery (1728)
Page St. and Lancaster Ave.

LYNN (1635)
City Hall, 3 City Hall Sq., Lynn, Mass. 01901, Tel: (781)-598-4000
Cemetery Department, (781)-477-7049

Ahavath Achim Anshe Sfard–Pride of Lynn Cemetery (1920)
Lake Shore Rd.

Chevra Mishna of Chelsea
(a section of the Ahavath Achim Anshe Sfard Cemetery)

Eastern Burial Ground (aka) Woodend Burying Ground (1813)
89 Union St.
+ [G.R. 2] *Vital Records of Lynn, Massachusetts to the year 1850* (1905).

Friends Burying Ground (aka) New Light Cemetery (1722)
behind 80 Sillsbee St.
[remains of 111 Quakers buried at Congress St. in Boston reinterred here 1826]
+ [G.R. 3] *Vital Records of Lynn, Massachusetts to the year 1850* (1905).
+ [G.R. 10] *Vital Records of Lynn, Massachusetts to the year 1850* (1905).

Havrah Mishna Sphard Cemetery
end of Moray St.

Pine Grove Cemetery (1850)
145 Boston St.
Tel: (781)-477-7049
+ [G.R. 9] *Vital Records of Lynn, Massachusetts to the year 1850* (1905).

St. Jean Baptiste Cemetery (1913)
140 Broadway St.
Tel: St. Mary's Rectory, 226 North St., Salem, Mass. (508)-744-2722

St. Joseph's Catholic Cemetery (1879)
134 Broadway St.
Tel: St. Mary's Church, 226 North St., Salem, Mass. (508)-744-2722

St. Mary's Catholic Cemetery (1858)
190 Lynnfield St.
Tel: St. Mary's Church, 226 North St., Salem, Mass. (508)-744-2722
Tel: Archives of the Archdiocese of Boston, 2121 Commonwealth Ave., Brighton, Mass. 02135, (617)-254-0100.
The Boston Archdiocese Archives has grave lot sales 1860-1884.

Western Burying Ground (1637)
36 Market Sq.
+ [G.R. 1] *Vital Records of Lynn, Massachusetts to the year 1850* (1905).
+ Benjamin H. Jacob, *A Record of Interments in the Old or Western Burying*

Ground in Lynn, Mass. (Salem, Mass.:
Salem Press, 1891) [F74/L98/J33/1891]

LYNNFIELD (1782)
from Lynn
Town Hall, 55 Summer St., Lynnfield,
Mass. 01940, Tel: (781)-334-3128
Cemetery Department, (781)-334-3143

Forest Hills Cemetery (1844)
Forest Hills Ave.

Joseph Tapley Tomb (1820's)
Lowell and Chestnut Sts.
(original twelve burials have been
removed)

**Old Burying Ground (aka) Center
Cemetery (1728)**
South Common St.
+ [G.R. 6] *Vital Records of Lynn,
Massachusetts to the year 1850* (1905).
+ NEHGS [MS70/LYN/12] and
[MS70/LYN/74]
+ NSDAR [G.R.C./S1/v.363]

**Newhall Cemetery (aka) Salem
Street Cemetery (1751)**
Salem St.

West Burying Ground (1809)
Main and South Sts., near Middle School
+ NEHGS [MS70/LYN/12]
Willow Cemetery (1869)
Summer St.

South Lynnfield Cemetery
+ [G.R. 8] *Vital Records of Lynn,
Massachusetts to the year 1850* (1905).

MALDEN (1649)
City Hall, 200 Pleasant St., Malden,
Mass. 02148, Tel: (781)-388-0610

**Bell Rock Cemetery (aka) Common
Burying Ground at Sandy Bank
(1649)**
Green St.
+ *The Births, Marriages and Deaths recorded
in the town of Malden 1649-1850* (1903)
+ Thomas Waterman, "Malden Burying-
Ground." *NEHGR* 4:65-66.
+ Thomas B. Wyman, "Synopsis of the
Inscriptions in the Old Malden Burying
Ground."
NEHGR 9:319-328.
+ D.P. Corey, "Synopsis of the
Inscriptions in the Old Malden Burying
Ground."
NEHGR 18:118.
+ NEHGS [MS70/MAL/10]

**Forest Dale Cemetery (aka) Malden
City Cemetery (19th century)**
150 Forest St.
Tel: (781)-322-2360
+ *The Births, Marriages and Deaths recorded
in the town of Malden 1649-1850* (1903)

Holy Cross Cemetery (1860)
175 Broadway
Tel: (781)-322-6300
Tel: Archives of the Archdiocese of
Boston, 2121 Commonwealth Ave.,
Brighton, Mass. 02135, (617)-254-
0100. The Boston Archdiocese Archives
has burial records 1864-1874, and grave
lot sales 1864-1874 with an index 1864-
1898.

**Maplewood Free Burying Ground
and Lebanon Street Jewish
Cemetery (1847)**
297 Lebanon St.

Salem Street Cemetery (1832)
Salem St.
Tel: Forest Dale Cemetery, (781)-322-
2360
+ *The Births, Marriages and Deaths recorded
in the town of Malden 1649-1850* (1903)

MANCHESTER-BY-THE-SEA (1645)
from Salem

Town Hall, 10 Central St., Manchester-by-the-Sea, Mass. 01944, Tel: (978)-526-2040

Cemetery Department, Pleasant St. Ext., Manchester-by-the-Sea, (978)-526-7260

Forster Cemetery
a section of the Old Burying Ground

Knight Family Cemetery (1875)
part of the Rosedale Cemetery

Old Burying Ground (aka) Tappan Cemetery (1661)
Washington and Summer Sts.
+ [G.R.] *Vital Records of Manchester, Massachusetts to the year 1850* (1903).

Pleasant Grove Cemetery (1952)
School and Pleasant Sts.

Rosedale Cemetery (1854)
Arabella Rd.

Rosedale Extension Cemetery (1909)
Pleasant St. Ext.

Union Cemetery (1845)
opposite 79 School St.

MANSFIELD (1770)
from Norton

Town Hall, 6 Park Row, Mansfield, Mass. 02048, Tel:(508)-261-7345

Codding Cemetery
West Mansfield
+ [G.R.5] *Vital Records of Mansfield, Massachusetts to the year 1850* (1933).

East Mansfield Cemetery
East St.
+ [G.R. 3] *Vital Records of Mansfield, Massachusetts to the year 1850* (1933).

Ephraim Leonard Family Burial Ground (1740)
East St.

Furnace Cemetery
440 Franklin St.

Gilbert Street Cemetery
Gilbert St.
+ [G.R. 11] *Vital Records of Mansfield, Massachusetts to the year 1850* (1933).

Happy Hollow Cemetery (1776)
Oak St., West Mansfield
+ [G.R. 8] *Vital Records of Mansfield, Massachusetts to the year 1850* (1933).

Hodges Cemetery
West Mansfield
+ [G.R.4] *Vital Records of Mansfield, Massachusetts to the year 1850* (1933).

Jewel Street Cemetery
Jewell St.

Leonard Cemetery
East Mansfield
+ [G.R. 9] *Vital Records of Mansfield, Massachusetts to the year 1850* (1933).

Morton Church Cemetery
West Mansfield
+ [G.R. 7] *Vital Records of Mansfield, Massachusetts to the year 1850* (1933).

Old Mansfield Cemetery (18th century)
Union St.
+ NEHGS [MS70/MAN/31], [Mss/SG/LIN/5/23], and [Mss/SG/HOD/6/60]
+ NSDAR [G.R.C./S1/v. 84]

St. Mary's Cemetery (1890)
off Rte. 106, Franklin St.
Tel: St. Mary's Rectory, 330 Pratt St.,
Mansfield (508)-339-2981

Spring Brook Cemetery (1807)
88 School St.
Tel: (508)-339-6830
+ [G.R.2] *Vital Records of Mansfield,
Massachusetts to the year 1850* (1933).

Sweet Cemetery
West Mansfield
+ [G.R.6] *Vital Records of Mansfield,
Massachusetts to the year 1850* (1933).

White Farm Cemetery
next to old town hall
+ [G.R. 10] *Vital Records of Mansfield,
Massachusetts to the year 1850* (1933).

MARBLEHEAD (1633)

Town Hall, Abbott Hall, 188
Washington St., Marblehead, Mass.
01945, Tel: (781)-631-0528.
Cemetery Department, 294 West Shore
Drive, Marblehead, Mass., Tel:(781)-631-
1182

Brown Tomb Field
Elm St.

Green Street Cemetery (1790)
Elm, Cressey and Green Sts.
+ [G.R. 4] *Vital Records of Marblehead,
Massachusetts to the year 1850* (1903).

Harbor View Cemetery (1859)
Waterside Rd., next to Waterside
Cemetery

Harris Street Cemetery (1737)
Harris St.,
+ [G.R. 3] *Vital Records of Marblehead,
Massachusetts to the year 1850* (1903).

Hathaway Tomb (19th century)
corner of Highland Terr. and Village St.

Hooper Tomb (1807)
Harris St., across from Harris Street
Cemetery

Martin Tomb (1827)
Harris St.

Old Burial Hill (1629)
Orne St., on a hill behind Rodd's Pond.
+ [G.R. 1] *Vital Records of Marblehead,
Massachusetts to the year 1850* (1903).
+ NEHGS [MS70/MAR/2]
+ NSDAR [G.R.C./S1/v. 85]

St. Michael's Cemetery (1720)
Summer St., beside St. Michael's Church
+ [G.R. 5] *Vital Records of Marblehead,
Massachusetts to the year 1850* (1903).
+ NEHGS [MS70/MAR/8]
+ NSDAR [G.R.C./S1/v. 85]

**Star of the Sea Catholic Cemetery
(ca. 1850)**
120 Lafayette St.

Unitarian Cemetery (1729)
behind Unitarian Church on Mugford St.
+ [G.R. 2] *Vital Records of Marblehead,
Massachusetts to the year 1850* (1903).

Waterside Cemetery (1859)
294 West Shore Dr.

Wyman Family Cemetery (1800)
next to St. Andrew's Church, Lafayette St..

MARION (1852)
from Rochester

Town Hall, 2 Spring St., Marion, Mass.
02738, Tel: (508)-748-3505
Cemetery Department, (508)-748-3541

Blankenship Cemetery
Point Rd.
+ NSDAR [G.R.C./S1/v. 48]
+ NEHGS [Mss/CB/78], and
[Mss/SG/LIN/5/15]

Evergreen Cemetery
Converse Rd. and Rte. 6.
+ [G.R. 13] *Vital Records of Rochester, Massachusetts to the year 1850* (1914).
+ NEHGS [Mss/CB/78],
[Mss/SG/LIN/5/14], and
[Mss/SG/LIN/5/15].

Happy Alley Cemetery (aka) Quaker Cemetery
+ [G.R. 12] *Vital Records of Rochester, Massachusetts to the year 1850* (1914).
+ NEHGS [Mss/CB/78],
[Mss/SG/LIN/5/14], and
[Mss/SG/LIN/5/15].

Little Neck Cemetery (18th century)
Hermitage Rd.
+ Charles M. Thatcher, *Old Cemeteries of Southeastern Massachusetts.*(Middleborough, Mass., Middleborough Public Library,1995) [F63/T53/1995/also Loan]
+ [G.R. 11] *Vital Records of Rochester, Massachusetts to the year 1850* (1914).
+ NEHGS [Mss/CB/78],
[Mss/SG/LIN/5/14], and
[Mss/SG/LIN/5/15].

Cemetery at Handy's Corner,
opposite the church north side (1797)
+ Charles M. Thatcher, *Old Cemeteries of Southeastern Massachusetts.* (Middleborough, Mass., Middleborough Public Library, 1995) [F63/T53/1995/also Loan]

Cemetery at Handy's Corner, opposite the church south side (1799)
+ Charles M. Thatcher, *Old Cemeteries of Southeastern Massachusetts.* (Middleborough,

Mass., Middleborough Public Library, 1995) [F63/T53/1995/also Loan]

Marion Cemetery (18th century)
south end of Village
+ Charles M. Thatcher, *Old Cemeteries of Southeastern Massachusetts.* (Middleborough, Mass., Middleborough Public Library, 1995) [F63/T53/1995/also Loan]

North Marion Cemetery
County Rd.

Old Landing Cemetery
Mill St.
+ [G.R. 14] *Vital Records of Rochester, Massachusetts to the year 1850* (1914).
+ NEHGS [Mss/CB/78], and
[Mss/SG/LIN/5/14], and
[Mss/SG/LIN/5/15].

MARLBOROUGH (1660)
City Hall, 140 Main St., Marlborough, Mass. Tel: (508)-460-3775
Cemetery Department, 133 Wilson St.
Marlborough, Mass. Tel: (508)-624-6916

Brigham Cemetery (1793)
West Main St., opposite Broad St.
+ [G.R. 4] *Vital Records of Marlborough, Massachusetts to the year 1850* (1908).
+ Franklin Pierce Rice, *Marlborough, Massachusetts, burial ground inscriptions.* (Worcester, Ma., Franklin P. Rice, 1908) [F74/M32/R6/1908/also Loan]
+ NEHGS [MS70/MAR/20]

Evergreen Cemetery (1959)
Wilson St.

Immaculate Conception Roman Catholic Cemetery (1858)
Crescent and Beach St.
Tel: Immaculate Conception, 17 Washington Ct., Marlborough, (508)-485-0016

Tel: Archives of the Archdiocese of Boston, 2121 Commonwealth Ave., Brighton, Mass. 02135, (617)-254-0100.The Boston Archdiocese Archives has lot assignments 1857-1926, and grave lot sales 1847-1943.

Maplewood Cemetery (1835)
Pleasant St.
+ NEHGS [MS70/MAR/22]
+ NSDAR [G.R.C./S1/v. 310]

Old Common Cemetery (1706)
Central St.
+ [G.R. 2] *Vital Records of Marlborough, Massachusetts to the year 1850* (1908).
+ Franklin Pierce Rice, *Marlborough, Massachusetts, burial ground inscriptions.* (Worcester, Ma., Franklin P. Rice, 1908) [F74/M32/R6/1908/also Loan]
+ NEHGS [MS70/MAR/25]

Robin Hill Cemetery (1817)
Lynch Blvd.
+ NEHGS [F74/M32/M61]
Typescript in Mss
+ NSDAR [G.R.C./S1/v. 48]

Rocklawn Cemetery (aka) Chipman Cemetery (1813)
Stevens St.
+ [G.R. 3] *Vital Records of Marlborough, Massachusetts to the year 1850* (1908).
+ NEHGS [MS70/MAR/20]
+ NEHGS [F74/M32/M61]
Typescript in Mss

Spring Hill Cemetery (1675)
Brown and High Sts.
+ [G.R. 1] *Vital Records of Marlborough, Massachusetts to the year 1850* (1908).
+ Franklin Pierce Rice, *Marlborough, Massachusetts, burial ground inscriptions.* (Worcester, Ma., Franklin P. Rice, 1908) [F74/M32/R6/1908/also Loan]
+ NEHGS [MS70/MAR/20]

St. Mary's Roman Catholic (French) Cemetery (1879)
Beech St., off West Main St.
Tel: St. Mary's Rectory, 26 Broad St., Marlborough (508)-485-0390

Weeks Cemetery (1800)
Concord Rd. and Sunbury St.
+ NEHGS [F74/M32/M61]
Typescript in Mss
+ NSDAR [G.R.C./S1/v. 48]

Wilson Farm Cemetery (aka) Morse Cemetery (1764)
Wilson St.
+ [G.R. 5] *Vital Records of Marlborough, Massachusetts to the year 1850* (1908).
+ NEHGS [F74/M32/M61] Typescript in Mss

MARSHFIELD (1640)
Town Hall, 870 Moraine St., Marshfield, Mass. 02050, Tel: (781)-834-5540

Baker Family Cemetery
Acorn St., near Baker's Ln.

Cedar Grove Cemetery (1657)
Ocean St.
+ NEHGS [MS70/MAR/40]
+ *The Mayflower Descendant* (v. 12-13)
+ NSDAR [G.R.C./S1/v. 86]

Centre Marshfield Cemetery (1740)
Grove and Ferry Sts.
+ *Vital Records of Marshfield, Massachusetts to the year 1850* (1969), p. 369-372.
+ Charles M. Thatcher, *Old Cemeteries of Southeastern Massachusetts.* . (Middleborough, Mass., Middleborough Public Library, 1995) [F63/T53/1995/also Loan]
+ *The Mayflower Descendant* (v. 8)
+ NSDAR [G.R.C./S1/v. 86]

Chapel Cemetery (1793)
next to the Congregational Church, Rte.
139 near Webster Square, South
Marshfield
+ *Vital Records of Marshfield, Massachusetts
to the year 1850* (1969), p. 414-421.
+ Charles M. Thatcher, *Old Cemeteries of
Southeastern Massachusetts.* (Middleborough,
Mass., Middleborough Public Library,
1995) [F63/T53/1995/also Loan]

**Congregational Church Cemetery
(18th century)**
Marshfield Hills, South Marshfield
+ *Vital Records of Marshfield, Massachusetts
to the year 1850* (1969), p. 397-414.
+ Charles M. Thatcher, *Old Cemeteries of
Southeastern Massachusetts.* (Middleborough,
Mass., Middleborough Public Library,
1995) [F63/T53/1995/also Loan]

Couch Cemetery (1960)
Union St.

**Dingley Family Cemetery (19th
century)**
off Rayfield Rd.

**Little Cemetery (aka) Sea View
Cemetery (1718)**
Summer St.
+ *Vital Records of Marshfield, Massachusetts
to the year 1850* (1969), p. 394-397
+ Charles M. Thatcher, *Old Cemeteries of
Southeastern Massachusetts.* (Middleborough,
Mass., Middleborough Public Library,
1995) [F63/T53/1995/also Loan]

Magoun Cemetery (1840)
opposite 83 Union St.

Marshfield Hills Cemetery (1729)
Old Main St.
+ *Vital Records of Marshfield, Massachusetts
to the year 1850* (1969), p. 373-386
+ Charles M. Thatcher, *Old Cemeteries of
Southeastern Massachusetts.* (Middleborough,

Mass., Middleborough Public Library,
1995) [F63/T53/1995/also Loan]
+ *The Mayflower Descendant* (v. 9)
+ NEHGS [MS70/MAR/40]
+ NSDAR [G.R.C./S1/v. 86]

Plainville Cemetery (1788)
Rte. 139, Old Plain and School Sts.
+ *Vital Records of Marshfield, Massachusetts
to the year 1850* (1969), p. 421-425.
+ Charles M. Thatcher, *Old Cemeteries of
Southeastern Massachusetts.* (Middleborough,
Mass., Middleborough Public Library,
1995) [F63/T53/1995/also Loan]
+ *The Mayflower Descendant* (v. 14)
+ NEHGS [MS70/MAR/40]
+ NSDAR [G.R.C./S1/v. 86]

Adam Rogers Family Tomb
opposite 333 Highland St.

Two Mile Cemetery (1801)
Union St.
+ *Vital Records of Marshfield, Massachusetts
to the year 1850* (1969), p. 391-394.
+ Charles M. Thatcher, *Old Cemeteries of
Southeastern Massachusetts.* (Middleborough,
Mass., Middleborough Public Library,
1995) [F63/T53/1995/also Loan]
+ *The Mayflower Descendant* (v. 10)
+ NEHGS [MS70/MAR/40]

Winslow Cemetery (1640)
Winslow Cemetery Rd.
+ *Vital Records of Marshfield, Massachusetts
to the year 1850* (1969), p. 386-390.
+ *The Mayflower Descendant* (v. 10)
+ NEHGS [MS70/MAR/40]
+ NSDAR [G.R.C./S1/v. 86]

MASHPEE (1763)
Town Hall, 16 Great Neck Rd. North,
Mashpee, Mass. 02649, Tel: (508)-539-1400

**Ancient Cemetery (aka) Lakewood
Cemetery (1805)**
Lakewood Dr.

Avant–Amos–Coomb Cemetery (1838)
Rte. 130

Attaquin Cemetery (1849)
Rte. 130 near Ashumet Rd.

Francis Family Cemetery (1798)
Pimlico Pond Rd.
Hicks Cemetery
Falmouth-Sandwich Rd. [no stones]

Jones–Johnson–Fowler Cemetery (1851)
South Sandwich Rd. and Rte. 30, no stones.

Roxanna C. Mye Cemetery
Highview Ave. [no stones]

Pocknett-Stevens (1871)
Meetinghouse Rd.

Punkhorn Point (aka) Skipper–Simon–Holland Cemetery (1835)
Great Neck Rd.

Tobey Cemetery Site
Santuit Pond Estate Development

Town Cemetery–Old Indian Cemetery (1770)
Rte. 28

MATTAPOISETT (1857)
from Rochester.
Town Hall, 16 Main St., Mattapoisett, Mass. 02739, Tel: (508)-758-4103

Barlow Cemetery (1756)
off Park St. and Barlow Ln.

Cushing Cemetery
Acushnet and Medell Rds.
+ NEHGS [Mss/CB/78]

Ellis–Bolles Family Cemetery (1872)
Wolf Island Rd., near Long Plain Rd.
+ NEHGS [Mss/CB/78]
Fairhaven Road Cemetery
Fairhaven Rd.
+ Charles M. Thatcher, *Old Cemeteries of Southeastern Massachusetts*. (Middleborough, Mass., Middleborough Public Library, 1995) [F63/T53/1995/also Loan]

Hammond Cemetery (1740)
River Rd.

Mattapoisett Friends Meeting House Cemetery (1827)
Marion Rd.
+ Charles M. Thatcher, *Old Cemeteries of Southeastern Massachusetts*. (Middleborough, Mass., Middleborough Public Library, 1995) [F63/T53/1995/also Loan]

Pine Island Cemetery (19th century)
Marion Rd. Rte. 6, near Hillside Ave.

St. Anthony's Cemetery
North St.
Tel: St. Anthony's Rectory, 22 Barstow St., Mattapoisett (508)-758-3719

MAYNARD (1871)
from Stow and Sudbury
Town Hall, 195 Main St., Maynard, Mass. 01754, Tel: (978)-897-1000

Glenwood Cemetery (1872)
Parker St. and Great Rd.
+ NSDAR [G.R.C./S1/v. 111]

St. Bridget's Cemetery (1859)
Old Mill and Great Rds.
Tel: (978)-897-2171

MEDFIELD (1650)
from Dedham
Town Hall, 459 Main St., Medfield,
Mass. 02052, Tel: (508)-359-8505

Medfield State Hospital Cemetery (1900)
45 Hospital Rd.

Vine Lake Cemetery (1651)
Main St.
Tel: (508)-359-8505
+ "Medfield, Mass., Gravestone records
to 1850." *NEHGR* 58:343-7.
+ NEHGS [Mss/SL/TIS/3]

MEDFORD (1630)
City Hall, 85 George P. Hassett Dr.,
Medford, Mass. 02155, Tel: (781)-393-1895

Cross Street Cemetery Site (1816)
Cross St., graves moved to the Oak
Grove Cemetery in 1958.
+ [G.R. 2] *Vital Records of Medford,
Massachusetts to the year 1850* (1907).

Old Salem Street Burying Ground (1691)
Salem and River Sts., Medford Square
+ [G.R.3] *Vital Records of Medford,
Massachusetts to the year 1850* (1907).

Oak Grove Cemetery (aka) City Cemetery (1853)
230 Playstead Rd.
Tel: (617)-393-2487

MEDWAY (1713)
from Medfield.
Town Hall, 155 Village St., Medway,
Mass. 02053, Tel: (508)-533-3204

Evergreen Cemetery (aka) West Medway Cemetery (1749)
Cottage St.
+ [G.R. 2] *Vital Records of Medway,
Massachusetts to the year 1850* (1905).
+ *Epitaphs from the Old Burying Ground,
West Medway, Mass.* (Dedham, Mass.:
1900) [MS/MED/604]
+ Susan F. Salisbury, *Southern
Massachusetts Cemetery Collection,* Volume 1
(Bowie, Md., Heritage Books, 1995))
[F63/S25/1995/also Loan]
+ NEHGS [MS70/WES/300] and
[MS70/WES/301]

Oakland Cemetery (1865)
Barber St.

St. Joseph Cemetery (1876)
Oakland St.
Tel: St. Joseph's Rectory, 2 Barber St.,
Medway, Mass. (508)-533-6500

MELROSE (1850)
from Malden
City Hall, 562 Main St., Melrose, Mass.
02176, Tel: (781)-665-0200
Cemetery Dept., Sylvan St., Melrose,
Mass. (781)-665-0405

Agudas Achim of Malden
(a section of the Route 99–Jewish
Cemetery)
Route 1

Congregation Hadrath Israel
(a section of the Route 99–Jewish
Cemetery)
Route 1

Netherlands Cemetery
Lindwood Ave.

Onikchty
(a section of the Route 9–Jewish
Cemetery)

Route 99–Jewish Cemetery
Broadway St.

Vickomir
(a section of the Route 99–Jewish
Cemetery)

Workmen's Circle Cemetery
(a section of the Route 99–Jewish
Cemetery)

Wyoming Cemetery (1850)
205 Sylvan St., across from Linwood Ave.
Tel: (781)-665-0405
+ *The Births, Marriages and Deaths recorded
in the town of Malden 1649-1850* (1903)

MENDON (1667)
Town Hall, 20 Main St., Mendon, Mass.
01756, Tel: (508)-473-1085

Bicknell Cemetery (1828)
Hartford Ave. East Mendon
+ [G.R. 4] *Vital Records of Mendon,
Massachusetts to the year 1850* (1920).
+ Susan F. Salisbury, *Southern Massa-
chusetts Cemetery Collection*, Volume 1
(Bowie, Md., Heritage Books, 1995))
[F63/S25/1995/also Loan]

Gaskill Cemetery (1810)
George St. and Neck Hill Rd.
+ [G.R. 3] *Vital Records of Mendon,
Massachusetts to the year 1850* (1920).
+ Susan F. Salisbury, *Southern Massa-
chusetts Cemetery Collection*, Volume 1
(Bowie, Md., Heritage Books, 1995))
[F63/S25/1995/also Loan]
+ NEHGS [MS70/MEN/5]

George Street Cemetery (1820)
George St.
+ [G.R. 2] *Vital Records of Mendon,
Massachusetts to the year 1850* (1920).
+ Susan F. Salisbury, *Southern Massa-
chusetts Cemetery Collection*, Volume 1

(Bowie, Md., Heritage Books, 1995))
[F63/S25/1995/also Loan]
+ NEHGS [MS70/MEN/5]

Locust Hill Cemetery (1829)
North Ave.
+ Susan F. Salisbury, *Southern Massa-
chusetts Cemetery Collection*, Volume 1
(Bowie, Md., Heritage Books, 1995))
[F63/S25/1995/also Loan]

Old Cemetery (1702)
Main St.
+ [G.R. 1] *Vital Records of Mendon,
Massachusetts to the year 1850* (1920).
+ Susan F. Salisbury, *Southern Massa-
chusetts Cemetery Collection*, Volume 1
(Bowie, Md., Heritage Books, 1995)
[F63/S25/1995/also Loan]
+ NEHGS [MS70/MEN/5]

Park Street Cemetery (1883)
Park St.
+ Susan F. Salisbury, *Southern Massa-
chusetts Cemetery Collection*, Volume 1
(Bowie, Md., Heritage Books, 1995))
[F63/S25/1995/also Loan]

Pine Hill Cemetery (1757)
Providence Rd.
+ [G.R. 8] *Vital Records of Mendon,
Massachusetts to the year 1850* (1920).
+ Susan F. Salisbury, *Southern Massa-
chusetts Cemetery Collection*, Volume 1
(Bowie, Md., Heritage Books, 1995)
[F63/S25/1995/also Loan]
+ NEHGS [MS70/MEN/5] and
[Mss/C/13]

Pleasant Street Cemetery (1842)
Pleasant St.
+ Susan F. Salisbury, *Southern Massa-
chusetts Cemetery Collection*, Volume 1
(Bowie, Md., Heritage Books, 1995)
[F63/S25/1995/also Loan]

Quaker Friends Cemetery (1729)
George St.

+ Susan F. Salisbury, *Southern Massa-chusetts Cemetery Collection*, Volume 1 (Bowie, Md., Heritage Books, 1995) [F63/S25/1995/also Loan]

Swandale Cemetery (1812)
Cemetery St.
+ [G.R. 6] *Vital Records of Mendon, Massachusetts to the year 1850* (1920).
+ Susan F. Salisbury, *Southern Massa-chusetts Cemetery Collection*, Volume 1 (Bowie, Md., Heritage Books, 1995) [F63/S25/1995/also Loan]
+ NEHGS [MS70/MEN/5]

Taft-Lamothe Cemetery (1854)
Millville Rd.
+ Susan F. Salisbury, *Southern Massa-chusetts Cemetery Collection*, Volume 1 (Bowie, Md., Heritage Books, 1995) [F63/S25/1995/also Loan]
+ NEHGS [MS70/MEN/5]

Wood Cemetery (1851)
Thornton St., and Hartford Ave. West
+ [G.R. 11] *Vital Records of Mendon, Massachusetts to the year 1850* (1920).
+ Susan F. Salisbury, *Southern Massa-chusetts Cemetery Collection*, Volume 1 (Bowie, Md., Heritage Books, 1995) [F63/S25/1995/also Loan]

Chestnut Hill Cemetery
+ [G.R. 19] *Vital Records of Mendon, Massachusetts to the year 1850* (1920).

Cook Cemetery
+ [G.R. 7] *Vital Records of Mendon, Massachusetts to the year 1850* (1920).

Daniels Cemetery
+ [G.R. 10] *Vital Records of Mendon, Massachusetts to the year 1850* (1920).

Freeman Cemetery
+ [G.R. 9] *Vital Records of Mendon, Massachusetts to the year 1850* (1920).

Davenport Cemetery
+ [G.R. 5] *Vital Records of Mendon, Massachusetts to the year 1850* (1920).

Thornton Cemetery
+ [G.R. 12] *Vital Records of Mendon, Massachusetts to the year 1850* (1920).

MERRIMAC (1876)
from Amesbury
Town Hall, 2 School St., Merrimac, Mass. 01860, Tel: (978)-346-8013
Cemetery Department, 5 East Main St., Merrimac, Mass. 01860, Tel: (978)-346-4591

Church Street Cemetery (1731)
Church St., next to Pilgrim Congregational Church
+ [G.R. 3] *Vital Records of Amesbury, Massachusetts to the year 1850* (1913)
+ NSDAR [G.R.C./S1/v. 355]

Heath Family Cemetery (19th century)
Birchmeadow and Heath Rds.

Locust Grove Cemetery (1876)
Locust St.

Lower Corner Cemetery (18th century)
118 East Main St.
+ [G.R. 2]*Vital Records of Amesbury, Massachusetts to the year 1850* (1913).

METHUEN (1725)
from Haverhill.
City Hall, 41 Pleasant St., Methuen, Mass. 01844, Tel: (978)-794-3123

Daddy Frye's Hill Cemetery (1728)
East St.

Elmwood Cemetery (1772)
130 North Lowell St.
Tel: (978)-794-3282
+ [G.R. 3] *Vital Records of Methuen,
Massachusetts to the year 1850* (1909).

Lithuanian National Catholic Cemetery (1914)
North Lowell St.

Meeting House Hill Burying Ground (1728)
Berkeley St.
+ [G.R. 1] *Vital Records of Methuen,
Massachusetts to the year 1850* (1909).
+ Methuen Historical Society, *Ye catalog
of epitaphs from ye old burying ground on
Meeting-House Hill in Methuen, Massa-
chusetts.* (Methuen, Mass.: Methuen
Transcript Co., 1897)
[F74/M6/M65/1897/also Loan]

Polish National Catholic Cemetery (1927)
North Lowell St., opposite Elmwood
Cemetery

Searle's Estate Cemetery (1900)
209 Lawrence St.

St. Anthony's Syrian Cemetery (aka) Maronite Catholic Rites Parish Church Cemetery (1918)
North Lowell St.
Tel: St. Anthony's Maronite Rectory, 145
Amesbury St., Lawrence, Masss., (978)-
685-7233

St. Peter and St. Paul Russian Orthodox Cemetery (1950)
North Lowell St., opposite Elmwood
Cemetery

Village Burying Ground–Lawrence Street Cemetery (1832)
Lawrence St., opposite the Presentation
of Mary Academy

+ [G.R. 2] *Vital Records of Methuen,
Massachusetts to the year 1850* (1909).
+ NEHGS [Mss/SL/MET/5]

Walnut Grove Cemetery (1850)
Grove St.

MIDDLEBOROUGH (1669)
Town Hall, 20 Centre St.,
Middleborough, Mass. 02346, Tel: (508)-
946-2415

Benson Cemetery
South Middleboro

Central Cemetery (1819)
Center St.
+ Charles M. Thatcher, *Old Cemeteries of
Southeastern Massachusetts.* (Middleborough,
Mass., Middleborough Public Library,
1995) [F63/T53/1995/also Loan]

Drake Cemetery
Pleasant St., North Middleboro
+ Charles M. Thatcher, *Old Cemeteries of
Southeastern Massachusetts* (Middleborough,
Mass., Middleborough Public Library,
1995) [F63/T53/1995/also Loan]

East Cemetery
Highland St.

Eaton Cemetery
Old Center St.
+ Charles M. Thatcher, *Old Cemeteries of
Southeastern Massachusetts* (Middleborough,
Mass., Middleborough Public Library,
1995) [F63/T53/1995/also Loan]

Ewer Family Cemetery
Highland St.

Fall Brook Cemetery (1819)
Tispaquin St., Fall Brook

+ Charles M. Thatcher, *Old Cemeteries of Southeastern Massachusetts*. (Middleborough, Mass., Middleborough Public Library, 1995) [F63/T53/1995/also Loan]

Gammons Cemetery
Sachem St., Fall Brook
+ Charles M. Thatcher, *Old Cemeteries of Southeastern Massachusetts*. (Middleborough, Mass., Middleborough Public Library, 1995) [F63/T53/1995/also Loan]

Green Cemetery
Plympton St.

Highland Cemetery
Highland St.

Hope's Rest Cemetery (1884)
Highland St., Rock Village, next to Rock Village Cemetery.
+ Charles M. Thatcher, *Old Cemeteries of Southeastern Massachusetts* (Middleborough, Mass., Middleborough Public Library, 1995) [F63/T53/1995/also Loan]

Marion Road–Neck Cemetery (1985)
Marion Rd.

Middleboro Infirmary Cemetery (1933)
Wood St.

Nemansket Hill Burial Ground (1662)
Plymouth St.
+ Charles M. Thatcher, *Old Cemeteries of Southeastern Massachusetts*. (Middleborough, Mass., Middleborough Public Library, 1995) [F63/T53/1995/also Loan]

Parish Burial Ground at the Green (1717)
Plympton St.
+ Charles M. Thatcher, *Old Cemeteries of Southeastern Massachusetts*. (Middleborough,

Mass., Middleborough Public Library, 1995) [F63/T53/1995/also Loan]

Gilbert Peirce Cemetery (19th century)
Marion Rd., next to the Reed Cemetery

Poor House Cemetery (1832)
Wood and Old Wood Sts.
+ Charles M. Thatcher, *Old Cemeteries of Southeastern Massachusetts* (Middleborough, Mass., Middleborough Public Library, 1995) [F63/T53/1995/also Loan]

Purchade Cemetery (aka) Alden Cemetery (1728)
Plymouth St., Purchade
+ Charles M. Thatcher, *Old Cemeteries of Southeastern Massachusetts*. (Middleborough, Mass., Middleborough Public Library, 1995) [F63/T53/1995/also Loan]

Reed Cemetery (1813)
Marion Rd., next to the Gilbert Peirce Cemetery

Rock Cemetery (aka) Thomas Cemetery (1745)
Highland St., next to Hope's Rest Cemetery.

Sachem Street–Gammons Cemetery (1828)
Sachem St.

St. Mary's Cemetery (1891)
Wood St., off Rte. 128
Tel: Sacred Heart Rectory, 340 Center St., Middleboro, (508)-947-0444
Tel: Archives of the Archdiocese of Boston, 2121 Commonwealth Ave., Brighton, Mass. 02135, (617)-254-0100.The Boston Archdiocese Archives has burial records and grave lot sales 1891-1913.

Smallpox Cemetery (1777)
Brook and Soule Sts., Eddyville, near the
Plympton town line.
+ Charles M. Thatcher, *Old Cemeteries of
Southeastern Massachusetts* (Middleborough,
Mass., Middleborough Public Library,
1995) [F63/T53/1995/also Loan]

South Middleboro Cemetery (1768)
Wareham St.
+ Charles M. Thatcher, *Old Cemeteries of
Southeastern Massachusetts* (Middleborough,
Mass., Middleborough Public Library,
1995) [F63/T53/1995/also Loan]

Tack Factory Cemetery (aka)
Leonard Cemetery (1819)
Taunton St., over Rte. 495, near the
Lakeville town line.
+ Charles M. Thatcher, *Old Cemeteries of
Southeastern Massachusetts* (Middleborough,
Mass., Middleborough Public Library,
1995) [F63/T53/1995/also Loan]

Thomas Cemetery
Highland St.

Thomastown Cemetery (1806)
Purchase St., Thomastown, near the
Carver town line.
+ Charles M. Thatcher, *Old Cemeteries of
Southeastern Massachusetts*. (Middleborough,
Mass., Middleborough Public Library,
1995) [F63/T53/1995/also Loan]

Tispequin Street Cemetery (1838)
Tispequin St.

Titicut Parish Cemetery (1750)
Plymouth St., North Middleboro
+ Charles M. Thatcher, *Old Cemeteries of
Southeastern Massachusetts*. (Middleborough,
Mass., Middleborough Public Library,
1995) [F63/T53/1995/also Loan]
+ NEHGS [Mss/SG/HOD/6/60]

Vernon Street Smallpox Burial
Ground (1778)
Vernon St., North Middleboro
+ Charles M. Thatcher, *Old Cemeteries of
Southeastern Massachusetts*. (Middleborough,
Mass., Middleborough Public Library,
1995) [F63/T53/1995/also Loan]

Wall Street Gravesite
Wall St., Rock Meadow
+ Charles M. Thatcher, *Old Cemeteries of
Southeastern Massachusetts*. (Middleborough,
Mass., Middleborough Public Library,
1995) [F63/T53/1995/also Loan]

Wappanucket Cemetery (1832)
Vaughn St.
+ Charles M. Thatcher, *Old Cemeteries of
Southeastern Massachusetts*. (Middleborough,
Mass., Middleborough Public Library,
1995) [F63/T53/1995/also Loan]

Warrentown Cemetery (1744)
Summer St.
+ Charles M. Thatcher, *Old Cemeteries of
Southeastern Massachusetts*. (Middleborough,
Mass., Middleborough Public Library,
1995) [F63/T53/1995/also Loan]

Wood Cemetery (aka) Thomas
Wood Cemetery (1796)
Wood and East Grove Sts.
+ Charles M. Thatcher, *Old Cemeteries of
Southeastern Massachusetts*. (Middleborough,
Mass., Middleborough Public Library,
1995) [F63/T53/1995/also Loan]

MIDDLEFIELD (1783)
from Becket, Chester,
Washington, Worthington
Town Hall, 188 Skyline Trail,
Middlefield, Mass., 01243, Tel: (413)-
623-8966
Cemetery Commission, P.O. Box 295,
Middlefield, Mass 01243

Middlefield Village Cemetery (1798)
105 Arthur Pease and Bell Rds.
+ [G.R. 1] *Vital Records of Middfield,*
Massachusetts to the year 1850 (1907).
+ NEHGS [MS70/MID/11]

Bell Cemetery (1791)
182 Skyline Trail
+ [G.R. 3] *Vital Records of Middfield,*
Massachusetts to the year 1850 (1907).
+ NEHGS [MS70/MID/11]

Mack Cemetery (1775)
188 Skyline Dr., behind Middlefield
Town Hall
+ [G.R. 2] *Vital Records of Middfield,*
Massachusetts to the year 1850 (1907).
+ NEHGS [MS70/MID/11]

Pine Grove Cemetery (1914)
21 Clark Wright Rd.

Howard Smith Cemetery
Clark Wright Rd.
+ [G.R. 5] *Vital Records of Middfield,*
Massachusetts to the year 1850 (1907).
+ NEHGS [MS70/MID/11]

Clark Wright Cemetery (1816)
100 Clark Wright Rd.
+ [G.R. 4] *Vital Records of Middfield,*
Massachusetts to the year 1850 (1907).
+ NEHGS [MS70/MID/11]

MIDDLETON (1728)
from Andover, Boxford, Salem, and Topsfield
Town Hall, 48 South Main St.,
Middleton, Mass. 01949, Tel: (978-774-6927
Cemetery Department, 195 North Main
St., Middleton, Mass. 01949. Tel: (978)-777-0407

Roger Elliot Family Plot (1826)
Lower Mill St.

+ [G.R. 7] *Vital Records of Middleton,*
Massachusetts to the year 1850 (1904).

Flint Family Burying Ground (1802)
Boston St.
+ [G.R. 11] *Vital Records of Middleton,*
Massachusetts to the year 1850 (1904).
+ NEHGS [Mss/3/M/24] and
[Mss/C/3033]
+ NSDAR [G.R.C./S1/v. 363]

Middleton Colony Cemetery (aka) Gregory Street Cemetery
behind houses on Gregory St. [cement
markers with no inscription]

Ingalls Burying Ground (1801)
Essex St.

Jacob Fuller Cemetery (1779)
South Main St.

Merriam Cemetery (1803)
South Main St.
+ [G.R. 3] *Vital Records of Middleton,*
Massachusetts to the year 1850 (1904).

Oakdale Cemetery (1748)
Rte. 63, Maple St.
+ [G.R. 1] *Vital Records of Middleton,*
Massachusetts to the year 1850 (1904).

Old Fuller Family Burying Ground (1738)
Mt. Vernon St.
+ [G.R. 5] *Vital Records of Middleton,*
Massachusetts to the year 1850 (1904).

Hutchinson Family Cemetery (aka) River Street Cemetery (19th c.)
in a field off River St., oppposite
Middletown Dump

Old Richardson Burial Ground (1798)
located at Haswell Park

+ [G.R. 9] *Vital Records of Middleton, Massachusetts to the year 1850* (1904).

Peabody Family Burying Ground (1811)
East St., near Webber's Pond

Amos Peabody Tomb Site
off Old Coppermine Rd. [burials removed]

Nathaniel and Ruth Peabody Grave plot
at the end of Mill St., near Peabody St.

Tomb of the Family of the Rev. Elias Smith (1775)
Mt. Vernon St.
+ [G.R. 10] *Vital Records of Middleton, Massachusetts to the year 1850* (1904).

John Stiles Family Burying Ground (1820)
off Old Kenney Rd. [no stones]

Symonds Burial Ground–Old Rowley Village Cemetery (1785)
Thomas Rd.
+ [G.R. 4] *Vital Records of Middleton, Massachusetts to the year 1850* (1904).

Graves of Gustavus Tufts' Children (1851)
on the property of the last house on Essex St.

Timothy Fuller Cemetery
+ [G.R. 2] *Vital Records of Middleton, Massachusetts to the year 1850* (1904).

Cemetery near East School House
+ [G.R. 6] *Vital Records of Middleton, Massachusetts to the year 1850* (1904).

Fuller Cemetery on the Benjamin Richardson farm
+ [G.R. 8] *Vital Records of Middleton, Massachusetts to the year 1850* (1904).

Howe Cemetery–North District
+ [G.R. 12] *Vital Records of Middleton, Massachusetts to the year 1850* (1904).

MILFORD (1780)
from Mendon.
Town Hall, 52 Main St., Milford, Mass. 01757, Tel: (508)-634-2307

North Purchase Cemetery (1801)
Pinewood Rd.
+ [G.R. 4] *Vital Records of Milford, Massachusetts to the year 1850* (1917).

Pine Grove Cemetery (1776)
Dilla and Cedar Sts.
+ [G.R. 1] *Vital Records of Milford, Massachusetts to the year 1850* (1917).
+ Susan F. Salisbury, *Southern Massachusetts Cemetery Collection,* Volume 1 (Bowie, Md., Heritage Books, 1995) [F63/S25/1995/also Loan]

Purchase Street Cemetery (1847)
Pinewood Rd.
+ [G.R. 6] *Vital Records of Milford, Massachusetts to the year 1850* (1917).
+ NEHGS [MS70/MIL/1]

Sacred Heart Cemetery (1937)
Medway Rd., Rte. 109
Tel: Sacred Heart Rectory, 5 East Main St., Milford, 01757, (508)-473-0331

**St. Mary's Roman Catholic
Cemetery (1839)**
Cedar St.
Tel: St. Mary's Rectory, 27 Pearl St.,
Milford, (508)-473-2000
+ [G.R. 1] *Vital Records of Milford,
Massachusetts to the year 1850* (1917).
+ Susan F. Salisbury, *Southern Massa-
chusetts Cemetery Collection,* Volume 1
(Bowie, Md., Heritage Books, 1995)
[F63/S25/1995/also Loan]

Vernon Grove Cemetery (1741)
Vernon St.
+ [G.R. 1] *Vital Records of Milford,
Massachusetts to the year 1850* (1917).
+ Susan F. Salisbury, *Southern Massa-
chusetts Cemetery Collection,* Volume 1
(Bowie, Md., Heritage Books, 1995)
[F63/S25/1995/also Loan]

Warfield Cemetery
South Hopedale
+ [G.R. 5] *Vital Records of Milford,
Massachusetts to the year 1850* (1917).

MILLBURY (1813)
from Sutton
Town Hall, 127 Elm St., Millbury, Mass.
01527, Tel: (508)-865-9110

**Armory Village Cemetery (aka)
County Bridge Cemetery**
+ Reuben Rawson Dodge, *Inscriptions in
the Cemeteries of Sutton, Massachusetts.*
(Worcester, Mass.: Charles Hamilton,
1898) [F74/S98/D66/1898/also Loan]
+ NEHGS [MS70/MIL/120]
+ NSDAR [G.R.C./S1/v. 439]

Central Cemetery (1843)
off Water St., next to St. Bridet's
Cemetery.

County Bridge Cemetery (1795)
Providence St.

Dwinnel Cemetery (1749)
off McCracken Rd.

St. Brigid's Cemetery (1864)
Water St., next to the Central Cemetery.
Tel: St. Brigid's Rectory, 59 Main St.,
Millbury, (508)-865-6624

West Millbury Cemetery (1775)
South Oxford Rd.

MILLIS (1885)
from Medway
Town Hall, 900 Main St., Millis, Mass.
02054, Tel: (508)-376-7046

Old Churchyard Cemetery (1714)
+ NEHGS [MS70/MIL/543]

**Prospect Hill Cemetery (aka) Bare
Hill Cemetery (1724)**
Auburn Rd.
+ [G.R. 1] *Vital Records of Medway,
Massachusetts to the year 1850* (1905).
+ NEHGS [MS70/MED/22]

MILLVILLE (1916)
from Blackstone
Town Hall, Municipal Center, 8 Central
St., Millville, Mass. 01529, Tel: (508)-
883-5849

**Chestnut Hill Meeting House
Cemetery (1769)**
Chestnut Hill Rd. and Main St., behind
Chestnut Hill Meeting House
+ Susan F. Salisbury, *Southern
Massachusetts Cemetery Collection* - Volume
1 (Bowie, Md., Heritage Books, 1995)
[F63/S25/1995/also Loan]

Millville Cemetery (18th century)
Central St.
+ [G.R. 15] *Vital Records of Mendon,
Massachusetts to the year 1850* (1920).

Old Millville Cemetery (1745)
220 Main St., next to Chestnut Hill
Meeting House Cemetery
+ [G.R. 13] *Vital Records of Mendon,*
Massachusetts to the year 1850 (1920).
+ NEHGS [MS70/MIL/762]

Wilson Lot Cemetery (aka)
Providence Street Cemetery (1799)
85 Providence St.
+ [G.R. 14] *Vital Records of Mendon,*
Massachusetts to the year 1850 (1920).
+ Susan F. Salisbury, *Southern*
Massachusetts Cemetery Collection - Volume
1 (Bowie, Md., Heritage Books, 1995)
[F63/S25/1995/also Loan]
+ NEHGS [MS70/MIL/762]

MILTON (1662)
from Dorchester.
Town Hall, 525 Canton Ave., Milton,
Mass. 02186, Tel: (617)-696-5414

Milton Cemetery (1672)
211 Centre St.
Tel: (617)-698-0200
+ William B. Trask, "Burial Inscriptions,
Milton, Mass." *NEHGR* 7:89-92.
+ NEHGS [MS70/MIL/932A]
+ *Milton Cemetery, a catalogue of the*
proprietors of lots, together with a record of
ancient inscriptions on all tablets in the cemetery
prior and including A.D. 1800. (Boston,
Mass.: David Clapp & Sons, Boston,
1883) [F74/M66/M43/1883]

MONROE (1822)
from Rowe
Town Hall, 3-C School St., Monroe,
Mass. 01350, Tel: (413)-424-5272

Monroe West Cemetery (1850)
Main Rd.

Town Ballou Cemetery (1825)
Main Rd.

MONSON (1760)
from Brimfield
Town Hall, 110 Main St., Suite 4,
Monson, Mass. 01057, Tel: (413)-267-
4115
Cemetery Department, 32 Wilbraham
Rd., Monson, Ma (413)-267-4113

Bethany Catholic Cemetery (1879)
Bethany Rd.
Tel: St. Patrick's Rectory, 22 Green St.,
Monson, (413)-267-3622

Butler District Cemetery (1791)
Butler Rd.
+ NEHGS [MS70/MON/12] and
[Corbin Collection]

Colton Hollow Cemetery (aka) Day
Cemetery (1810)
Bennett Rd.
+ NEHGS [Corbin Collection]

Brimfield Road Cemetery (1836)
Aldrich and Brimfield Rd.

Gage District Cemetery (1817)
Gage St.
+ NEHGS [MS70/MON/12] and
[Corbin Collection]

Hillcrest Cemetery (1969)
32 Wilbraham Rd.
Hillside Cemetery (aka) Center Cemetery
(1778)
Mill and Main Sts.
+ NEHGS [Corbin Collection]

Main Cemetery (1762)
Bethany Rd., located within the Bethany
Catholic Cemetery.

Main Street Cemetery (1803)
Main St.
+ NEHGS [Corbin Collection]

Stafford Road Cemetery (aka) May Hill Cemetery
May Hill Rd., off of Stafford Rd.

Monson Developmental Center Cemetery (1940)
Monson State Hospital, 200 State Ave.
Tel: (413)-283-3411

Moulton Hill Cemetery (1779)
Old Wales Rd.
+ NEHGS [Corbin Collection]

North Main Street Cemetery (1760)
North Main St.
+ NEHGS [MS70/MON/10] and [Corbin Collection]

MONTAGUE (1754)
from Sunderland
Town Hall, One Avenue A., Turners Galls, Mass. 01376, Tel: (413)-863-3211

Burnham Cemetery
South High St., Turners Falls

Aaron Clark Memorial Cemetery (1937)
Turners Falls Rd.

Chestnut Hill Cemetery
West Chestnut Hill Rd.

Dry Hill Cemetery
Dry Hill Rd., Millers Falls

Elm Grove Cemetery
Turners Falls Rd.

Fairway Avenue Cemetery
Fairway Ave., Turners Falls

Highland Cemetery (19th century)
Millers Falls Rd., Millers Falls

Locust Hill Cemetery
Turners Falls Rd.

Mineral Road Cemetery
East Mineral Rd., Millers Falls

Old South Cemetery
Stage Rd.

Our Lady Czestochowa Cemetery
Turners Falls Rd.
Tel: Our Lady Czestochowa Rectory, 84 K. St., Turners Falls, (413)-863-4748

Poor Farm Cemetery (aka) Federal Street Cemetery
Federal St.

Springdale Cemetery
Turnpike Rd., Turners Falls

St. Ann's Cemetery (1884)
Turners Falls Rd.
Tel: St. Ann's Rectory, 90 Seventh St., Turners Falls, (413)-863-2585

St. Mary's Cemetery (1872)
Turners Falls Rd.
Tel: St. Ann's Rectory, 90 Seventh St., Turners Falls, (413)-863-2585

MONTEREY (1847)
from Tyringham
Town Hall, Grange # 291, 435 Main Rd., Monterey, Mass. 01245, Tel: (413)-528-5175

Chestnut Hill Road Cemetery (1782)
Chestnut Hill Rd.
+ NEHGS [MS70/EGR/10] and [Corbin Collection]
+ NSDAR [G.R.C./S1/v. 192]

Corashire Cemetery (1813)
Blue Hill Rd.
+ NEHGS [MS70/EGR/10] and
[Corbin Collection]
+ NSDAR [G.R.C./S1/v. 192]

William Gould Family Cemetery (1925)
at the Gould Farm

Mount Hunger Cemetery (1774)
Mt. Hunger Rd.
+ NEHGS [MS70/EGR/10] and
[Corbin Collection]
+ NSDAR [G.R.C./S1/v. 192]

Old Center Cemetery (1799)
Beartown Mountain Rd.
+ NEHGS [MS70/EGR/10] and
[Corbin Collection]
+ NSDAR [G.R.C./S1/v. 192]

Woods Cemetery (1757)
Beartown Mountain Rd.
+ NEHGS [MS70/EGR/10] and
[Corbin Collection]
+ NSDAR [G.R.C./S1/v. 192]
+ Cynthia T. Hoogs, *Cemetery Inscriptions Moneterey, Massachusetts.* (Great
Barrington, 1984) [F74/M695/H6/1984]

MONTGOMERY (1780)
from Southampton and Westfield
Town Hall, 161 Main Rd., Montgomery,
Mass. 01085, Tel: (413)-862-3386

Center Cemetery (aka) Village Cemetery (1795)
Russell Rd.
+ NEHGS [F74/M7/L4] Typescript in
Mss; and [Corbin Collection]
+ NSDAR [MASS
COUNTIES/HAMPDEN/MONTGO
MERY]

Elisha Clark Cemetery (1774)
Pomeroy Rd.
+ NEHGS [F74/M7/L4] Typescript in
Mss, and [Corbin Collection]
+ NSDAR [MASS COUNTIES/
HAMPDEN/MONTGOMERY]

Pitcher Cemetery (1820)
Pitcher St.
+ NEHGS [F74/M7/L4] Typescript in
Mss; and [Corbin Collection]
+ NSDAR [MASS COUNTIES/
HAMPDEN/MONTGOMERY] and
[G.R.C./1932/S1/v. 16]

Sand Knoll Cemetery (1813)
Old House Rd.
+ NEHGS [F74/M7/L4] Typescript in
Mss
+ NSDAR [MASS COUNTIES/
HAMPDEN/MONTGOMERY]

MOUNT WASHINGTON (1779)
Town Hall, 118 East St., Mount
Washington, Mass. 01258, Tel: (413)-
528-2839

Alander Cemetery (aka) City Hill Cemetery (1798)
Cross Rd. and West St.
+ Rollin H. Cooke Collection)
[F72/B5/B473 (roll - 1)] microfilm at
N.E.H.G.S.
+ NEHGS [MS70/MOU/21] and
[MS70/EGR/10]
+ NSDAR [G.R.C./S1/v. 192]

Cross Road Cemetery (aka) Center Cemetery (1800)
Cross Rd., near Church
+ Rollin H. Cooke Collection)
[F72/B5/B473 (roll - 1)] microfilm at
N.E.H.G.S.
+ NEHGS [MS70/MOU/21]
+ NSDAR [G.R.C./S1/v. 192]

Lamson–Patterson–Whitbeck Family Cemetery (1833)
Bear Rock Rd.
+ Rollin H. Cooke Collection [F72/B5/B473 (roll #1)] microfilm at N.E.H.G.S.

Anna Lee Cemetery (aka) Benjamin Osborn Cemetery (1772)
West St.

Samson Cemetery (1884)
East St. near Mt. Everett Rd.

North of Hughes Farm Cemetery (1772)
near the West Rd.
+ Mt. Washington Cemetery Inscriptions 1760-1898, (Rollin H. Cooke Collection) [F72/B5/B473 (roll - 1)] microfilm at N.E.H.G.S.
+ NEHGS [MS70/MOU/21]

NAHANT (1853)
from Lynn.
Town Hall, 334 Nahant Rd., Nahant, Mass. 01908, Tel: (781)-581-0018

Greenlawn Cemetery (1858)
Nahant Rd., across from Nahant Police Station.
+ [G.R. 5] *Vital Records of Lynn, Massachusetts to the year 1850* (1905).
+ NEHGS [MS70/NAH/1]

Josephand Caleb Johnson Family Cemetery Site (19th century)
Pleasant St.
+ NEHGS [MS70/NAH/1]

NANTUCKET (1687)
Town Hall, 16 Broad St., Nantucket, Mass. 02554, Tel: (508)-238-7217

African American Cemetery (1821)
off Prospect St., across from the Old Mill
+ [G.R. 6] *Vital Records of Nantucket, Massachusetts to the year 1850* (1925).

First Settlers Cemetery (1706)
off Cliff Rd., near Maxcey's Pond.

Old Polpis Burying Ground (17th century)
Polpis Rd.

Friends Quaker Burying Ground (1708)
Quaker and Madaket Rds.
+ [G.R. 5] *Vital Records of Nantucket, Massachusetts to the year 1850* (1925).

Miacomet Indian Burying Ground Site
Sufside Rd.

Mill Hills Cemetery
Vesper Ln.

New North Cemetery (1820's)
across from Old North Cemetery, New Ln.
+ [G.R. 2] *Vital Records of Nantucket, Massachusetts to the year 1850* (1925).

Newtown Cemetery (aka) South Cemetery (1775)
Sparks Ave.
+ [G.R. 4] *Vital Records of Nantucket, Massachusetts to the year 1850* (1925).

Old North Cemetery (1746)
west side of New Ln.
+ [G.R. 1] *Vital Records of Nantucket, Massachusetts to the year 1850* (1925).

Prospect Hill Cemetery (1811)
Milk and Vestal Sts.
+ [G.R. 3] *Vital Records of Nantucket, Massachusetts to the year 1850* (1925).

Quaise Asylum Cemetery (aka) Poor Farm Burying Ground (19th century)
near Altar Rock Rd.

St. Mary's Cemetery (19th century)
Joy and Vestal Sts.
Tel: St. Mary's Rectory, 6 Orange St.,
Nantucket, (508)-228-4852

Unitarian Cemetery (20th Century)
Somerset Rd., attached to the Prospect
Hill Cemetery

NATICK (1650)

Town Hall, 13 Central St., Natick, Mass.
01760, Tel: (508)-647-6432

Boden Lane Cemetery (1793)
after 162 Boden Ln.
+ [G.R. 2] *Vital Records of Natick,
Massachusetts to the year 1850* (1910).
+ Brown, Mrs. Lyman R., *Grave Records
from Three Old Cemeteries, Natick, Mass.
Cemeteries.* (Natick, Mass.: Natick Chapter
D.A.R., 1937) [F74/N2/B88/1937a]
+ NEHGS [MS70/NAT/2]

Dell Park Cemetery
163 Pond St., off of Rte. 27 South
Tel: (508)-655-1271
+ [G.R. 1] *Vital Records of Natick,
Massachusetts to the year 1850* (1910).
+ Brown, Mrs. Lyman R., *Natick
Cemeteries: Glenwood, New Dell Park, Old
Dell Park, St. Patrick's.* (Natick, Mass.:
Natick Chapter D.A.R., 1937)
[F74/N2/B88/1937]
+ NEHGS [MS70/NAT/3]

Eliot Square Cemetery (1731)
end of Union St., off of Rte. 116 East,
South Natick
+ [G.R. 3] *Vital Records of Natick,
Massachusetts to the year 1850* (1910).

+ Brown, Mrs. Lyman R., *Grave Records
from Three Old Cemeteries, Natick, Mass.
Cemeteries.* (Natick, Mass.: Natick Chapter
D.A.R., 1937) [F74/N2/B88/1937a]
+ NEHGS [MS70/NAT/1] and
[MS70/NAT/1]
+ NSDAR [G.R.C./S1/v. 59]

Framingham–Natick Jewish Cemetery
Windsor Ave., off of Rte. 27 South and
West St.
Tel: Temple Israel, 145 Hartford St.,
Natick, (508)-650-3521

Glenwood Cemetery (1840)
Glenwood St., South Natick
Tel: (508)-651-1797
+ [G.R. 4] *Vital Records of Natick,
Massachusetts to the year 1850* (1910).
+ Brown, Mrs. Lyman R., *Natick
Cemeteries: Glenwood, New Dell Park, Old
Dell Park, St. Patrick's.* (Natick, Mass.:
Natick Chapter D.A.R., 1937)
[F74/N2/B88/1937]
+ NEHGS [MS70/NAT/2]

Indian Burial Ground (17th century)
Eliot St., Rte. 16 East
+ NEHGS [MS70/NAT/1]

Indian Cemetery (1750)
Pond St., next to Dell Park Cemetery
+ NSDAR [G.R.C./S1/v. 59]

North Natick Cemetery (1744)
North Main St., Rte. 27
+ [G.R. 5] *Vital Records of Natick,
Massachusetts to the year 1850* (1910).
+ George Kuhn Clarke, *Epitaphs from
Graveyards in Wellesley (formerly West
Needham), North Natick, and Saint Mary's
Churchyard in Newton Lower Falls,
Massachusetts with Genealogical and
Biographical notes.* (Boston, Mass.:
Privately printed, 1900)
[F74/W38/C55/1900]

+ Brown, Mrs. Lyman R., *Grave Records from Three Old Cemeteries, Natick, Mass. Cemeteries.* (Natick, Mass.: Natick Chapter D.A.R., 1937) [F74/N2/B88/1937a]
+ NEHGS [MS70/NAT/2]
+ NSDAR [G.R.C./S1/v. 59]

St. Patrick's Cemetery
164 Pond St., across the street from the Dell Pond Cemetery
Tel: St. Patricks Rectory, 44 E. Central St., Natick (508)-653-1093
+ [G.R. 6] *Vital Records of Natick, Massachusetts to the year 1850* (1910).
+ Brown, Mrs. Lyman R., *Natick Cemeteries: Glenwood, New Dell Park, Old Dell Park, St. Patrick's.* (Natick, Mass.: Natick Chapter D.A.R., 1937) [F74/N2/B88/1937]

NEEDHAM (1711)
from Dedham
Town Hall, 1471 Highland Ave., Needham, Mass. 02492, Tel: (781)-455-4571

Needham Cemetery (1711)
128 Nehoiden St.
Tel: (781)-444-0529
+ [G.S.] Robert B. Hanson, *Vital Records of Needham, Mass. 1711-1845* (1997)
+ Charles Curtis Greenwood, *Epitaphs from the Old Burying Ground, Needham, Massachusetts, with notes.* (Dedham, Mass.: H.H. McQuillen, 1898) [MS/NEE/36]
+ NEHGS [MS70/NEE/1], [SL/NEE/1] and [SL/NEE/1a]
+ NSDAR [G.R.C./S1/v.177] Soldier burials only.

St. Mary's Cemetery (1878)
1 Wellesley Street, near the Wellesley town line.
Tel:(781)-235-1841

NEW ASHFORD (1781)
Town Hall, 188 Mallery Rd., New Ashford, Mass., Tel: (413)-458-5461

New Ashford Cemetery (1776)
Mallery and Cemetery Rds.
+ Cooke Collection
+ NEHGS [MS70/NEW/1]

NEW BEDFORD (1787)
from Dartmouth
City Hall, 133 William St., New Bedford, Mass. 02740, Tel: (508)-979-1450

Ahavath Achim Jewish Cemetery
1345 Plainville Rd.

Casey Farm Gravesite
Hathaway Rd.
"*a single grave on the farm of Mrs. Emma G. Casey*"
+ [G.R. 15] *Vital Records of New Bedford, Massachusetts to the year 1850* (1932).

Congregational Church Cemetery
Lund's Corner
+ [G.R. 5] *Vital Records of New Bedford, Massachusetts to the year 1850* (1932).
+ NSDAR [G.R.C./S1/v.128]

Friends Cemetery (1853)
149 Dartmouth St.
+ [G.R. 2] *Vital Records of New Bedford, Massachusetts to the year 1850* (1932).
+ NEHGS [Mss/SL/NEW/252] and [F74/N5/L3] Typescript in Mss.
+ NSDAR [G.R.C./S1/v. 255]

Griffin Street Cemetery (1804)
Griffin St.
+ NEHGS [MS70/NEW/14] and[Mss/NEW/252]
+ NSDAR [G.R.C./S1/v.94], and [MASS/MILITARY/1775-1783/G.R.C./S1/v. 196] containing Revolutionary War Soldiers only

Hebrew Cemetery
1345 Plainville Rd.

Nye Family Burying Ground
Nye's Lane
+ [G.R. 7] *Vital Records of New Bedford,
Massachusetts to the year 1850* (1932).

Oak Grove Cemetery (1843)
185 Parker St.
+ [G.R. 3] *Vital Records of New Bedford,
Massachusetts to the year 1850* (1932).
+ NEHGS [Mss/NEW/252],
and[MASS/MILITARY/1775-
1783/G.R.C./S1/v. 196] containing
Revolutionay War Soldiers only

Old Burying Ground (1802)
South Water and Griffin Sts.
+ [G.R. 4] *Vital Records of New Bedford,
Massachusetts to the year 1850* (1932).

Peckham West Cemetery
395 Mt. Pleasant St.
+ [G.R. 6] *Vital Records of New Bedford,
Massachusetts to the year 1850* (1932).
+ NSDAR [MASS/MILITARY/1775-
1783/G.R.C./S1/v. 196] containing
Revolutionary War Soldiers only

**Pine Grove Cemetery (aka) Tarklin
Hill Burying Ground**
1055 Ashley Blvd.
+ [G.R. 9] *Vital Records of New Bedford,
Massachusetts to the year 1850* (1932).
+ NSDAR [G.R.C./S1/v. 175], and
[MASS/MILITARY/1775-1783/
G.R.C./S1/v. 196] containing
Revolutionary War Soldiers only

Polish National Cemetery
Phillips Rd.
Tel: Polish National Rectory, 839 County
St., New Bedford, (508)-992-1790

Rockdale Avenue Cemetery
Rockdale Ave.

+ [G.R. 16] *Vital Records of New Bedford,
Massachusetts to the year 1850* (1932).

Rural Cemetery (19th century)
149 Dartmouth St.
+ [G.R. 1] *Vital Records of New Bedford,
Massachusetts to the year 1850* (1932).
+ NEHGS [Mss/NEW/252]
+ NSDAR [MASS/MILITARY/1775-
1783/G.R.C./S1/v. 196]containing
Revolutionary War Soldiers only

Sacred Heart Cemetery (1854)
559 Mount Pleasant St.

St. John's Cemetery (1886)
664 Allen St.
Tel: (508)-992-1071
+ Gil and Pat Amaral, *St. John's Cemetery
Gravestone Inscriptions.*
[F74/N5/A53/199-]

St. Mary's Cemetery
559 Mount Pleasant St.
Tel: (508)-993-5077

Tobey Family Burying Ground
Sassaquin
+ [G.R. 8] *Vital Records of New Bedford,
Massachusetts to the year 1850* (1932).

Private Burying Ground
on the farm formerly owned by John W.
Gifford, Shawmut Avenue
+ [G.R. 10] *Vital Records of New Bedford,
Massachusetts to the year 1850* (1932).

NEW BRAINTREE (1751)
from Brookfield and Hardwick
Town Hall, 20 Memorial Dr., New
Braintree, Mass 01531, Tel: (413)-867-
4952

Church Cemetery
Hardwick Rd.

Evergreen Cemetery (1800)
Cemetery Rd. and Barre Rd.

North Cemetery
Hardwick Rd.

South East Cemetery
Webb Rd.

South West Cemetery
West Rd.

NEW MARLBOROUGH (1759)

Town Hall, Mill River South Field Rd., Mill River, Mass. 01244, Tel: (413)-229-8116

Arnold Cemetery (1848)
Great Barrington Mill River Rd.

Basset Cemetery (1850)
Mill River Hartsville Rd.

Carroll-Sisson-Blodgett Cemetery (1842)
Southfield Mill River Rd.
+ NEHGS [MS/82/25], and [Corbin Collection]
+ NSDAR [G.R.C./S1/v. 138]

Clayton Cemetery (1801)
Clayton Mill River Rd.
+ NEHGS [MS/82/25]
+ NSDAR [G.R.C./S1/v. 138]

Hadsell Cemetery (1846)
Konkapot Rd. and Canaan Southfield Rd.
+ NEHGS [MS/82/25]
+ NSDAR [G.R.C./S1/v. 138]

Hart Cemetery (1838)
Route 57
+ NEHGS [MS/82/25], and [Corbin Collection]
+ NSDAR [G.R.C./S1/v. 138]

Hartsville Cemetery (1822)
near Lake Buell, Hartsville
+ NEHGS [MS/82/25]
+ NSDAR [G.R.C./S1/v. 138]

Huxley Cemetery (1775)
Norfolk Rd.
+ NEHGS [MS/82/25]
+ NSDAR [G.R.C./S1/v. 138]

William Henry Lee Memorial (1859)
Norfolk Rd.
+ NSDAR [G.R.C./S1/v. 138]

Old Center Cemetery (1755)
Rte. 57 and New Marlborough - Southfield Rd.
+ NSDAR [G.R.C./S1/v. 138]

Old Mill River Cemetery (1758)
Hartsville Rd.
+ NEHGS [MS/82/25]
+ NSDAR [G.R.C./S1/v. 138]

Old Southfield Cemetery (1794)
Norfolk Rd.
+ NSDAR [G.R.C./S1/v. 138]

NEW SALEM (1753)

Town Hall, 15 South Main St., New Salem, Mass. 01355, Tel: (978)-544-2731

Center Cemetery (1745)
South Main St.
Tel: (978)-544-2303
+ [G.R. 1] *Vital Records of New Salem, Massachusetts to the year 1850* (1927).

Golden Lake Cemetery Site
All burials were removed to Quabbin Park Cemetery, Ware, Massachusetts 1938
+ [G.R. 2] *Vital Records of New Salem, Massachusetts to the year 1850* (1927).
+ NEHGS [MS/70/WAR/15]

North New Salem Cemetery (1820)
Fay Rd.

NEWBURY (1635)
Town Hall, 25 High Rd., Newbury,
Mass. 01951, Tel: (978)-462-2332

Evergreen Cemetery (1786)
Cottage Rd.

First Parish Cemetery (1647)
High Rd., across from the First Parish
Church
+ Elias Nason, "The Burial-Place at
"Old Town", Newbury, Ms." *NEHGR*
1:371-376.

First Settlers Burying Ground (1635)
High Rd., one half mile north after
Parker River Bridge
+ H.G.S., "Newbury Burying Ground"
NEHGR 12:73

Newbury Neck Cemetery (1742)
Newbury Neck Rd.

**South Byfield Parish Burying
Ground (1702)**
Elm St., near Byfield Parish Church at
the Georgetown town line

Thomas G. Parker Cemetery
High Rd.

**Turner's Eden Cemetery (aka)
Rogers Family Cemetery (ca. 1860)**
off Fruit St., Byfield

NEWBURYPORT (1764)
from Newbury.
City Hall, 60 Pleasant St., Newburyport,
Mass. 01950, Tel: (978)-465-4407
Cemetery Department, Perry Way,
Newburyport, Ma 01950 (978)-465-4464

Highland Cemetery (1800)
Highland St.
Tel: (508)-465-4464
+ Noreen C. Pramberg, *Etched in Stone,
Newburyport, Mass., Cemeteries, Volume Two.*
(Newburyport, Mass.: Noreen C.
Pramberg, 1991)
[F74/N55/P73/1991/v. 2]

Oak Hill Cemetery (1842)
State and Parker Sts.
+ *Oak Hill Cemetery in Newburyport, from its
establishment and consecration to 1878.*
(Newburyport, Mass.: William H. Huse
& Co., 1878) [F74/N55/019/1878]
+ Noreen C. Pramberg, *Etched in Stone,
Newburyport, Mass., Cemeteries, Volume One.*
(Newburyport, Mass.: Noreen C.
Pramberg, 1991) [F74/N55/P73/1991]

Old Burying Hill (1729)
Greenleaf, Pond and Auburn Sts.,
Bartlett Sts.
+ Noreen C. Pramberg, *Etched in Stone,
Newburyport, Mass., Cemeteries, Volume One.*
(Newburyport, Mass.: Noreen C.
Pramberg, 1991) [F74/N55/P73/1991]

**Queen Anne's Chapel Burying
Ground (aka) Belleville Cemetery
(1720)**
Storey Ave.
+ Noreen C. Pramberg, *Etched in Stone,
Newburyport, Mass., Cemeteries, Volume One.*
(Newburyport, Mass.: Noreen C.
Pramberg, 1991) [F74/N55/P73/1991]

St. Mary's Cemetery (1875)
Storey Ave.
+ Noreen C. Pramberg, *Etched in Stone,
Newburyport, Mass., Cemeteries, Volume Two.*
(Newburyport, Mass.: Noreen C.
Pramberg, 1991)
[F74/N55/P73/1991/v. 2] Veterans
only.

St. Paul's Episopal Cemetery (1742)
High and Market Sts.

+ Noreen C. Pramberg, *Etched in Stone, Newburyport, Mass., Cemeteries, Volume One.* (Newburyport, Mass.: Noreen C. Pramberg, 1991) [F74/N55/P73/1991]

Sawyer's Hill Burial Ground (1630)
Curzon Mill Rd.
+ Noreen C. Pramberg, *Etched in Stone, Newburyport, Mass., Cemeteries, Volume One.* (Newburyport, Mass.: Noreen C. Pramberg, 1991) [F74/N55/P73/1991]

NEWTON (1691)

City Hall, 1000 Commonwealth Ave., Newton, Mass. 02459, Tel: (617)-552-7030

Centre Street Cemetery (aka) East Parish Burial Ground (1655)
Centre and Cotton Sts.
+ [G.R. 1] *Vital Records of Newton, Massachusetts to the year 1850* (1905).
+ NEHGS [Mss/SL/NEW/2408] and [F74/N56/A4] Typescript in Mss
+ NSDAR [MASS/COUNTIES/MIDDLESEX/NEWTON/S1/V 90]
+ NSDAR [G.R.C./S1/v. 90]

Newton Cemetery and Crematory (1855)
791 Walnut St.
Tel:(617)-332-0047
+ NEHGS [F74/N56/A4] Typescript in Mss
+ NSDAR [G.R.C./S1/v. 90]

River Street Cemetery (aka) West Parish Burial Ground (1777)
River St., West Newton
+ [G.R. 2] *Vital Records of Newton, Massachusetts to the year 1850* (1905).
+ NEHGS [F74/N56/A4] Typescript in Mss
+ NSDAR [G.R.C./S1/v. 90]

St. Mary's Cemetery (aka) Lower Falls Cemetery (1813)
258 Concord St., Newton Lower Falls
Tel: St. Mary's Episcopal Rectory, 258 Concord St., Newton, Mass., (617)-527-4769
+ [G.R. 4] *Vital Records of Newton, Massachusetts to the year 1850* (1905).
+ Beverly E. Hurney, *St. Mary's Cemetery, Newton, Massachusetts: Epitaphs.* (Boston, Mass.: NEHGS, 2000)
+ George Kuhn Clarke, *Epitaphs from Graveyards in Wellesley (formerly West Needham), North Natick, and Saint Mary's Churchyard in Newton Lower Falls, Massachusetts with Genealogical and Biographical notes.* (Boston, Mass.: Privately printed, 1900) [F74/W38/C55/1900]+ NEHGS [F74/N56/A4] Typescript in Mss
+ NEHGS [Mss/SL/WEL/10]
+ NSDAR [G.R.C./S1/v. 90]

Winchester Street (aka) South Burial Ground (1803)
Winchester St., Newton Highlands
+ [G.R. 3] *Vital Records of Newton, Massachusetts to the year 1850* (1905).
+ NEHGS [F74/N56/A4] Typescript in Mss

NORFOLK (1870)
from Franklin and Medway.
Town Hall, One Liberty Ln., Norfolk, Mass. 02056, Tel: (508)-528-1400
Cemetery Department, 33 Medwat Branch, Norfolk, Ma 02056 Tel: (508)-528-4990

Norfolk Cemetery (aka) Old North Wrentham Cemetery (1777)
Main St.
Tel: (508)-528-4990
+ [G.R. 1] *Vital Records of Wrentham, Massachusetts to the year 1850* (1910).

Pondville Cemetery (18th century)
Everett St.
+ [G.R. 7] *Vital Records of Wrentham,*
Massachusetts to the year 1850 (1910).

NORTH ADAMS (1878)
from Adams
City Hall, 10 Main St.., North Adams,
Ma 01247, Tel: (413)-662-3015

Advent Cemetery (1835)
Old Military Rd. off Veazie St.

Beth Israel Cemetery (19th Century)
Walker St.

Blackinton Cemetery (1813)
Massachusetts Ave.
+ Massachusetts Society of Genealogists
- Northern Berkshire Chapter, *Blackinton*
Cemetery interment record, North Adams
(Pittsfield, Mass.: Mass. Society of
Genealogists, 1984)
[F74/N8/B5/1984/also Loan]

**Chilson–Gates–Hewett Cemetery
(1811)**
off Myers Ave.
+ NEHGS [Mss/3/N/34]
+ NSDAR [G.R.C./S1/v. 346]

East Hoosac Cemetery
South State St.

**Old Congregational Burial Ground
(1830)**
South State St.

Hillside Cemetery (1830)
168 W. Main St.
Tel: (413)-662-3048

**North Church Street Cemetery
(1802)**
North Church St.
+ NEHGS [MS70/NOR/3]

**Southview Cemetery (aka) Old
Phillips Cemetery (1813)**
975 Church St.
+ NEHGS [MS70/NOR/3]

St. Joseph's Cemetery (1900)
Rte. 8A, Ashland St. Across from
Southview Cemetery.
Tel: St. Francis Rectory, Union St.,

Wilbur Family Burial Ground (1813)
West Mountain Rd.

NORTH ANDOVER
(1855)
from Andover.
Town Hall, 120 Main St., North
Andover, Mass. 01845, Tel: (978)-688-
9502

Averill Farm Cemetery (1818)
Forest St.
+ NEHGS [Mss/SL/AND/6]

Berry Farm Cemetery (1764)
Berry St.
+ NEHGS [Mss/SL/AND/6]

Seth Farnham Gravesite (1845)
off the Salem Turnpike
+ NEHGS [Mss/SL/AND/6]

First Settlers Burying Ground (1662)
Academy Rd. and Court St.
+ [G.R. 1]*Vital Records of Andover,*
Massachusetts to the year 1850 (1912).
+ NEHGS [MS70/NOR/50]

Holy Sepulchre Cemetery (1889)
Waverly Rd.
+ NEHGS [MS70/NOR/53]
+ NSDAR [G.R.C./S1/v. 167]

Moses Kimball Farm (1848)
Forest St.
+ NEHGS [Mss/SL/AND/6]

Ridgewood Cemetery (1850)
177 Salem St.
+ [G.R. 7]*Vital Records of Andover, Massachusetts to the year 1850* (1912).
+ NEHGS [MS70/NOR/52], and [MS70/NOR/54]

Second Burial Ground (1817)
Academy Rd.
+ [G.R. 6]*Vital Records of Andover, Massachusetts to the year 1850* (1912).
+ NEHGS [MS70/NOR/53]
+ NSDAR [G.R.C./S1/v. 167]

NORTH ATTLEBOROUGH (1887)
from Attleborough
Town Hall, 32 South Washington St., North Attleborough, Mass., Tel: (508)-699-0108

Carpenter Family Cemetery (1810)
near 335 Mendon Rd.
+ Susan F. Salisbury, *Southern Massachusetts Cemetery Collection* - Volume 2 (Bowie, Md., Heritage Books, 1996) [F63/S25/1995/also Loan]

Falls Cemetery, North Attleborough (1731)
+ [G.R. 4] *Vital Records of Attleborough, Massachusetts to the year 1850* (1934).
+ NEHGS [MS70/NOR/60]

Mann Burial Grounds (1778)
off Draper Ave.
+ [G.R. 6] *Vital Records of Attleborough, Massachusetts to the year 1850* (1934).
+ NEHGS [MS70/NOR/60]
+ NSDAR [G.R.C./S1/v. 151]

Mount Hope Cemetery (1852)
565 Mount Hope St.
Tel: (508)-699-2141
+ [G.R. 5] *Vital Records of Attleborough, Massachusetts to the year 1850* (1934).

+ NEHGS [MS70/NOR/61]
+ NSDAR [G.R.C./S1/v. 151]

Old North Cemetery (aka) Woodcock Cemetery (1676)
Park and Washington Sts., junction Routes 1 and 1A
+ [G.R. 11] *Vital Records of Attleborough, Massachusetts to the year 1850* (1934).
+ NEHGS [F74/A89/D2] Typescript in Mss
+ NSDAR [G.R.C./S1/v. 151]

Paine Cemetery (1826)
Paine Rd., off Rte. 1
+ [G.R. 10] *Vital Records of Attleborough, Massachusetts to the year 1850* (1934).
+ NEHGS [MS70/NOR/60], and [F74/A89/D2] Typescript in Mss
+ NSDAR [G.R.C./S1/v. 151]

Robinson Cemetery (1773)
Towne St., Attleboro Falls, behind the Central Congregational Church.
+ Susan F. Salisbury, *Southern Massachusetts Cemetery Collection* - Volume 2 (Bowie, Md., Heritage Books, 1996) [F63/S25/1995/also Loan]
+ NEHGS [F74/A89/C3/1928] and [F74/A89/D2] Typescripts in Mss
+ NSDAR [G.R.C./S1/v. 151]

St. Mary's Roman Catholic Cemetery (1871)
Towne St., off Mt. Hope St.
Tel: (508)-695-1173
+ Susan F. Salisbury, *Southern Massachusetts Cemetery Collection* - Volume 2 (Bowie, Md., Heritage Books, 1996) [F63/S25/1995/also Loan]

NORTH BROOKFIELD (1812)
from Brookfield
Town Hall, 185 North Main St., North Brookfield, Mass., Tel: (508)-867-0203

Cutter Cemetery (18th century)
off Hanson Rd.

Indian Cemetery
Old West Brookfield Rd., near Bates Rd. and Rte. 67

Maple Street Cemetery (19th century)
Elm St.

North Brookfield Cemetery (1770)
Hill Rd. and Middle St.
+ NEHGS [Mss/SL/NOR/17]

St. Joseph's Cemetery
102 Bell St.
Tel: St. John's Rectory, 28 Mt. Pleasant St., North Brookfield, Mass. (508)-867-6811

Tyler Burying Ground (1777)
+ NEHGS [Mss/SL/NOR/17]

Walnut Grove Cemetery
+ NEHGS [Mss/SL/NOR/17]

NORTH READING (1853)
from Reading
Town Hall, 235 North St., North Reading, Mass. 01864, Tel: (508)-664-6048
Cemetery Department, 235 North St., North Reading, Mass. 01864, Tel: (508)-664-6027

Congregation Beth Israel of Malden Cemetery
241 Main St.

Harmonyvale Cemetery
98 Chestnut St.
+ [G.R. 4] *Vital Records of Reading, Massachusetts to the year 1850* (1912).

Lynn City Lodge Cemetery
Main St.

Park Street Cemetery
211 Park St.
+ [G.R. 2] *Vital Records of Reading, Massachusetts to the year 1850* (1912).
+ NEHGS [MS70/NOR/370]

Riverside Cemetery
171 Elm St.
+ [G.R. 3] *Vital Records of Reading, Massachusetts to the year 1850* (1912).

NORTHBOROUGH (1766)
from Westborough.
Town Hall, 63 Main St., Northborough, Mass. 01532, Tel: (508)-393-6996

First Buryng Ground (aka) Brigham Street Cemetery
All burials moved to the Howard Street Cemetery.
Brigham St.
+ NEHGS [Mss/3/N/29]

Mary Goodenow's Gravesite (1707)
Rte. 20, East Main St.

Howard Street Cemetery (1727)
50 Howard St.
+ NEHGS [Mss/CB/4], and [Mss/3/N/29]

NORTHBRIDGE (1772)
from Uxbridge
Town Hall, 7 Main St., Northbridge, Mass. 01588, Tel: (508)-234-2001

Benson Cemetery
Benson Rd.
+ [G.R. 4] *Vital Records of Northbridge, Massachusetts to the year 1850* (1916).

Cooper Road Cemetery (1795)
Cooper Rd., Whitinsville
+ [G.R. 9] *Vital Records of Northbridge,
Massachusetts to the year 1850* (1916).
+ Susan F. Salisbury, *Southern
Massachusetts Cemetery Collection* - Volume
1 (Bowie, Md., Heritage Books, 1995)
[F63/S25/1995/also Loan]

Hill Street Cemetery (18th century)
Batchelder Rd and Hill St., Whitinsville

Lackey Cemetery
Carr St.
+ [G.R. 10] *Vital Records of Northbridge,
Massachusetts to the year 1850* (1916).
+ NSDAR [G.R.C./S1/v. 234]

**Old Cemetery (aka) Northbridge
Center Cemetery**
Hills St. and Batchelder Rd.
+ [G.R. 8] *Vital Records of Northbridge,
Massachusetts to the year 1850* (1916).
+ NEHGS [Mss/C/3037]
+ NSDAR [G.R.C./S1/v. 234]

Pine Grove Cemetery (1785)
241 Linwood Ave., Whitinsville
Tel: (508)-234-2793
+ [G.R. 1] *Vital Records of Northbridge,
Massachusetts to the year 1850* (1916).
+ Susan F. Salisbury, *Southern
Massachusetts Cemetery Collection* - Volume
1 (Bowie, Md., Heritage Books, 1995)
[F63/S25/1995/also Loan]
+ NSDAR [G.R.C./S1/v. 234]

**Plummer Street–Quaker Cemetery
(1830)**
Plummer and Church St., Whitinsville
+ [G.R. 6] *Vital Records of Northbridge,
Massachusetts to the year 1850* (1916).
+ Susan F. Salisbury, *Southern
Massachusetts Cemetery Collection* - Volume
1 (Bowie, Md., Heritage Books, 1995)
[F63/S25/1995/also Loan]

Riverdale Cemetery (1802)
Providence Rd., Whitinsville
+ [G.R. 2] *Vital Records of Northbridge,
Massachusetts to the year 1850* (1916).
+ Susan F. Salisbury, *Southern
Massachusetts Cemetery Collection* - Volume
1 (Bowie, Md., Heritage Books, 1995)
[F63/S25/1995/also Loan]

St. Patrick's Cemetery
Providence Rd.
Tel: St. Patrick's Rectory, 7 Eash St.,
Whitinsville, Mass. (508)-234-5656
+ [G.R. 3] *Vital Records of Northbridge,
Massachusetts to the year 1850* (1916).

Fowler Cemetery
+ [G.R. 7] *Vital Records of Northbridge,
Massachusetts to the year 1850* (1916).

NORTHFIELD (1714)
Town Hall, 69 Main St., Northfield,
Mass. 01360, Tel: (413)-498-2901

Center Cemetery (1769)
Parker Ave.
+ NEHGS [Corbin Collection]

Coller Cemetery
Coller Cemetery Rd

**Dwight and Emma Moody
Gravesite (1897)**
Main St.
Mount Herman Cemetery
Gill Rd., West Northfield

Northfield Farm Cemetery
Rte. 63

Pentecost Road Cemetery
Pentecost Rd.

St. Mary's Cemetery
St. Mary Street

Tel: St. Patrick's Rectory, Main St., Northfield, Mass. (413)-498-2728

South Mountain Cemetery (1815)
South Mountain Rd.

West Northfield Cemetery
River Rd.
+ NEHGS [Corbin Collection]

NORTHAMPTON (1656)
City Hall, 210 Main St., Northampton, Mass. 01060, Tel: (413)-587-1222

Bridge Street Cemetery (1683)
156 Bridge St.
+ Thomas Bridgman, *Inscriptions on the Grave stones in the grave yard of Northampton, and of other towns in the valled of Connecticut.* (Northampton, Mass.: Hopkins, Bridgman & Co., 1850)
[RB/F74/N86/B74/1850]
+ NEHGS [MS70/NOR/43] and [Corbin Collection]

Congregation B'nai Israel Cemetery (aka) Joseph B'nai Lodge #395 Cemetery (1895)
473 North King St.
Tel: Congregation B'nai Israel, 253 Prospect St., Northampton, Mass. (413)-584-3593

Park Street Cemetery (1825)
44 Park St., Florence
+ NEHGS [MS70/FLO/1], and [Corbin Collection]
+ NSDAR [G.R.C./S1/v.177]

St. Mary's Roman Catholic Cemetery (1850)
235 North Elm and Hatfield Sts.
Tel: (413)-584-3257

St. Mary's Roman Catholic Cemetery (1891)
Haydenville Rd

St. Peter and Paul Russian Orthodox Cemetery (1931)
33 Mountain St.

Spring Grove Cemetery (1883)
300 North Maple St.
+ NEHGS [Corbin Collection]

West Farms Cemetery (1788)
200 West Farms Rd.
+ NEHGS [MS70/NOR/40] and [Corbin Collection]
+ NSDAR [G.R.C./S1/v.177]

NORTON (1710)
from Taunton
Town Hall, 70 East Main St., Norton, Mass. 02766, Tel: (508)-285-0232

Babbit–Cobb Cemetery (1739)
opposite 93 Newcomb St.
+ [G.R. 5] *Vital Records of Norton, Massachusetts to the year 1850* (1906).

Briggs Cemetery Site
Oak St., all burials moved.
+ [G.R. 18] *Vital Records of Norton, Massachusetts to the year 1850* (1906).

George Codding Burial Place (1862)
North Worcester St., near Richardson Ave.
+ [G.R. 19] *Vital Records of Norton, Massachusetts to the year 1850* (1906).

Crane Cemetery (1800)
North Worcester St., near Richardson Ave.
+ [G.R. 10] *Vital Records of Norton, Massachusetts to the year 1850* (1906).

Crane–Newcomb Burial Place (1815)
53 Hill St.
+ [G.R. 13] *Vital Records of Norton, Massachusetts to the year 1850* (1906).

Dyer Family Burial Place (1833)
opposite 475 S. Worcester St.
+ [G.R. 20] *Vital Records of Norton, Massachusetts to the year 1850* (1906).

John Eddy Burial Place (1768)
between 55-61 Hill St.
+ [G.R. 14 *Vital Records of Norton, Massachusetts to the year 1850* (1906).

Eddy–Lincoln Cemetery (1839)
172 South Washington St.
+ [G.R. 12] *Vital Records of Norton, Massachusetts to the year 1850* (1906).

First Burial Place Cemetery (aka) Settlers Cemetery (1724)
Bay Rd., behind the First Settlers Monument.
+ [G.R. 1] *Vital Records of Norton, Massachusetts to the year 1850* (1906).

Hall Cemetery (1794)
Reservoir St. and Birch Ln.
+ [G.R. 15 *Vital Records of Norton, Massachusetts to the year 1850* (1906).

Hodges Family Cemetery Site (19th century)
East Hodge St., area developed no stones.

Keith–Leonard Gravestones (1716)
36 Elm St.

Seneca Lincoln Burying Ground (1762)
next to 281 Taunton Ave. on Rte. 140
+ [G.R. 9] *Vital Records of Norton, Massachusetts to the year 1850* (1906).

Lincoln Burial Place at the Gaffney Farm Site
South Worcester St., site on the location of a golf course.
+ [G.R. 21] *Vital Records of Norton, Massachusetts to the year 1850* (1906).

Josiah Newcomb Cemetery (1796)
Holmes St., between Rte. 123 East Main and Burt Sts. Near the Easton town line.
+ [G.R. 17] *Vital Records of Norton, Massachusetts to the year 1850* (1906).

Norton Center Cemetery (aka) Church Cemetery, Pine Street Cemetery (1710)
Pine St.
+ [G.R. 3] *Vital Records of Norton, Massachusetts to the year 1850* (1906).
+ NEHGS [Mss/SG/LIN/5/23]

Norton Common Cemetery (1702)
Rte. 123, opposite 199 West Main St.
+ [G.R. 2] *Vital Records of Norton, Massachusetts to the year 1850* (1906).
+ NEHGS [Mss/SG/HOD/6/60]

Timothy Plain Cemetery (1742)
opposite 173 Plain St.
+ [G.R. 4] *Vital Records of Norton, Massachusetts to the year 1850* (1906).
+ NEHGS [MS/NOR/101], [MS70/NOR/465], [Mss/SG/LIN/5/23], and [Mss/SG/HOD/6/60]

Poor Farm Cemetery Site
land located behind the Hall Cemetery, land was developed.

Quaker Cemetery on Isaac Woodward Farm
272 South Washington St., on the top of a hill.

Titus Family Cemetery Site
Dean and South Worcester Sts.

Abraham White Cemetery (1801)
at the Norton Commerce Center, South Washington St.
+ [G.R. 11] *Vital Records of Norton, Massachusetts to the year 1850* (1906).

White Cemetery (aka) East Norton Cemetery, and Rte. 123 Cemetery (1801)
Rte. 123, opposite 285 East Main St.
+ [G.R. 16 *Vital Records of Norton, Massachusetts to the year 1850* (1906).

Winnicunett New Cemetery (1774)
across from Winnicunett Second Cemetery, Toad Island Rd. near Bay Rd.
+ [G.R. 7] *Vital Records of Norton, Massachusetts to the year 1850* (1906).
+ Mrs. Wendell B. Presbrey, *Inscriptions from Eight Cemeteries in Bristol, County, Massachusetts.* (---, Massachusetts D.A.R., 1987) [F72/B8/I57/1987]
+ NEHGS [MS70/NOR/470], [Mss/SG/LIN/5/23], and [Mss/SG/HOD/6/60]
+ NSDAR [G.R.C./S2/v. 1]

Winnicunett Second Cemetery (1817)
Toad Island Rd. and Bay St.
+ *Eight Cemeteries of Bristol County*
+ [G.R. 6] *Vital Records of Norton, Massachusetts to the year 1850* (1906).

Hanna Woodward Gravesite
Harvey St., gravestone missing.

Woodward–Willis Cemetery (1800)
opposite 228 Old Taunton Ave.
+ [G.R. 8] *Vital Records of Norton, Massachusetts to the year 1850* (1906).

NORWELL (1849)
from Scituate
Town Hall, 345 Main St., Norwell, Mass. 02061, Tel: (781)-659-8073
Cemetery Department, (781)-659-8072

Bowker Cemetery (1812)
across from 278 Bowker St.
+ [G.R. 17] *Vital Records of Scituate, Massachusetts to the year 1850* (1909).

Church Hill Cemetery (1725)
Church St., off of Common Ave., between River and Church Sts., South Norwell
+ [G.R. 15] *Vital Records of Scituate, Massachusetts to the year 1850* (1909).
+ Charles M. Thatcher, *Old Cemeteries of Southeastern Massachusetts.* (Middleborough, Mass., Middleborough Public Library, 1995) [F63/T53/1995/also Loan]

Damon Cemetery
off Grove St.
+ [G.R. 18] *Vital Records of Scituate, Massachusetts to the year 1850* (1909).

First Parish of Norwell Cemetery (1720)
Main St.
+ South Shore Genealogical Society, *An index to the First Parish Cemetery of Norwell.* (Norwell, Mass.: South Shore Genealogical Society, 1988) [F74/N98/S68/1988]
+ Charles M. Thatcher, *Old Cemeteries of Southeastern Massachusetts.* (Middleborough, Mass., Middleborough Public Library, 1995) [F63/T53/1995/also Loan]

Dr. Joseph Jacobs Cemetery (aka) Assinippi Cemetery (1779)
Assinippi
+ Charles M. Thatcher, *Old Cemeteries of Southeastern Massachusetts, Old Cemeteries of Southeastern Massachusetts.* (Middlebor-

ough, Mass., Middleborough Public
Library, 1995) [F63/T53/1995/also Loan]
+ NEHGS [MS70/SAN/18]

Old Second Church Cemetery (1680)
Main St., east of Bridge St.
+ [G.R. 13] *Vital Records of Scituate,
Massachusetts to the year 1850* (1909).
+ NEHGS [MS70/SCI/2]

Otis Cemetery
Pleasant St.
+ [G.R. 21] *Vital Records of Scituate,
Massachusetts to the year 1850* (1909).

Pinehurst Cemetery (1870)
off Common St.

Quaker Cemetery
on the banks of the North River, near
the Wanton Shipyard
+ [G.R. 20] *Vital Records of Scituate,
Massachusetts to the year 1850* (1909).

Stockbridge Cemetery (1700)
Mount Blue St., across from School St.
+ [G.R. 16] *Vital Records of Scituate,
Massachusetts to the year 1850* (1909).

Washington Street Cemetery (1892)
Washington St., Rte. 53
+ [G.R. 19] *Vital Records of Scituate,
Massachusetts to the year 1850* (1909).

South Parish Cemetery
+ [G.R. 14] *Vital Records of Scituate,
Massachusetts to the year 1850* (1909).
+ NEHGS [MS70/SAN/18]

NORWOOD (1872)
from Dedham and Walpole
Town Hall, 566 Washington St.,
Norwood, Mass. 02062, Tel: (781)-762-
1240

Highland Cemetery (1880)
380 Winter St
Tel: (781)-762-1149

Old Parish Cemetery (1741)
Washington St
Tel: Highland Cemetery, (781)-762-1149
+ NEHGS [MS70/NOR/490]

OAK BLUFFS (1880)
from Edgartown
Town Hall, Oak Bluffs Ave., Oak Bluffs,
Mass. 02557, Tel: (508)-693-5515

Lagoon–Marine Cemetery (1804)
Shirley Ave.

Benjamin Luce Cemetery (1810)
Vineyard Haven Rd.

Norton Cemetery (1764)
Harbor Ln.

Oak Grove Cemetery (1759)
School St.

**Sea View Hill–Sacred Heart
Cemetery (1892)**
Vineyard Ave.

Smith Cemetery (1831)
Barnes Rd.

Wilbur Cemetery (1875)
Vineyard Haven Rd.

OAKHAM (1762)
from Rutland
Town Hall, 2 Coldbrook Rd., Oakham,
Mass. 01068, Tel: (508)-882-5549

Clapp–Boyd Cemetery (1827)
off South Rd.

+ [G.S. 5] *Vital Records of Sandwich,*
Massachusetts to the year 1850 (1905).
+ NEHGS [MS70/OAK/20]

Coldbrook Hill Cemetery (aka) First Cemetery, Smallpox Cemetery (1761)
Coldbrook Hill, MDC River Watershed

Green Hollow Cemetery (1819)
Crawford Rd.
+ [G.S. 6] *Vital Records of Sandwich,*
Massachusetts to the year 1850 (1905).

Oakham Cemetery (19th century)
MDC River Watershed property,
Coldbrook

Old Burying Ground (aka) Center Cemetery Churchyard (1770)
Coldbrook Rd.
+ [G.S. 1] *Vital Records of Sandwich,*
Massachusetts to the year 1850 (1905).
+ NEHGS [MS70/OAK/20]

Pine Grove Cemetery (aka) West Cemetery (1812)
Old Turnpike Rd.
+ [G.S. 3] *Vital Records of Sandwich,*
Massachusetts to the year 1850 (1905).

South Cemetery (1810)
Rte. 148, North Brookfield Rd.
+ [G.S. 4] *Vital Records of Sandwich,*
Massachusetts to the year 1850 (1905).
+ NEHGS [MS70/OAK/20]

Southwest Cemetery (1818)
Lincoln Rd.
+ [G.S. 2] *Vital Records of Sandwich,*
Massachusetts to the year 1850 (1905).
+ NEHGS [MS70/OAK/20]

ORANGE (1783)
from Athol, Royalston, and Warwick
Town Hall, 6 Prospect St., Suite 1,
Orange, Mass. 01364, Tel: (978)-544-
2254
Cemetery Department, P.O. Box 56,
Orange, Mass. 01364 Tel: 978-544-3681

Branch Bridge Road Cemetery (1785)
Branch Bridge Rd.
+ NSDAR [G.R.C./1932/S1/v. 16]

Central Cemetery (1850)
85 Grove St.
Tel: (508)-544-3681

Holtshire Cemetery (18th century)
Holtshire and Chestnut Hill Rds., across
from Lake Matawa
+ [G.R. 3] *Vital Records of New Salem,*
Massachusetts to the year 1850 (1927).
+ NEHGS [MS70/ORA/1]
+ NSDAR [G.R.C./1932/S1/v. 16]

Jones Cemetery (18th century)
Jones Cemetery Rd., off of Wheeler Ave.
+ NEHGS [MS70/ORA/1]
+ NSDAR [G.R.C./1932/S1/v. 16]

North Orange Cemetery (1776)
Main St., the end of Wheeler Ave.
+ NEHGS [MS70/NOR/340], and
[MS70/ORA/1]
+ NSDAR [G.R.C./1932/S1/v. 16]

South Orange Cemetery (1923)
585 South Main St., Rte. 122

Tully Cemetery (18th century)
Warwick Rd., near Tully Center
+ NEHGS [MS70/ORA/1]

West Orange Cemetery (19th c.)
West Orange Rd., Rte. 2A
+ NEHGS [MS70/ORA/1]

ORLEANS (1797)
from Eastham
Town Hall, 19 School Rd., Orleans, Mass. 02653, Tel: (508)-240-3700

East Orleans Cemetery (aka) Meetinghouse Road Cemetery (1812)
east of Meetinghouse Rd.

Freeman Smallpox Cemetery
off Rte. 28 near Pleasant Bay, South Orleans.

Methodist Meeting House Cemetery (aka) Orleans Center Cemetery (1818)
Rte. 6A and Main St., Orleans Center

Orleans Cemetery (1723)
Rte. 6A, Main St., East Orleans
+ Josiah Paine, "Inscriptions upon Gravestones in the old cemetery at Orleans, Mass.,
NEHGS 21:212-215.

Rogers Family Cemetery (1816)
Harwich Rd., between Rte. 28 and 39

OTIS (1773)
from Tyringham
Town Hall, One North Main Rd., Otis, Mass. 01253, Tel: (508)-240-3700

Free Meeting House Cemetery (aka) West Otis Cemetery (1802)
Nash Rd., West Otis

Gulf Bridge Cemetery (aka) Clark Cemetery (1840)
Tolland State Forest, State Forest Rd.
+ NEHGS [MS70/OTI/1], and [Corbin Collection]
New East Cemetery (1815)

Route 23, behind the Otis Baptist Church, East Otis
+ NEHGS [MS70/OTI/1], [Corbin Collection]
+ NSDAR [G.R.C./S1/v. 217]

Old East Cemetery (aka) Norton Cemetery (1815)
Blandford Rd.
+ NEHGS [MS70/OTI/1],[MS70/OTI/2], and [Corbin Collection].
+ NSDAR [G.R.C./S1/v. 217]

Otis Center Cemetery (1743)
Rte. 23 West, Otis Center
+ NEHGS [MS70/OTI/2], and [Corbin Collection].
+ NSDAR [G.R.C./S1/v. 217]

Snow Cemetery
off Algerie Rd., East Otis

Watson Cemetery (1831)
near Haley Pond, Algerine Rd., East Otis
+ NEHGS [MS70/OTI/1], and [Corbin Collection]

West Center Cemetery (1790)
Stebbins Rd., West Otis
+ NEHGS [MS70/OTI/1], and [Corbin Collection].
+ NSDAR [G.R.C./S1/v. 217]

OXFORD (1693)
Town Hall, 325 Main St., Oxford, Mass. 01540, Tel: (508)-987-6032

Brookside Cemetery
Edmunds Rd.

Church Street Burial Ground (1713)
Church St.
+ Susan F. Salisbury, *Southern Massachusetts Cemetery Collection* - Volume

1 (Bowie, Md., Heritage Books, 1995)
[F63/S25/1995/also Loan]

North Cemetery (1847)
Main St.

North Gore Cemetery (1761)
Pleasant St.

St. Roch's Roman Catholic Cemetery (1858)
Federal Hill Rd.
Tel: St. Roch's Rectory, (508)-987-8987

South Cemetery
Main St.

PALMER (1752)
Town Hall, 4417 Main St., Palmer, Mass. 01069, Tel: (413)-283-2637
Cemetery Department, 4417 Main St., Palmer, Mass. 01069, Tel: (413)-283-2665

Four Corners Cemetery
Main St., Thorndike

Oak Knoll Cemetery
Thorndike St., across from St. Thomas the Apostle Church

Old Palmer Center Cemetery (1737)
Warren St.
+ [G.R. 1] *Vital Records of Palmer, Massachusetts to the year 1850* (1905).
+ Orrin Peer Allen, *Inscriptions from the two ancient cemeteries of Palmer, Massachusetts 1729-1901* (Palmer, Mass., The Journal Print, 1902) [MS70/PAL/4]

Old Three Rivers Cemetery
East Main St., across from St. Ann's Church, Three Rivers

St. Anne's Cemetery (19th century)
121 E. Main St., Three Rivers

Tel: St. Anne's Rectory, 2230 Main St., Palmer, Mass. (413)-283-5041

St. Peter's and St. Paul's Cemetery (1905)
Fuller Rd.
Tel: St. Peter's and St. Paul's Rectory, 2267 Main St., Palmer, Mass. (413)-283-6030

St. Thomas Cemetery (1855)
Thorndike St.
Tel: St. Thomas the Apostle Rectory, 1076 Thorndike St., Palmer, Mass. (413)-283-5091

PAXTON (1765)
from Leicester and Rutland
Town Hall, 697 Pleasant St., Paxton, Mass. 01612, Tel: 508-799-7347

Mooreland Cemetery (1767)
239 Richards Ave.

Paxton Center Cemetery (1765)
Church St., rear of the Paxton Congregational Church
+ Franklin Pierce Rice, *Paxton, Massachusetts, burial ground inscriptions : to the end of the year 1849* (Worcester, Mass.: Franklin P. Rice, 1906)
[F74/P3/R52/1906/also Loan]

Worcester County Memorial Park Cemetery
217 Richards Ave.

PEABODY (1855)
from Danvers.
City Hall, 24 Lowell St., Peabody, Mass. 01960, Tel: (978)-532-2000
Cemetery Dept., 3 Cedar Grove, Oak Grove, Monumental, Peabody Hist. (978)-531-1073

Bnai Brith of Somerville Cemetery
Off Rte. 128. Located between Peabody
and Endicott Sts.

Brown–Southwick Cemetery (1800)
Nichols Ln., West Peabody
Bryant Cemetery
rear 281 Lynnfield St., South Peabody

Buxton–Osborne Cemetery Site
Sparrow Lane, Center Peabody

Cedar Grove Cemetery (1851)
Cedar Grove Ave.
Tel: (978)-531-1073

Curtis–Very Cemetery (1736)
21 Lynn St.

Danforth Cemetery Site
Lowell St.

Douty–Newhall Cemetery (1816)
Newbury St., Rte. 1 South

**Emerson (aka) Allen's Lane
Cemetery (1799)**
corner of Washington St. and Allen's Ln.

Felton Cemetery (1790)
Prospect and Brooksby Sts.

Flint Burying Ground (1796)
rear of 1 LeBlanc Dr. and Nichols Rd,
West Peabody

Flint Memorial Cemetery (1873)
108 Newbury St., Rte. 1 South

Gardner Burial Ground (1818)
opposite 10 Birch St., West Peadbody

Gibbs Cemetery Site (1871)
Newbury St., Rte. 1 South

Jacobs Family Cemetery (1775)
opposite 437 Lowell St.

+ [G.R. 5] *Vital Records of Salem,
Massachusetts to the year 1850* (1916).

King Cemetery (1774)
240 Lowell St.

King–Hussey Cemetery (1821)
Summit St.

Larrabee Family Cemetery (1844)
rear of 14 Larrabee Terr., West Peabody

Larrabee–Marsh Cemetery Site
off Summit St.

Lebanon Memorial Cemetery
(a section of the Bnai Brith of Somerville
Cemetery)

Eleazer Lindsey Memorial (1782)
Lakeshore Rd. and Fairview Ave., South
Peabody

Maple Hill Cemetery (1913)
North Central St.

James Marsh Cemetery Site (1750)
Forest St.

Marsh Tomb (1844)
Centennial Dr.

**Marsh–Dunkley Cemetery Site
(1802)**
Lowell St.

Marsh–Shaw Cemetery Site (1774)
Lowell St.

Monumental Cemetery
Wallis St., Center Peabody

Moulton Family Cemetery (1827)
near 128 Newbury St., Rte. 1 South

Needham Burying Ground (1801)
Goodale St., South Peabody

John Needham Family Cemetery (1806)
behind Rose Cir., South Peabody

New Russell Cemetery (1839)
Intervale St.

Newhall Cemetery (1818)
Needham's Crossing, South Precinct

Oak Grove Cemetery (1817)
Pine and Johnson Sts., West Peabody

Oak Hill Cemetery–Chevra Kadusha Cemetery (1900)
North Central St.

Old Jacobs Cemetery (1813)
Colonial Rd.

Boston Street Cemetery (aka) Trask Cemetery (1689)
Main St., Peabody Center
+ [G.R. 6]*Vital Records of Salem, Massachusetts to the year 1850* (1916).

Phelp's Cemetery Site
Hoover Terrace, West Peabody

Pope Burial Ground (1755)
rear of Newbury St., Rte. 1 South

Prescott Family Cemetery (1718)
3 Tremont St., Peabody Center

Proctor Cemetery (1821)
Lowell St., at Rte. 128 North

Puritan Lawn Memorial Park (1934)
185 Lake Street
Tel: (978)-535-3660

Quaker Cemetery Site (1678)
Western and Goodhue Sts.
All burial removed in 1924 to the Quaker Friends Cemetery, Essex St., Salem, Mass.

Raddin Cemetery Site (1844)
Lynnfield St., Center Peabody

Russell-Upton Cemetery (1772)
left of 33 Glen Dr., West Peabody

Taylor Cemetery (1825)
Pine St., West Peabody

Temple Beth El Cemetery (1938)
Lowell St., opposite Bourbon St., West Peabody

Temple Israel of Swampscott Cemetery (1955)
Lowell St. and Peabody Rd., West Peabody

Temple Shalom of Medford
(a section of the Bnai Brith of Somerville Cemetery)

Temple Tifereth Israel Cemetery
(a section of the Bnai Brith of Somerville Cemetery)

Twiss Family Cemetery (1862)
rear of 8 Amy Rd., near Yoland Rd., West Peabody

Upton Cemetery (1757)
Peterson Rd., West Peabody

Jonathan Wilson Monument (1815)
located on the grounds of the North Shore Shopping Center

Wilson Cemetery (1776)
rear of Andover St., near Pulaski St.

Workmen's Circle Cemetery (1940)
Rte. 114, North Central St.

PELHAM (1743)
Town Hall, 351 Amherst Rd., Pelham, Mass. 01002, Tel: (413)-253-7129

Ruben Allen Cemetery (aka) Johnson Family Burial Ground (1837)
in the woods off Packardville Rd.

Arnold Burial Ground (1806)
in the woods north of 192 Amherst Rd.
+ NEHGS [Corbin Collection]

Harkness Cemetery (1830)
Amherst and Jones Rds.

Knight's Corner Burial Ground (1832)
185 Packardville Rd.
+ NEHGS [Corbin Collection]

Knightville Cemetery
County Rd.

Pelham Hill Cemetery (1739)
Pelham Center, Amherst Rd. and Daniel Shays Highway Rte. 202
+ NEHGS [MS70/PEL/1] and [Corbin Collection]
+ NSDAR [G.R.C./S1/v. 16]

Quaker Cemetery (1808)
no gravestones
in the woods north of Amherst Rd., and crossing of Metacomet and Monadnock Trail

Stevens Cemetery (aka) Smith Family Burial Ground (1818)
131 Packardville Rd.
+ NEHGS [Corbin Collection]

Valley Village Cemetery (1848)
173 North Valley Rd.
+ NEHGS [Corbin Collection]

West Burial Ground (aka) Cook–Johnson Cemetery (1771)
in the woods near 275 North Valley Rd.
+ NEHGS [Corbin Collection]

PEMBROKE (1712)
from Duxbury
Town Hall, 100 Center St., Pembroke, Mass. 02359, Tel: (781)-293-7211
Cemetery Department, 100 Center St., Pembroke Tel: (781)-293-5649

Briggs Cemetery (aka) Barker Burial Ground (18th century)
Rte. 53, Washington St., North Pembroke
+ [G.R. 5] *Vital Records of Pembroke, Massachusetts to the year 1850* (1911).
+ Charles M. Thatcher, *Old Cemeteries of Southeastern Massachusetts*. (Middleborough, Mass., Middleborough Public Library, 1995) [F63/T53/1995/also Loan]

Centre Cemetery (1715)
Center and Curve Sts., Pembroke Center
+ [G.R. 1] *Vital Records of Pembroke, Massachusetts to the year 1850* (1911).
+ NEHGS [MS70/PEM/1]

Brown Cemetery (19th century)
High St., across from Mountain Ave.
+ NEHGS [MS70/FRE/10]

Friends Burying Ground (18th century)
Washington and Schooset St., North Pembroke
+ [G.R. 9] *Vital Records of Pembroke, Massachusetts to the year 1850* (1911).
+ Charles M. Thatcher, *Old Cemeteries of Southeastern Massachusetts*. (Middleborough, Mass., Middleborough Public Library, 1995) [F63/T53/1995/also Loan]

Seth Hatch Family Cemetery (1799)
Water St., Two Mile

Luther Magoun Family Cemetery (18th century)
Water St., Two Mile

Paul Magoun Family Cemetery (19th century)
Water St., Two Mile

Silas Morton–Barstow Tomb (19th century)
Water St., Two Mile

Mount Pleasant Cemetery (19th century)
Mattakeesett St., Bryantville
+ [G.R. 3] *Vital Records of Pembroke, Massachusetts to the year 1850* (1911).
+ Charles M. Thatcher, *Old Cemeteries of Southeastern Massachusetts.* (Middleborough, Mass., Middleborough Public Library, 1995) [F63/T53/1995/also Loan]
+ NEHGS [MS70/PEM/1]

Pine Grove Cemetery (aka) East Pembroke Cemetery (19th century)
Spring St.
+ [G.R. 6] *Vital Records of Pembroke, Massachusetts to the year 1850* (1911).

Randall Lot Cemetery (1871)
Water St., Two Mile

Sachem Lodge Cemetery (aka) High Street Cemetery (19th century)
High St.
+ [G.R. 7] *Vital Records of Pembroke, Massachusetts to the year 1850* (1911).

Stetson Burial Ground
+ [G.R. 2] *Vital Records of Pembroke, Massachusetts to the year 1850* (1911).
+ NEHGS [MS70/PEM/1]

Two Mile Cemetery
perhaps this refers to one of the Magoun family cemeteries.

+ [G.R. 4] *Vital Records of Pembroke, Massachusetts to the year 1850* (1911).

Chapel Ground Cemetery
Chapel St., near the Kingston town line.
+ [G.R. 8] *Vital Records of Pembroke, Massachusetts to the year 1850* (1911).

PEPPERELL (1753)
from Groton.
Town Hall, One Main St., Pepperell, Mass. 01463, Tel: (978)-433-0339
Cemetery Department, 40 Heald St., Pepperell, Ma 01463 Tel: (978)-433-0323

Lawrence Cemetery
this cemetery is now located in the town of Hollis, N.H.
+ [G.R. 5] *Vital Records of Pepperell, Massachusetts to the year 1850* (1985).

Pepperell Cemetery (1890)
9-11 Park St., off Rte. 113
+ [G.R. 3] *Vital Records of Pepperell, Massachusetts to the year 1850* (1985).
+ NSDAR [G.R.C./S1/v. 61]

St. Joseph's Cemetery
Jersey St., off Rte. 113
Tel: St. Joseph's Rectory, 28 Tarbell St., Pepperell, Mass. (978)-433-5737
+ [G.R. 4] *Vital Records of Pepperell, Massachusetts to the year 1850* (1985).

Walton Cemetery (1746)
5-7 Park St., next to Pepperell Cemetery
+ [G.R. 1] *Vital Records of Pepperell, Massachusetts to the year 1850* (1985).
+ NEHGS [MS70/PEP/1]

Woodlawn Cemetery (1805)
44-48 Heald St.
+ [G.R. 2] *Vital Records of Pepperell, Massachusetts to the year 1850* (1985).

PERU (1771)

Town Hall, 4 North Rd., Peru, Mass. 01235, Tel: (413)-655-8312

Center Cemetery (1776)
South Rd., near the First Congregational Church
+ NEHGS [MS70/PER/2], [Corbin Collection], and [F74/F45/L4] Typescript in Mss
+ NSDAR [G.R.C./S1/v. 436]

Ford Family Cemetery (1831)
Rte. 143, on the property of Camp Danbee, near the Hinsdale town line.
+ NEHGS [MS70/PER/2], and [F74/F45/L4] Typescript in Mss
+ NSDAR [G.R.C./S1/v. 436]

North Cemetery (aka) Pierce Cemetery (1797)
Pierce Rd., near East Windsor Rd.
+ NEHGS [F74/F45/L4] Typescript in Mss, and [Corbin Collection]
+ NSDAR [G.R.C./S1/v. 436]

South Cemetery (aka) Wheeler Cemetery (1829)
Middlefield Rd.
+ NEHGS [F74/F45/L4] Typescript in Mss
+ NSDAR [G.R.C./S1/v. 436]

South Road Extension Cemetery (19th Century)
South Road Extension

South Thompson Burial Ground Site (1827)
Rte. 143, near South and North St. intersection
+Mrs. Max Lederer, *Tombstone inscriptions of Peru, Massachusetts*. (Southampton, Mass. 1948) [F74/P45/L4/1948]
+ NEHGS [Corbin Collection]

PETERSHAM (1754)

Town Hall, 3 South Main St., Petersham, Mass. 01366, Tel: (978)-724-6649

Coolidge Cemetery (1816)
Hardwick Rd.

East Street Cemetery (1862)
East St.

Harvard Cemetery (1814)
North Main St.

Indian Cemetery (1777)
Hubbardston Rd.

Nichewaug Cemetery (1834)
Glen Valley Rd.

Northwest Cemetery (1834)
Flat Rock Rd.

Old Centre Cemetery (1751)
South Main St.
Second East Street Cemetery (1804)
East St.

Shaker Cemetery Site
All burials were removed to Quabbin Park Cemetery, Ware, Massachusetts 1938
+ NEHGS [MS/70/WAR/15]

Snow Cemetery Site
All burials were removed to Quabbin Park Cemetery, Ware, Massachusetts 1938
+ NEHGS [MS/70/WAR/15]

West Street Cemetery (1803)
West St.

PHILLIPSTON (1786)
from Athol and Templeton
Town Hall, 50 The Common, Phillipston, Mass. 01331, Tel: (978)-249-1733

Betsey Ainsworth Gravesite (1829)
Narrow Lane Rd.
+ NSDAR [G.R.C./S1/v. 354]

Baldwin Hill Cemetery (1776)
between 75 and 95 Baldwin Hill Rd.
+ Central Mass. Gen. Society, *Cemetery Inscriptions of Philipston, Mass.*, (Westminster, Mass.: Massachusetts Genealogical Society, 1999) [F74/P56/C46/1999]

Lower Cemetery (aka) Valley Cemetery (1831)
Athol Rd.
+ Central Mass. Gen. Society, *Cemetery Inscriptions of Philipston, Mass.*, (Westminster, Mass.: Massachusetts Genealogical Society, 1999) [F74/P56/C46/1999]

Petersham Road Cemetery
Petersham Rd., East Phillipston
+ NEHGS [MS70/PHI/1]
+ NSDAR [G.R.C./S1/v.94]

Phillipston Center Cemetery (1803)
Athol and Baldwinville Rds.
+ Central Mass. Gen. Society, *Cemetery Inscriptions of Philipston, Mass.*, (Westminster, Mass.: Massachusetts Genealogical Society, 1999) [F74/P56/C46/1999]

Royalston Road Cemetery (1840)
across from 800 Royalston Rd.
+ Central Mass. Gen. Society, *Cemetery Inscriptions of Philipston, Mass.*, (Westminster, Mass.: Massachusetts Genealogical Society, 1999) [F74/P56/C46/1999]

South Cemetery (1777)
Searles Hill Rd.
+ Central Mass. Gen. Society, *Cemetery Inscriptions of Philipston, Mass.*, (Westminster, Mass.: Massachusetts Genealogical Society, 1999) [F74/P56/C46/1999]

PITTSFIELD (1761)
City Hall, 70 Allen St., Pittsfield, Mass. 01201, Tel: (413)-499-9361

Ahavath Sholem Cemetery (1912)
Churchill St.

Anshe Amunim Cemetery (1869)
Onota St. (a section of the Pittsfield Cemetery)

East Part Cemetery (1812)
Williams St.
+ NEHGS [Corbin Collection]

Knesset Israel Cemetery (1893)
290 Pecks Rd.
Tel: Knesset Israel Synagogue, 16 Colt Rd., Pittsfield, Mass. (413)-445-4872

Pittsfield Cemetery (1762)
203 Wahconah St.

St. Joseph's Cemetery (1840)
222 Pecks Rd.
Tel: (413)-499-1317

Shaker Cemetery (1813)
West Housatonic St., on the grounds of the Shaker Village.

James Taylor's Gravesite (1823)
725 Churchill St.

West Part Cemetery (1813)
West St.
+ NEHGS [MS70/PIT/5] and [Corbin Collection]
+ NSDAR [G.R.C./S1/v.94]

Sarah Deming Cemetery
+ NEHGS [MS70/PIT/2]
+ NSDAR [G.R.C./S1/v. 436]

PLAINFIELD (1785)
from Cummington.
Town Hall, 344 Main St., Plainfield,
Mass. 01070, Tel: (413)-634-5417
Cemetery Committe, Tel: (413)-634-5417

Ancient Cemetery (1792)
in pasture off West Hill Rd.

**East Street Cemetery (aka)
Stockwell Cemetery (aka) Baptist
Cemetery (1839)**
East St.

Hilltop Cemetery (1808)
Central and Union Sts.
+ NEHGS [Corbin Collection]

**North Street Cemetery Site (18th
century) [no gravestones]**
in woods north of 71 North St.

**Pleasant Street (aka) Dyer Cemetery
(1812)**
Pleasant St.

**South Central Street Cemetery Site
(18th century) [no gravestones]**
54 South Central St.

**South Central Street Cemetery Site
[no gravestones]**
on slope behind 288 South Central St.

**Union Street Cemetery (aka) Old
Village Cemetery (1792)**
Union St.
+ NEHGS [Vertical
File/F74/P7/B7/1980]

**West Hill Cemetery (aka) Summit
Street Cemetery (1801)**
Summit St.
+ NEHGS [Corbin Collection]

**West Mountain Cemetery (aka)
Allis–Barton Cemetery (1815)**
Upper Liberty St.
+ NSDAR [G.R.C./S1/v. 48]

West Street Cemetery (1829)
West St. near Windsor Ave.

Haskins Family Cemetery
+ NEHGS [Corbin Collection]

McCloud Cemetery
+ NEHGS [Corbin Collection]

PLAINVILLE (1905)
fromWrentham
Town Hall, 142 South St., Plainville,
Mass. 02762, Tel: (508)-695-3142

New Plainville Cemetery (1851)
Rte. 106 and Rte. 1A, West Bacon St,
near Plainville Center.
+ Susan F. Salisbury, *Southern
Massachusetts Cemetery Collection* - Volume
2 (Bowie, Md., Heritage Books, 1996)
[F63/S25/1995/also Loan]

Old South Burial Ground (1808)
West Bacon St.
+ [G.R. 3] *Vital Records of Wrentham,
Massachusetts to the year 1850* (1910).
+ Susan F. Salisbury, *Southern
Massachusetts Cemetery Collection* - Volume
2 (Bowie, Md., Heritage Books, 1996)
[F63/S25/1995/also Loan]
+ NEHGS [MS70/PLA/10]
+ NSDAR [G.R.C./S1/v. 151]

Shepardville Cemetery (1730)
Rte. 152 and Rte. 1, Taunton St.

+ [G.R. 4] *Vital Records of Wrentham,
Massachusetts to the year 1850* (1910).
+ Susan F. Salisbury, *Southern
Massachusetts Cemetery Collection* - Volume
2 (Bowie, Md., Heritage Books, 1996)
[F63/S25/1995/also Loan]
+ NEHGS [MS70/PLA/12]
+ NSDAR [G.R.C./S1/v. 151]

PLYMOUTH (1620)

Town Hall, 9 Stafford St., Plymouth,
Mass. 02360, Tel: (508)-830-4050
Plymouth Cemetery Dept., 11 Lincoln
St., Plymouth, Mass. 02360, Tel: (508)-
830-4078

Bates Burial Ground (1867)
Timberlane Rd., off Lond Pond Rd.

Bassett Cemetery (1835)
Herring Way

Blackmar Hill Burial Ground (1830)
off West Lond Pond Rd., near Halfway
Pond Rd.

Brailey Burial Ground (1900)
Brailey Ln., off of South St.

Burial Hill Cemetery (1622)
School St., behind Town Square
Tel: (508)-830-4079
+ Bradford Kingman, *Epitaphs from
Burial Hill, Plymouth, Massachusetts, from
1657 to 1892 : with biographical and historical
dates.* (Baltimore, Mass.: Genealogical
Publishing Co., 1977 reprint of 1892
edition) [F74/P8/K5/1977]
+ Benjamin Drew, *Burial Hill, Plymouth,
Massachusetts : its monuments and gravestones
numbered and briefly described, and the
inscriptions and epitaphs thereon carefully
copied.* (Plymouth, Mass.: Avery & Doten,
1894) [F74/P8/D7/1894/also Loan]
+ Barbara J. Bradford Robinson,
Howard E. Robinson, Cynthia L.
Robinson, *Burial Hill in the 1990s*

*Plymouth, Massachusetts a six-year cemetery
mapping project with descriptions, conditions,
and some photographs.* (Plymouth, Mass.:
Plymouth Public Library Corp., 2000).
+ NEHGS [MS70/PLY/3], and
[MS70/PLY/12].

Cedarville Cemetery (1833)
Herring Pond Rd.
+ Charles M. Thatcher, *Old Cemeteries of
Southeastern Massachusetts.*(Middleborough,
Mass., Middleborough Public
Library,1995) [F63/T53/1995/also
Loan]

Chiltonville Cemetery (1729)
behind 6 River St., next to Plimoth
Plantation

Coles Hill Burial Ground (1620)
Carver St. and Water St.

Douglas Burying Ground (1828)
Halfway Pond Rd., Long Pond
+ Charles M. Thatcher, *Old Cemeteries of
Southeastern Massachusetts.* (Middlebor-
ough, Mass., Middleborough Public
Library, 1995) [F63/T53/1995/also Loan]

Faunce Memorial Burial Park (1959)
behind the Faunce Memorial Union
Church, Halfway Pond Rd.

Fawn Pond Cemetery
Fawn Pond Rd.

Harlow–Savery Cemetery (1806)
Old Sandwich Rd.

**Herring Pond Wampanoag Indian
(aka) Bournedale Cemetery (1849)**
Sandy Point Rd, located in Plymouth and
Bourne

Indian Cemetery (1818)
Bartlett Rd., Manomet

King Cemetery (1838)
West Long Pond Rd.
+ Charles M. Thatcher, *Old Cemeteries of Southeastern Massachusetts*. (Middleborough, Mass., Middleborough Public Library, 1995) [F63/T53/1995/also Loan]

Lakewood Cemetery (aka) Hirsch Indian Cemetery (1831)
Elmer Ramond Playground, Long Pond Rd.
+ NEHGS [F72/P7/N2] Typescript in Mss

Lower Herring Pond Cemetery (1825)
Herring Pond Rd.

Lucas Cemetery (1818)
Carver Rd., near Carver town line.

Lucas–Thrasher Cemetery (1800)
off Morgan Rd., off Long Pond Rd., near Long Pond

Manomet Cemetery (1806)
State Rd., Rte 3A, White Horse Beach
+ Charles M. Thatcher, *Old Cemeteries of Southeastern Massachusetts*. (Middleborough, Mass., Middleborough Public Library, 1995) [F63/T53/1995/also Loan]

Nickerson Burial Ground (1800)
Packard St., Buttermilk Bay

Nightingale Cemetery (1874)
Lakewood Dr., off Long Pond Rd.

Oak Grove Cemetery (1803)
Summer and James Sts.
+ Charles M. Thatcher, *Old Cemeteries of Southeastern Massachusetts*. (Middleborough, Mass., Middleborough Public Library, 1995) [F63/T53/1995/also Loan]

Parting Ways Cemetery (18th century)
Plympton Rd., Rte. 80

Plymouth County Memorial Cemetery (1970's)
next to 265 South Meadow Rd.

Raymond–Newcomb Cemetery (1800)
Long Pond Rd., between Clark Rd. and Halfway Pond Rd.

Redding Cemetery (aka) Bloody Pond Cemetery (1851)
Long Pond Rd., south of Halfway Pond Rd.

Russell Mills Cemetery (1825)
Jordan Rd., Chiltonville
+ Charles M. Thatcher, *Old Cemeteries of Southeastern Massachusetts*.(Middleborough, Mass., Middleborough Public Library,1995) [F63/T53/1995/also Loan]

St. Joseph's Roman Catholic Cemetery (1863)
Summer St. and Westerly Rd.

Shurtleff Burial Ground (1776)
Fawn Pond Rd., near Fawn Pond Cemetery

South Pond Cemetery (1783)
Cemetery Hill Rd., off Lond Pond Rd.

Valler Cemetery (1845)
Hay Rd., off State Rd., Manomet

Vine Hill Cemetery (1800)
Samoset St., Rte. 44

Watson Cemetery (1853)
Clarks Island, Plymouth Harbor near Duxbury

Whitehorse Cemetery (1717)
Cedar Rd., off Rocky Hill Rd., Manomet
+ NEHGS [MS70/PLY/12]

PLYMPTON (1707)
from Plymouth
Town Hall, 5 Palmer Rd., Plympton, Mass. 02367, Tel: (781)-585-3220

Hillcrest Cemetery (1711)
Main St.
+ [G.R. 1] *Vital Records of Plympton, Massachusetts to the year 1850* (1923).

Isaac Loring Gravesite (1778)
County Rd., near Halifax town line.

Plympton Green Cemetery (1732)
Plympton Center
+ [G.R. 4] *Vital Records of Norton, Massachusetts to the year 1850* (1906).

Plympton Congregational Church Cemetery (1856)
Main St., behind the Congregational Church. Tel: (781)-585-5764

Small Pox cemetery (18th century)

Plympton Center.
+ [G.R. 3] *Vital Records of Norton, Massachusetts to the year 1850* (1906).

Small cemetery in the northern part of Plympton
+ [G.R. 2] *Vital Records of Norton, Massachusetts to the year 1850* (1906).

PRESCOTT (1822)
from New Salem and Pelham
This town flooded in 1938 for the Quabbin Reservoir. All burials in the following cemeteries were removed to Quabbin Park Cemetery, Ware, Mass. 1938
+ NEHGS [MS/70/WAR/15]

Bobbinville Burial Ground (1784)
+ NEHGS [Corbin Collection]

Center Cemetery
+ NEHGS [Corbin Collection]

North Prescott Cemetery
+ NEHGS [Corbin Collection]

Northeast Cemetery
+ NEHGS [Corbin Collection]

Northwest Cemetery
+ NEHGS [Corbin Collection]

Fish Hill Cemetery Site
Isaac Linzie Cemetery Site
Thomas S. Mann Family Cemetery Site
Pelham Hollow Road Cemetery (aka) East Burying Ground (1778)
Pine Grove Cemetery Site
Jason Powers Cemetery Site
Town House Cemetery Site

PRINCETON (1759)
from Rutland
Town Hall, 6 Town Hall Dr., Princeton, Mass. 01541, Tel: (978)-464-2103

Meeting House Hill Cemetery (1765)
Mountain Rd.
+ NSDAR [G.R.C./S1/v. 439]

North Cemetery (1826)
Mirick Rd.
+ NSDAR [G.R.C./S1/v. 439]

Parker 1 Burying Ground (1831)
Parker Pl.

Parker 2 Cemetery
Beaman Rd.

South Burying Ground (1848)
Ball Hill Rd.
+ NEHGS [MS70/PRI/3]

West Cemetery (1794)
Wheeler Rd.
+ NEHGS [MS70/PRI/2]

Woodlawn Cemetery (1852)
Connor Ln.
+ NEHGS [MS70/PRI/3]

Cedar Knoll Cemetery
+ NEHGS [MS70/PRI/3]

Oakwoods Cemetery
+ NEHGS [MS70/PRI/3]

PROVINCETOWN (1727)
Town Hall, 260 Commercial St.,
Provincetown, Mass. 02657, Tel: (508)-
487-7013
Cemetery Department, 26 Alden St.,
Provincetown, Mass. Tel: (508)-487-7070

Shank Painter Cemetery (aka) Old Cemetery Number 2 (1817)
Cemetery Rd.
+ Lurana Higgins Cook, *Provincetown, Massachusetts Cemeter Inscriptions.* (Bowie, Md., Heritage Books, 1980)
[F74/P96/P76/also Loan]

Gifford Cemetery (1818)
Cemetery Rd. (next to Hamilton Cemetery)
+ Lurana Higgins Cook, *Provincetown, Massachusetts Cemeter Inscriptions.* (Bowie, Md., Heritage Books, 1980)
[F74/P96/P76/also Loan]
Hamilton Cemetery (1833)
Cemetery Rd. (next to Gifford Cemetery)
+ Lurana Higgins Cook, *Provincetown, Massachusetts Cemeter Inscriptions.* (Bowie, Md., Heritage Books, 1980)
[F74/P96/P76/also Loan]

Old Cemetery (1723)
Winthrop and Court Sts.
+ *The Mayflower Descendant* (vols. 8-10)

St. Peter's Catholic Cemetery (19th Century)
Winslow and Jerome Smith Rds. [early burial from 1801 from farm is earliest stone].

Smallpox Cemetery
off Rte. 6
+ Lurana Higgins Cook, *Provincetown, Massachusetts Cemeter Inscriptions.* (Bowie, Md., Heritage Books, 1980)
[F74/P96/P76/also Loan]

QUINCY (1792)
from Braintree and Dorchester
City Hall, 1305 Hancock St., Quincy, Mass. 02169, Tel: (617)-376-1131

Christ Church Episcopal Burial Ground (1725)
54-60 School St., near Phipps St.
Tel: Christ Church, 12 Quincy Ave., Quincy, Mass. (617)-773-0310
+ NEHGS [MS70/QUI/14],
[MS70/QUI/16], [Mss/A/345], and
[MS70/BRA/34]
+ NSDAR [G.R.C./S1/v.177]

Hall Place Cemetery (1841)
61 Crescent St., next to St. Mary's Cemetery, West Quincy
+ NEHGS [MS/QUI/27],
[Mss/A/345], and [MS70/BRA/34]
Tel: Mount Wollaston Cemetery, (617)-376-1294

Hancock Cemetery (1640)
1325 Hancock St.
+ William S. Pattee, "Quincy Inscriptions" *NEHGR* 9:151-5, 296.

+ NEHGS [MS70/QUI/11],
[MS70/QUI/14], [Mss/A/345], and
[MS70/BRA/34]
+ NSDAR [G.R.C./S1/v.120]
Tel: Mount Wollaston Cemetery, (617)-376-1294

Mount Wollaston Cemetery (1856)
20 Sea St.
Tel: (617)-376-1294

National Sailor's Home Cemetery (1861)
off Fenno St., Wollaston
+ NEHGS [MS70/QUI/16], and
[F74/W894/D2] Typescript Mss

Pine Hill Cemetery (1966)
815 Willard St.
Tel: Mount Wollaston Cemetery, (617)-376-1294

Sailor's Snug Harbor Cemetery (1856)
Palmer St., Germantown
+ NEHGS [MS70/QUI/15]

St. Mary's Cemetery (1840)
115 Crescent St., next to Hall Place
Cemetery, West Quincy
Tel: St. Mary's Rectory, 245 North St.,
Quincy, Mass. (617)-773-0120
Archives of the Archdiocese of Boston,
2121 Commonwealth Ave., Brighton,
Mass. 02135, (617)-254-0100. The
Boston Archdiocese Archives has grave
lot sales 1885-1920.

United First Parish Church Tomb
1306 Hancock St.
Tel: (617)-773-1290
Contains the tombs of Presidents John
Adams and John Quincy Adams and
their wives.

RANDOLPH (1793)
from Braintree
Town Hall, 41 South Main St.,
Randolph, Mass. 02368, Tel: (781)-961-0900

Central Cemetery (1743)
North St.
+ NEHGS [MS70/RAN/2],
[MS70/RAN/8], [Mss/A/345], and
[MS70/BRA/34]

Kehillath Israel Cemetery (a section of the Lindwood Memorial Park Cemetery)

Lindwood Memorial Park–Jewish Cemetery (1952)
497 North Street
Tel: (781)-963-2822

Moses Mendelsohn Cemetery
(a section of the Lindwood Memorial Park Cemetery) (1983)

Oakland Cemetery (1792)
Oak and Orchard Sts.
+ NEHGS [MS70/RAN/1],
[MS70/RAN/4], [MS70/RAN/5],
[Mss/A/345], and [MS70/BRA/34]
+ NSDAR [G.R.C./S1/v. 89]

St. Mary's Cemetery (1845)
245 North St.
Tel: (781)-961-9323

Temple Emanuel of Newton Cemetery
(a section of the Lindwood Memorial Park Cemetery)

RAYNHAM (1731)
from Taunton
Town Hall, 53 Orchard St., Raynham,
Mass. 02767, Tel: (508)-824-2700

Britton Cemetery
Britton St., one marked gravestone.
+ Charles M. Thatcher, *Old Cemeteries of Southeastern Massachusetts*. (Middleborough, Mass., Middleborough Public Library, 1995) [F63/T53/1995/also Loan]
+ NEHGS [Mss/SL/RAY/7]

Horatio Dean Family Cemetery (1850)
+ NEHGS [Mss/SL/RAY/7]

Fields Cemetery
Britton St.

Gilmore Cemetery
Britton St.

Britton Cemetery
Center St.

Hall Cemetery
off Leonard St.
+ Charles M. Thatcher, *Old Cemeteries of Southeastern Massachusetts*.(Middleborough, Mass., Middleborough Public Library,1995) [F63/T53/1995/also Loan]
+ NEHGS [MS70/RAY/3]

Hall Cemetery
off Pine St.
+ Charles M. Thatcher, *Old Cemeteries of Southeastern Massachusetts*.(Middleborough, Mass., Middleborough Public Library,1995) [F63/T53/1995/also Loan]
+ NEHGS [Mss/SL/RAY/7] and [Mss/SL/RAY/3]

Haskins Cemetery
off Pine St.

King Cemetery
Hall St.
+ Charles M. Thatcher, *Old Cemeteries of Southeastern Massachusetts*. (Middleborough,

Mass., Middleborough Public Library, 1995) [F63/T53/1995/also Loan]

King Cemetery
South St., a dead end street.
+ Charles M. Thatcher, *Old Cemeteries of Southeastern Massachusetts*. (Middleborough, Mass., Middleborough Public Library, 1995) [F63/T53/1995/also Loan]
+ NEHGS [Mss/SL/RAY/7], and [Mss/SG/HOD/6/60]

Leonard Cemetery (1778)
Leonard and Judson Sts.
+ NEHGS [Mss/SL/RAY/7]

North Raynham Cemetery (18th century)
Elm St. West and Bridge St.
+ NEHGS [Mss/SG/LIN/5/23], and [Mss/SG/HOD/6/60]

Johnson Pond Island Cemetery Site
Rte. 104, no gravestones

Lincoln Cemetery
off Elm St.

Pleasant Street Cemetery (1726)
Pleasant St.
+ NEHGS [Mss/SL/RAY/7]

River Street Cemetery
near Taunton River, River St.

Robinson Cemetery
Church and Dean Sts.
+ Charles M. Thatcher, *Old Cemeteries of Southeastern Massachusetts*. (Middleborough, Mass., Middleborough Public Library, 1995) [F63/T53/1995/also Loan]
+ NEHGS [Mss/SL/RAY/7]

Shaw Cemetery (1718)
Rte. 138, near Elm St.
+ Charles M. Thatcher, *Old Cemeteries of Southeastern Massachusetts*. (Middleborough,

Mass., Middleborough Public Library,
1995) [F63/T53/1995/also Loan]
+ NEHGS [Mss/SG/LIN/5/23], and
[Mss/SG/HOD/6/60]

Smallpox Cemetery
off Titicut Rd.

Smallpox Cemetery Site
off King St., (no marked stones)

Smith Cemetery
Hill St.
+ NEHGS [Mss/SL/RAY/7]

South Street Cemetery (1718)
South St.
+ Charles M. Thatcher, *Old Cemeteries of
Southeastern Massachusetts.*(Middleborough,
Mass., Middleborough Public
Library,1995) [F63/T53/1995/also
Loan]
+ NEHGS [Mss/SL/RAY/7], and
NEHGS [Mss/SG/LIN/5/23]

Williams Cemetery
Church St.
+ Charles M. Thatcher, *Old Cemeteries of
Southeastern Massachusetts.*(Middleborough,
Mass., Middleborough Public
Library,1995) [F63/T53/1995/also
Loan]
+ NEHGS [Mss/SL/RAY/7]

READING (1644)
from Lynn
Town Hall, 16 Lowell St., Reading, Mass.
01867, Tel: (781)-942-9050
Cemetery Department, 16 Lowell St.,
Reading, Mass. 01867, Tel: (781)-942-
9086

Charles Lawn Memorial Park (1982)
Charles St.

Forest Glen Cemetery (1924)
Forest Glen Rd.

Laurel Hill Cemetery (1736)
Lowell St.
+ [G.R. 1] *Vital Records of Reading,
Massachusetts to the year 1850* (1912).

Wood End Cemetery (1997)
Franklin St.

REHOBOTH (1645)
Town Hall, Peck St., Rehoboth, Mass.
02769, Tel: (508)-252-6502

**Baker Cemetery (aka) Cole's Brook
Cemetery (1774)**
Spring St., near Cole's Brook
+ Susan F. Salisbury, *Southern
Massachusetts Cemetery Collection,* Volume 2
(Bowie, Md., Heritage Books, 1996)
[F63/S25/1995/also Loan]
+ NEHGS [MS70/REH/3],
[MS70/REH/12], and [MS70/REH/13]

Bliss Family Burying Ground (1800)
Agriculture Ave., near Fairfield St.
+ Susan F. Salisbury, *Southern
Massachusetts Cemetery Collection,* Volume 2
(Bowie, Md., Heritage Books, 1996)
[F63/S25/1995/also Loan]
+ NEHGS [MS70/REH/12], and
[MS70/REH/13]

Bosworth Family Cemetery (1820)
Hornbine Rd. near Baker St.
+ Susan F. Salisbury, *Southern
Massachusetts Cemetery Collection,* Volume 2
(Bowie, Md., Heritage Books, 1996)
[F63/S25/1995/also Loan]
+ NEHGS [MS70/REH/12]

**Ichabod Bosworth Family Cemetery
(1820)**
Purchase St.

+ Susan F. Salisbury, *Southern Massachusetts Cemetery Collection,* Volume 2 (Bowie, Md., Heritage Books, 1996) [F63/S25/1995/also Loan] + NEHGS [MS70/REH/12]

Brook Street Cemetery
across from the Hix Family Cemetery, marked with field stones.

Buffington Family Cemetery Site (1838)
Martin St., burial were perhaps moved to Swansea, Mass. + NEHGS [MS70/REH/12], and [MS70/REH/13]

Burial Place Hill (1716)
Providence and Peckham Sts. + Susan F. Salisbury, *Southern Massachusetts Cemetery Collection* - Volume 2 (Bowie, Md., Heritage Books, 1996) [F63/S25/1995/also Loan] + NEHGS [MS70/REH/12], [MS70/REH/13], [Mss/A/313], and [Mss/345]

Carruthers Family Cemetery (1834)
Providence St., near East St. + NEHGS [MS70/REH/12], and [MS70/REH/13]

Case Family Cemetery (1777)
Baker St., near the Swansea town line. + NEHGS [MS70/REH/12], and [MS70/REH/13]

Terry Diddle Cemetery (1802)
Kelton St. + NEHGS [MS70/REH/12], and [MS70/REH/13]

James Gardiner Family Cemetery
Hornbine Rd.

Goff and Wheeler Cemetery (1786)
Bay State Rd.

+ Susan F. Salisbury, *Southern Massachusetts Cemetery Collection*, Volume 2 (Bowie, Md., Heritage Books, 1996) [F63/S25/1995/also Loan] + NEHGS [MS70/REH/12], and [MS70/REH/13]

Charles Goff Cemetery (1740)
Chestnut St. + NEHGS [MS70/REH/13]

Lovel Goff Cemetery
Elm St. near Summer and Moulton Sts. + Susan F. Salisbury, *Southern Massachusetts Cemetery Collection* - Volume 2 (Bowie, Md., Heritage Books, 1996) [F63/S25/1995/also Loan] + NEHGS [MS70/REH/12], and [MS70/REH/13]

Greenwood Cemetery (aka) Oak Swamp Cemetery (19th century)
Plain St. + Susan F. Salisbury, *Southern Massachusetts Cemetery Collection* - Volume 2 (Bowie, Md., Heritage Books, 1996) [F63/S25/1995/also Loan] + NEHGS [MS70/REH/12]

Judge Haile Family Cemetery (1786)
Wood St. near Providence and Brook Sts. + NEHGS [MS70/REH/12], and [MS70/REH/13]

Hix Cemetery (18th century)
Brook St. + NEHGS [MS70/REH/12]

Horton Burial Ground (1828)
Pierces Ln. + Susan F. Salisbury, *Southern Massachusetts Cemetery Collection* - Volume 2 (Bowie, Md., Heritage Books, 1996) [F63/S25/1995/also Loan] + NEHGS [MS70/REH/12], and [MS70/REH/13]

Horton Family Cemetery
Spring St., across from the Baker Cemetery.

Ariel Horton Family Cemetery (1846)
Pleasant St., near the Pleasant Street School

James Horton Family Cemetery (1849)
Pleasant St. near Chestnut St.
+ Susan F. Salisbury, *Southern Massachusetts Cemetery Collection* - Volume 2 (Bowie, Md., Heritage Books, 1996) [F63/S25/1995/also Loan]
+ NEHGS [MS70/REH/12]

Jonathan Horton Family Cemetery (1774)
Pleasant St., between Davis St. and Pierce Ln.
+ NEHGS [MS70/REH/3]

Orrem N. Horton Family Cemetery
County St.

Otis Horton Family Cemetery (1828)
Pleasant St., near Davis St.

Isaiah Hunt Cemetery Site (1775)
Broad and Salisbury Sts. (no stones)
+ NEHGS [MS70/REH/12]

Elkanah Ingalls Family Cemetery (1806)
Cedar St.
+ Susan F. Salisbury, *Southern Massachusetts Cemetery Collection* - Volume 2 (Bowie, Md., Heritage Books, 1996) [F63/S25/1995/also Loan]

Kilton Family Cemetery Site
Kelton St., burial moved to the Oak Swamp Cemetery

Lake Family Cemetery Site (1861)
near the Palmer's River Churchyard. All burials removed to the Village Cemetery.
+ NEHGS [MS70/REH/12], and [MS70/REH/13]

Otis J. Martin Family Cemetery (1813)
Providence St.
+ NEHGS [MS70/REH/12], and [MS70/REH/13]

Medbury Family Cemetery (1825)
Pine St. near Homestead Ave.
+ Susan F. Salisbury, *Southern Massachusetts Cemetery Collection* - Volume 2 (Bowie, Md., Heritage Books, 1996) [F63/S25/1995/also Loan]
+ NEHGS [MS70/REH/12], and [MS70/REH/13]

Millerd Family Cemetery (1806)
Cedar St.
+ Susan F. Salisbury, *Southern Massachusetts Cemetery Collection* - Volume 2 (Bowie, Md., Heritage Books, 1996) [F63/S25/1995/also Loan]
+ NEHGS [MS70/REH/13]

Munroe Family Cemetery Site
Mason St. near Providence St., burial moved to the Thomas Cemetery in Swansea, Mass.

Nichols, Cole and Moulton Cemetery (1798)
Moulton St.
+ Susan F. Salisbury, *Southern Massachusetts Cemetery Collection*, Volume 2 (Bowie, Md., Heritage Books, 1996) [F63/S25/1995/also Loan]
+ NEHGS [MS70/REH/12], and [MS70/REH/13]

Capt. Israel Nichols Cemetery (1800)
Moulton St.

+ NEHGS [MS70/REH/12], and
[MS70/REH/13]

Oak Knoll Cemetery (aka) Briggs Corner Cemetery (18th century)
Park and Tremont Sts., North Rehoboth
+ Susan F. Salisbury, *Southern Massachusetts Cemetery Collection* - Volume 2 (Bowie, Md., Heritage Books, 1996)
[F63/S25/1995/also Loan]
+ NEHGS [MS70/REH/12],
[MS70/REH/13] and [Mss/A/313]

Palmer's River Burial Ground (1717)
Lake St. near Winter St.
+ NEHGS [MS70/REH/12]

Abel F. Pearce Family Cemetery (1848)
Larson Ln., near Moulton St.

Arikim Pearce Family Cemetery (1740)
Chestnut St.

Peck Family Cemetery (1736)
on the west bank of the Palmer River near Summer St.
+ NEHGS [MS70/REH/13]

Esek Pierce Family Cemetery (1770)
Horbine Rd.

Isaac Pierce Family Cemetery
Pierce Ln. near Pleasant St.
+ NEHGS [MS70/REH/12]

Joseph Stillman Pierce Cemetery (1802)
Kelton St.
+ Susan F. Salisbury, *Southern Massachusetts Cemetery Collection* - Volume 2 (Bowie, Md., Heritage Books, 1996)
[F63/S25/1995/also Loan]

Joshua Pierce Family Cemetery (1804)
Spring St., next to the Horton Family Cemetery, and across from the Baker Cemetery.
+ Susan F. Salisbury, *Southern Massachusetts Cemetery Collection* - Volume 2 (Bowie, Md., Heritage Books, 1996)
[F63/S25/1995/also Loan]
+ NEHGS [MS70/REH/3],
[MS70/REH/12], and [MS70/REH/13]

Nathan Pierce Family Cemetery (1853)
Purchase St., near the Dighton and Swansea town lines.

Peleg Pierce Family Cemetery (1790)
Pierce Ln.
+ NEHGS [Mss/3/S/38]

Rounds Family Cemetery (1791)
Plain St., near Swansea town line.
+ NEHGS [MS70/REH/12],
[MS70/REH/13], and [Mss/3/S/38]

Eneas Rounds Yard Cemetery (1848)
Anawan St., near Tremont St.
+ Susan F. Salisbury, *Southern Massachusetts Cemetery Collection* - Volume 2 (Bowie, Md., Heritage Books, 1996)
[F63/S25/1995/also Loan]
+ NEHGS [MS70/REH/12], and
[MS70/REH/13]

Simmons Family Cemetery (1795)
Cedar St.

Stevens Corner Cemetery (aka) Hix Cemetery (1759)
Anawan St.
+ Susan F. Salisbury, *Southern Massachusetts Cemetery Collection* - Volume 2 (Bowie, Md., Heritage Books, 1996)
[F63/S25/1995/also Loan]

+ NEHGS [MS70/REH/12], and [MS70/REH/13]

Village Cemetery (1774)
Bay State Rd.
+ Susan F. Salisbury, *Southern Massachusetts Cemetery Collection* - Volume 2 (Bowie, Md., Heritage Books, 1996) [F63/S25/1995/also Loan]

Jonathan Wheeler Cemetery (1832)
Wheeler St. near Summer St.
+ Susan F. Salisbury, *Southern Massachusetts Cemetery Collection* - Volume 2 (Bowie, Md., Heritage Books, 1996) [F63/S25/1995/also Loan]

Samuel T. Wheeler Family Cemetery (1832)
Pleasant St., across from the James Horton Family Cemetery.
+ Susan F. Salisbury, *Southern Massachusetts Cemetery Collection*, Volume 2 (Bowie, Md., Heritage Books, 1996) [F63/S25/1995/also Loan]
+ NEHGS [MS70/REH/12], and [MS70/REH/13]

Shubael Wheeler Family Cemetery (aka) Horton Cemetery (19th century)
Chestnut St.
+ Susan F. Salisbury, *Southern Massachusetts Cemetery Collection* - Volume 2 (Bowie, Md., Heritage Books, 1996) [F63/S25/1995/also Loan]
+ NEHGS [MS70/REH/12], and [MS70/REH/13]

Tamerline Wheeler Horton Family Cemetery Site
All burials were believed moved to the Village Cemetery.
+ Gravestone inscriptions [Mss/A/313]

REVERE (1846)
from Chelsea
City Hall, 281 Broadway St., Revere, Mass. 02151, Tel: (781)-286-8110.

Unitarian Church Tomb Site (1805)
Eustis Street, demolished in 1912. Burial removed to Rumney Marsh Burying Ground.
+ Benjamin Shurtleff, *The History of the town of Revere.* (Boston, Mass., Barker Press, 1938) [F74/R4/55/1938/also Loan]

Rumney Marsh Burying Ground (1693)
Butler St.
+ Benjamin Shurtleff, *The History of the town of Revere.* (Boston, Mass., Barker Press, 1938) [F74/R4/55/1938/also Loan] p. 438-62.
+ J.W.T., "Inscriptions in Chelsea Old Burial-Ground." *NEHGR*, 31:117.
+ NEHGS [MS70/REV/1]

Capt. James Stoners Family Tomb Site (1795)
Payson St., demolished in 1910.
+ Benjamin Shurtleff, *The History of the town of Revere.* (Boston, Mass., Barker Press, 1938) [F74/R4/55/1938/also Loan], p. 462.

RICHMOND (1765)
Town Hall, 1529 State Rd., Richmond, Mass. 01254, Tel: (413)-698-3315

Burghardt Family Cemetery (1816)
1987 State Rd., Rte. 41
+ [G.R. 1] *Vital Records of Richmond, Massachusetts to the year 1850* (1913).
+ NEHGS [MS70/RIC/1]

Center Cemetery (1766)
across from 1188 State Rd., Rte. 41

+ [G.R. 2] *Vital Records of Richmond, Massachusetts to the year 1850* (1913).
+ NEHGS [MS70/RIC/1]

Cole Cemetery (1838)
off Summit Rd.
+ [G.R. 5] *Vital Records of Richmond, Massachusetts to the year 1850* (1913).

Cone Hill Cemetery (aka) Southwest Cemetery (1782)
across from 337 Cone Hill Rd.
+ [G.R. 3] *Vital Records of Richmond, Massachusetts to the year 1850* (1913).
+ NEHGS [MS70/RIC/1]

North Cemetery (1796)
across from 81-123 State Rd.., Rte. 41
+ [G.R. 7] *Vital Records of Richmond, Massachusetts to the year 1850* (1913).

Northeast–Lindsay Cemetery (1771)
next to 45 Cemetery Rd.
+ [G.R. 4] *Vital Records of Richmond, Massachusetts to the year 1850* (1913).
+ NEHGS [MS70/RIC/1]
+ NSDAR [G.R.C./S1/v.94]

Deacon Silas Parmalee Gravesite (1776)
526 State Rd., Rte. 41

West Road Cemetery
1040 West Rd.

Inscription in a field belonging to Mr. Coleman, on the Pittsfield road
+ [G.R. 6] *Vital Records of Richmond, Massachusetts to the year 1850* (1913).

ROCHESTER (1686)
Town Hall, One Constitution Way, Rochester, Mass. 02770, Tel: (508)-763-3866

Ashley Cemetery (1788)
North Ave., near Freetown line.
+ [G.R. 9] *Vital Records of Rochester, Massachusetts to the year 1850* (1914).
+ Charles M. Thatcher, *Old Cemeteries of Southeastern Massachusetts*.(Middleborough, Mass., Middleborough Public Library,1995) [F63/T53/1995/also Loan]
+ NEHGS [MS70/ROC/10]

Braley Family Cemetery (1838)
between 135 and 155 Featherbed Ln.

Ellis Family Burying Ground (1840)
in the woods behind 69 Mattapoisett Rd.
+ [G.R. 8] *Vital Records of Rochester, Massachusetts to the year 1850* (1914).
+ NEHGS [MS70/ROC/10]

Hillside Cemetery (aka) East Rochester Cemetery (1824)
off High St.
+ [G.R. 3] *Vital Records of Rochester, Massachusetts to the year 1850* (1914).
+ [G.R. 7 *Vital Records of Rochester, Massachusetts to the year 1850* (1914).
+ NEHGS [MS70/ROC/10]

North Rochester Cemetery (aka) Central Cemetery
North Ave., opposite Benson Rd., North Rochester
+ [G.R. 5] *Vital Records of Rochester, Massachusetts to the year 1850* (1914).
+ Charles M. Thatcher, *Old Cemeteries of Southeastern Massachusetts*.(Middleborough, Mass., Middleborough Public Library,1995) [F63/T53/1995/also Loan]
+ NEHGS [MS70/ROC/10]

Old Parish Cemetery
opposite 305 Braley Hill Rd., North Rochester
+ [G.R. 4] *Vital Records of Rochester, Massachusetts to the year 1850* (1914).

+ NEHGS [MS70/ROC/10]
+ NSDAR [MASS
COUNTIES/PLYMOUTH/ROCHES
TER/RYD]

Rochester First Parish Cemetery (1701)
enter on Dexter's Ln., Rochester Center
+ [G.R. 1] *Vital Records of Rochester, Massachusetts to the year 1850* (1914).
+ NEHGS [Mss/SG/LIN/5/18]

Sherman Cemetery
Pine St., Long Plain, opposite Rochester Memorial School
+ [G.R. 7] *Vital Records of Rochester, Massachusetts to the year 1850* (1914).
+ Charles M. Thatcher, *Old Cemeteries of Southeastern Massachusetts.*(Middleborough, Mass., Middleborough Public Library,1995) [F63/T53/1995/also Loan]
+ NEHGS [MS70/ROC/10]

Union Cemetery
opposite 422 Walnut Plain Rd.
+ [G.R. 2] *Vital Records of Rochester, Massachusetts to the year 1850* (1914).
+ Charles M. Thatcher, *Old Cemeteries of Southeastern Massachusetts.*(Middleborough, Mass., Middleborough Public Library,1995) [F63/T53/1995/also Loan]
+ NEHGS [MS70/ROC/10]

Woodside Cemetery (aka) Pierceville Cemetery (1828)
County Rd., next to the Congregational Church
+ [G.R. 10] *Vital Records of Rochester, Massachusetts to the year 1850* (1914).
+ Charles M. Thatcher, *Old Cemeteries of Southeastern Massachusetts.*(Middleborough, Mass., Middleborough Public Library,1995) [F63/T53/1995/also Loan]

ROCKLAND (1874)
from Abington
Town Hall, 242 Union St., Rockland, Mass. 02370, Tel: (781)-871-1892

Beal Family Cemetery (18th century)
near 417 Webster St., near East Water Sts.
+ [G.R. 8] *Vital Records of Abington, Massachusetts to the year 1850* (1912).
+ NEHGS [MS70/ABI/3], and [Mss/A/352]

Nat Beal Cemetery
near 354 Webster St.

Ellis Family Burying Ground (1778)
opposite 542 Summer St.
+ NEHGS [Mss/A/352]

Holy Family Catholic Cemetery (1907)
116 Centre Ave.
Tel: Holy Family Rectory, 403 Union St., Rockland, Mass. (781)-878-2306

Jenkins Family Burying Ground
Summer and Concord Sts.

Lane Family Cemetery
Liberty and East Water Sts.
+ [G.R. 6] *Vital Records of Abington, Massachusetts to the year 1850* (1912).
+ NEHGS [MS70/ABI/3], and [Mss/A/352]

Maplewood Cemetery (1746)
Webster St., near Hanover town line.
+ [G.R. 2] *Vital Records of Abington, Massachusetts to the year 1850* (1912).
+ NEHGS [MS70/ABI/3], and [Mss/A/352]

Mount Pleasant Cemetery (1848)
Liberty St., across from the Old Town Cemetery.

+ [G.R. 9] *Vital Records of Abington, Massachusetts to the year 1850* (1912).
+ NEHGS [MS70/ABI/3], and [Mss/A/352]

Old Town Cemetery (aka) Liberty Street Cemetery (1770)

Liberty St., across from Mount Pleasant Cemetery.
+ [G.R. 5] *Vital Records of Abington, Massachusetts to the year 1850* (1912).
+ NEHGS [MS70/ABI/3]

St. Patrick's Cemetery (1848)

125 Central St.
Tel: St. Bridget's Rectory, 455 Plymouth St., Rockland, Mass. (617)-878-0900

Small Pox Cemetery

Beech Hill, Beech St.
"*Stones on north side of Beech Hill, Rockland, said to have been victims of small pox.*"
+ [G.R. 15] *Vital Records of Abington, Massachusetts to the year 1850* (1912).
+ NEHGS [Mss/A/352]

Spring Lake Cemetery (aka) Samuel Reed Cemetery (1804)

near Reed's Pond
+ [G.R. 4] *Vital Records of Abington, Massachusetts to the year 1850* (1912).
+ NEHGS [Mss/A/352]

Spring Street Cemetery (aka) Evergreen Cemetery (aka) Abiah Reed Cemetery (1834)

Spring St.
+ [G.R. 3] *Vital Records of Abington, Massachusetts to the year 1850* (1912).
+ NEHGS [MS70/ABI/3] Mount Vernon; Maplewood, Main St.; Abiah Reed, Springfield St. + NEHGS [Mss/A/352]

Stetson Family Burying Ground

Market St., near Hanover town line.

Stoddard Family Burying Ground

near 133 Spring St.

Torrey Tomb

Market and Liberty Sts.

Wilkes Cemetery (1830)

+ [G.R. 7] *Vital Records of Abington, Massachusetts to the year 1850* (1912).
+ NEHGS [MS70/ABI/3], and [Mss/A/352]

ROCKPORT (1840)
from Gloucester

Town Hall, 34 Broadway St., Rockport, Mass. 01966, Tel: (978)-546-6894
Cemetery Department, 34 Broadway St., Rockport, Ma. 01966 Tel: (978)-546-3525

Beech Grove Cemetery (1856)

Pleasant St.
+ [G.R. 2] *Vital Records of Rockport, Massachusetts to the year 1850* (1924).

Locust Grove–Folly Cove Cemetery (1811)

1201 Washington St.
+ [G.R. 3] *Vital Records of Rockport, Massachusetts to the year 1850* (1924).
+ [G.R. 14] *Vital Records of Gloucester, Massachusetts to the year 1850* (1924).

Old Parish Cemetery (aka) Sandy Bay Cemetery (1754)

10 ½ Beach St.
+ [G.R. 1] *Vital Records of Rockport, Massachusetts to the year 1850* (1924).

Union Cemetery (18th century)

Union Ln.

ROWE (1785)
Town Hall, 321 Zoar Rd., Rowe, Mass. 01367, Tel: (413)-339-5520

Cressy Cemetery (1828)
off Tunnel Rd.
+ NEHGS [F74/R86/L4] Typescript in Mss, and [Corbin Collection]
+ NSDAR [G.R.C./S1/v. 341]

East Cemetery
Cyrus Stage Rd.
+ NEHGS [F74/R86/L4] Typescript in Mss, and [Corbin Collection]
+ NSDAR [G.R.C./S1/v. 341]

North Cemetery
Ford Hill Rd.
+ NEHGS [F74/R86/L4] Typescript in Mss, and [Corbin Collection]
+ NSDAR [G.R.C./S1/v. 341]

West Cemetery
Hazelton Rd.
+ NEHGS [F74/R86/L4] Typescript in Mss, and [Corbin Collection]
+ NSDAR [G.R.C./S1/v. 341]

ROWLEY (1639)
Town Hall, 139 Main St., Route 1A, Rowley, Mass. 01969, Tel: (978)-948-2081

Chaplin–Clark Homestead Cemetery (1730)
Rte. 133 West, Bradford St., field stone markers.

Hutt Cemetery Site (1971)
private cemetery at 541 Haverhill St., body removed to Canada.

Linebrook Burial Ground (1747)
Meeting House and Leslie Rds.

Metcalf Rock Pasture Burial Ground (aka) Smallpox Cemetery (1775)
Haverhill St.

Old Burying Ground (1639)
Main St., next to Rowley Town Hall
+ [G.R. 1] *Vital Records of Rowley, Massachusetts to the year 1850* (1928).
+ George B. Blodgette, *Inscriptions from the Old Cemetery in Rowley, Mass.* (Salem, Mass.: The Salem Press Publishing and Printing Co., 1893) [F74/R88/R61/1893] and [MS/ROW/328].
+ NEHGS [MS70/ROW/10]

ROYALSTON (1765)
Town Hall, The Common, Royalston, Mass. 01368, Tel: (978)-249-0493

Jonas Alliene Cemetery (1982)
Winchendon Rd., off Woods and Brown Rds.

Butterworth Cemetery (1838)
Butterworth Rd., west of Athol-Richmond Rd.
Gales and Gates Cemetery (1786)
Bliss Hill Rd., south of Warwich Rd.

Hillside Cemetery (1795)
Main St. Rte. 68, South Royalston

Lawrence Brook Cemetery (1837)
south of Royalston Common on Rte. 68.

Maple Cemetery (1856)
Athol-Royalston Rd., south of Royalston Common.

Newton Cemetery (1794)
Athol-Richmond Rd. (Rte. 32), ½ miles south of Richmond, N.H. line.

Old Center Cemetery (1753)
Athol-Royalston Rd., south of Royalston Common

Riverside Cemetery (1831)
River Rd., South Royalston

Under the Hill Cemetery (1777)
Warwick Rd. (Rte. 68)

RUSSELL (1792)
from Montgomery and Westfield
Town Hall, Main St., Russell, Mass. 01071, Tel: (413)-862-3265
Cemetery Department, Municipal Office, 200 Main St., Russell, Ma 01071

Birch Hill Cemetery (aka) Russell Pond Cemetery (1793)
Birch Hill Rd.
+ NEHGS [MS70/RUS/1]

Abraham Bradley Cemetery
Rte. 2
+ NEHGS [MS70/RUS/2]

Crescent Mills Cemetery (1831)
1172 Huntington Rd.
+ NEHGS [MS70/RUS/2]

Hazard Pond Cemetery
+ NEHGS [MS70/RUS/2]

Palmer Cemetery (1804)
Tekoa Ave.
+ NEHGS [MS70/RUS/2]

Russell Center Cemetery (1794)
Rte. 20
+ NEHGS [MS70/RUS/2]

RUTLAND (1714)
Town Hall, 250 Main St., Rutland, Mass. 01543, Tel: (508)-886-4104

Chanock Hill Road Cemetery
Chanock Hill Rd.

Goose Hill Cemetery
Old Boston Highway

Old Rutland Cemetery (1717)
Main St.
+ David Everett Phillips, *Monumental Inscriptions in the Old Cemetery at Rutland, Worcester, County, Mass., "Laid out" June 7, 1717.* (Columbus, Oh: The "Old Northwest" Genealogical Society, 1902) [F74/R97/P5/1902]
+ Edward H. Duane, *The Old Burial Ground, Rutland, Mass. 1717-1888.* (Rutland, Mass.: The Rutland Historical Society, 1980) [F74/R97/D8]

Rural Cemetery of Rutland (1848)
Main St.

West Rutland Cemetery (19th century)
Rte. 122, near Long Pond

SALEM (1630)
City Hall, 93 Washington St., Salem, Mass. 01970, Tel: (978)745-9595

Broad Street Cemetery (1655)
5 Broad St.
Tel: (978)-745-0195
+ [G.R. 7]*Vital Records of Salem, Massachusetts to the year 1850* (1916).
+ NEHGS [F74/S1/D21] Typescript in Mss

Charter Street Cemetery (1637)
51 Charter St.
+ [G.R. 1]*Vital Records of Salem, Massachusetts to the year 1850* (1916).
+ "Inscriptions from the Burying Ground in Salem, Mass.", *NEHGR* 3:128-132, 3:276-278.

Friends Cemetery (1718)
396 ½ Essex St.
+ [G.R. 11]*Vital Records of Salem,*
Massachusetts to the year 1850 (1916).

Greenlawn Cemetery (1807)
57 Orne St
Tel: (978)-745-0195
+ [G.R. 10]*Vital Records of Salem,*
Massachusetts to the year 1850 (1916).

Harmony Grove Cemetery (1840)
30 Grove Street
Tel: (978)-744-0554
+ [G.R. 9]*Vital Records of Salem,*
Massachusetts to the year 1850 (1916).
+ *Harmony Grove Cemetery, Salem, Mass.*
(Salem, Mass.: G.M. Whipple & A.A.
Smith, 1866) [F74/S1/H24/1866]

Howard Street Cemetery (1801)
29 Howard St.
+ [G.R. 8]*Vital Records of Salem,*
Massachusetts to the year 1850 (1916).
+ NEHGS [MS70/SAL/10]

St. Mary's Cemetery (1845)
226 North St.
+ [G.R. 12]*Vital Records of Salem,*
Massachusetts to the year 1850 (1916).
Tel: Archives of the Archdiocese of
Boston, 2121 Commonwealth Ave.,
Brighton, Mass. 02135, (617)-254-0100.

St. Peter's Cemetery
22-24 St. Peter St.

SALISBURY (1639)
Town Hall, 5 Beach Rd., Salisbury, Mass.
01952, Tel: (978)-462-7591

Belleview Cemetery
30 Seabrook Rd.

Long Hill Cemetery (ca. 1856)
Beach Rd.

Maplewood Cemetery (1639)
Ferry Rd.

**Newburyport Hebrew Cemetery
(1920)**
Lafayette Rd.

Old Burying Ground (1662)
Beach and Ferry Sts.

P.A. True Farm Cemetery
Lafayette Rd.

SANDISFIELD (1762)
Town Hall, 3 Silverbrook Rd.,
Sandisfield, Mass. 01255, Tel: (413)-258-
4711

Beech Plain Cemetery (1775)
Beech Plain Rd.
+ NEHGS [MS70/SAN/15]
+ NSDAR [G.R.C./S1/v. 184]

**Center Cemetery (aka) Montville
Cemetery (1758)**
Sandisfield Rd., Rte. 57
+ Charles D. Townsend, *Border Town
Cemeteries of Massachusetts.* (West Hartford,
Ct., Chedwato Service, 1953)
[F63/T69/1953/also Loan]
+ NEHGS [MS70/SAN/15]

Clam River Cemetery
+ NEHGS [MS70/SAN/18]
+ NSDAR [G.R.C./S1/v. 184]

Crescent Hill Cemetery
+ NEHGS [MS70/SAN/15]

**Dubois Family Cemetery Site (aka)
River Cemetery Site**
off Rose Rd. This cemetery site is now
underwater, burials were moved to the
Sandisfield Cemetery.
+ NEHGS [F74/R86/L4] Typescript in
Mss

Roberts Road Cemetery (1797)
Roberts Rd.

Joshua Smith Gravesite (1793)
Dodd Rd.

South Sandisfield Cemetery (1836)
Sandy Brook Rd.
+ NEHGS [MS70/SAN/15], and
[MS70/SAN/18]
+ NSDAR [G.R.C./S1/v. 184]

Twining Family Cemetery (19th century)
off West St.

West New Boston Cemetery (1831)
Rte. 57, West St.
+ NEHGS [MS70/SAN/15], and
[MS70/SAN/18]
+ NSDAR [G.R.C./S1/v. 184]

SANDWICH (1638)
Town Hall, 145 Main St., Sandwich,
Mass. 02563, Tel: (508)-888-0340

Bay View Cemetery (1864)
Main St.
+ *Vital Records of Sandwich, Massachusetts to the year 1850* (1996).

Cedarville Cemetery (1805)
Rte. 6A
+ *Vital Records of Sandwich, Massachusetts to the year 1850* (1996).

Forestdale Cemetery (1826)
Falmouth Rd.
+ *Vital Records of Sandwich, Massachusetts to the year 1850* (1996).

Freeman Cemetery (1806)
Grove St.
+ *Vital Records of Sandwich, Massachusetts to the year 1850* (1996).

Mount Hope Cemetery (1775)
Rte. 6A
+ *Vital Records of Sandwich, Massachusetts to the year 1850* (1996).

New Town Cemetery (1977)
Rte. 130

Old Quaker Cemetery (ca. 1670s)
end Quaker Rd. [no stones]

Old Town Cemetery (1683)
Grove St.
+ NEHGS [MS70/SAN/10], and
[Mss/280].
+ NSDAR [G.R.C./S1/v.128]

Percival–Hablin Family Cemetery (1831)
Farmersville Rd.

Poor Farm Cemetery (1823)
Crowell and Charles Sts. [no stones]

Quaker Cemetery (1694)
behind Quaker Meetinghouse
+ *Vital Records of Sandwich, Massachusetts to the year 1850* (1996).

Saddle and Pillion Cemetery (1676)
at the end of Wilson Rd.

St. Peters Cemetery (1865)
Grove and Pine Sts.
+ *Vital Records of Sandwich, Massachusetts to the year 1850* (1996).

South Sandwich Cemetery (1811)
Boardley St.

Spring Hill Cemetery (1812)
Rte. 6A
+ *Vital Records of Sandwich, Massachusetts to the year 1850* (1996).

Tobey Cemetery (ca. 1788)
Quaker Meetinghouse Rd.

+ *Vital Records of Sandwich, Massachusetts to the year 1850* (1996).

Joe Wilson Family Cemetery (1886)
off Rte. 130

Wakeby–Goodspeed Family Cemetery (1803)
Cotuit Rd.
+ *Vital Records of Sandwich, Massachusetts to the year 1850* (1996).

SAUGUS (1815)
from Lynn
Town Hall, 298 Central St., Saugus, Mass. 01906, Tel: (781)-231-4101

First Parish Cemetery (aka) Center Cemetery (1741)
Main St. at Monument Square
+ [G.R. 1] *Vital Records of Saugus, Massachusetts to the year 1850* (1907).
+ [G.R. 7] *Vital Records of Lynn, Massachusetts to the year 1850* (1905).
+ NEHGS [MS70/SAU/10]
+ NSDAR [G.R.C./S1/v.177]

Riverside Cemetery (1844)
164 Winter St.
Tel: (781)-231-4170
+ [G.R. 2] *Vital Records of Saugus, Massachusetts to the year 1850* (1907).

SAVOY (1797)
Town Hall, 720 Main Rd., Savoy, Mass. 01256, Tel: (413)-743-4290

Babbit Cemetery (1815)
Bannis Rd.
+ NEHGS [MS70/SAV/1], and [Corbin Collection]

Center Burying Ground
Savoy Center

+ NEHGS [MS70/SAV/1], and [Corbin Collection]

Comfort Bates Lot Cemetery (1811)
Old Cross Path
+ NEHGS [F74/S2/C6] Typescript in Mss, and [Corbin Collection]

Dexter B. Bates Cemetery (1800)
Windsor Rd.
+ NEHGS [MS70/SAV/1], [F74/S2/C6] Typescript in Mss, and [Corbin Collection]

Carter–Burnett Pond Cemetery (1835)
New State Rd.
+ NEHGS [F74/S2/C6] Typescript in Mss, and [Corbin Collection]

Deming Family Burial Ground (1816)
1130 Main Rd., Rte. 116
+ NEHGS [MS70/SAV/1], [F74/S2/C6] Typescript in Mss, and [Corbin Collection]

Estes Burial Ground (1817)
Tannery Rd., State Forest
+ NEHGS [MS70/SAV/1], [F74/S2/C6] Typescript in Mss, and [Corbin Collection]

Center Hathaway Burial Ground (1814)
Adams Rd.
+ NEHGS [MS70/SAV/1], [F74/S2/C6] Typescript in Mss, and [Corbin Collection]

Ingraham Cemetery (1798)
Rte. 116, Loop Rd., near Chapel Rd.
+ NEHGS [MS70/SAV/1], [F74/S2/C6] Typescript in Mss, and [Corbin Collection]

Millard Burial Ground (1834)
off Rte. 116, near Plainfield town line.
+ NEHGS [MS70/SAV/1],
[F74/S2/C6] Typescript in Mss, and
[Corbin Collection]

Miller Cemetery (1827)
Adams Rd., near Center Rd., Savoy
Center
+ NEHGS [MS70/SAV/1],
[F74/S2/C6] Typescript in Mss, and
[Corbin Collection]

New State Cemetery (1809)
New State Rd
+ NEHGS [MS70/SAV/1],
[F74/S2/C6] Typescript in Mss, and
[Corbin Collection]

Remington Family Lot (1848)
Loop Rd. near Rte. 116
+ NEHGS [MS70/SAV/1],
[F74/S2/C6] Typescript in Mss, and
[Corbin Collection]

**Second Hathaway Burial Ground
(1854)**
off Rte. 116
+ NEHGS [F74/S2/C6] Typescript in
Mss

**Shaker Cemetery (aka) Dunham
Burying Ground (1818)**
Lewis Hill Trail, State Forest

**Spruce Corner Cemetery (aka) Brier
Cemetery (1802)**
Barner Rd., Brier
+ NEHGS [F74/S2/C6] Typescript in
Mss, and [Corbin Collection]

Staples Cemetery (1826)
off Brown Rd. near Tomb Cemetery
+ NEHGS [F74/S2/C6] Typescript in
Mss, and [Corbin Collection]

Prince Starkes Grave Lot (1862)
Loop Rd., near Ingraham Cemetery
+ NEHGS [MS70/SAV/1],
[F74/S2/C6] Typescript in Mss, and
[Corbin Collection]

**The Tomb Cemetery (aka) Cherry
Hill Cemetery (1815)**
Rte. 116, Main Rd.
+ NEHGS [MS70/SAV/1],
[F74/S2/C6] Typescript in Mss, and
[Corbin Collection]

Tower Cemetery (1851)
Bannis Rd.
+ NEHGS [F74/S2/C6] Typescript in
Mss, and [Corbin Collection]

Turner Cemetery (1843)
Adams Rd., Savoy Center
+ NEHGS [MS70/SAV/1],
[F74/S2/C6] Typescript in Mss, and
[Corbin Collection]
+ Walter E. Corbin, *Tombstone inscriptions
of the town of Savoy, Berkshire County,
Massachusetts.* [F74/S2/C6]

Dunham Burying Ground
+ NEHGS [MS70/SAV/1],
[F74/S2/C6] Typescript in Mss, and
[Corbin Collection]

SCITUATE (1633)
Town Hall, 600 Chief Justice Cushing
Way, Scituate, Mass. 02066, Tel: (781)-
545-8473

Clapp Burying Ground (1774)
Union St., Greenbush
+ [G.R. 12]*Vital Records of Scituate,
Massachusetts to the year 1850* (1909).

**Cudworth Cemetery (aka) Veterans
Cemetery (1823)**
Cudworth Rd., Scituate Centre, off
Country Way

+ [G.R. 9]*Vital Records of Scituate,
Massachusetts to the year 1850* (1909).

Judge Cushing's Cemetery (1757)
off Rte. 3, Neal Gate St., Greenbush
+ [G.R. 3]*Vital Records of Scituate,
Massachusetts to the year 1850* (1909).
+ Charles M. Thatcher, *Old Cemeteries of
Southeastern Massachusetts.* (Middlebor-
ough, Mass., Middleborough Public
Library, 1995) [F63/T53/1995/also
Loan]

Fairview Cemetery (1800)
Fairview Ave., Scituate Centre
+ [G.R. 7]*Vital Records of Scituate,
Massachusetts to the year 1850* (1909).
+ Charles M. Thatcher, *Old Cemeteries of
Southeastern Massachusetts.* (Middleborough,
Mass., Middleborough Public Library,
1995) [F63/T53/1995/also Loan]

Groveland Cemetery (1720)
Mann Lot Rd., North Scituate
+ [G.R. 2]*Vital Records of Scituate,
Massachusetts to the year 1850* (1909).
+ Charles M. Thatcher, *Old Cemeteries of
Southeastern Massachusetts.*(Middleborough,
Mass., Middleborough Public Library,
1995) [F63/T53/1995/also Loan]

Hatch Burying Ground (1796)
off Rte. 3A, Greenbush
+ [G.R. 4]*Vital Records of Scituate,
Massachusetts to the year 1850* (1909).
+ Charles M. Thatcher, *Old Cemeteries of
Southeastern Massachusetts.*(Middleborough,
Mass., Middleborough Public Library,
1995) [F63/T53/1995/also Loan]
+ NEHGS [F74/A89/C3/1928]
Typescript in Mss

James–Clapp Family Burying Ground (19th century)
off the Driftway, Greenbush
+ [G.R. 5]*Vital Records of Scituate,
Massachusetts to the year 1850* (1909).

Kilborn Merritt Cemetery (1816)
Clapp Rd., North Scituate
+ [G.R. 11]*Vital Records of Scituate,
Massachusetts to the year 1850* (1909).

Men of Kent Cemetery (1624)
Meetinghouse Ln.
+ [G.R. 1]*Vital Records of Scituate,
Massachusetts to the year 1850* (1909).
+ NEHGS [MS70/SCI/1]

Mount Hope Cemetery (1786)
Clapp Rd., North Scituate
Tel: (617)-545-1851
+ [G.R. 8]*Vital Records of Scituate,
Massachusetts to the year 1850* (1909).

New St. Mary's Cemetery (1880)
Stockbridge St.

Old St. Mary's Cemetery
off Stockbridge Rd, a part of Union
Cemetery
+ [G.R. 10]*Vital Records of Scituate,
Massachusetts to the year 1850* (1909).

Union Cemetery
off Stockbridge Rd., Scituate Harbor
+ [G.R. 6]*Vital Records of Scituate,
Massachusetts to the year 1850* (1909).
+ Charles M. Thatcher, *Old Cemeteries of
Southeastern Massachusetts.*(Middleborough,
Mass., Middleborough Public Library,
1995) [F63/T53/1995/also Loan]

SEEKONK (1812)
from Rehoboth
Town Hall, 100 Peck St., Seekonk, Mass.
02771, Tel: (508)-336-2920

Church of the Holy Ghost Cemetery (1916)
Dexter St.

William Handy Gravesite (1845)
behind 1495 Fall River Ave.

Munroe Cemetery (1758)
Lake and Lincoln Sts.

Polish Cemetery
West Ave.

Town of Seekonk Cemetery (1880)
Newman Ave. and Water St.

SHARON (1765)
from Stoughton
Town Hall, 90 South Main St., Sharon,
Mass. 02067, Tel: (781)-784-1505
Cemetery Department, 217 South Main
St., Sharon, Mass. (781)-784-1525

Chestnut Tree Burial Ground (1733)
Richards and Canton Sts.
+ NEHGS [MS70/SHA/1]

**Capt. Friend Drake Family Burial
Ground (1837)**
Mountain St.
+ NEHGS [MS70/SHA/1], and
[F74/S886/J6] Typescript in Mss

**George Drake Family Burial
Ground (1810)**
Mansfield St.
+ NEHGS [MS70/SHA/1]

Eastside Cemetery
Bay Rd.

Esty Family Burial Ground (1804)
East Foxboro St.
+ NEHGS [MS70/SHA/1]

Oliver Lothrop Grave Site (1823)
Moose Hill St.
+ NEHGS [MS70/SHA/1]

Moose Hill Burial Ground (1775)
Walpole and Moose Hill Sts.
+ NEHGS [MS70/SHA/1]

Rock Ridge Cemetery (1760)
East and Mountain Sts.
+ NEHGS [MS70/SHA/1]

**Sharon Memorial Park–Jewish
Cemetery (1950)**
Dedham and Walpole Sts.
Tel: (781)-828-7216

Tisdale Cemetery (1724)
Mountain St.
+ NEHGS [MS70/SHA/1]

**Village Tomb Site (aka) Curtis
Family Tomb Site.**
All burials moved to the Chestnut Tree
Burial Ground.
+ NEHGS [MS70/SHA/1]

West–Billings Burial Ground (1717)
South Main St., near the Foxboro town
line.
+ NEHGS [MS70/SHA/1]

SHEFFIELD (1733)
Town Hall, 21 Depot Sq., Sheffield,
Mass. 01257, Tel: (413)-229-8752

**Ashley Falls Cemetery (aka) Sackett
Cemetery (1840)**
Clayton Rd., between East Main St. and
Rte. 7
+ NEHGS [MS70/SHE/2]

**Barnard Cemetery (aka) South
Cemetery (1756)**
South Main St., across from Root Lane
+ NEHGS [MS70/SHE/1], and
[MS70/SHE/2]

**Bow Wow Cemetery (aka) Pine
Grove Cemetery and Curtiss
Cemetery (1758)**
Bow Wow Rd.
+ NEHGS [MS70/SHE/1]

Brush Hill Cemetery (aka) Clark Cemetery (1813)
Brush Hill Rd.

Brush Hill Road Private Cemetery (1985)
Brush Hill Rd., next to the Brush Hill Cemetery

Cande–Sage Family Cemetery (1776)
in the woods off Under Mountain Rd., Rte. 41. Near the Connecticut state line.
+ NEHGS [MS70/SHE/2]

Center Cemetery (1816)
Berkshire School Rd., between Salisbury Rd. and South Main St.
+ NEHGS [MS70/SHE/2]

Churchill Cemetery (1813)
Salisbury Rd.
+ NEHGS [MS70/SHE/2]

Hewins Street Cemetery (1774)
Hewins St., near Hulett Rd.
+ NEHGS [MS70/SHE/2]

Huggins Cemetery (aka) Home Road Cemetery (1814)
Home Rd.

Methodist Cemetery (aka) Old Ashley Falls Cemetery (1839)
behind the church in Ashley Falls section of town.

Our Lady of the Valley Cemetery (1874)
Salisbury Rd., near Barnum St.

Sheffield Plain Cemetery (aka) Noble Cemetery (1760)
south end of Sheffield Plain, Rte. 7, near the Shears Cemetery
+ NEHGS [MS70/SHE/1]

Shears Cemetery (aka) Kellogg Cemetery (1819)
Rte. 7, near Covered Bridge Ln.
+ NEHGS [MS70/SHE/2]

Spoor Cemetery (1814)
Rte. 41 near the Berkshire School
+ NEHGS [MS70/SHE/2]

John Spoor Smallpox Gravesite (1776)
on the old road between Great Barrington and Sheffield.

Zebulon Stevens Gravesite (1776)
buried on the West road to Sheffield

Ward Burial Ground (1757)
Barnum Rd., near Foley Rd.
+ NEHGS [MS70/SHE/2]

SHELBURNE (1768)
from Deerfield
Town Hall, 51 Bridge St., Shelburne, Mass. 01370, Tel: (413)-625-0301

Arms Cemetery (1854)
Shelburne Falls
+ [G.R. 5] *Vital Records of Shelburne, Massachusetts to the year 1850* (1931).

Center Cemetery (1774)
Shelburne Center
Tel: (413)-625-9595
+ [G.R. 3] *Vital Records of Shelburne, Massachusetts to the year 1850* (1931).

East Shelburne Cemetery
+ [G.R. 1] *Vital Records of Shelburne, Massachusetts to the year 1850* (1931).

Hill–Old North Cemetery
+ [G.R. 4] *Vital Records of Shelburne, Massachusetts to the year 1850* (1931).
+ NSDAR [G.R.C./S1/v. 360] only Revolutionary War soldiers

South Shelburne Cemetery (1813)
South Sherburne
+ [G.R. 2]*Vital Records of Shelburne, Massachusetts to the year 1850* (1931).

Private burying ground on boundary between Deerfield and Shelburne
+ [G.R. 6]*Vital Records of Shelburne, Massachusetts to the year 1850* (1931).

SHERBORN (1674)
Town Hall, 19 Washington St., Sherborn, Mass. 01770, Tel: (508)-651-7853

Children of Female Inmates of Framingham Prison Cemetery (1920s)
Perry St., next to Brush Hill Cemetery

Clara Barton–Framingham Prison Female Prisoner Cemetery (1950s)
Perry St., across from Brush Hill Cemetery

Brush Hill Cemetery (1785)
Perry St.
+ [G.R. 4]*Vital Records of Sherborn, Massachusetts to the year 1850* (1907).
+ NEHGS [MS70/SHE/40], and [MS70/SHE/41]

Central Cemetery (1686)
Main St., Rte. 16 and 27
+ NEHGS [MS70/SHE/40], [MS70/SHE/41], and [Mss/C/3040]

Farm Cemetery (1688)
Farm Rd., near Forest St.
+ [G.R. 8]*Vital Records of Sherborn, Massachusetts to the year 1850* (1907).
+ NEHGS [MS70/SHE/40], and [MS70/SHE/41]

New South Cemetery (1790)
South Main St., near Cedar Hill Rd.
South Sherborn
+ [G.R. 1]*Vital Records of Sherborn, Massachusetts to the year 1850* (1907).
+ NEHGS [MS70/SHE/40], and [MS70/SHE/41]

Old South Sherborn Cemetery (1655)
South Main St., Rte. 27 near Rte. 115
+ [G.R. 7]*Vital Records of Sherborn, Massachusetts to the year 1850* (1907).
+ NEHGS [MS70/SHE/40], and [MS70/SHE/41]

Pine Hill Cemetery (1852)
Cemetery Lane, on Rtes. 16 and 27
+ [G.R. 2]*Vital Records of Sherborn, Massachusetts to the year 1850* (1907).
+ NEHGS [MS70/SHE/41]

Plain Cemetery (1790)
Rte. 27, North Main St.
+ [G.R. 3]*Vital Records of Sherborn, Massachusetts to the year 1850* (1907).
+ NEHGS [MS70/SHE/40]

West Cemetery (1791)
Maple St. near Bear Hill Rd., West Sherborn
+ [G.R. 5]*Vital Records of Sherborn, Massachusetts to the year 1850* (1907).
+ NEHGS [MS70/SHE/40], and NEHGS [MS70/SHE/41]

SHIRLEY (1753)
from Groton
Town Hall, Municipal Building, 7 off Hospital Rd., Shirley, Mass. 01464, Tel: (978)-425-2610

Shirley Centre Cemetery (1754)
cor Horse Pond and Brown Rds.
+ [G.R. 1] *Vital Records of Shirley, Massachusetts to the year 1850* (1918).

+ Ethel Standwood Bolton,
"Inscriptions from the Cemetery at
Shirley Centre, Mass., from 1754 to
1850." *NEHGR* 57:68-75, 200-207.

St. Anthony Cemetery (1907)
Harvard Rd.
Tel: St. Anthony's Rectory, 14 Phoenix
St., Shirley, Mass. (508)-425-4588

Shirley Village Cemetery (1849)
Shaker Rd.
+ [G.R. 2] *Vital Records of Shirley,
Massachusetts to the year 1850* (1918).

French Cemetery
+ [G.R. 4] *Vital Records of Shirley,
Massachusetts to the year 1850* (1918).

SHREWSBURY (1720)
Town Hall, 100 Maple Ave., Shrewsbury,
Mass. 01545, Tel: (508)-841-8507

Mountain View Cemetery (1721)
Church Rd. and Boylston Sts.
Tel: (508)-842-8626

Grafton State Hospital (aka) Hillcrest Cemetery (1901)
Westborough Rd.

Hillside Cemetery (aka) for Worcester State Hospital Cemetery
Lake Street

Johnson Family Cemetery (18th century)
West Main St., near the corner of Old
Mill Rd.

St. Anne's Cemetery (19th century)
across from 130 Boston Worcester
Turnpike, Rte. 9
Tel: St. Anne's Rectory, 130 Boston
Worcester Tunpike, Shrewsbury, Mass.
(508)-757-5154

South Cemetery
Grove and Grafton Sts.

SHUTESBURY (1761)
Town Hall, One Cooleyville Rd.,
Shutesbury, Mass. 01072, Tel: (413)-259-
1204

Centre Cemetery
all burials were moved in 1938 to the
West Cemetery

Hamilton Family Cemetery Site
All burials were removed to Quabbin
Park Cemetery, Ware, Mass. 1938
+ NEHGS [MS/70/WAR/15], and
[Corbin Collection]

Luther Henry Tomb
now part of the West Cemetery

Jewish Community Association of Amherst Cemetery (1980's)
opposite 215 Leverett Rd.
Tel: Jewish Community Assoc. of
Amherst, 742 Main St., Shutesbury,
Mass. (413)-256-0160

Locks Pond Cemetery
Locks Pond Rd., opposite Lake Dr.
+ NEHGS [Corbin Collection]

Pratt's Corner Cemetery
Pratt's Corner and Sand Hill Rds.
+ NEHGS [Corbin Collection]

West Cemetery
158 Leverett Rd.
+ NEHGS [Corbin Collection], and
[Mss/3/A/9] for Revolutionary War
soldiers only.

SOMERSET (1790)
from Swansea
Town Hall, 140 Wood St., Somerset,
Mass. 02726, Tel: (508)-646-2818

David Anthony Cemetery (1796)
Lee's River Ave.

John Anthony Cemetery (1822)
Lee's River Ave.

Bourne Cemetery (1810)
sout of County St.

Bowers Cemetery (1750)
South St. and Riverside Ave.

Brayton Cemetery (1799)
Caroline Ave., west of Brayton Ave.

Buffington Cemetery
3671 County St.

Buffinton-Wilbur Cemetery (1741)
Lawton St., near Maple St.

Chaves-Dudley Cemetery
between Elm and County Sts.

Davis-Dudley Cemetery
between Elm and County Sts.

Deardon-Perry Cemetery
south of Old Colony Ave.

Eddy Cemetery
Pleasant St., south of Brown Simmons
Cemetery

Eddy Farm Cemetery
south of 4 Old Colony Ave.

Gibbs Cemetery (1804)
Buffinton St.

Hathaway-Chase Cemetery
south side of Marble St.

Lee Cemetery
off Cleveland St.

Lee Cemetery (1819)
east side of Lee's River Ave., south of
Rte. 6

Newhill Avenue Burial Ground
Newhill Ave.

Palmer Street Cemetery (1797)
Palmer St.

Perry-Deardon Cemetery (1730)
Simms St.

Pierce-Chace Cemetery (1728)
Marble St.

Purinton-Pierce Cemetery (1843)
County St., near Christian Church

Purinton-Weaver Cemetery (1809)
Arnold St.

St. Patrick's Cemetery (1886)
3340 County St.
Tel: St. Patrick's Rectory, 306 South St.,
Somerset, Mass. (508)-672-1523

Sherman Burial Ground
Lee's River Ave., near Lee's River

Brown Simmons Cemetery (1817)
Pleasant St., south of Sandy Point Rd.

Slade-Earl Cemetery (1723)
near Brightman St. Bridge
+ NEHGS [MS70/SOM/5]
+ NSDAR [G.R.C./1932/S1/v. 16]

Slade-Pierce Cemetery (1810)
Whetstone Hill, west of County St.

Slade Cemetery (1851)
O'Neill Rd.

Charles Slade Cemetery (1700)
south of Wilbur St., opposite Lee's River
Ave.

Edward Slade Cemetery (1864)
Old North St., east of Elm St.

Jonathan Slade Cemetery (1701)
Riverside Ave., near bridge

Nathan Slade Cemetery (1817)
east side of Prospect St.

William Slade Cemetery
Wilbur Ave.

Slade–Wilbur Cemetery (1810)
Whetstone Hill.

Slave Burial Ground
between Lee's River Ave., and Lees
River. Near Sherman Burial Ground

Society of Friends Cemetery (1830)
Prospect St.

SOMERVILLE (1842)
from Charlestown
City Hall, 93 Highland Ave., Somerville,
Mass. 02143, Tel: (617)-625-6600

New Veterans Cemetery (1948)
1327 Broadway St., Clarendon Hill

**Old Cemetery (aka) Milk Row
Cemetery (1804)**
420 Somerville Ave.
+ The Somerville Historical Society,
Historic Leaves Vol. VII (Somerville,
Mass., The Somerville Historical Society,
1909) [MS/SOM/101/7]
+ NSDAR [G.R.C./S1/v. 62]

SOUTH HADLEY (1753)
from Hadley
Town Hall, 116 Main St., South Hadley,
Mass. 01075, Tel: (413)-538-5023

Evergreen Cemetery (1868)
87 Hadley St.
+ NEHGS [Corbin Collection]
+ NSDAR [G.R.C./S1/v. 433]
Mater Dolorosa Cemetery (1892)
63 Maple St.

Notre Dame Cemetery
63 Lyman St.
Tel: Our Lady of Perpetual Help
Recotry, 271 Chestnut St., Holyoke
(413)-534-4407

**Old South Hadley Burial Ground
Site (1728)**
41 College St., all burials were moved to
the Evergreen Cemetery in 1902-3.
+ *The Old South Hadley Burial Ground*
1976, a conservation project coordinated
by Jessie Lie and supported by the South
Hadley Bicentennial Committee. (South
Hadley, Mass.: South Hadley Historical
Society, 1976) [F74/S735/S68/1976].
+ NEHGS [Corbin Collection]
+ NSDAR [G.R.C./S1/v. 433]

Precious Blood Cemetery (1874)
Willimansett St. and off Rte. 202, next to
the St. Rose Cemetery
Tel: Our Lady of Perpetual Help
Rectory, 271 Chestnut St., Holyoke
(413)-534-4407

John Preston Gravesite (1727)
behind the Gaylord Memorial Library,
College St.
last burial on the site of the Old South
Hadley Cemetery

St. Rose Cemetery (1884)
Rte. 202, next to Precious Blood
Cemetery

Tel: St. Patrick's Rectory, 30 Main St.,
South Hadley, Mass. (413)-532-2850

South Hadley Village Cemetery (1826)
South Main and Spring St., South Hadley
Falls
+ NEHGS [Corbin Collection]
+ NSDAR [G.R.C./S1/v. 433]

SOUTHAMPTON (1753)
from Northampton
Town Hall, 8 East St., Southampton,
Mass. 01073, Tel: (413)-527-8392

Gridley Family Cemetery (1835)
Main St., College Highway, near Clark St.
+ NEHGS [MS70/SOU/20] and
[Corbin Collection]
+ NSDAR [G.R.C./S1/v. 58]

Southampton Center Cemetery (1738)
Main St., College Highway
Tel: (413)-527-3688
+ NEHGS [MS70/SOU/20], and
[Corbin Collection]
+ NSDAR [G.R.C./S1/v. 58]

West Part Cemetery (1788)
Fomer Rd.
+ NEHGS [MS70/SOU/20], and
[Corbin Collection]
+ NSDAR [G.R.C./S1/v. 58]

SOUTHBOROUGH (1727)
from Marlborough
Town Hall, 17 Common St.,
Southborough, Mass. 01772, Tel: (508)-485-0710

Burnett Burial Park Cemetery
27 Main St.

Old Burial Ground (1730)
Common and St. Marks St., next to the
Southborough Library
+ NEHGS [F74/S72/D2] Typescript in
Mss

St. Mark's Churchyard Cemetery (1982)
27 Main St.
Tel: St. Mark's Rectory, 27 Main St.,
Southborough, Mass. (508)-481-1917

Southborough Rural Cemetery (1842)
Rte. 85, 11 Cordaville Rd.

SOUTHBRIDGE (1816)
from Charlton, Dudley, and Southbridge
Town Hall, 41 Elm St., Southbridge,
Mass. 01550, Tel: (508)-764-5408

Morse Cemetery (1787)
Crops Rd.

New Notre Dame Cemetery
Woodstock Rd.
Tel: Catholic Diocese Cemetery Office,
260 Cambridge St., Worcester, Mass.
(508)-757-7415

Oak Ridge Cemetery (1801)
Oak Ridge Ave.

Old Notre Dame Cemetery
Charlton St.
Tel: Catholic Diocese Cemetery Office,
260 Cambridge St., Worcester, Mass.
(508)-757-7415

St. George's Cemetery
Paige Hill Rd.
Tel: Catholic Diocese Cemetery Office,
260 Cambridge St., Worcester, Mass.
(508)-757-7415

St. Mary's Cemetery
Charlton St.
Tel: St. Mary's Rectory, 263 Hamilton
St., Southbridge, Mass. (508)-764-3226

SOUTHWICK (1770)
from Westfield
Town Hall, 454 College Highway,
Southwick, Mass. 01077, Tel: (413)-569-
5504

New Southwick Cemetery (1912)
Rte. 202, College Highway

Old Southwick Cemetery (1771)
Rte. 202, College Highway
+ Charles D. Townsend, *Border Town
Cemeteries of Massachusetts*. (West Hartford,
Ct., Chedwato Service, 1953)
[F63/T69/1953/also Loan]
+ NEHGS [MS70/SOU/40]

SPENCER (1753)
from Leicester
Town Hall, 157 Main St., Spencer, Mass.
01562, Tel: (508)-885-7500

Old Spencer Burial Ground (1742)
Main and North Sts.

Pine Grove Cemetery (1845)
North Spencer Rd. and Pleasant St..

**Mary Queen of the Rosary Parish
Cemetery (1872)**
West Main St. and Meadow Rd.
Tel: Mary Queen of the Rosary Rectory,
60 Maple St., Spencer, Mass. (508)-885-
3111

SPRINGFIELD (1641)
City Hall, 36 Court St.,
Springfield, Mass. 01103, Tel:
(413)-787-6094

Cherry Lane Cemetery
28 Cherry St.
+ NEHGS [F74/S8/D2] Typescript in
Mss

City of Homes Cemetery
(part of the Congregation Kesser Israel
Cemetery)

**Congregation Kesser Israel and
Congregational Sons of Israel
Cemetery (1933)**
904 Wilbraham St.

Elm Street Cemetery Site
burial were removed in 1848 to the
Springfield Cemetery.
+ NEHGS [MS70/SPR/1], and
[MS70/SPR/3]

Gate of Heaven Cemetery (1971)
421 Tinkham Rd.
Tel: (413)-782-4731

**Hillcrest Park Cemetery and
Mausoleum (1925)**
895 Parker St.
Tel: (413)-782-2311

Maplewood Cemetery
759 Parker St.

Oak Grove Cemetery (1882)
426 Bay St.
Tel: (413)-739-2127

**St. Aloysius–French Catholic
Cemetery (1880)**
1273 Berkshire Ave.
Tel: St. Judes Rectory, 1326 Worcester
St., Springfield, Mass. (413)-543-3739

St. Benedict's Catholic Cemetery
Liberty St.
Tel: St. Michael's Cemetery (413)-733-0659

St. Joseph's Cemetery
Prospect St.
Tel: (413)-734-7013

St. Michael's Roman Catholic Cemetery (1871)
1601 State St.
Tel : (413)-733-0659

Sinai Memorial Park (1940)
650 Cottage St.
Tel: Sinai Temple Reformed, 1100 Dickinson St., Springfield, Mass. (413)-736-3619

Springfield Cemetery (1841)
171 Maple St.
Tel: (413)-732-0712
Waschogue Cemetery
1402 Allen St.
Tel: (413)-787-6440

STERLING (1781)
from Lancaster
Town Hall, 1 Park St., Sterling, Mass. 01564, Tel: (978)-422-8111

Chocksett Cemetery (aka) Reed Cemetery (1736)
Redstone Hill Rd.
+ *Birth, Marriage and Death Register, Church Records and Epitaphs of Lancaster* (1890) [p. 416].
+ Esther K. Whitcomb, *Inscriptions from burial grounds of the Nashaway towns : Lancaster, Harvard, Bolton, Leominster, Sterling, Berlin, West Boylston, and Hudson, Massachusetts.* (Bowie, Md: Heritage Books, 1989) [F74/L2/I57/1989/also Loan]

+ NEHGS [MS70/STE/9], [MS70/STE/30] and [MS70/LAN/1]
+ NSDAR [G.R.C./S1/v. 106], and [G.R.C./S1/v. 267]

Cookshire Cemetery (1782)
Boutelle Rd.
+ Esther K. Whitcomb, *Inscriptions from burial grounds of the Nashaway towns : Lancaster, Harvard, Bolton, Leominster, Sterling, Berlin, West Boylston, and Hudson, Massachusetts.* (Bowie, Md: Heritage Books, 1989) [F74/L2/I57/1989/also Loan]
+ NEHGS [MS70/STE/6] and [MS70/STE/30]

Fairbanks Cemetery (1760)
Chase Hill Rd.
+ Esther K. Whitcomb, *Inscriptions from burial grounds of the Nashaway towns : Lancaster, Harvard, Bolton, Leominster, Sterling, Berlin, West Boylston, and Hudson, Massachusetts.* (Bowie, Md: Heritage Books, 1989) [F74/L2/I57/1989/also Loan]
+ NEHGS [MS70/STE/27] and [MS70/STE/30]

Hillside Cemetery (1953)
Sterling and Clinton Rds.

Legg Cemetery (1725)
Dana Hill Rd., off Rte. 140
+ Esther K. Whitcomb, *Inscriptions from burial grounds of the Nashaway towns : Lancaster, Harvard, Bolton, Leominster, Sterling, Berlin, West Boylston, and Hudson, Massachusetts.* (Bowie, Md: Heritage Books, 1989) [F74/L2/I57/1989/also Loan]
+ NEHGS [MS70/STE/8] and [MS70/STE/30]

Oak Hill Cemetery
Clinton Rd.
+ Esther K. Whitcomb, *Inscriptions from burial grounds of the Nashaway towns :*

Lancaster, Harvard, Bolton, Leominster, Sterling, Berlin, West Boylston, and Hudson, Massachusetts. (Bowie, Md: Heritage Books, 1989) [F74/L2/I57/1989/also Loan]
+ NEHGS [MS70/SOU/131]

General Cemetery Reference for Sterling:
+ NSDAR [G.R.C./S1/v.98] Inscription Index for Sterling.

STOCKBRIDGE (1739)
Town Hall, 6 Main St., Stockbridge, Mass. 01262, Tel: (413)-298-4568

Center Cemetery (1807)
Main St.
+ NEHGS [MS70/STO/5]
+ NSDAR [G.R.C./S1/v. 243]

Deming Family Cemetery (1789)
South St.
+ NEHGS [MS70/STO/51]

Indian Burial Ground
Main St.

Old Interlaken Cemetery (aka) Curtisville Cemetery (1782)
Mahkeenac Rd.
+ NEHGS [MS70/STO/5]
+ NSDAR [G.R.C./S1/v. 243]

St. Joseph's Roman Catholic Cemetery (1853)
Church St.

Village Cemetery (1745)
Main St.

Sedgwick Cemetery
+ NSDAR [G.R.C./S1/v. 243]

STONEHAM (1725)
from Charlestown
Town Hall, 35 Central St., Stoneham, Mass. 02180, Tel: (781)-279-2560
Cemetery Department, 16 Pine St., Stoneham, Mass. 02180, Tel: (781)-438-0760

Lindenwood Cemetery (1861)
Montvale Ave.

Old Burying Ground (1728)
Pleasant St.
+ Rev. John A. Vinton, "Inscription in the Old Cemetery in Stoneham, Ms." *NEHGR* 12:307-10.
+ NEHGS [F74/S88/D21] Typescript in Mss

Pleasant Street Cemetery
Pleasant St.

St. Patrick's Cemetery
Elm St.
Tel: (781)-729-1445

General Cemetery Reference for Stoneham:
+ NEHGS [Mss/A/B8] *Account Book of Burials in Stoneham 1812-1871.*

STOUGHTON (1726)
from Dorchester
Town Hall, 10 Pearl St., Stoughton, Mass. 02072, Tel: (781)-341-1300

Curtis Family Cemetery (1827)
Page St.
+ NEHGS [F74/S886/J6] Typescript in Mss

Drake Family Cemetery Site (19th century)
southeast corner of Bay Rd. and Old Central St., Cobb's Corner, site demolished.

Dry Pond Cemetery (1749)
Plain St. and Bay Rd., on Stoughton
Sharon town line.
+ NEHGS [MS70/SHA/1],
[MS70/STO/56], and [F74/S886/J6]
Typescript in Mss.
+ NSDAR [G.R.C./S1/v.54]

Evergreen Cemetery (1855)
Rte. 138, 1100 Washington St., across
from Plain St.
+ NEHGS [Mss/266] Inscriptions by
Bradford Kingman
+ NSDAR [G.R.C./S1/v.54]

Holy Sepulchre Catholic Cemetery (1850s)
Central St.
Tel: Immaculate Conception Rectory,
122 Canton St., Stoughton, Mass (781)-
344-2073

Maplewood Cemetery (1840)
Rte. 139, entrance near 946 Pleasant St.
Marshall Bird Cemetery (1819)
next to 1873 Washington St., near
Easton town line.
+ NEHGS [MS70/STO/54]
+ NSDAR [G.R.C./S1/v.54]

Methodist Meeting House Cemetery (aka) Drake Cemetery (1815)
near 1819 Central St., near West St.
+ NEHGS [MS70/STO/52], and
[F74/S886/J6] Typescript in Mss
+ NSDAR [G.R.C./S1/v.54]

Pearl Street Cemetery (1737)
Pearl St., near Stoughton Center
+ NEHGS [MS70/STO/58], [Mss/266],
[F74/S886/J6] Typescript in Mss.
+ NSDAR [G.R.C./S1/v.54]

Poor Farm Cemetery (19th century)
in the woods near 660 School St. [no
stones other than boundary markers]

Porter Family Cemetery (1808)
South St., beside the Pride of Brockton
Cemetery

Pride of Brockton Jewish Cemetery (1903)
South St.

STOW (1683)
Town Hall, 380 Great Rd., Stow, Mass.
01775, Tel: (978)-897-4514

Brookside Cemetery (1841)
Gleasondale Rd.
+ NSDAR [G.R.C./S1/v. 111]

Hillside Cemetery (aka) Pilot Grove Hill Cemetery (1812)
Crescent St.
+ NSDAR [G.R.C./S1/v. 111]
Lower Village Cemetery (1711)
Pompositticut Rd.
+ NSDAR [G.R.C./S1/v. 111]

STURBRIDGE (1738)
Town Hall, 308 Main St., Sturbridge,
Mass. 01566, Tel: (508)-347-2510

North Cemetery (1790)
44 Maple St., across from Gardner Ave.
+ [G.R. 2] *Vital Records of Sturbridge,
Massachusetts to the year 1850* (1906).
+ NEHGS [MS70/STU/2]

Old Sturbridge Common Cemetery (1750)
293 Main St., Rte. 131 across from
Sturbridge Common
+ [G.R. 1] *Vital Records of Sturbridge,
Massachusetts to the year 1850* (1906).
+ NEHGS [MS70/STU/1]

St. Anne's and St. Patrick's Cemetery
33 Arnold Rd., Fiskdale

Tel: Archdiocese of Worcester, 49 Elm St., Worcester, Mass. (508)-791-7171

SUDBURY (1639)

Town Hall, 322 Concord Rd., Sudbury, Mass. 01776, Tel: (978)-443-8891

Mount Pleasant Cemetery (1840)
Concord Rd., northeast of the First Parish Church. Across from Revolutionary Cemetery.

Mount Wadsworth Cemetery (1833)
Concord Rd.
New North Cemetery (1955)
Pantry Rd., across from Old North Cemetery

New Town Cemetery (1868)
Concord Rd., next to Old Town Cemetery

Nobscot Smallpox Cemetery Site (1792)
Nobscot Boy Scout Reservation, 1 Nobscot Rd., South Sudbury

Old North Sudbury Cemetery (1843)
Pantry Rd., south of Rte. 117

Old Town Cemetery (1857)
Concord Rd., next to Mount Pleasant Cemetery

Old Center Cemetery (aka) Revolutionary Cemetery (1716)
Concord Rd., east of Presbyterian Church. Across from Mount Pleasant Cemetery.
+Lucy Hall Greenlaw, "Inscriptions at Sudbury, Mass.", *NEHGR* 61:14-25, 120-7.

Wadsworth Cemetery (1676)
Concord Rd., north of Rte. 20, Green Hill

SUNDERLAND (1714)

Town Hall, 12 School St., Sunderland, Mass. 01375, Tel: (413)-665-1442

North Sunderland Cemetery (1813)
Rte. 47
+ NEHGS [Corbin Collection]

Riverside Cemetery (1714)
Cemetery Rd.
+ NEHGS [Corbin Collection]

SUTTON (1714)

Town Hall, 4 Uxbridge Rd., Sutton, Mass. 01590, Tel: (508)-865-8725

Armsby Cemetery (1792)
Armsby Rd.
+ [G.R. 17] *Vital Records of Sutton, Massachusetts to the year 1850* (1907).
+ Susan F. Salisbury, *Southern Massachusetts Cemetery Collection* - Volume 1 (Bowie, Md., Heritage Books, 1995) [F63/S25/1995/also Loan]
+ Reuben Rawson Dodge, *Inscriptions in the Cemeteries of Sutton, Massachusetts.* (Worcester, Mass.: Charles Hamilton, 1898) [F74/S98/D66/1898/also Loan]
+ NEHGS [MS70/SUT/2]

Brigham Hill Cemetery
West Sutton
+ [G.R. 1] *Vital Records of Sutton, Massachusetts to the year 1850* (1907).
+ NEHGS [MS70/SUT/2]

Sutton Town Cemetery (aka) Centre Cemetery (1719)
Uxbridge and Boston Rd., behind the Town Hall.
+ [G.R. 11] *Vital Records of Sutton, Massachusetts to the year 1850* (1907).
+ Reuben Rawson Dodge, *Inscriptions in the Cemeteries of Sutton, Massachusetts.* (Worcester, Mass.: Charles Hamilton, 1898) [F74/S98/D66/1898/also Loan]

+ Susan F. Salisbury, *Southern
Massachusetts Cemetery Collection* - Volume
1 (Bowie, Md., Heritage Books, 1995)
[F63/S25/1995/also Loan]
+ NEHGS [MS70/SUT/2], and
[MS70/SUT/6]
+ NSDAR [G.R.C./S1/v. 159]

Cole–Woodbury Cemetery (1813)
off Boston Rd.
+ [G.R. 10] *Vital Records of Sutton,
Massachusetts to the year 1850* (1907).
+ NEHGS [MS70/SUT/2]

John Darling Cemetery (19th c.)
Darling Ln., Manchaug
+ [G.R. 1] *Vital Records of Sutton,
Massachusetts to the year 1850* (1907).

Dodge Cemetery (1791)
Leland Hill Rd.
+ [G.R. 16] *Vital Records of Sutton,
Massachusetts to the year 1850* (1907).
+ Susan F. Salisbury, *Southern
Massachusetts Cemetery Collection* - Volume
1 (Bowie, Md., Heritage Books, 1995)
[F63/S25/1995/also Loan]
+ Reuben Rawson Dodge, *Inscriptions in
the Cemeteries of Sutton, Massachusetts.*
(Worcester, Mass.: Charles Hamilton,
1898) [F74/S98/D66/1898/also Loan]
+ NEHGS [MS70/SUT/2]

Doe Valley Cemetery
Pleasant St.

Fuller Cemetery (19th century)
Torey Rd., near Manchaug Pond
+ [G.R. 5] *Vital Records of Sutton,
Massachusetts to the year 1850* (1907).

Fuller Cemetery
"in Dist. No. 2"
+ [G.R. 9] *Vital Records of Sutton,
Massachusetts to the year 1850* (1907).
+ NEHGS [MS70/SUT/2]

Hall Cemetery
"on Levi Griggs' Farm"
+ [G.R. 4] *Vital Records of Sutton,
Massachusetts to the year 1850* (1907).

Harback Cemetery (1782)
Rte. 146
+ NEHGS [MS70/SUT/7]

Levi Holt Cemetery
near Manchaug Pond
+ [G.R. 1] *Vital Records of Sutton,
Massachusetts to the year 1850* (1907).

New Howard Street Cemetery (1862)
Armsby Rd.
+ Reuben Rawson Dodge, *Inscriptions in
the Cemeteries of Sutton, Massachusetts.*
(Worcester, Mass.: Charles Hamilton,
1898) [F74/S98/D66/1898/also Loan]
+ NEHGS [MS70/SUT/4]
+ NSDAR [G.R.C./S1/v.128]

Old Howard Cemetery (1823)
off Armsby Rd.
+ Susan F. Salisbury, *Southern
Massachusetts Cemetery Collection* - Volume
1 (Bowie, Md., Heritage Books, 1995)
[F63/S25/1995/also Loan]

Marble–Freegrace Farm Cemetery (1786)
80 Burbank Rd.
+ [G.R. 1] *Vital Records of Sutton,
Massachusetts to the year 1850* (1907).

Old Plan Cemetery
"near Saw-mill site"
+ [G.R. 12] *Vital Records of Sutton,
Massachusetts to the year 1850* (1907).
+ NEHGS [MS70/SUT/2]

Pigeon Hill Cemetery (19th century)
off Mendon Rd.
+ [G.R. 15] *Vital Records of Sutton,
Massachusetts to the year 1850* (1907).
+ NEHGS [MS70/SUT/2]

Putnam–Hutchinson Cemetery
Hutchinson Rd.
+ [G.R. 1] *Vital Records of Sutton,
Massachusetts to the year 1850* (1907).

South Sutton Cemetery (1803)
Hough Rd.
+ [G.R. 14] *Vital Records of Sutton,
Massachusetts to the year 1850* (1907).
+ NEHGS [MS70/SUT/2]

West Sutton Cemetery (18th century)
West Sutton Rd.
+ [G.R. 18] *Vital Records of Sutton,
Massachusetts to the year 1850* (1907).
+ NEHGS [MS70/SUT/2]

Wilkinsonville Cemetery (19th century)
Boston Rd., and Dodge Hill Rd.
+ [G.R. 19] *Vital Records of Sutton,
Massachusetts to the year 1850* (1907).
+ Susan F. Salisbury, *Southern
Massachusetts Cemetery Collection* - Volume
1 (Bowie, Md., Heritage Books, 1995)
[F63/S25/1995/also Loan]
+ Reuben Rawson Dodge, *Inscriptions in
the Cemeteries of Sutton, Massachusetts.*
(Worcester, Mass.: Charles Hamilton,
1898) [F74/S98/D66/1898/also Loan]
+ NEHGS [MS70/SUT/2] and
[MS70/SUT/5]
+ NSDAR [G.R.C./S1/v.128]

Arnold Family Cemetery
+ [G.R. 13] *Vital Records of Sutton,
Massachusetts to the year 1850* (1907).

Carpenter Family Cemetery
+ [G.R. 7] *Vital Records of Sutton,
Massachusetts to the year 1850* (1907).

General Cemetery Reference for Sutton:
+ NSDAR [G.R.C./S1/v.98] Inscription
Index for Sutton.

SWAMPSCOTT (1852)
from Lynn
Town Hall, 22 Monument Ave.,
Swampscott, Mass. 01907, Tel: (781)-
596-8856

Swampscott Cemetery (1744)
400 Essex St.
Tel: (781)-596-8863
+ [G.R. 4] *Vital Records of Lynn,
Massachusetts to the year 1850* (1905).

SWANSEA (1667)
from Rehoboth
Town Hall, 81 Main St., Swansea, Mass.
02777, Tel: (508)-678-9389

Arnold–Gardner Cemetery (1825)
Gardners Neck Rd., near Wilbur Ave.
+ Robert S. Trim, *Swansea Massachusetts
Gravestone Records.* (Boston, Mass.,
NEHGS) [F74/S995/T74]

Elisha Baker Family Cemetery
Hortonville Rd., near Wood St.
+ Robert S. Trim, *Swansea Massachusetts
Gravestone Records.* (Boston, Mass.,
NEHGS) [F74/S995/T74]

Baptist Church Cemetery (1737)
Fall River Ave., across from the Thomas
Cemetery, North Swansea
+ Robert S. Trim, *Swansea Massachusetts
Gravestone Records.* (Boston, Mass.,
NEHGS) [F74/S995/T74]
+ Susan F. Salisbury, *Southern
Massachusetts Cemetery Collection* - Volume
2 (Bowie, Md., Heritage Books, 1996)
[F63/S25/1995/also Loan]
+ NEHGS [MS70/SWA/12]

Bleachery Grave Yard (aka) Center Cemetery (1723)
Swansea Center

+ NEHGS [MS70/NOR/410],
[MS70/SWA/10], and Vertical File
[F74/S995/M6]
+ NSDAR [G.R.C./S1/v.128] and
[G.R.C./1932/S1/v. 16]

John Brown Family Cemetery (1832)
off Old Warren Rd., near Warren, Rhode
Island border.
+ Robert S. Trim, *Swansea Massachusetts
Gravestone Records*. (Boston, Mass.,
NEHGS) [F74/S995/T74]

Seth Brown Family Cemetery (1775)
off Pearse Rd.
+ Robert S. Trim, *Swansea Massachusetts
Gravestone Records*. (Boston, Mass.,
NEHGS) [F74/S995/T74]

Buffington Family Cemetery (1835)
Cedar St.
+ Robert S. Trim, *Swansea Massachusetts
Gravestone Records*. (Boston, Mass.,
NEHGS) [F74/S995/T74]

Asa Chace Family Cemetery (1857)
Baker Rd.
+ Robert S. Trim, *Swansea Massachusetts
Gravestone Records*. (Boston, Mass.,
NEHGS) [F74/S995/T74]
+ Susan F. Salisbury, *Southern
Massachusetts Cemetery Collection* - Volume
2 (Bowie, Md., Heritage Books, 1996)
[F63/S25/1995/also Loan]

Enoch Chace Family Cemetery
(1805)
Baker Rd.
+ Robert S. Trim, *Swansea Massachusetts
Gravestone Records*. (Boston, Mass.,
NEHGS) [F74/S995/T74]
+ Susan F. Salisbury, *Southern
Massachusetts Cemetery Collection* - Volume
2 (Bowie, Md., Heritage Books, 1996)
[F63/S25/1995/also Loan]

Chace Family Cemetery (1805)
Sharp's Lot Rd.

+ Robert S. Trim, *Swansea Massachusetts
Gravestone Records*. (Boston, Mass.,
NEHGS) [F74/S995/T74]

Christ Church Cemetery (1811)
Main St.
+ Robert S. Trim, *Swansea Massachusetts
Gravestone Records*. (Boston, Mass.,
NEHGS) [F74/S995/T74]
+ Susan F. Salisbury, *Southern
Massachusetts Cemetery Collection* - Volume
2 (Bowie, Md., Heritage Books, 1996)
[F63/S25/1995/also Loan]

Aaron Cole Family Cemetery (1807)
off Old Warren Rd.
+ Susan F. Salisbury, *Southern
Massachusetts Cemetery Collection* - Volume
2 (Bowie, Md., Heritage Books, 1996)
[F63/S25/1995/also Loan]

Davis–Luther–Riley Cemetery
(1815)
Old Warren Rd.
+ Robert S. Trim, *Swansea Massachusetts
Gravestone Records*. (Boston, Mass.,
NEHGS) [F74/S995/T74]

Capt. Charles Eddy Family
Cemetery (1807)
rear of the St. Louis Church, 56
Buffington St.
+ Robert S. Trim, *Swansea Massachusetts
Gravestone Records*. (Boston, Mass.,
NEHGS) [F74/S995/T74]
+ Susan F. Salisbury, *Southern
Massachusetts Cemetery Collection*, Volume 2
(Bowie, Md., Heritage Books, 1996)
[F63/S25/1995/also Loan]

Old Eddy Cemetery (1687)
off Cole River
+ Robert S. Trim, *Swansea Massachusetts
Gravestone Records*. (Boston, Mass.,
NEHGS) [F74/S995/T74]
+ Susan F. Salisbury, *Southern
Massachusetts Cemetery Collection*, Volume 2

(Bowie, Md., Heritage Books, 1996)
[F63/S25/1995/also Loan]

Gardner Cemetery (1769)

Gardner Neck Rd.
+ Robert S. Trim, *Swansea Massachusetts
Gravestone Records.* (Boston, Mass.,
NEHGS) [F74/S995/T74]

Hale Family Cemetery (1784)

off Locust St.
+ Robert S. Trim, *Swansea Massachusetts
Gravestone Records.* (Boston, Mass.,
NEHGS) [F74/S995/T74]
+ Susan F. Salisbury, *Southern
Massachusetts Cemetery Collection* - Volume
2 (Bowie, Md., Heritage Books, 1996)
[F63/S25/1995/also Loan]

Hortonville Road Cemetery

Hortonville Rd.
+ Robert S. Trim, *Swansea Massachusetts
Gravestone Records.* (Boston, Mass.,
NEHGS) [F74/S995/T74]
+ Susan F. Salisbury, *Southern
Massachusetts Cemetery Collection* - Volume
2 (Bowie, Md., Heritage Books, 1996)
[F63/S25/1995/also Loan]

Ingalls Family Cemetery (1806)

Breslin Path, near Rehoboth town line.
+ Robert S. Trim, *Swansea Massachusetts
Gravestone Records.* (Boston, Mass.,
NEHGS) [F74/S995/T74]

Kingsley Family Cemetery (1805)

Milford Rd., near Rte. 6
+ Robert S. Trim, *Swansea Massachusetts
Gravestone Records.* (Boston, Mass.,
NEHGS) [F74/S995/T74]
+ Susan F. Salisbury, *Southern
Massachusetts Cemetery Collection* , Volume 2
(Bowie, Md., Heritage Books, 1996)
[F63/S25/1995/also Loan]

Lawton–Johnson Family Cemetery (1835)

near 333 Sharp's Lot Rd.

+ Robert S. Trim, *Swansea Massachusetts
Gravestone Records.* (Boston, Mass.,
NEHGS) [F74/S995/T74]

Stephen Lee Family Cemetery (1821)

off Purchase St.
+ Robert S. Trim, *Swansea Massachusetts
Gravestone Records.* (Boston, Mass.,
NEHGS) [F74/S995/T74]

Nathaniel Lewin Family Cemetery (1861)

old Stevens Rd.
+ Robert S. Trim, *Swansea Massachusetts
Gravestone Records.* (Boston, Mass.,
NEHGS) [F74/S995/T74]

Benjamin M. Lewis Family Cemetery (1846)

off Dillon Ln.
+ Robert S. Trim, *Swansea Massachusetts
Gravestone Records.* (Boston, Mass.,
NEHGS) [F74/S995/T74]

Lydia Lewis Family Cemetery (1795)

off Dillon Ln.
+ Robert S. Trim, *Swansea Massachusetts
Gravestone Records.* (Boston, Mass.,
NEHGS) [F74/S995/T74]

Luther Family Cemetery (1755)

Wood St.
+ Robert S. Trim, *Swansea Massachusetts
Gravestone Records.* (Boston, Mass.,
NEHGS) [F74/S995/T74]

Luther Family Cemetery (1776)

Milford Rd. and Spring St.
+ Robert S. Trim, *Swansea Massachusetts
Gravestone Records.* (Boston, Mass.,
NEHGS) [F74/S995/T74]

Martin Family Cemetery I (1787)

Hortonville Rd., near Rte. 118

+ Robert S. Trim, *Swansea Massachusetts Gravestone Records.* (Boston, Mass., NEHGS) [F74/S995/T74]
+ Susan F. Salisbury, *Southern Massachusetts Cemetery Collection,* Volume 2 (Bowie, Md., Heritage Books, 1996) [F63/S25/1995/also Loan]

Martin Family Cemetery II (1792)
Hortonville Rd., near the bridge
+ Robert S. Trim, *Swansea Massachusetts Gravestone Records.* (Boston, Mass., NEHGS) [F74/S995/T74]
+ Susan F. Salisbury, *Southern Massachusetts Cemetery Collection,* Volume 2 (Bowie, Md., Heritage Books, 1996) [F63/S25/1995/also Loan]

Martin Family Cemetery III (1855)
next to 178 Hortonville Rd.
+ Robert S. Trim, *Swansea Massachusetts Gravestone Records.* (Boston, Mass., NEHGS) [F74/S995/T74]

Christopher Mason Cemetery (1771)
Stephen French Rd.
+ Robert S. Trim, *Swansea Massachusetts Gravestone Records.* (Boston, Mass., NEHGS) [F74/S995/T74]

Elisha Mason Cemetery (1760)
Locust St.
+ Robert S. Trim, *Swansea Massachusetts Gravestone Records.* (Boston, Mass., NEHGS) [F74/S995/T74]

Mason–Bushee–Kingsley Cemetery (1731)
off Fall River Ave., Rte. 6
+ Robert S. Trim, *Swansea Massachusetts Gravestone Records.* (Boston, Mass., NEHGS) [F74/S995/T74]
+ Susan F. Salisbury, *Southern Massachusetts Cemetery Collection* - Volume 2 (Bowie, Md., Heritage Books, 1996) [F63/S25/1995/also Loan]
+ NEHGS [MS70/SWA/12]

Elder Daniel Martin Cemetery (1739)
Vinicum Rd., near Read St.
+ Robert S. Trim, *Swansea Massachusetts Gravestone Records.* (Boston, Mass., NEHGS) [F74/S995/T74]

Mason Reed Cemetery
+ Susan F. Salisbury, *Southern Massachusetts Cemetery Collection* - Volume 2 (Bowie, Md., Heritage Books, 1996) [F63/S25/1995/also Loan]

Milford Road Cemetery (1753)
Milford Rd.
+ Robert S. Trim, *Swansea Massachusetts Gravestone Records.* (Boston, Mass., NEHGS) [F74/S995/T74]

Monroe Family Cemetery (1843)
rear of 237 Burnside St., near Bushee Rd.
+ Susan F. Salisbury, *Southern Massachusetts Cemetery Collection* - Volume 2 (Bowie, Md., Heritage Books, 1996) [F63/S25/1995/also Loan]

Mount Hope Cemetery (19th c.)
Nortonville and Milford Rds.
+ Susan F. Salisbury, *Southern Massachusetts Cemetery Collection* - Volume 2 (Bowie, Md., Heritage Books, 1996) [F63/S25/1995/also Loan]
+ Robert S. Trim, *Swansea Massachusetts Gravestone Records.* (Boston, Mass., NEHGS) [F74/S995/T74]
+ [G.R.] *Vital Records of Taunton, Massachusetts to the year 1850* (1928).
Old Warren Road Cemetery
Old Warren Rd.
+ Susan F. Salisbury, *Southern Massachusetts Cemetery Collection* - Volume 2 (Bowie, Md., Heritage Books, 1996) [F63/S25/1995/also Loan]

Jabez Pierce Family Cemetery (1828)
off Purchase St., Rehoboth, located within Swansea.

+ Susan F. Salisbury, *Southern Massachusetts Cemetery Collection* - Volume 2 (Bowie, Md., Heritage Books, 1996) [F63/S25/1995/also Loan]

Sisson Cemetery (1776)
Seaview Ave., off Brayton Ave.
+ Robert S. Trim, *Swansea Massachusetts Gravestone Records.* (Boston, Mass., NEHGS) [F74/S995/T74]

Col. Peleg Slade Burying Ground (1813)
Hortonville Rd.
+ Susan F. Salisbury, *Southern Massachusetts Cemetery Collection* - Volume 2 (Bowie, Md., Heritage Books, 1996) [F63/S25/1995/also Loan]
+ NEHGS [MS70/NOR/410] and Vertical File [F74/S995/M6]
+ NSDAR [G.R.C./S1/v.128]

Thomas Cemetery
Fall River Ave., G.A.R. Highway Rte. 6, North Swansea
+ Susan F. Salisbury, *Southern Massachusetts Cemetery Collection* - Volume 2 (Bowie, Md., Heritage Books, 1996) [F63/S25/1995/also Loan]

Town Hall Cemetery (1758)
Main St.
+ Susan F. Salisbury, *Southern Massachusetts Cemetery Collection* - Volume 2 (Bowie, Md., Heritage Books, 1996) [F63/S25/1995/also Loan]

Wheaton Family Cemetery (1791)
Brescia Way, off Chace Rd.
+ Robert S. Trim, *Swansea Massachusetts Gravestone Records.* (Boston, Mass., NEHGS) [F74/S995/T74]

White Church Cemetery (1828)
Maple and Fall River Avc.
+ Robert S. Trim, *Swansea Massachusetts Gravestone Records.* (Boston, Mass., NEHGS) [F74/S995/T74]

Winslow Cemetery (1813)
Stevens Rd.
+ Robert S. Trim, *Swansea Massachusetts Gravestone Records.* (Boston, Mass., NEHGS) [F74/S995/T74]

Wood Family Cemetery (1777)
Reed St.
+ Robert S. Trim, *Swansea Massachusetts Gravestone Records.* (Boston, Mass., NEHGS) [F74/S995/T74]

Noah Wood Family Cemetery (1787)
Wood St., near the Swansea Reservoir.
+ Robert S. Trim, *Swansea Massachusetts Gravestone Records.* (Boston, Mass., NEHGS) [F74/S995/T74]

TAUNTON (1639)
City Hall, 15 Summer St., Taunton, Mass. 02780, Tel: (508)-821-1024

Almshouse Cemetery Site (1771)
near site of old Taunton Almshouse
+ NEHGS [Mss/SG/LIN/5/23], and [Mss/SG/HOD/6/60]

African American Cemetery (aka) Talbot Family Cemetery (1830)
Sherwood Ave., near Precinct St.
+ Eight Cemeteries of Bristol County
+ [G.R. 45] *Vital Records of Taunton, Massachusetts to the year 1850* (1928).
+ Mrs. Wendell B. Presbrey, *Inscriptions from Eight Cemeteries in Bristol, County, Massachusetts,* Massachusetts D.A.R., 1987) [F72/B8/I57/1987]
+ NEHGS [Mss/SL/RAY/7]
+ NSDAR [G.R.C./S2/v. 1] and [G.R.C./S1/v. 433]

Bassett Burying Ground (1817)
12 Field St., opposite North Taunton Cemetery

+ [G.R. 20] *Vital Records of Taunton, Massachusetts to the year 1850* (1928).
+ NEHGS [MS70/TAU/2]

Bassett Family Burying Ground (1845)
820 South Crane Ave., near Harvey St.
+ [G.R.22] *Vital Records of Taunton, Massachusetts to the year 1850* (1928).
+ NEHGS [MS70/TAU/2], and [F74/T2/P7] Typescript in Mss
+ NSDAR [G.R.C./S1/v. 417.5]

Burt–Gulliver-Crane-Walker Burying Ground (1739)
Gulliver St. near Burt St., West Taunton
+ [G.R. 12] *Vital Records of Taunton, Massachusetts to the year 1850* (1928).
+ NEHGS [MS70/TAU/2], and [F74/T2/P7] Typescript in Mss

Burt Street Cemetery
in woods off Burt St.

Caswell–Fairbanks Burying Ground (1805)
409-411 Middleboro Ave.
+ [G.R. 8] *Vital Records of Taunton, Massachusetts to the year 1850* (1928).
+ Charles M. Thatcher, *Old Cemeteries of Southeastern Massachusetts*. (Middleborough, Mass., Middleborough Public Library, 1995) [F63/T53/1995/also Loan]
+ NEHGS [MS70/TAU/2]
+ NSDAR [G.R.C./S2/v. 1]

Caswell Street Cemetery (1741)
Caswell St., opposite Staples St., East Taunton
+ Charles M. Thatcher, *Old Cemeteries of Southeastern Massachusetts*. (Middleborough, Mass., Middleborough Public Library, 1995) [F63/T53/1995/also Loan]
+ Mrs. Wendell B. Presbrey, *Inscriptions from Eight Cemeteries in Bristol, County, Massachusetts.* (---, Massachusetts D.A.R., 1987) [F72/B8/I57/1987]

+ [G.R. 7] *Vital Records of Taunton, Massachusetts to the year 1850* (1928).
+ NEHGS [Mss/SG/LIN/5/23], and [Mss/SG/HOD/6/60]
+ NSDAR [G.R.C./S1/v. 433]

Cedar Knoll Cemetery (1981)
175 Staples St., East Taunton
Tel: (508)-872-7229

Cobb-Bragg Cemetery Site (site destroyed)
near 300 Burt St.

Cooper Family Burying Ground (1745)
behind 228 Berkley St., near Pratt St.
+ [G.R. 28] *Vital Records of Taunton, Massachusetts to the year 1850* (1928).
+ NEHGS [Mss/SG/LIN/5/23], and [Mss/SG/HOD/6/60]

County Street Cemetery (1850)
1797 County St.

Country Way Cemetery Site
in woods near Country Way

Crane Avenue Burying Ground (1750)
Crane Ave., near the Norton town line.
+ [G.R. 2] *Vital Records of Taunton, Massachusetts to the year 1850* (1928).

East Weir Cemetery (1797)
rear 59 Plain St.
+ [G.R. 14] *Vital Records of Taunton, Massachusetts to the year 1850* (1928).

Field Cemetery (1815)
between 34 and 48 Field St.
+ [G.R. 23] *Vital Records of Taunton, Massachusetts to the year 1850* (1928).
+ NEHGS [F74/T2/P7] Typescript in Mss
+ NSDAR [G.R.C./S1/v. 417.5]

Gilbert Burying Ground (1746)
Pratt and Berkley Sts.
+ [G.R. 43] *Vital Records of Taunton, Massachusetts to the year 1850* (1928).

Greenwood Cemetery (aka) Quaker Burial Ground
near 223 Fremont St.

Happy Hollow–Locust Grove Cemetery (1850)
Pratt St.
Joel Harvey Gravesite
east of Round St.

Havey Cemetery (aka) Abraham White Cemetery (1801)
off Fremont St., near Bassett St. Behind the Dever School Building 1.
+ NEHGS [F74/T2/P7] Typescript in Mss

Harvey Family–Friends Burying Ground (1835)
opposite 820 South Crane Ave.
+ [G.R. 21, 25] *Vital Records of Taunton, Massachusetts to the year 1850* (1928).

Hathaway Burying Ground (1805)
1600 Somerset Ave., between Railroad Ave. and the Taunton River.
+ [G.R. 13] *Vital Records of Taunton, Massachusetts to the year 1850* (1928).

Howard Burying Ground (1750)
across from 408 Tremont St.

King's Furnace Cemetery (1811)
1300 Middleboro Ave., across from Massasoit State Park, East Taunton
+ [G.R. 5] *Vital Records of Taunton, Massachusetts to the year 1850* (1928).

Knapp Burying Ground (1779)
rear 494 Tremont St., near Segregansett Rd., West Taunton

+ [G.R. 35] *Vital Records of Taunton, Massachusetts to the year 1850* (1928).
+ NEHGS [Mss/SG/LIN/5/23], and [Mss/SG/HOD/6/60].

Lincoln Burying Ground (1850)
Bassett St., near Bay St.
+ [G.R. 24] *Vital Records of Taunton, Massachusetts to the year 1850* (1928).

Bezer Lincoln Burying Ground (1832)
off 1360 Watson St. near Bay St.
+ [G.R. 26] *Vital Records of Taunton, Massachusetts to the year 1850* (1928).

Lincoln Burying Ground (1802)
Davis St., near Shores St.
+ [G.R. 49] *Vital Records of Taunton, Massachusetts to the year 1850* (1928).
+ NEHGS [F74/T2/P7] Typescript in Mss, [Mss/SG/LIN/5/23], and [Mss/SG/HOD/6/60].
+ NSDAR [G.R.C./S1/v. 417.5]

Mayflower Hill Cemetery (1840)
235 Broadway St., corner of Washington St., Rte. 138
Tel: (508)-821-1021
+ [G.R. 50] *Vital Records of Taunton, Massachusetts to the year 1850* (1928).

Mount Nebo Cemetery (1885)
19 Glebe St.

Mount Pleasant Cemetery (1710)
19 Crocker St., near Cohannet and Barnum St. intersection.
+ [G.R. 17] *Vital Records of Taunton, Massachusetts to the year 1850* (1928).

Neck–of–Land Cemetery (1689)
81 Summer St.
+ [G.R. 9] *Vital Records of Taunton, Massachusetts to the year 1850* (1928).
+ NEHGS [MS70/TAU/10], [Mss/SG/HOD/6/60],

[Mss/SG/LIN/5/23], and[F74/T2/P7]
Typescript in Mss.
+ NSDAR [G.R.C./S1/v. 417.5]

North Taunton Cemetery

1863-1871 Bay St, and Field St.
+ [G.R. 10] *Vital Records of Taunton,
Massachusetts to the year 1850* (1928).
+ NEHGS [F74/T2/P7] Typescript in
Mss, [Mss/SG/LIN/5/23], and
[Mss/SG/HOD/6/60].
+ NSDAR [G.R.C./S1/v. 417.5]

Oakland Cemetery (aka) Glebe Street Cemetery (1728)

20 Glebe St.
Tel: Mayflower Hill Cemetery, (508)-821-
1021
+ [G.R. 3] *Vital Records of Taunton,
Massachusetts to the year 1850* (1928).
+ NEHGS [F74/T2/P7] Typescript in
Mss, [Mss/SG/LIN/5/23], and
[Mss/SG/HOD/6/60]
+ NSDAR [G.R.C./S1/v. 417.5]

Ox Bow Farm Cemetery (1785)

Williams St., behind Taunton High
School
+ [G.R. 52] *Vital Records of Taunton,
Massachusetts to the year 1850* (1928).
+ NSDAR [G.R.C./S1/v. 417.5]

Seth Padelford Grave Site (1778)

County St.
+ [G.R. 18] *Vital Records of Taunton,
Massachusetts to the year 1850* (1928).

Padelford Cemetery (1792)

Middleboro Ave., near Airport Hanger.
+ Charles M. Thatcher, *Old Cemeteries of
Southeastern Massachusetts*. (Middleborough,
Mass., Middleborough Public Library,
1995) [F63/T53/1995/also Loan]

Phillips Cemetery

Pratt St. near Berkley St.

Phillips Burying Ground (1819)

near 433 Staples St.
+ [G.R. 35] *Vital Records of Taunton,
Massachusetts to the year 1850* (1928).

Pine Hill Street Cemetery (1750)

Stevens and Pine Hill Sts.
+ [G.R. 4] *Vital Records of Taunton,
Massachusetts to the year 1850* (1928).
+ Charles M. Thatcher, *Old Cemeteries of
Southeastern Massachusetts*. (Middleborough,
Mass., Middleborough Public Library,
1995) [F63/T53/1995/also Loan]
+ NEHGS [Mss/SG/LIN/5/23], and
[Mss/SG/HOD/6/60]

Plain Cemetery (1725)

141-143 Broadway and Washington Sts.
+ [G.R. 1] *Vital Records of Taunton,
Massachusetts to the year 1850* (1928).
+ NEHGS [Mss/SG/HOD/6/60]

Reed Cemetery (1801)

in woods opposite Railroad Ave.
+ [G.R. 32] *Vital Records of Taunton,
Massachusetts to the year 1850* (1928).
+ NEHGS [Mss/SG/LIN/5/23], and
[Mss/SG/HOD/6/60]

Asa Richmond Gravesite

1678 Middleboro Ave.

Richmond Cemetery (1793)

Taunton River area, near the Richmond
Street Cemetery
+ [G.R. 44] *Vital Records of Taunton,
Massachusetts to the year 1850* (1928).
+ Charles M. Thatcher, *Old Cemeteries of
Southeastern Massachusetts*. (Middleborough,
Mass., Middleborough Public Library,
1995) [F63/T53/1995/also Loan]
+ NEHGS [Mss/SG/LIN/5/23]

Richmond Street Cemetery (1819)

near 545 Richmond St.
+ [G.R. 19] *Vital Records of Taunton,
Massachusetts to the year 1850* (1928).

Rockwoods Cemetery (aka) Glebe Street Cemetery

near Rocky Woods and Glebe Sts.

St. Francis Catholic Cemetery (1894)

24 Glebe St., West Taunton
Tel: Taunton Catholic Cemetery Office,
475 E. Britannia St., Taunton, Mass.
(508)-824-9570
+ [G.R. 39] *Vital Records of Taunton, Massachusetts to the year 1850* (1928).

St. James Catholic Cemetery (1850)

44 Liberty St.
Tel: Taunton Catholic Cemetery Office,
475 E. Britannia St., Taunton, Mass.
(508)-824-9570
+ [G.R. 37] *Vital Records of Taunton, Massachusetts to the year 1850* (1928).

St. Joseph's Catholic Cemetery (1850)

475 East Britannia St.
Tel: Taunton Catholic Cemetery Office,
475 E. Britannia St., Taunton, Mass.
(508)-824-9570
+ [G.R. 40] *Vital Records of Taunton, Massachusetts to the year 1850* (1928).

St. Mary's Catholic Cemetery (1850)

100 East Brittannia St.
Tel: Taunton Catholic Cemetery Office,
475 E. Britannia St., Taunton, Mass.
(508)-824-9570
+ [G.R. 41] *Vital Records of Taunton, Massachusetts to the year 1850* (1928).

St. Thomas Episcopal Church Burying Ground (1765)

227 Tremont St., near Three Mile River
+ [G.R. 15] *Vital Records of Taunton, Massachusetts to the year 1850* (1928).
+ NEHGS [Mss/SG/LIN/5/23], and [Mss/SG/HOD/6/60]

Sandy Hill Cemetery (1804)

off Somerset Ave., at the end of Seventh St.

+ [G.R. 34] *Vital Records of Taunton, Massachusetts to the year 1850* (1928).
+ NEHGS [MS70/TAU/1],
[Mss/SG/LIN/5/23],
[Mss/SG/HOD/6/60], and
[F74/T2/P7] Typescript in Mss
+ NSDAR [G.R.C./S1/v. 417.5]

Soper Burying Ground

near 318 County St., near Johnson St.

Staples Street Burying Ground (1732)

Staples St., at the junction of Seekell St.,
East Taunton
+ [G.R. 6] *Vital Records of Taunton, Massachusetts to the year 1850* (1928).
+ NEHGS [Mss/SG/LIN/5/23], and
[Mss/SG/HOD/6/60]

William L. Walker Burying Ground (1835)

two separate cemeteries off Lanesway St.
at 113 Burt St.
+ [G.R. 30, 31] *Vital Records of Taunton, Massachusetts to the year 1850* (1928).
+ Mrs. Wendell B. Presbrey, *Inscriptions from Eight Cemeteries in Bristol, County, Massachusetts.* (---, Massachusetts D.A.R., 1987) [F72/B8/I57/1987]
+ NEHGS [Mss/SG/LIN/5/23], and
[Mss/SG/HOD/6/60].
+ NSDAR [G.R.C./S1/v. 433]

Walker–Blake Cemetery (1650)

end of Baker Rd. and Taunton Ave.
+ [G.R. 33] *Vital Records of Taunton, Massachusetts to the year 1850* (1928).
+ NEHGS [F74/T2/P7] Typescript in Mss, [Mss/SG/LIN/5/23], and [Mss/SG/HOD/6/60]
+ NSDAR [G.R.C./S2/v. 1], and [G.R.C./S1/v. 417.5]

Westville Cemetery (1787)

1291 Cohannet St., near Winthrop St.
Tel: (508)-822-0489

+ [G.R. 11] *Vital Records of Taunton, Massachusetts to the year 1850* (1928).
+ Mrs. Wendell B. Presbrey, *Inscriptions from Eight Cemeteries in Bristol, County, Massachusetts.* (---, Massachusetts D.A.R., 1987) [F72/B8/I57/1987]
+ NSDAR [G.R.C./S2/v. 1]

Wetherell Cemetery (1781)
Lothrop and Prospect Sts.
+ [G.R. 27] *Vital Records of Taunton, Massachusetts to the year 1850* (1928).
+ NEHGS [Mss/SG/HOD/6/60]

White Cemetery (1841)
34 South St., opposite Railroad Ave.
+ NSDAR [G.R.C./S1/v. 417.5]

Williams–Padelford Cemetery (1814)
between 62 and 78 Seaver St., off Viking St.
+ [G.R. 46] *Vital Records of Taunton, Massachusetts to the year 1850* (1928).

Willis Burying Ground (1850)
28 Worcester St.
+ [G.R. 16] *Vital Records of Taunton, Massachusetts to the year 1850* (1928).

Father Wilson Cemetery (1846)
123 ½ Broadway St.
+ [G.R. 38] *Vital Records of Taunton, Massachusetts to the year 1850* (1928).

Franklin Woodward Burying Ground (1838)
in the woods behind 1396 Norton Ave., between Short St. and Norton, Mass.
+ [G.R. 42] *Vital Records of Taunton, Massachusetts to the year 1850* (1928).

TEMPLETON (1762)
Town Hall, 9 Main St., Baldwinville, Mass. Tel: (508)-939-5678

Baptist Common Cemetery (1795)
Baldwinville and Baptist Common Rds.
+ [G.S. 1] *Vital Records of Templeton, Massachusetts to the year 1850* (1907).
+ Central Mass. Gen. Society, *Cemetery Inscriptions of Baldwinville and Templeton, Mass.*, (1999), p. 7
+ NSDAR [G.R.C./S1/v. 354]

Center Burial Ground (1763)
Rte. 101, Dudley Rd., behind the First Church of Templeton
+ Central Mass. Gen. Society, *Cemetery Inscriptions of Baldwinville and Templeton, Mass.*, (1999), p. 15

Greenlawn Cemetery (1820)
Bridge St., Baldwinville
+ Central Mass. Gen. Society, *Cemetery Inscriptions of Baldwinville and Templeton, Mass.*, (1999), p. 43
+ NEHGS [Mss/A/315], [MS70/BAL/1] and [Mss/A/315].
+ NSDAR [G.R.C./S1/v. 216]

Pine Grove Cemetery (1779)
Rte. 2A
Tel: (508)-939-5678
+ Central Mass. Gen. Society, *Cemetery Inscriptions of Baldwinville and Templeton, Mass.*, (1999), p. 135

Sawyer–Norcross Family Burial Ground (1834)
off Norcross Hill Rd.

Burial on road to Baldwinville
+ [G.S. 2] *Vital Records of Templeton, Massachusetts to the year 1850* (1907).

TEWKSBURY (1734)
from Billerica
Town Hall, 1009 Main St., Tewksbury,
Mass. 01876, Tel: (978)-640-4355

Kendall Road Cemetery
Kendall Rd., near Andover town line.
+ NEHGS [MS70/TEW/2]

Oblate Fathers Cemetery (1895)
486 Chandler St.
Tel: (978)-851-7258

Old Centre Cemetery (18th century)
Lee St.
+ [G.R. 1] *Vital Records of Tewksbury,
Massachusetts to the year 1850* (1903).
+ NEHGS [MS70/TEW/1], and
[MS70/TEW/2]

Pine Hill Cemetery
the end of Indian Hill Rd., off 744
Chandler St.
St. Mary's Cemetery (1830)
90 River Rd., off 910 Andover St. Rte.
133
Tel: (978)-851-2248

South Tewksbury Cemetery
Shawsheen and Main Sts., South
Tewksbury
+ [G.R. 3] *Vital Records of Tewksbury,
Massachusetts to the year 1850* (1903).
+ NEHGS [MS70/TEW/2]

Tewksbury Cemetery
172 East St.
+ [G.R. 2] *Vital Records of Tewksbury,
Massachusetts to the year 1850* (1903).

Tewksbury Hospital Cemetery (1854)
365 East St.
Tel: (978)-851-7321

Northwest Cemetery
+ [G.R. 3] *Vital Records of Tewksbury,
Massachusetts to the year 1850* (1903).

TISBURY (1671)
Town Hall, 51 Spring St., Tisbury, Mass.
02568, Tel: (508)-696-4215

Boston Seaman's Friend Society Cemetery (19th century)
Sailors Burying Ground Rd., Vineyard
Haven

Cemetery near United States Marine Hospital, Vineyard Haven
+ [G.R. 8] *Vital Records of Tisbury,
Massachusetts to the year 1850* (1910).

Company Place Cemetery (aka) South End and Crossways Cemetery (1719)
30 Villa Dr., off Causeway Rd., Vineyard
Haven.
+ [G.R. 6] *Vital Records of Tisbury,
Massachusetts to the year 1850* (1910).

Daggett Family Cemetery (1779)
325 West Spring St., Vineyard Haven.
+ [G.R. 9] *Vital Records of Tisbury,
Massachusetts to the year 1850* (1910).

Holmes Hole Cemetery (aka) West Chop Cemetery (1791)
485 Main St. and Grove Ave.
+ [G.R. 7] *Vital Records of Tisbury,
Massachusetts to the year 1850* (1910).
+ NEHGS [Mss/SL/TIS/1]

Oak Grove Cemetery (1814)
299-303 State Rd., and West Spring St.
+ [G.R. 5] *Vital Records of Tisbury,
Massachusetts to the year 1850* (1910).
+ NEHGS [Mss/SL/TIS/1]

Village Cemetery (aka) Proprietors' Burying Ground (1776)
60 Center St., near Franklin St., behind the Tisbury Town Hall.
+ [G.R. 4] *Vital Records of Tisbury, Massachusetts to the year 1850* (1910).
+ NEHGS [Mss/SL/TIS/3]

TOLLAND (1810)
Town Hall, 241 West Granville Rd., Tolland, Mass. 01034, Tel: (413)-258-4794

Blandford Road Cemetery (1833)
Blandford Rd.

Clark–Marshall Family Cemetery (1836)
Burt Hill Rd.

Granger Family Cemetery (1822)
Rivers Rd.

Rivers Road Cemetery
Rivers Rd.

Tolland Cemetery (1776)
Route 57
+ Charles D. Townsend, *Border Town Cemeteries of Massachusetts.* (West Hartford, Ct., Chedwato Service, 1953)
[F63/T69/1953/also Loan]

Tolland Main Cemetery (1747)
West Granville Rd.

Twining Family Cemetery (1815)
New Boston Rd.

TOPSFIELD (1648)
from Ipswich
Town Hall, 8 West Common St., Topsfield, Mass. 01983, Tel: (978)-887-1505

Boston Street Cemetery (1833)
216 Boston St., near Maple St.

Cummings Burying Ground (1843)
83 Asbury St.

Lake Burying Ground (19th c.)
River Rd. and Prospect St.

Pine Grove Cemetery (1717)
8 Haverhill Rd.
+ [G.R. 1] *Vital Records of Topsfield, Massachusetts to the year 1850* (1903).

South Side Cemetery (1741)
196 Rowley Bridge St.
+ [G.R. 2] *Vital Records of Topsfield, Massachusetts to the year 1850* (1903).

TOWNSEND (1732)
Town Hall, Memorial Hall, 272 Main St., Townsend, Mass. 01469, Tel: (978)-597-1704
Cemetery Department, 29 Highland St., Townsend, Mass. 01469

God's Little Acre (aka) The Old Burial Ground (18th century)
Highland St.
+ NEHGS [Mss/F74/T7/B3]
+ NSDAR [G.R.C./S1/v. 382]

Hillside Cemetery (19th century)
Highland St.
+ NSDAR [G.R.C./S1/v. 382]

Riverside Cemetery (19th century)
Dudley Rd., West Townsend

TRURO (1709)
Town Hall, 24 Town Hall Rd., Truro, Masss. 02666, Tel: (508)-349-3860

Ball Cemetery (1923)
in the woods at the end of Higgins Hollow Rd. (2 burials)

Cobb Family Cemetery (1779)
in the woods off Old County Rd., South Truro (2 burials)

H. Doane Grave Site (1781)
off Savage Rd.

First Congregational Parish Cemetery (1813)
Town Hall Rd.
+ NEHGS [Mss/A/60]
+ NSDAR [G.R.C./S1/v. 303]

Methodist Cemetery (1810)
Bridge and Meetinghouse Rds.

New South Cemetery (1994)
Old County Rd.

Old North Cemetery (aka) First Church of Christ Cemetery (1713)
Rte. 6 and Aldrich Rd., near Provincetown town line.
+ Warren and Kathryn Rich, *Wellfleet, Truro, & Cape Cod Cemetery Inscriptions, Section Four, North Truro Cemetery, North Truro, Massachusetts.* (Wellfleet, Mass.: The Rich Family Assoc., 1971) [F74/W39/R5/v. 5]
+ *The Mayflower Descendant* (vols. 12-14)
+ NEHGS [MS70/TRU/2]
+ NSDAR [G.R.C./S1/v. 353]

Pine Grove Cemetery (1796)
off County Rd., South Truro
+ *Wellfleet, Truro, & Cape Cod Cemetery Inscriptions, Section Seven, Pine Grove Cemetery, South Truro, Massachusetts, with biographical and genealogical notes.* (Wellfleet,

Mass.: Pine Grove Cemetery Assoc., 1983) [F74/W39/R5/v. 7]

Benjamin Rich Family Cemetery (1780)
in the woods off Holsberry Rd. (two burials)

T. Ridley Gravesite (1776)
in the woods off Rte. 6

William and Miriam Rollins Cemetery (1925)
near Pilgrim Lake

Sacred Heart Cemetery (1868)
Bridge and Meetinghouse Rds.

Snow Cemetery (1817)
Bridge Rd.

South Pamet Cemetery
South Pamet Rd.

TYNGSBOROUGH (1789)
from Dunstable
Town Hall, 25 Bryants Ln., Tyngsborough, Mass. 01879, Tel: (978)-649-2300

Drake–Tyng Cemetery (1834)
Middlesex Rd.
+ [G.R. 2] *Vital Records of Tyngsborough, Massachusetts to the year 1850* (1912).
+ [G.R. 6] *Vital Records of Dunstable, Massachusetts to the year 1850* (1913).
+ NEHGS [MS70/TYN/1]

Fletcher Cemetery (1818)
Frost Rd.
+ [G.R. 3] *Vital Records of Tyngsborough, Massachusetts to the year 1850* (1912).
+ [G.R. 9] *Vital Records of Dunstable, Massachusetts to the year 1850* (1913).
+ NEHGS [MS70/TYN/1]

Flint's Corner Cemetery (1867)
Westford Rd.
+ [G.R. 5] *Vital Records of Tyngsborough, Massachusetts to the year 1850* (1912).
+ NEHGS [MS70/TYN/1], and [MS70/TYN/2]

Gould Burial Grounds (1750)
Norris Rd.
+ [G.R. 6] *Vital Records of Tyngsborough, Massachusetts to the year 1850* (1912).
+ [G.R. 10] *Vital Records of Dunstable, Massachusetts to the year 1850* (1913).
+ NEHGS [MS70/TYN/1], and [MS70/TYN/2]

Sherburne Cemetery (1822)
Sherburne Ave., East Tyngsborough
Tel: (978)-251-3197
+ [G.R. 4] *Vital Records of Tyngsborough, Massachusetts to the year 1850* (1912).
+ [G.R. 8] *Vital Records of Dunstable, Massachusetts to the year 1850* (1913).
+ NEHGS [MS70/TYN/1], and [MS70/TYN/2]

Thompson Cemetery (1757)
Old Kendall Rd.
+ [G.R. 1] *Vital Records of Tyngsborough, Massachusetts to the year 1850* (1912).
+ [G.R. 7] *Vital Records of Dunstable, Massachusetts to the year 1850* (1913).
+ NEHGS [MS70/TYN/1], and [MS70/TYN/2]

Tyng Family Cemetery
80 Tyng Rd.

Tyngsboro Memorial Cemetery (1965)
Fletcher Dr.

TYRINGHAM (1762)
Town Hall, 116 Main St., Tyringham, Mass. 01264, Tel: (413)-243-1749

Sgt. Solomon Heath Gravesite (aka) Small Pox Cemetery
Town Center opposite Jerusalem Rd.
+ NSDAR [G.R.C./S1/v.72]

McLennan-Titus Cemetery
off Fenn Rd. on Round Mountain

Paper Mill Cemetery (1784)
Main Rd., near Webster Rd.
+ Cynthia Tryon Hoogs, *Cemetery Inscriptions, Tyringham, Massachusetts.* (Great Barrington, Mass.: Cythia T. Hoogs, 1985) [F74/T98/H6/1985]
+ NSDAR [G.R.C./S1/v.72]

Powder Mill Cemetery (1821)
off George Canon Rd.

Shaker Cemetery (1791)
Jerusalem Rd.

Village Center Cemetery (1802)
Church Rd.
+ Cynthia Tryon Hoogs, *Cemetery Inscriptions, Tyringham, Massachusetts.* (Great Barrington, Mass.: Cythia T. Hoogs, 1985) [F74/T98/H6/1985]
+ NEHGS [MS70/TYR/20]
+ NSDAR [G.R.C./S1/v. 368]

UPTON (1735)
from Hopkinton, Mendon, Sutton and Uxbridge
Town Hall, One Main St., Upton, Mass. 01568, Tel: (508)-529-3565

Bradish Cemetery (aka) Old North Cemetery (1776)
128 Westborough Rd.
+ Susan F. Salisbury, *Southern Massachusetts Cemetery Collection* - Volume 1 (Bowie, Md., Heritage Books, 1995) [F63/S25/1995/also Loan]

Lakeview Cemetery (1849)
45 North Main St., across from Pine
Grove Cemetery
+ Susan F. Salisbury, *Southern
Massachusetts Cemetery Collection* - Volume
1 (Bowie, Md., Heritage Books, 1995)
[F63/S25/1995/also Loan]

Maplewood Cemetery (1865)
Maple Ave.
+ Susan F. Salisbury, *Southern
Massachusetts Cemetery Collection*, Volume 1
(Bowie, Md., Heritage Books, 1995)
[F63/S25/1995/also Loan]

Old First Church Cemetery (1735)
106 Grove St.
+ NEHGS [MS70/UPT/1]

Pine Grove Cemetery (1756)
46 North Main St., across from
Lakeview Cemetery

Daniel Wood Cemetery (1793) (two gravestones)
South and Chestnut Sts.
+ Susan F. Salisbury, *Southern
Massachusetts Cemetery Collection*, Volume 1.
1995

UXBRIDGE (1727)
from Mendon
Town Hall, 21 South Main St., Uxbridge,
Mass. 01569, Tel: (508)-278-8608

Albee Cemetery (1818)
160 Albee Rd.
+ [G.R. 24] *Vital Records of Uxbridge,
Massachusetts to the year 1850* (1916).
+ Susan F. Salisbury, *Southern
Massachusetts Cemetery Collection* - Volume
1 (Bowie, Md., Heritage Books, 1995)
[F63/S25/1995/also Loan]

Aldrich Cemetery (1827)
748 West St.

+ [G.R. 10] *Vital Records of Uxbridge,
Massachusetts to the year 1850* (1916).
+ Susan F. Salisbury, *Southern
Massachusetts Cemetery Collection* - Volume
1 (Bowie, Md., Heritage Books, 1995)
[F63/S25/1995/also Loan]
+ NEHGS [MS70/MIL/762]

Aldrich–Buxton Cemetery
971 Quaker Highway

George Aldrich Cemetery
22 Glendale Rd.
+ [G.R. 16] *Vital Records of Uxbridge,
Massachusetts to the year 1850* (1916).

Almshouse Cemetery
80 Almshouse Rd.

Bassett Cemetery
172 Rockmeadow Rd.
+ [G.R. 4] *Vital Records of Uxbridge,
Massachusetts to the year 1850* (1916).

Buffum Family Cemetery (1827)
115 Buffum Rd., near Douglas line.
+ [G.R. 25] *Vital Records of Uxbridge,
Massachusetts to the year 1850* (1916).
+ Susan F. Salisbury, *Southern
Massachusetts Cemetery Collection* , Volume 1
(Bowie, Md., Heritage Books, 1995)
[F63/S25/1995/also Loan]
Baalis Bullard Cemetery
347 West River Rd.

Chestnut Street Cemetery [field stone markers]
500 Chestnut St.

Cook Cemetery
220 Quaker Highway
+ [G.R. 7] *Vital Records of Uxbridge,
Massachusetts to the year 1850* (1916).

Daniels Cemetery (1810)
224 Henry St.
+ [G.R. 3] *Vital Records of Uxbridge,
Massachusetts to the year 1850* (1916).

+ Susan F. Salisbury, *Southern Massachusetts Cemetery Collection* - Volume 1 (Bowie, Md., Heritage Books, 1995) [F63/S25/1995/also Loan]

Darling Repose Cemetery (1833)
rear of Millville Rd., East Uxbridge
+ [G.R. 5] *Vital Records of Uxbridge, Massachusetts to the year 1850* (1916).
+ NEHGS [MS70/MIL/762]

DeWolfe Cemetery
30 Erickson St.
+ [G.R. 18] *Vital Records of Uxbridge, Massachusetts to the year 1850* (1916).

Royal Farnum Cemetery
20 Albee Rd.

Friends Quaker Cemetery (1749)
Quaker Meeting House
Rte. 146, 500 Quaker Highway
+ [G.R. 21] *Vital Records of Uxbridge, Massachusetts to the year 1850* (1916).
+ Susan F. Salisbury, *Southern Massachusetts Cemetery Collection* - Volume 1 (Bowie, Md., Heritage Books, 1995) [F63/S25/1995/also Loan]

Gary Lane Cemetery
[field stone markers]
27 Gary Ln.

Gifford Cemetery (1799)
620 Quaker Highway
+ [G.R. 22] *Vital Records of Uxbridge, Massachusetts to the year 1850* (1916).
+ NEHGS [MS70/MIL/762]

Stephen Holbrook Cemetery
52 Albee Rd.

King Street Cemetery
195 King St.

Morse Cemetery
382 Elmwood St., South Uxbridge

+ [G.R. 17] *Vital Records of Uxbridge, Massachusetts to the year 1850* (1916).

A. Mowry Tomb
672 Hartford Ave.

Gideon Mowry Cemetery
92 Glendale Rd., South Uxbridge
+ [G.R. 15] *Vital Records of Uxbridge, Massachusetts to the year 1850* (1916).

Norden–Swedish Cemetery (1833)
Rte. 122, 994 Millville Rd.
+ [G.R. 6] *Vital Records of Uxbridge, Massachusetts to the year 1850* (1916).
+ Susan F. Salisbury, *Southern Massachusetts Cemetery Collection* - Volume 1 (Bowie, Md., Heritage Books, 1995) [F63/S25/1995/also Loan]
+ NEHGS [MS70/MIL/762]

Old Burying Ground Site (1737)
site of Uxbridge Town Hall. All burials were moved to Prospect Hill Cemetery
+ NEHGS [MS70/UXB/1]

Prospect Hill Cemetery (1737)
Rte. 16, 35 Mendon St.
+ [G.R. 1] *Vital Records of Uxbridge, Massachusetts to the year 1850* (1916).
+ Susan F. Salisbury, *Southern Massachusetts Cemetery Collection* - Volume 1 (Bowie, Md., Heritage Books, 1995) [F63/S25/1995/also Loan]
+ NEHGS [MS70/UXB/1]

Providence Street Cemetery (1828)
Providence St.
[Aldrich and Southwick families]
+ Susan F. Salisbury, *Southern Massachusetts Cemetery Collection* - Volume 1 (Bowie, Md., Heritage Books, 1995) [F63/S25/1995/also Loan]

Quaker City Cemetery
50 Providence St.
+ [G.R. 23] *Vital Records of Uxbridge, Massachusetts to the year 1850* (1916).

Richardson Cemetery (1837)
175 South St.
+ [G.R. 19] *Vital Records of Uxbridge,*
Massachusetts to the year 1850 (1916).
+ Susan F. Salisbury, *Southern*
Massachusetts Cemetery Collection, Volume 1
(Bowie, Md., Heritage Books, 1995)
[F63/S25/1995/also Loan]

Joseph Richardson Cemetery
195 King St.
+ [G.R. 14] *Vital Records of Uxbridge,*
Massachusetts to the year 1850 (1916).

Hannah Seagrave Cemetery
266 West St.

St. Mary's Catholic Cemetery
88 Granite St.
Tel: (508)-278-6592
+ [G.R. 2] *Vital Records of Uxbridge,*
Massachusetts to the year 1850 (1916).

Shove Family Cemetery (1847)
555 Chocolog Rd.
+ [G.R. 11] *Vital Records of Uxbridge,*
Massachusetts to the year 1850 (1916).
+ Susan F. Salisbury, *Southern*
Massachusetts Cemetery Collection, Volume 1
(Bowie, Md., Heritage Books, 1995)
[F63/S25/1995/also Loan]

David Southwick Cemetery
255 Chocolog Rd.
+ [G.R. 20] *Vital Records of Uxbridge,*
Massachusetts to the year 1850 (1916).

Royal Taft Family Cemetery (1810)
35 Johnson Rd.
+ [G.R. 12] *Vital Records of Uxbridge,*
Massachusetts to the year 1850 (1916).
+ Susan F. Salisbury, *Southern*
Massachusetts Cemetery Collection - Volume
1 (Bowie, Md., Heritage Books, 1995)
[F63/S25/1995/also Loan]

Tiffany Cemetery
50 Buffum Rd.

+ [G.R. 9] *Vital Records of Uxbridge,*
Massachusetts to the year 1850 (1916).

Tucker Cemetery
560 West St.
+ [G.R. 8] *Vital Records of Uxbridge,*
Massachusetts to the year 1850 (1916).

White Cemetery
992 Aldrich St.
+ [G.R. 13] *Vital Records of Uxbridge,*
Massachusetts to the year 1850 (1916).

WAKEFIELD (1812)
from Reading
Town Hall, One Lafayette St., Wakefield,
Mass. 01880, Tel: (781)-246-6384

Adath Israel Cemetery
(a section of the Temple Israel
Cemetery)

Amos Lodge # 27 B'Nai Brith
(a section of the Temple Israel
Cemetery)

B'nai Israel Cemetery
(a section of the Temple Israel
Cemetery)

Forest Glade Cemetery (1898)
454 Lowell St.
Tel: (617)-246-6313

Lakeside Cemetery (1847)
near 507 North Ave. and Beacon St.
Tel: 781-246-2256
+ [G.R. 2] *Vital Records of Wakefield,*
Massachusetts to the year 1850 (1903).

Lynn Hebrew Benevolent (a section of the Temple Israel Cemetery)

Old Burial Ground (1688)
Church St.

+ [G.R. 1] *Vital Records of Wakefield, Massachusetts to the year 1850* (1903).
+ Lilley Eaton, "Inscriptions, from the most Ancient Burial Ground, in South Reading, Ms." *NEHGR* 7:25-27.
+ NSDAR [G.R.C./S1/v. 95]

Temple Emanuel Cemetery
(a section of the Temple Israel Cemetery)

Temple Israel Cemetery (1860)
North Ave.

WALES (1762)
from Brimfield
Town Hall, 3 Hollow Rd., Wales, Mass. 01081, Tel: (413)-245-7571

Hessian Cemetery
Peck Rd.

Houghton's Farm Family Cemetery (1829)
Holland Rd.
+ NEHGS [Corbin Collection]

Number 1 Cemetery (1763)
Union Rd.
+ NEHGS [MS70/WAL/1] and [Corbin Collection]
+ NSDAR [G.R.C./S1/v. 66, 107, 297]

Number 2 Cemetery (aka) Old Baptist Cemetery (1823)
Main St.
+ NEHGS [MS70/WAL/2], and [Corbin Collection].

Number 3 Cemetery (aka) Laurel Hill Cemetery (1826)
Laurel Hill Rd., Shawville
+ NEHGS [MS70/WAL/3], [MS70/WAL/18], and [Corbin Collection]

Number 4 Cemetery (aka) South Laurel Hill Cemetery (1883)
Laurel Hill Rd.
+ NEHGS [MS70/WAL/3], [MS70/WAL/18], and [Corbin Collection]

Walker Burying Ground (1816)
Peck Rd.

WALPOLE (1724)
from Dedham
Town Hall, 135 School St., Walpole, Mass. 02081, Tel: (508)-660-7296
Cemetery Department, 135 School St., Walpole, Mass. 02081, (508)-660-7354

Abigail (Hartshorne) Smith Tomb(1784)
1385 Washington St.

Blake Family Cemetery (1789)
South St., located within the Walpole Town Forest

East Walpole Cemetery (1730)
Pleasant St.

Guild Family Cemetery (1793)
Old Post Rd.

Maple Grove Cemetery (1817)
Kendall St.

Morse Cemetery (18th century)
Norfolk and West Sts.

Old Burial Place (1718)
Main and Kendall Sts.
+ NEHGS [MS70/WAL/10]

Plains Cemetery (1741)
Kingsbury St., West Walpole
+ NEHGS [Mss/SL/WAL/2]

Terrace Hill Cemetery (1775)
South and Washington Sts.

Walpole Rural Cemetery (1843)
Pemberton St.

WALTHAM (1738)
from Watertown
City Hall, 610 Main St., Waltham, Mass.
02452, Tel: (781)-893-4040

Beth Israel Memorial Park
South St.
Tel: Jewish Cemetery Association, 1320
Centre St., Newton Center, Mass. (617)-
244-6509

Calvary Cemetery (1850)
250 High Street
Tel: (781)-893-5646

**Grove Hill Cemetery (aka) Old
Burial Ground (1703)**
290 Main St.
Tel: Mount Feake Cemetery, (617)-893-
1680
+ [G.R.] *Vital Records of Warren,
Massachusetts to the year 1850* (1910).
+ J. B. Bright, "Waltham Grave-Yard"
NEHGR 5:249 -50.
+ NSDAR [G.R.C./S1/v. 110]

**Metropolitan State Hospital
Cemetery (1930)**
475 Trapelo Rd.

Mount Feake Cemetery (1857)
203 Prospect St.
Tel: (617)-893-1680

WARE (1761)
Town Hall, 126 Main St., Ware, Mass.
01082, Tel: (413)-967-4471

Aspen Grove Cemetery (1852)
95 Pleasant St.
+ NEHGS [Corbin Collection]

East Church Cemetery
Church St.
+ NEHGS [Corbin Collection]

**East Congregational Church
Cemetery (1826)**
Park St.
+ NEHGS [Corbin Collection]

Holy Cross Cemetery (1929)
West Main St.
Tel: Holy Cross Rectory, 61 Maple St.,
Ware, Mass. (413)-967-5233
Mt. Carmel Cemetery
Greenwich Rd.
Tel: Mount Carmel Rectory, 17 Convent
Hill Rd., Ware, Mass. (413)-967-5704

Quabbin Park Cemetery (1750)
Rte. 9
Tel: Quabbin Visitor's Center, 485 Ware
Rd., Belchertown, Mass. (413)-323-7221
Containing burials from the following
cemeteries: Packardville Cemetery (1787-
1938) Enfield; Packardville Church
Cemetery (1859-1938) Enfield; Pelham
Hollow Cemetery (1778-1938) Prescott.
+ NEHGS [MS70/WAR/15]
+ NSDAR [G.R.C./S1/v. 143]

St. Mary's Cemetery
60 South St.
Tel: (413)-967-5913

**Old and New St. William's
Cemetery (1851)**
West St.
Tel: (413)-967-4963

Ware Center Burial Ground (1751)
Greenwich Plains Rd
+ NEHGS [Corbin Collection]

West Cemetery
Ware Center

West Street Burial Ground (1786)
West St.

WAREHAM (1739)
from Rochester
Town Hall, 54 Marion Rd., Wareham,
Mass. 02571, Tel: (508)-291-3140
Cemetery Department, 95 Charge Pond
Rd., Tel: (508)-295-5300

Agawam Neck Cemetery (1685)
Great Neck Rd., and R.D. Stillman
Memorial Dr.
+ Charles M. Thatcher, *Old Cemeteries of
Southeastern Massachusetts*. (Middleborough,
Mass., Middleborough Public
Library,1995) [F63/T53/1995/also Loan]
+ NEHGS [Mss/SG/LIN/5/27],
[Mss/SG/LIN/5/25], and index
[Mss/SG/LIN/5/26].

**Briggs Lane Cemetery (aka) Pierce
Mill Cemetery**
Briggs Ln.
+ NEHGS [Mss/SG/LIN/5/27],
NEHGS [Mss/SG/LIN/5/25], and
index [Mss/SG/LIN/5/26].

**Center Cemetery (aka) Parker Mills
Cemetery (1810)**
Tihonet Rd.
+ Charles M. Thatcher, *Old Cemeteries of
Southeastern Massachusetts*. (Middleborough,
Mass., Middleborough Public Library,
1995) [F63/T53/1995/also Loan]
+ NEHGS [Mss/SG/LIN/5/28],
[Mss/SG/LIN/5/25], and index
[Mss/SG/LIN/5/26]

Long Neck Cemetery (1823)
Long Neck Rd., off Onset Ave.
+ Charles M. Thatcher, *Old Cemeteries of
Southeastern Massachusetts*. (Middleborough,

Mass., Middleborough Public Library,
1995) [F63/T53/1995/also Loan]
+ NEHGS [Mss/SG/LIN/5/27],
[Mss/SG/LIN/5/25], and index
[Mss/SG/LIN/5/26]

Nickerson Family Cemetery (1835)
Red Brook
+ NEHGS [Mss/SL/LIN/5/25]

Packard Family Cemetery (1852)
Red Brook
+ NEHGS [Mss/SL/LIN/5/25]

St. Patrick's Cemetery
Tel: St. Patricks Rectory, 82 High St.,
Wareham, Mass. (508)-295-2411
+ NEHGS [Mss/SG/LIN/5/28],
[Mss/SG/LIN/5/25],
[Mss/SG/LIN/5/25], and index
[Mss/SG/LIN/5/26].

**Tobey–Fearing–Bliss Burial Ground
(1819)**
Main St.
+ Charles M. Thatcher, *Old Cemeteries of
Southeastern Massachusetts*. (Middleborough,
Mass., Middleborough Public Library,
1995) [F63/T53/1995/also Loan]
+ NEHGS [Mss/SG/LIN/5/25]

WARREN (1742)
from Brimfield and Brookfield
Town Hall, 48 High St., Warren, Mass.
01083, Tel: (413)-436-5702

**Baker Cemetery (aka) South Warren
Cemetery**
+ [G.R. 1] *Vital Records of Warren,
Massachusetts to the year 1850* (1910).
+ NEHGS [Mss/SL/WAR/5], and
[Corbin Collection, *see Brimfield, Mass.*]

Hodges Corner Cemetery (ca. 1787)
Southbridge Rd.
+ NEHGS [Mss/SL/WAR/5]

Pine Grove Cemetery (1746)
Maple St.
+ [G.R. 1] *Vital Records of Warren,*
Massachusetts to the year 1850 (1910).
+ NEHGS [Mss/SL/WAR/5]

St. Paul's Cemetery (1877)
Maple St.

WARWICK (1763)
Town Hall, 12 Athol Rd., Warwick,
Mass. 01378, Tel: (978)-544-8304

Warwick Center Cemetery (1762)
Orange Rd., Rte. 78

Cemetery near Kelton Farm
near Royalston, Massachusetts town line
+ NEHGS [Mss/C/3042]

General Cemetery Reference for
Warwick:
+ NSDAR : Peter Puget Chapter D.A.R.,
Cemetery inscriptions of Warwick, Franklin County,
Massachusetts to 1865. (Edmonds, Wa.)

WASHINGTON (1777)
Town Hall, 8 Summit Hill Rd.,
Washington, Mass. 01223, Tel: (413)-
623-8878

Chapel Road Cemetery (aka) City
Cemetery (1811)
West Branch Rd.
+ NEHGS [MS70/WAS/1]
+ NSDAR [G.R.C./S1/v.94]

Kent Cemetery (1848)
Ryan Rd.

Stonehouse Cemetery (1798)
Stone House Rd.

Town Hall Cemetery (1776)
Washington Mountain Rd.

WATERTOWN (1630)
Town Hall, 149 Main St., Watertown,
Mass. 02472, Tel: (617)-972-6486
Cemetery Department, 124 Orchard St.,
Watertown, Mass. 02472 Tel: (617)-972-
6420

Arlington Street Cemetery
Mout Auburn and Arlington Sts.

Common Street Burial Ground
(aka) Village Cemetery (1754)
Mount Auburn and Common Sts.
+ NEHGS [MS70/WAT/1],
[MS/WAT/2], and [Mss/SL/WAT/15]
+ NSDAR [G.R.C./S1/v. 48]

Mount Auburn Catholic Cemetery
(1850)
580 Mt. Auburn St.
Tel: (781)-893-5646
Archives of the Archdiocese of Boston,
2121 Commonwealth Ave., Brighton,
Mass. 02135, (617)-254-0100.The Boston
Archdiocese Archives has burial records
1854-1882, and grave lot sales 1854-
1858.
+ Marie E. Daly, *Gravestone Inscriptions*
from Mount Auburn Catholic Cemetery
Watertown. (Waltham, Mass.: Marie E.
Daly, 1983) [F74/W33/D35/1983/also
Loan]
+ NSDAR [MASS. COUNTIES/
MIDDLESEX/WATERTOWN]

Old Burying Place (1642)
Mount Auburn and Arlington Sts.
+ William Thaddeus Harris,
+ NEHGS [MS70/WAT/1]

Ridgelawn Cemetery (1902)
191 Highland Ave., near Stuart St.
+ NEHGS [F74/W33/D2] Typescript
in Mss
+ NSDAR [G.R.C./S1/v. 142]

St. Patricks Cemetery (1893)
Belmont and Lexington Sts.
Tel: (781)-893-5646

WAYLAND (1780)
from Sudbury
Town Hall, 41 Cochituate Rd., Wayland,
Mass. 01778, Tel: (508)-358-3631

Lakeview Cemetery (1871)
Commonwealth Rd., Rte. 30
+ [G.R. 3] *Vital Records of Wayland,*
Massachusetts to the year 1850 (1910).
+ NEHGS [Mss/SL/WAY/5]

North Cemetery (1643)
Old Sudbury Rd., Rte. 27
+ [G.R. 1] *Vital Records of Wayland,*
Massachusetts to the year 1850 (1910).
+ NEHGS [MS70/WAY/1], and
[Mss/SL/WAY/512]
St. Zepherins Cemetery
Mitchell St.

South Cemetery
Rte. 27
+ [G.R. 2] *Vital Records of Wayland,*
Massachusetts to the year 1850 (1910).

Draper Family Cemetery
located within North Cemetery
+ [G.R. 4] *Vital Records of Wayland,*
Massachusetts to the year 1850 (1910).
+ NEHGS [Mss/SL/WAY/512]

WEBSTER (1832)
from Dudley and Oxford
Town Hall, Main St., Webster, Mass.
01570, Tel: (508)-949-3850

Lakeside Cemetery
Lower Gore St.

Mount Zion Cemetery (18th century)
Rte. 12 Worcester Rd.

Sacred Heart Cemetery
Worcester Rd.
Tel: Sacred Heart Rectory, 18 E. Main
St., Webster, Mass. (508)-943-3140

St. Anthony's Cemetery
Worcester Rd.
Tel: Catholic Diocese Cemetery Office,
260 Cambridge St., Worcester, Mass.
(508)-757-7415

St. Joseph's Polish Cemetery
Worcester Rd.
Tel: St. Joseph's Rectory, Whitcomb St.,
Webster, Mass. (508)-943-0467

Webster–Dudley Cemetery
East Webster
+ [G.S. 7] *Vital Records of Dudley,*
Massachusetts to the year 1850 (1908).

WELLESLEY (1881)
from Needham
Town Hall, 525 Washington St.,
Wellesley, Mass. 02482, Tel: (781)-431-
1019.

St. Mary's Cemetery
Hunnewell St.
Tel : (781)-235-1841

Woodlawn Cemetery (1882)
148 Brook St.
Tel: (781)-235-7133
+ [GSW2]*Vital Records of Needham, Mass.*
1711-1845 (1997)
+ George Kuhn Clarke, *Epitaphs from*
graveyards in Wellesley (formerly West
Needham), North Natick, and Saint Mary's
Churchyard in Newton Lower Falls,
Massachusetts : with genealogical and

biographical notes. (Boston, 1900)
[F74/W38/C55/1900/also Loan]

WELLFLEET(1763)
from Eastham
Town Hall, 300 Main St., Wellfleet,
Mass. 02667, Tel: (508)-349-0301

Chapel of Saint James the Fisherman (1956)
Rte. 6
Tel: Chapel of Saint James the
Fisherman

Duck Creek Cemetery (1740)
Cahoon Hollow Rd., next to Our Lady
of Lourdes Cemetery
+*Wellfleet, Truro, & Cape Cod Cemetery
Inscriptions, Section Nine, Pleasant Hill and
Oak Dale Cemeteries, Wellfleet* (Wellfleet,
Mass.: The Rich Family Assoc., 1986)
[F74/W39/R5/v. 9]
+ *The Mayflower Descendant* (vols. 10-12)

French Catholic Cemetery (1880)
Berrio Farm, Sandpiper Hill Rd.

Lombard Family Cemetery (1859)
Bound Brook Island Rd.

Oak Dale Cemetery (1825)
Gross Hill Rd.
+*Wellfleet, Truro, & Cape Cod Cemetery
Inscriptions, Section Nine, Pleasant Hill and
Oak Dale Cemeteries, Wellfleet* (Wellfleet,
Mass.: The Rich Family Assoc., 1986)
[F74/W39/R5/v. 9]

Our Lady of Lourdes Roman Catholic Cemetery (1899)
Cahoon Hollow Rd.

Pleasant Hill Cemetery (1819)
Gross Hill Rd.
+*Wellfleet, Truro, & Cape Cod Cemetery
Inscriptions, Section Nine, Pleasant Hill and*

Oak Dale Cemeteries, Wellfleet (Wellfleet,
Mass.: The Rich Family Assoc., 1986)
[F74/W39/R5/v. 9]

Chequesset Neck Burial Ground (1716)
Chequesset Neck Rd.

South Wellfleet Cemetery (1822)
State Highway Rte. 6
+Kenneth Cole, *Wellfleet, Truro, & Cape
Cod Cemetery Inscriptions, Section One, South
Wellfleet Cemetery, Wellfleet* (Wellfleet,
Mass.: The Rich Family Assoc., 1986)
[F74/W39/R5/v.9]

Robert Young Cemetery (1799)
Paine Hollow Rd.

WENDELL (1781)
from Shutesbury
Town Hall, 270 Wendell Depot Rd.,
Wendell, Mass., Tel: (978)-544-6682

Lock's Village Cemetery (1900)
Jennison Rd., near Shutesbury town line.

Mormon Hollow Cemetery (1795)
Farley Rd.

Small Pox Cemetery (1833)
Morse Village Rd.

Wendell Center Cemetery (1782)
Center Rd.

South Cemetery
+ NEHGS [Corbin Collection]

WENHAM (1643)
Town Hall, 138 Main St., Wenham,
Mass. 01984, Tel: (978)-468-5520
Cemetery Department, 91 Grapevine
Rd., Wenham, Mass. (978)-468-5530

Fairfield Family Cemetery (1691)
William Fairfield Dr., off Cherry St.
+ [G.R. 2] *Vital Records of Wenham,
Massachusetts to the year 1850* (1903).

Wenham Cemetery (1710)
Main St., Rte. 1A
+ [G.R. 1] *Vital Records of Wenham,
Massachusetts to the year 1850* (1903).

WEST BOYLSTON (1808)
from Boylston, Holden and Sterling
Town Hall, 120 Prescott St., West
Boylston, Mass. 01583, Tel: (508)-835-6240

Beaman Cemetery Site (1757)
Site now in the Wachusett Reservoir,
burials moved to the Mount Vernon
Cemetery in 1901.

St. Luke's Catholic Cemetery (1860's)
near 260 Lancaster St., Rte. 110
Tel: Our Lady of Good Counsel, 111
Worcester St.

High Plain Cemetery (19th c.)
High St., Oakdale
+ [G.R. 3] *Vital Records of West Boylston,
Massachusetts to the year 1850* (1903).

Mount Vernon Cemetery (1750s)
Church and Worcester Sts.
+ [G.R. 2] *Vital Records of West Boylston,
Massachusetts to the year 1850* (1903).
+ Esther K. Whitcomb, *Inscriptions from
burial grounds of the Nashaway towns :
Lancaster, Harvard, Bolton, Leominster,
Sterling, Berlin, West Boylston, and Hudson,
Massachusetts.* (Bowie, Md: Heritage
Books, 1989) [F74/L2/I57/1989/also
Loan]
+ NEHGS [MS70/WES/736]

Town Cemetery (a section of the Mount Vernon Cemetery) (1790's)
+ [G.R. 1] *Vital Records of West Boylston,
Massachusetts to the year 1850* (1903).
+ NEHGS [MS70/WES/736]

WEST BRIDGEWATER (1822)
from Bridgewater
Town Hall, 65 North Main St., West
Bridgewater, Mass. 02379, Tel: (508)-894-1200

Alger Cemetery
Wolf Trap Hill
+ [G.R. 4] *Vital Records of West
Bridgewater, Massachusetts to the year 1850*
(1907).

Ames Family Burying Ground
Cross St.
+ [G.R.5] *Vital Records of West Bridgewater,
Massachusetts to the year 1850* (1907).

Dunbar Family Cemetery (1749)
Walnut St.

Jerusalem Graveyard (1749)
Manley St.
+ [G.R. 3] *Vital Records of West
Bridgewater, Massachusetts to the year 1850*
(1907).

Methodist Church Cemetery (aka) Cochesett Cemetery
Rte. 106
+ [G.R. 7] *Vital Records of West
Bridgewater, Massachusetts to the year 1850*
(1907).
+ NEHGS [MS70/WES/91]

Old Graveyard (1692)
South St.
+ [G.R. 1] *Vital Records of West
Bridgewater, Massachusetts to the year 1850*
(1907).

Pine Hill Cemetery (1870)
North Main St.
Tel: (508)583-5466
+ [G.R. 6] *Vital Records of West Bridgewater, Massachusetts to the year 1850* (1907).
+ NEHGS [MS70/WES/90], and [MS70/WES/91]

Pleasant Hill Cemetery
Cochesett St., Cochesett
+ [G.R. 8] *Vital Records of West Bridgewater, Massachusetts to the year 1850* (1907).
+ NEHGS [MS70/WES/91]

Powder House Cemetery (1747)
Matfield St.
+ [G.R. 2] *Vital Records of West Bridgewater, Massachusetts to the year 1850* (1907).

Walnut Street Cemetery
Walnut St.

WEST BROOKFIELD (1848)
from Brookfield
Town Hall, 2 East Main St., West Brookfield, Mass. 01585, Tel: (508)-867-1415

Barnes Memorial Cemetery (1820)
Wickaboag Valley Rd.

Catholic Cemetery (1873)
West Main St.

Indian Cemetery (1710)
50 Cottage St.

Pine Grove Cemetery (1771)
41 Church St.
+ NEHGS [Mss/SL/WES/8]

Ragged Hill Cemetery (1812)
Lyons Rd.

Sacred Heart Cemetery
Rte. 9
Tel: Catholic Diocese Cemetery Office, 260 Cambridge St., Worcester, Mass. (508)-757-7415
+ NEHGS [MS70/WES/110]

WEST NEWBURY (1819)
from Newbury
Town Hall, 381 Main St., West Newbury, Mass. 01985, Tel: (978)-363-1100

Bridge Street Cemetery (1724)
Bridge St.
+ [G.R. 2] *Vital Records of West Newbury, Massachusetts to the year 1850* (1918).
+ Susan Follansbee, *Cemetery Records of West Newbury, Massachusetts.* (Camden, Me: Picton Press, 1997) [F74/W48/F65/1997]

Crane Neck Hill Cemetery (1747)
Crane Neck Rd.
+ [G.R. 5] *Vital Records of West Newbury, Massachusetts to the year 1850* (1918).
+ NEHGS [MS70/WES/330], and [Mss/C/3044]

Goodridge Farm Cemetery
Indian Hill St.
+ [G.R. 8] *Vital Records of West Newbury, Massachusetts to the year 1850* (1918).

Merrimack Cemetery (1803)
Pleasant St.
+ [G.R. 3] *Vital Records of West Newbury, Massachusetts to the year 1850* (1918).

Quaker Cemetery (1808)
off Turkey Hill Rd.
+ [G.R. 6] *Vital Records of West Newbury, Massachusetts to the year 1850* (1918).
+ NEHGS [Mss/C/4252]

Rural Cemetery (1832)
Chase St.
+ [G.R. 4] *Vital Records of West Newbury, Massachusetts to the year 1850* (1918).

Sawyer Burying Ground
Indian Hill St.
+ [G.R. 7] *Vital Records of West Newbury, Massachusetts to the year 1850* (1918).

Walnut Hill Cemetery (1725)
Bachellor St.
+ [G.R. 1] *Vital Records of West Newbury, Massachusetts to the year 1850* (1918).

West Newbury Graveyard # 2 (1843)
Indian Hill St.

C.W. Ordway Farm Cemetery
on C.W. Ordway Farm
+ [G.R. 9] *Vital Records of West Newbury, Massachusetts to the year 1850* (1918).

WEST SPRINGFIELD (1774)
from Springfield
Town Hall, 26 Central St., West Springfield, Mass. 01089, Tel: (413)-263-3012

Ashleyville Cemetery
Riverdale St., near Ashley Ave.
+ [G.R. 4] *Vital Records of West Springfield, Massachusetts to the year 1850* (1944).
+ NEHGS [Mss/SL/WES/18] and [Corbin Collection]
+ NSDAR [G.R.C./S1/v. 144]

Beth El Cemetery (1912)
near 300 Kings Highway, next to St. Thomas Cemetery
Tel: Temple Beth El, 979 Dickinson St., Springfield, Ma 01108. (413)-733-4149

Beth Israel Cemetery
part of the Beth El Cemetery

B'Nai Jacob Cemetery
part of the Beth El Cemetery

Kodimoh Cemetery
part of the Beth El Cemetery

Meeting House Hill Cemetery (1808)
Elm St, behind Masonic Hall
+ [G.R. 12] *Vital Records of West Springfield, Massachusetts to the year 1850* (1944).
+ NEHGS [Mss/SL/WES/18]
+ NSDAR [G.R.C./S1/v. 144] and [G.R.C./1932/S1/v. 16]

Old Meadow Cemetery (aka) Union Street Cemetery (1711)
Union St.
+ [G.R. 1] *Vital Records of West Springfield, Massachusetts to the year 1850* (1944).
+ NEHGS [MS70/WES/380], and [Corbin Collection]
+ NSDAR [G.R.C./S1/v. 144] and [G.R.C./1932/S1/v. 16]

Park Street Cemetery (19th century)
Park St.
+ [G.R. 3] *Vital Records of West Springfield, Massachusetts to the year 1850* (1944).
+ NEHGS [Mss/SL/WES/18] and [Corbin Collection]
+ NSDAR [G.R.C./S1/v. 144]

Paucautuck Cemetery (aka) Tatham Cemetery (1702)
Sibley Ave., off of Dewey St.
+ [G.R. 2] *Vital Records of West Springfield, Massachusetts to the year 1850* (1944).
+ NEHGS [Corbin Collection]
+ NSDAR [G.R.C./S1/v. 144]

St. Thomas Cemetery
Kings Highway, next to Beth El Cemetery
Tel: St. Thomas Rectory, 47 Pine St., West Springfield, (413)-739-4779

WEST STOCKBRIDGE (1774)
from Stockbridge
Town Hall, 9 Main St., West Stockbridge, Mass. 01266, Tel: (413)-232-0318

Cobb Burial Ground
Cobb Rd.

Slauter Cemetery (aka) South Cemetery and Rockdale Cemetery (1783)
Great Barrington Rd.
+ [G.R. 2] *Vital Records of West Stockbridge, Massachusetts to the year 1850* (1907).
+ NEHGS [MS70/WES/390]

St. Patrick's Catholic Cemetery (1870)
Richmond St.
+ [G.R. 4] *Vital Records of West Stockbridge, Massachusetts to the year 1850* (1907).
+ NEHGS [MS70/WES/390]

Village Cemetery (1792)
Richmond Rd.
+ [G.R. 3] *Vital Records of West Stockbridge, Massachusetts to the year 1850* (1907).
+ NEHGS [MS70/WES/390]

West Center Road Cemetery (1793)
West Center Rd.
+ [G.R. 1] *Vital Records of West Stockbridge, Massachusetts to the year 1850* (1907).
+ NEHGS [MS70/WES/390], [MS70/WES/392]
+ NSDAR [G.R.C./S1/v. 302]

WEST TISBURY (1892)
from Tisbury
Town Hall, 1059 State Rd., West Tisbury, Mass. 02575, Tel: (508)-696-0148

Christiantown Burial Ground (1847)
Christiantown Rd., Indian Hill

Lambert's Cove Road Cemetery (1762)
Lambert's Cove Rd.
+ [G.R. 2] *Vital Records of Tisbury, Massachusetts to the year 1850* (1910).

Middletown–West Tisbury Cemetery (1670)
off State Rd., near South Rd.
+ [G.R. 3] *Vital Records of Tisbury, Massachusetts to the year 1850* (1910).

Mingo Family Burial Ground (1880)
Christiantown Rd., Christiantown

North Tisbury Burial Ground (1809)
State Rd.

Village Cemetery
Franklin and Center Sts.
+ [G.R. 1] *Vital Records of Tisbury, Massachusetts to the year 1850* (1910).

WESTBOROUGH (1717)
from Marlborough
Town Hall, 34 West Main St., Westborough, Mass. 01581, Tel: (508)-366-3020
Cemetery Department, 131 Oak St., Westborough, Mass. 01581, Tel: (508)-366-3070

Midland Cemetery (1812)
57 South St.
+ NEHGS [MS70/WES/50]

Old Burial Ground (aka) Memorial Cemetery (1725)
West Main St.
+ NEHGS [MS70/WES/50]

Pine Grove Cemetery (1844)
106 South St., Rte. 135

St. Luke's Cemetery (19th century)
Hopkinton Rd.
Tel: (508)-366-5502
+ NEHGS [MS70/WES/50]

WESTFIELD (1669)
from Springfield
City Hall, 59 Court St., Westfield, Mass. 01085, Tel: (413)-572-6235
Cemetery Department, 4 Holcomb St., Westfield, Mass. 01085

Middle Farms Cemetery (1790)
Russellville Rd.
+ NEHGS [MS70/WES/201]
+ NSDAR [G.R.C./S1/v. 214]

Mundale Parish Cemetery (1811)
in the woods off Granville Rd.
+ NEHGS [MS70/WES/201]
+ NSDAR [G.R.C./S1/v. 214]

Old Burying Ground (1648)
Mechanic St.
+ NEHGS [MS70/WES/200], [MS70/WES/202], and [Corbin Collection]
+ NSDAR [G.R.C./S1/v. 214]

East Mountain Road Cemetery (aka) Owen District Cemetery (1808)
East Mountain Rd.
+ NSDAR [G.R.C./S1/v. 214]

Pine Hill Cemetery (1780)
Upper Court St., and Western Ave.
Tel: (413)-568-7026

St. John's Lutheran Cemetery
Lock House Rd., and Twiss St.
Tel: St. John's Rectory, 60 Broad St., Westford, Mass. (413)-568-1417

St. Joseph's Polish National Catholic Cemetery
Southampton Rd., Rte. 202
Tel: St. Joseph's Rectory, 44 Prospect St., Springfield, Mass. (413)-734-7013

St. Mary's Cemetery (1862)
30 Bartlett St., Rte. 202
Tel: (413)-568-7775

WESTFORD (1729)
from Chelmsford

Town Hall, 55 Main St., Westford, Mass.01886, Tel: (978)-692-5515
Cemetery Department, 55 Main St., Westford, Mass. Tel: (508)-692-5526

Fairview Cemetery (aka) East Burying Ground and Snow's Cemetery (1702)
Tadmuck and Main Sts.
+ [G.R. 1] *Vital Records of Westford, Massachusetts to the year 1850* (1915).
+ William P. Prescott, *A Register of the dead buried in the East Burying Ground by Levi Snow commencing April 17, 1835.* (Bound Brook, N.J.: William B. Prescott, 1985) [F74/W69/S66/1985]
+ NEHGS [MS70/WES/220]

Hillside Cemetery (aka) North Burying Ground and Nutting Cemetery (1753)
Nutting Rd. and Depot St.
+ [G.R. 3] *Vital Records of Westford, Massachusetts to the year 1850* (1915).

Old Pioneer Burying Ground Site
Old Lowell and Carlisle Rds.

Russian Brotherhood Cemetery (1918)
Patten Rd.

St. Catherine's Cemetery
Pine Ridge Rd.

Westlawn Cemetery (aka) West Burying Ground and Day's Cemetery (1761).
Rte. 225 Concord and Country Rds.
+ [G.R. 2] *Vital Records of Westford, Massachusetts to the year 1850* (1915).

Wright Family Cemetery (19th century)
Rte. 40, Groton Rd.
+ [G.R. 4] *Vital Records of Westford, Massachusetts to the year 1850* (1915).

WESTHAMPTON (1778)
from Northampton
Town Hall, One South Rd., Westhampton, Mass. 01027, Tel: (413)-527-0463

Damon Family Cemetery
Northwest Rd.

Theophilus Edwards Family Tomb Site
all burials moved to Westhampton Center Cemetery.
+ NSDAR [G.R.C./S1/v. 322]

Kingsley Cemetery Site (1780)
all burials moved in 1866 to Westhampton Center Cemetery.
+ NSDAR [G.R.C./S1/v. 322]

Westhampton Center Cemetery (1791)
Cemetery Rd.
Tel: (413)-527-5252
+ NEHGS [Corbin Collection]
+ NSDAR [G.R.C./S1/v. 322]

WESTMINSTER (1759)
Town Hall, 3 Bacon St., Westminster, Mass. 01473, Tel: (978)-874-7406
Cemetery Dept., 9 Narrows Rd., Westminster, Mass. 01473, Tel: (978)-874-7415

Mount Pleasant Cemetery (1803)
Knower and Ellis Rds.
+ [G.R. 2] *Vital Records of Winchendon, Massachusetts to the year 1850* (1909).
+ NEHGS [Mss/SL/WES/9], and [MS70/WES/310].

Old Cemetery
near Westminster Common, Dawley Rd.
+ [G.R. 1] *Vital Records of Westminster, Massachusetts to the year 1850* (1908).
+ NEHGS [Mss/SL/WES/9]

Whitmanville Cemetery (1828)
across from 228 South Ashburnham Rd.
+ [G.R. 3] *Vital Records of Winchendon, Massachusetts to the year 1850* (1909).
+ NEHGS [Mss/SL/WES/9]

Woodside Cemetery (aka) Lower Cemetery (1742)
9 Narrows Rd.
+ NSDAR [G.R.C./S1/v. 317]

WESTON (1713)
from Watertown
Town Hall, Town House Rd., Weston, Mass. 02493, Tel: (781)-893-7320

Farmers' Burying Ground (1703)
Colpitts and Boston Post Rd.
+ NEHGS [Mss/SL/WES/20]

Central Cemetery (1792)
Lindwood Ave. and Boston Post Rd.

Linwood Cemetery (1874)
near 190 Boston Post Rd.

South Burying Ground (1791)
South Ave. near Wellesley St.

WESTPORT (1787)
from Dartmouth
Town Hall, 816 Main St., Westport,
Mass. 02790 Tel: (508)-636-1000
Cemetery Department, 947 Main St.,
Westport, Mass. Tel: (508)-634-1025

Allen Family Cemetery (1818)
*"on road from Gifford's Corner to Westport
Point"*
+ [G.R. 14] *Vital Records of Westport,
Massachusetts to the year 1850* (1918).
+ NEHGS [Mss/SL/WES/26]

**James Allen and Abner Wilcox
Cemetery**
South Westport
+ [G.R. 65] *Vital Records of Westport,
Massachusetts to the year 1850* (1918).
+ NEHGS [Mss/SL/WES/26]

Almy Family Cemetery (1782)
Horseneck Rd.
+ [G.R. 53] *Vital Records of Westport,
Massachusetts to the year 1850* (1918).
+ NEHGS [Mss/SL/WES/26]

John R. Baker Gravesite (1882)
Forge Rd.
+ NEHGS [Mss/SL/WES/26]

Beech Grove Cemetery
Main Rd., Central Village
+ [G.R. 1] *Vital Records of Westport,
Massachusetts to the year 1850* (1918).
+ NEHGS [Mss/SL/WES/26]

Peter Borden Gravesite (1845)
Sanford Rd.
+ [G.R. 41] *Vital Records of Westport,
Massachusetts to the year 1850* (1918).
+ NEHGS [Mss/SL/WES/26]

Borden Family Cemetery (1801)
Sanford Rd.
+ [G.R. 44] *Vital Records of Westport,
Massachusetts to the year 1850* (1918).
+ NEHGS [Mss/SL/WES/26]

**Christopher Borden Family
Cemetery (3)**
Sanford Rd.
+ [G.R. 45] *Vital Records of Westport,
Massachusetts to the year 1850* (1918).
+ NEHGS [Mss/SL/WES/26]

**Maria Brawley Family Gravesite
(1836)**
Gifford Rd.
+ [G.R. 56] *Vital Records of Westport,
Massachusetts to the year 1850* (1918).
+ NEHGS [Mss/SL/WES/26]

**Gardner Brightman Family
Cemetery (1834)**
Horseneck Rd.
+ [G.R. 52] *Vital Records of Westport,
Massachusetts to the year 1850* (1918).
+ NEHGS [Mss/SL/WES/26]

Henry Brightman Cemetery (1827)
Cornell Town Rd.
+ [G.R. 32] *Vital Records of Westport,
Massachusetts to the year 1850* (1918).
+ NEHGS [Mss/SL/WES/26]

Brownell Family Cemetery
"on road from Central Village to Adamsville"
+ [G.R. 16] *Vital Records of Westport,
Massachusetts to the year 1850* (1918).
+ NEHGS [Mss/SL/WES/26]

Brownell Family Cemetery (1740)
near Westport Harbor
+ [G.R. 30] *Vital Records of Westport,
Massachusetts to the year 1850* (1918).
+ NEHGS [Mss/SL/WES/26]

Ezekiel Brownell Cemetery
Brownell's Corner

+ [G.R. 8] *Vital Records of Westport,
Massachusetts to the year 1850* (1918).
+ NEHGS [Mss/SL/WES/26]

George Cook Brownell Cemetery (1848)
Old County Rd.
+ [G.R. 39] *Vital Records of Westport,
Massachusetts to the year 1850* (1918).
+ NEHGS [Mss/SL/WES/26]

Centre Friends Cemetery
Gifford's Corner
+ [G.R. 6] *Vital Records of Westport,
Massachusetts to the year 1850* (1918).

Cory Family Cemetery (1801)
Cornell Town Rd.
+ [G.R. 31] *Vital Records of Westport,
Massachusetts to the year 1850* (1918).
+ NEHGS [Mss/SL/WES/26]

Davis Family Cemetery
Cornell Town Rd.
+ [G.R. 33 *Vital Records of Westport,
Massachusetts to the year 1850* (1918).
+ NEHGS [Mss/SL/WES/26]

Davis Family Cemetery (1787)
Davis Rd.
+ [G.R. 47] *Vital Records of Westport,
Massachusetts to the year 1850* (1918).
+ NEHGS [Mss/SL/WES/26]

Alice Dennis Gravesite (1834)
Gifford Rd.
+ [G.R. 54] *Vital Records of Westport,
Massachusetts to the year 1850* (1918).
+ NEHGS [Mss/SL/WES/26]

Elizabeth Devall Gravesite (1838)
Sodom Rd.
+ [G.R. 26] *Vital Records of Westport,
Massachusetts to the year 1850* (1918).
+ NEHGS [Mss/SL/WES/26]

Daniel Devol Family Cemetery (1844)
Sodom Rd.
+ [G.R. 25] *Vital Records of Westport,
Massachusetts to the year 1850* (1918).
+ NEHGS [Mss/SL/WES/26]

Elisha Francis Family Cemetery (1839)
Sanford Rd.
+ [G.R. 42] *Vital Records of Westport,
Massachusetts to the year 1850* (1918).

Friends Cemetery
Central Village
+ [G.R. 5] *Vital Records of Westport,
Massachusetts to the year 1850* (1918).

Hannah Gammons Gravesite (1848)
"from Handy's Corner to Head of Westport"
+ [G.R. 19] *Vital Records of Westport,
Massachusetts to the year 1850* (1918).
+ NEHGS [Mss/SL/WES/26]

William H. Gifford Cemetery (1819)
Blossom Rd., North Westport
+ [G.R. 49] *Vital Records of Westport,
Massachusetts to the year 1850* (1918).
+ NEHGS [Mss/SL/WES/26]

Gifford and Richmond Cemetery (1815)
+ [G.R. 11] *Vital Records of Westport,
Massachusetts to the year 1850* (1918).
+ NEHGS [Mss/SL/WES/26]

Gifford, White and Cornell Family Cemetery (1794)
South Westport
+ [G.R. 22] *Vital Records of Westport,
Massachusetts to the year 1850* (1918).
+ NEHGS [Mss/SL/WES/26]

Green and Allen Family Cemetery (1847)
Drift Rd.

+ [G.R. 20] *Vital Records of Westport, Massachusetts to the year 1850* (1918).
+ NEHGS [Mss/SL/WES/26]

Samuel Hart Gravesite (1848)
"*on road from Handy's Corner to Head of Westport*"
+ [G.R. 59] *Vital Records of Westport, Massachusetts to the year 1850* (1918).

Hicks Family Cemetery (1798)
"*on road from Gifford's Corner to Westport Point*"
+ [G.R. 35] *Vital Records of Westport, Massachusetts to the year 1850* (1918).
+ NEHGS [Mss/SL/WES/26]

Naomi Howard Family Cemetery (1836)
Old County Rd.
+ [G.R. 57] *Vital Records of Westport, Massachusetts to the year 1850* (1918).
+ NEHGS [Mss/SL/WES/26]

Howland Family Cemetery (1838)
"*from Handy's Corner to Head of Westport*"
+ [G.R. 18] *Vital Records of Westport, Massachusetts to the year 1850* (1918).
+ NEHGS [Mss/SL/WES/26]

Howland Family Cemetery (1838)
Old County Rd.
+ [G.R. 38] *Vital Records of Westport, Massachusetts to the year 1850* (1918).
+ NEHGS [Mss/SL/WES/26]

Silas Kirby Cemetery (1798)
Drift Rd.
+ [G.R. 21] *Vital Records of Westport, Massachusetts to the year 1850* (1918).
+ NEHGS [Mss/SL/WES/26]

Kirby Family Cemetery (1851)
Kirby's Corner
+ [G.R. 13] *Vital Records of Westport, Massachusetts to the year 1850* (1918).
+ NEHGS [Mss/SL/WES/26]

Kirby Family Cemetery (1836)
"*from Drift Road to Main Road*"
+ [G.R. 17] *Vital Records of Westport, Massachusetts to the year 1850* (1918).
+ NEHGS [Mss/SL/WES/26]

Lawton Cemetery
Old County Rd.
+ [G.R. 9] *Vital Records of Westport, Massachusetts to the year 1850* (1918).
+ NEHGS [Mss/SL/WES/26]

Linden Grove Cemetery
"*Head of Westport*"
+ [G.R. 2] *Vital Records of Westport, Massachusetts to the year 1850* (1918).
+ NEHGS [Mss/SL/WES/26]

Lyon Family Cemetery
"*on road from Handy's Corner to Head of Westport*"
+ [G.R. 10] *Vital Records of Westport, Massachusetts to the year 1850* (1918).
+ NEHGS [Mss/SL/WES/26]

Noah Macomber Gravesite (1848)
North Westport
+ [G.R. 46] *Vital Records of Westport, Massachusetts to the year 1850* (1918).
+ NEHGS [Mss/SL/WES/26]

Maple Grove Cemetery
Reed Rd., Head of Westport
+ [G.R. 3] *Vital Records of Westport, Massachusetts to the year 1850* (1918).
+ NEHGS [Mss/SL/WES/26]

Milk, Walk and Brightman Family Cemetery (1814)
"*on road from Handy's Corner to Head of Westport*"
+ [G.R. 63] *Vital Records of Westport, Massachusetts to the year 1850* (1918).
+ NEHGS [Mss/SL/WES/26]

John Mosher Gravesite (1839)
Sodom Rd.
+ [G.R. 24] *Vital Records of Westport, Massachusetts to the year 1850* (1918).
+ NEHGS [Mss/SL/WES/26]

Potter Family Cemetery (1827)
Sodom Rd.
+ [G.R. 28] *Vital Records of Westport, Massachusetts to the year 1850* (1918).
+ NEHGS [Mss/SL/WES/26]

Records Family Cemetery (1811)
Westport Harbor
+ [G.R. 29] *Vital Records of Westport, Massachusetts to the year 1850* (1918).
+ NEHGS [Mss/SL/WES/26]

Reynolds Family Cemetery (1868)
Gifford Rd.
+ [G.R. 55] *Vital Records of Westport, Massachusetts to the year 1850* (1918).
+ NEHGS [Mss/SL/WES/26]

Thaddeus Reynolds Gravesite (1842)
Old County Rd.
+ [G.R. 58] *Vital Records of Westport, Massachusetts to the year 1850* (1918).

David Sanford Family Cemetery (1809)
Sanford Rd.
+ [G.R. 43] *Vital Records of Westport, Massachusetts to the year 1850* (1918).
+ NEHGS [Mss/SL/WES/26]

J. L. Sherman Cemetery (1821)
"on road from Gifford's Corner"
+ [G.R. 34] *Vital Records of Westport, Massachusetts to the year 1850* (1918).
+ NEHGS [Mss/SL/WES/26]

Wilson Sherman Cemetery
Blossom Rd., North Westport
+ [G.R. 50] *Vital Records of Westport, Massachusetts to the year 1850* (1918).
+ NEHGS [Mss/SL/WES/26]

Sisson Cemetery
Pinehill Rd.
+ [G.R. 23] *Vital Records of Westport, Massachusetts to the year 1850* (1918).

David Sisson Family Cemetery (1818)
Pinehill Rd.
+ [G.R. 23] *Vital Records of Westport, Massachusetts to the year 1850* (1918).
+ NEHGS [Mss/SL/WES/26]

Ruhamahy Sowle Gravesite (1771)
"on road from Gifford's Corner to Westport Point"
+ [G.R. 36] *Vital Records of Westport, Massachusetts to the year 1850* (1918).
+ NEHGS [Mss/SL/WES/26]

Tripp Family Cemetery (1803)
Drift Rd.
+ [G.R. 37] *Vital Records of Westport, Massachusetts to the year 1850* (1918).
+ NEHGS [Mss/SL/WES/26]

Tripp and Booth Burying Ground
Brownell's Corner
+ [G.R. 7] *Vital Records of Westport, Massachusetts to the year 1850* (1918).
+ NEHGS [Mss/SL/WES/26]

Tripp Family Cemetery (1785)
"on road from Central Village to Adamsville"
+ [G.R. 15] *Vital Records of Westport, Massachusetts to the year 1850* (1918).
+ NEHGS [Mss/SL/WES/26]

Tripp Family Cemetery (1832)
"on road from Handy's Corner to Head of Westport"
+ [G.R. 61] *Vital Records of Westport, Massachusetts to the year 1850* (1918).
+ NEHGS [Mss/SL/WES/26]

Tripp and Sisson Family Cemetery (1838)
"on road from Handy's Corner to Head of Westport"

+ [G.R. 60] *Vital Records of Westport,
Massachusetts to the year 1850* (1918).
+ NEHGS [Mss/SL/WES/26]

Westport Point Cemetery
Main Rd.
+ [G.R. 4] *Vital Records of Westport,
Massachusetts to the year 1850* (1918).
+ NEHGS [Mss/SL/WES/26]

Elizabeth White Gravesite (1827)
Charlotte White Rd.
+ [G.R. 64] *Vital Records of Westport,
Massachusetts to the year 1850* (1918).
+ NEHGS [Mss/SL/WES/26]

Mary White Gravesite (1835)
*"on road from Handy's Corner to Head of
Westport"*
+ [G.R. 62] *Vital Records of Westport,
Massachusetts to the year 1850* (1918).
+ NEHGS [Mss/SL/WES/26]

Winde Grove Cemetery
Reed Rd.

George Wing Cemetery
*"on road from Handy's Corner to Head of
Westport"*
+ [G.R. 12] *Vital Records of Westport,
Massachusetts to the year 1850* (1918).
+ NEHGS [Mss/SL/WES/26]

Hannah Wood Gravesite (1843)
Sodom Rd.
+ [G.R. 27] *Vital Records of Westport,
Massachusetts to the year 1850* (1918).
+ NEHGS [Mss/SL/WES/26]

Wood and King Family Cemetery
Horseneck Rd.
+ [G.R. 51] *Vital Records of Westport,
Massachusetts to the year 1850* (1918).
+ NEHGS [Mss/SL/WES/26]

Rufus E. Wordell Cemetery (1809)
North Westport
+ [G.R. 48] *Vital Records of Westport,
Massachusetts to the year 1850* (1918).
+ NEHGS [Mss/SL/WES/26]

WESTWOOD (1897)
from Dedham
Town Hall, 580 High St., Westwood,
Mass. 02090, Tel: (781)-326-3964
Cemetery Department, 580 High St.,
Westwood, Mass. 02090.,Tel: (617)-326-
8661

New Westwood Cemetery (1979)
High St., across from Westwood
Cemetery.

Westwood Cemetery (1752)
Nahatan St., at the intersection of High
and Pond Sts.

WEYMOUTH (1635)
Town Hall, 75 Middle St., Weymouth,
Mass. 02189, Tel: (781)-335-2000

Ashwood Cemetery Cemetery (1819)
Broad and Front Sts., Weymouth
Landing
+ [G.R. 5] *Vital Records of Weymouth,
Massachusetts to the year 1850* (1910).
+ NEHGS [MS70/WEY/1], and
[Mss/SL/WEY/2]

East Weymouth Cemetery (aka)
Old Burying Ground (1795)
Pleasant St. near Lambert Ave., East
Weymouth
+ [G.R. 11] *Vital Records of Weymouth,
Massachusetts to the year 1850* (1910).
+ NEHGS [MS70/WEY/1], and
[Mss/SL/WEY/2]

Elmwood Cemetery (1756)

580 Union St., South Weymouth, near the Rockland town line.
Tel: (617)-331-2459
+ [G.R. 6] *Vital Records of Weymouth, Massachusetts to the year 1850* (1910).
+ NEHGS [MS70/WEY/1], and [Mss/SL/WEY/2]

Fairmount Cemetery (1795)

1436 Pleasant Street, East Weymouth
Tel : (781)-335-3223
+ [G.R. 10] *Vital Records of Weymouth, Massachusetts to the year 1850* (1910).
+ NEHGS [MS70/WEY/1], and [Mss/SL/WEY/2]

Highland Cemetery (1751)

901 Main St., South Weymouth
Tel: (781)-331-2459
+ [G.R. 1] *Vital Records of Weymouth, Massachusetts to the year 1850* (1910).
+ NEHGS [MS70/WEY/1], and [Mss/SL/WEY/2]

Lakeview Cemetery (1751)

335 Pond St., South Weymouth
Tel: (781)-335-0911
+ [G.R. 9] *Vital Records of Weymouth, Massachusetts to the year 1850* (1910).
+ NEHGS [MS70/WEY/1], and [Mss/SL/WEY/2]

Martin Burying Ground

South Weymouth
+ [G.R. 13] *Vital Records of Weymouth, Massachusetts to the year 1850* (1910).
+ NEHGS [Mss/SL/WEY/2]

Mount Hope Cemetery (1799)

Main St., South Weymouth
+ [G.R. 8] *Vital Records of Weymouth, Massachusetts to the year 1850* (1910).
+ NEHGS [MS70/WEY/1], and [Mss/SL/WEY/2]

Old Burying Ground (1730)

Pleasant St., South Weymouth

+ [G.R. 12] *Vital Records of Weymouth, Massachusetts to the year 1850* (1910).
+ NEHGS [MS70/WEY/1], and [Mss/SL/WEY/2]

Old Cemetery (1811)

Randolph St., South Weymouth
+ [G.R. 7] *Vital Records of Weymouth, Massachusetts to the year 1850* (1910).
+ NEHGS [MS70/WEY/1], [Mss/SL/WEY/2], and [MS70/SOU/430]

Old North Cemetery (1676)

North St., North Weymouth
+ [G.R. 14] *Vital Records of Weymouth, Massachusetts to the year 1850* (1910).
+ John J. Loud, "Epitaphs from the older half 'Burying Hill,' Weymouth, Mass."
NEHGR 23:118-20, 292-4, 423-5.
+ NEHGS [MS70/WEY/1], and [Mss/SL/WEY/2]

Reed Cemetery (1769)

550 Front St., South Weymouth
+ [G.R. 3] *Vital Records of Weymouth, Massachusetts to the year 1850* (1910).
+ NEHGS [MS70/WEY/1], and [Mss/SL/WEY/2]

St. Francis Xavier Cemetery (1850)

726 Washington St.
Tel: (781)-337-3144

Village Cemetery (1840)

Front and Washington Sts.
Tel: (781)-337-4799
+ [G.R. 2] *Vital Records of Weymouth, Massachusetts to the year 1850* (1910).
+ NEHGS [MS70/WEY/1], and [Mss/SL/WEY/2]

Wessagusset Colony Tomb Site (1622)

43 Bicknell Rd.
+ Jack Frost and G. S. Lord, *Two Forts ... to Destiny.* (North Scituate, Mass.:

Hawthorne Press, 1972) p. 75-76.
[F74/P8/F76/1972]

White Family Cemetery (1760)
off Summer St., South Weymouth
+ [G.R. 4] *Vital Records of Weymouth,*
Massachusetts to the year 1850 (1910).
+ NEHGS [MS70/WEY/1], and
[Mss/SL/WEY/2]

WHATELY (1771)
from Hatfield.
Town Hall, 218 Chestnut Plain Rd.,
Whately, Mass. 01093, Tel: (413)-665-
9560

Center Cemetery (aka) Central
Cemetery (1762)
215 Chestnut Plain Rd.
+ NEHGS [Corbin Collection]

Eastern Whately Cemetery (aka)
Hope Hill Cemetery (1772)
202 Christian Ln.
+ NEHGS [Corbin Collection]

Holy Ghost Ukranian Cemetery
(1920)
373 Long Plain Rd.

Western Whately Cemetery (1776)
122 Webber Rd.
+ NEHGS [Corbin Collection]

WHITMAN (1875)
from Abington and East
Bridgewater
Town Hall, 54 South Ave., Whitman,
Mass. 02382, Tel: (781)-447-7607
Cemetery Department, 100 Essex St.,
Whitman, Mass. 02382 (781)-447-7630

Colebrook Cemetery (1849)
45 Essex St., and Park Ave.

Tel: (781)-447-5117
+ [G.R. 13] *Vital Records of Abington,*
Massachusetts to the year 1850 (1912).
+ NEHGS [MS70/ABI/3], and
[Mss/A/352]

Hersey Children's Burying Ground
behind 685 Washington St.

High Street Cemetery (aka) Noyes
Family Burying Ground (1805)
behind 182 High St., across from
Hutchinson Terr.
+ [G.R. 10] *Vital Records of Abington,*
Massachusetts to the year 1850 (1912).
+ NEHGS [MS70/ABI/3] and
[Mss/A/352]

Jenkins Family Burying Ground
Pleasant St.

Mount Zion Cemetery (1740)
next to 751 Washington St.
Tel: Holy Ghost Church Rectory, 518
Washington St., Whitman (781)-447-
7630
+ [G.R. 12] *Vital Records of Abington,*
Massachusetts to the year 1850 (1912).
+ [G.R. 14] *Vital Records of Abington,*
Massachusetts to the year 1850 (1912).
+ NEHGS [MS70/ABI/3],
[Mss/A/352], and [Mss/SL/WHI/11]

St. James Cemetery
across from 491 Harvard St., near
Auburn St.
Tel: Holy Ghost Rectory, 518
Washington St., Whitman (781)-447-
7630

Small Pox House Cemetery Site
(1778)
Franklin St., at the site of the Whitman-
Hanson School
+ [G.R. 11] *Vital Records of Abington,*
Massachusetts to the year 1850 (1912).
+ NEHGS [MS70/ABI/3] and
[Mss/A/352]

Amos Whitmarsh Cemetery
+ NEHGS [MS70/ABI/3]

WILBRAHAM (1763)
from Springfield.
Town Hall, 240 Springfield St.,
Wilbraham, Mass. 01095, Tel: (413)-
596-2809
Cemetery Department, 240 Springfield
St., Wilbraham, Mass. 01095.

Adams Cemetery (1741)
Tinkham Rd., near Main St.

**East Wilbraham Cemetery (aka)
Butler Hill Cemetery (1779)**
Boston Rd., Rte. 20 near the Palmer
town line.
+ NEHGS [Corbin Collection]

Glendale Cemetery (1787)
Glendale and Monson Rds.

Woodland Dell Cemetery (1851)
Woodland Dell St., off of Main St.
+ NEHGS [Corbin Collection]

WILLIAMSBURG (1771)
from Hatfield
Town Hall, 141 Main St., Williamsburg,
Mass. 01039, Tel: (413)-268-8402

Haydenville Cemetery (1826)
High St.
+ NEHGS [Corbin Collection]

High Street Cemetery
5 High St., Haydenville

Mountain Street Cemetery
Mountain St.
+ NEHGS [Corbin Collection]

**Williamsburg Center Cemetery
(aka) Old Cemetery (aka) Village
Hill Cemetery (1771)**
Village Hill Rd.
+ NEHGS [Corbin Collection]

WILLIAMSTOWN (1765)
Town Hall, 31 North St., Williamstown,
Mass. 01267, Tel: (413)-458-9341
Cemetery Department, 31 North St.,
Williamstown, Mass. Tel: (413)-458-8657

**Bacon Cemetery (aka) Hopper
Road Cemetery (1825)**
Hopper Rd.
+ [G.R. 5] *Vital Records of Williamstown,
Massachusetts to the year 1850* (1907).
+ NEHGS [Mss/V/4173]

Comstock Cemetery (1796)
off Rte. 43, South Williamstown
+ [G.R. 6] *Vital Records of Williamstown,
Massachusetts to the year 1850* (1907).
+ NEHGS [Mss/V/4173]

**Eastlawn Cemetery (aka)
Williamstown Cemetery (1820)**
605 East Main St.
Tel: (413)-458-8657
+ [G.R. 3] *Vital Records of Williamstown,
Massachusetts to the year 1850* (1907).
+ NEHGS [Mss/V/4173]

Moon Family Burying Ground
off Bulkeley St.Hopkins Memorial Forest
[marked by field stones]

Oak Hill Burying Ground
+ [G.R. 4] *Vital Records of Williamstown,
Massachusetts to the year 1850* (1907).
+ NEHGS [Mss/V/4173]

**Southlawn Cemetery (aka) South
Williamstown Cemetery (1777)**
New Ashford Rd.

+ [G.R. 8] *Vital Records of Williamstown, Massachusetts to the year 1850* (1907).
+ Rollin H. Cooke Collection [F72/B5/B473 (roll - 3)] microfilm at N.E.H.G.S.
+ NEHGS [Mss/V/4173]

Sweet Burying Ground (1813)
Hancock Rd., near Hancock town line.
+ [G.R. 7] *Vital Records of Williamstown, Massachusetts to the year 1850* (1907).
+ NEHGS [Mss/V/4173]

Westlawn Cemetery (aka) West Williamstown Cemetery (1762)
West Main St.

Williams College Cemetery (1833)
Lynde Ln.
+ [G.R. 2] *Vital Records of Williamstown, Massachusetts to the year 1850* (1907).
+ NEHGS [Mss/V/4173]

WILMINGTON (1730)
from Reading
Town Hall, 121 Glen Rd., Wilmington, Mass. 01887, Tel: (978)-658-2030

Old Burial Ground (1731)
Middlesex Ave., across from Wildwood Cemetery
+ NEHGS [MS70/WIL/60]
+ NSDAR [G.R.C./S1/v. 60]

Wildwood Cemetery (1857)
Wildwood St and Middlesex Ave., across from the Old Burial Ground.
Tel: (978)-658-3901

WINCHENDON (1764)
Town Hall, 109 Front St., Winchendon, Mass. 01475, Tel: (978)-297-2766
Cemetery Department, 109 Front St., Winchendon, Mass. Tel: (978)-297-0170

Calvary Cemetery (1871)
Glenallan St., across from Riverside Cemetery
Tel: Immaculate Heart of Mary Rectory, 525 Spruce St., Winchendon, Mass. (508)-297-0280

Lucy May Gravesite (1844)
near the Massachusetts state border.
+ NEHGS [Mss/SL/WIN/4]

Massachusetts Veteran's Cemtery (2002)
Glenallen St.
Tel: (413)-821-9500
contact Agawan Veteran's Cemetery

New Boston Cemetery (1791)
Beaman Pond and Baldwinville Rds.
+ [G.R. 2] *Vital Records of Winchendon, Massachusetts to the year 1850* (1909).
+ NEHGS [Mss/SL/WIN/4]
+ NSDAR [G.R.C./S1/v. 354]

Old Centre Cemetery (1755)
Hall Rd., and High St.
+ [G.R. 1] *Vital Records of Winchendon, Massachusetts to the year 1850* (1909).
+ NEHGS [Mss/SL/WIN/4]

Riverside Cemetery (1858)
Glenallan St., across from Calvary Cemetery.
+ [G.R. 3] *Vital Records of Winchendon, Massachusetts to the year 1850* (1909).
+ NEHGS [Mss/SL/WIN/4]

WINCHESTER (1850)
from Medford, Woburn.
Town Hall, 71 Mt. Vernon St., Winchester, Mass. 01890, Tel: (781)-721-7130

Calvary Cemetery
686 Washington St., a section is located in Woburn, Mass.

Tel: Catholic Diocese Cemetery Office, 260 Cambridge St., Worcester, Mass. (508)-757-7415

Wildwood Cemetery (1805)
34 Palmer St.
Tel: (781)-721-7142
+ [G.R. 1] *Vital Records of Windsor, Massachusetts to the year 1850* (1910).

WINDSOR (1771)
Town Hall, 3 Hinsdale Rd., Windsor, Mass. 01270, Tel: (413)-684-3977

Bush Cemetery (1795)
Windego Rd.
+ [G.R. 2] *Vital Records of Windsor, Massachusetts to the year 1850* (1917).
+ NEHGS [MS70/WIN/32], and [F74/W86/A87] Typescript Mss
+ NSDAR [G.R.C./S1/v. 135]

East Windsor Cemetery (1863)
Westfield Rd.
+ [G.R. 4] *Vital Records of Windsor, Massachusetts to the year 1850* (1917).
+ NEHGS [F74/W86/A87] Typescript Mss
+ NSDAR [G.R.C./S1/v. 135]

Samuel Eddy Family Cemetery (1796)
Savoy Hollow Rd.
+ NEHGS [F74/W86/A87] Typescript Mss

Shaw Cemetery (1790)
Shaw Rd.
+ [G.R. 4] *Vital Records of Windsor, Massachusetts to the year 1850* (1917).
+ NEHGS [F74/W86/A87] Typescript Mss
+ NSDAR [G.R.C./S1/v. 135]

Windsor Center Cemetery (1774)
Rte 8A, Windsor Hill

+ [G.R. 1] *Vital Records of Windsor, Massachusetts to the year 1850* (1917).
+ NEHGS [F74/W86/A87] Typescript Mss
+ NSDAR [G.R.C./S1/v. 135]

WINTHROP (1846)
from Chelsea and Woburn.
Town Hall, One Metcalf Sq., Winthrop, Mass. 02152, Tel: (617)-846-1742

Belle Isle Section Cemetery (1993)
100 Kennedy Rd.
Tel: (617)-846-0610

Cross Street Section Cemetery (1940)
Cross St.
Tel: Belle Isle Section Cemetery (617)-846-0610

New Cemetery (aka) Middle Cemetery (1919)
River Rd., across from Winthrop Cemetery
Tel: Belle Isle Section Cemetery (617)-846-0610

Winthrop Cemetery (1835)
Bowdoin St.
Tel: Belle Isle Section Cemetery (617)-846-0610

WOBURN (1642)
City Hall, 10 Common St., Woburn, Mass. 01801, Tel: (781)-932-4450

Agudath Achim
(a section of the Woburn Jewish Cemetery)

American Austrian
(a section of the Woburn Jewish Cemetery)

Beth David
(a section of the Woburn Jewish
Cemetery)

Beth Jacob
(a section of the Woburn Jewish
Cemetery)

Beth Joseph # 1 thru 3
(sections of the Woburn Jewish
Cemetery)

Calvary Cemetery
Central St.,a section is located in
Winchester, Mass.
Tel: (781)-729-1445

Chevra Kadusha of Boston
(a section of the Woburn Jewish
Cemetery)

Chevra Mishnias–Agudas Achim
(a section of the Woburn Jewish
Cemetery)

Congregation Anshe Lebovitz
(sections of the Woburn Jewish
Cemetery)

Congregation Anshe Poland
(a section of the Woburn Jewish
Cemetery)

First Burial Ground (1642)
Park St., across from the Baptist Church

Independent Golden Crown
(a section of the Woburn Jewish
Cemetery)

Independent Pride of Boston
(a section of the Woburn Jewish
Cemetery)

Kenesseth Israel
(a section of the Woburn Jewish
Cemetery)

Meretz
(a section of the Woburn Jewish
Cemetery)

Montefiore
(a section of the Woburn Jewish
Cemetery)

Pride of Boston
(a section of the Woburn Jewish
Cemetery)

Puritan Cemetery
(a section of the Woburn Jewish
Cemetery)

Roxbury Mutual Cemetery
(a section of the Woburn Jewish
Cemetery)

**Second Burial Ground (aka) First
Parish Cemetery (1789)**
Montvale Ave., behind the Peterson
School

Shari Jerusalem Cemetery
(a section of the Woburn Jewish
Cemetery)

Wall Street Shule Cemetery
(a section of the Woburn Jewish
Cemetery)

Woburn Hebrew Center Cemetery
(a section of the Woburn Jewish
Cemetery)

Woburn Jewish Cemetery
Montvale Ave.
Tel: Jewish Cemetery Association, 1320
Centre St., Newton Center, Mass. (617)-
244-6509

Woodbrook Cemetery (1845)
100 Salem St.
Tel: (781)-937-8297

+ *Manual of Woburn Cemetery containing lists of the lots and their owners arranged numerically and alphabetically, with the by-laws, town votes, and other matters relating to the cemetery.* (Woburn, Mass.: Cemetery Committee, 1877) [MS/WOB/3]

WORCESTER (1684)
City Hall, 455 Main St., Worcester, Mass. 01608, Tel: (508)-799-1121

All Faiths Cemetery (aka) New Swedish Cemetery (1885)
7 Island Rd.
Tel: (508)-753-8842

B'Nai Brith Jewish Cemetery
30 Sutton Ln.

Hope Cemetery (1795)
119 Webster St.
Tel: (508)-799-1531
+ NSDAR [G.R.C./S1/v.324]
Revolutionary War soldiers only.

Mechanic Street Burying Ground Site (1795)
Mechanic St., all burial were moved to Hope Cemetery.
+ NEHGS [MS70/WOR/3]
+ NEHGS [MS70/WOR/5]

Notre Dame Cemetery (1870)
162 Webster St.
Tel: (508)-753-7692

Old Swedish Cemetery
154 Webster St.
Tel: All Faiths Cemetery, (508)-753-8842

Rural Cemetery and Crematory (1838)
180 Grove St.
Tel: (508)-754-1313

St. John's Cemetery (1847)
260 Cambridge St.
Tel: (508)757-7415

Worcester Common Cemetery (1717)
Worcester Common
+ NSDAR: William Sumner Barton, *Epitaphs from the cemetery on Worcester Common, with occasional notes, references, and an index.* (Worcester, 1848).

General Cemetery Reference for Worcester:
+ William Sumner Barton, *Inscriptions from the old burial grounds in Worcester, Massachusetts, from 1727 to 1859 : with biographical and historical notes.* (Worcester, 1878) [F74/W9/W86/1878/also Loan]

WORTHINGTON (1768)
Town Hall, 160 Huntington Rd., Worthington, Mass. 01098, Tel: (413)-238-5578

Adams Cemetery
West St.

Converse Cemetery (1845)
Rte. 112
Huntington Road

Guard–Hazen Cemetery
Guard St.

North Cemetery
Cold St.
+ [G.R. 8] *Vital Records of Worthington, Massachusetts to the year 1850* (1911).

Parker Four Corners Cemetery
West St.

Ringville Cemetery
Witt Hill Rd.
+ [G.R. 2] *Vital Records of Worthington, Massachusetts to the year 1850* (1911).

Worthington Center Cemetery (18th century)
Sam Hill Rd, Worthington Center
+ [G.R. 6] *Vital Records of Worthington, Massachusetts to the year 1850* (1911).

Cemetery near Curtis Place
+ [G.R. 4] *Vital Records of Worthington, Massachusetts to the year 1850* (1911).

Cemetery near Johnson Place
+ [G.R. 3] *Vital Records of Worthington, Massachusetts to the year 1850* (1911).

South Worthington Cemetery
+ [G.R. 1] *Vital Records of Worthington, Massachusetts to the year 1850* (1911).

WRENTHAM (1673)
Town Hall, 79 South St., Wrentham, Mass. 02093, Tel: (508)-384-5415
Cemetery Department, 360 Taunton St., Wrentham, Mass. 02093 Tel: (508)-384-5477

Center Cemetery (1647)
Dedham and East Sts., Rte.1A
+ [G.R. 1] *Vital Records of Wrentham, Massachusetts to the year 1850* (1910).
+ Susan F. Salisbury, *Southern Massachusetts Cemetery Collection*, Volume 2 (Bowie, Md., Heritage Books, 1996) [F63/S25/1995/also Loan]

Cook Cemetery (1784)
West St.
+ Susan F. Salisbury, *Southern Massachusetts Cemetery Collection* - Volume 2 (Bowie, Md., Heritage Books, 1996) [F63/S25/1995/also Loan]

Gerould Cemetery (aka) Great Plain Cemetery (1756)
High and South Sts., Rte 1A
+ [G.R. 2] *Vital Records of Wrentham, Massachusetts to the year 1850* (1910).
+ NEHGS [F74/W95/D2] Typescript Mss

Sheldonville Cemetery (aka) Burnt Swamp Cemetery (1828)
Burnt Swamp Rd. and West St., Rte. 121
+ [G.R. 5] *Vital Records of Wrentham, Massachusetts to the year 1850* (1910).
+ Susan F. Salisbury, *Southern Massachusetts Cemetery Collection*-Volume 2 (Bowie, Md., Heritage Books, 1996) [F63/S25/1995/also Loan]

Trinity Church Burying Ground
47 East St. Rte. 140

West Wrentham Cemetery (1757)
West and Williams Sts.
+ [G.R. 6] *Vital Records of Wrentham, Massachusetts to the year 1850* (1910).
+ NEHGS [Mss/C/1802a-b]

Wrentham State School Cemetery (aka) Louise Johnson Memorial Cemetery (1906)
Emerald St.
Tel: Wrentham Developmental Center, P.O. Box 144, Wrentham, Mass. (508)-384-3116

YARMOUTH (1639)
Town Hall, 1146 Route 28, Yarmouth, Mass. 02664, Tel: (508)-398-2231
Cemetery Department, 161 Old Mill Way, West Yarmouth, Mass. 02673, Tel: (508)-778-6624

Ancient Cemetery (ca. 1639)
Centre St., off Rte. 6A, Yarmouthport
+ George Ernest Bowman, *Gravestone record in the Ancient cemetery and the*

Woodside cemetery, Yarmouth. (Boston, Mass., Thomas Todd, 1906)
[F74/Y2/B68/1906/also Loan]
Bass River Baptist Cemetery (1813)
88 Old Main St., on the grounds of Bass River Community Baptist Church, South Yarmouth
+ NEHGS [MS70/YAR/10]
+ NSDAR [G.R.C./S1/v. 403]

Civil War Graves Site
(no gravestones)
off Union St., near Rte. 6A

Eldredge–Matthews–Taylor Smallpox Cemetery (1796)
North Dennis Rd., Yarmouthport

Georgetown Cemetery (1820)
High Bank Rd., next to Bass River Golf Course, South Yarmouth
+ NEHGS [MS70/YAR/10]
+ NSDAR [G.R.C./S1/v. 403]

Chandler Gray Cemetery (1988)
161 Old Mill Way, at the end of Chandler Gray Rd., West Yarmouth

Gideon Gray Cemetery
near Wild Rose Terr, off Dinah's Pond, South Yarmouth

Methodist Cemetery (1812)
Willow St., South Yarmouth
+ NEHGS [MS70/YAR/10]
+ NSDAR [G.R.C./S1/v. 403]

Pine Grove Cemetery (1820)
29 Station Ave., South Yarmouth

Quaker Cemetery (1811)
58 North Main St., South Yarmouth
+ NEHGS [MS70/SOU/460], and [MS70/YAR/10]
+ NSDAR [G.R.C./S1/v. 403]

Smallpox Cemetery
Bray Farm Rd., off Rte. 6A, Yarmouthport

Smallpox Cemetery (1779)
Weir Rd., off Rte. 6A, Yarmouthport
+ NEHGS [MS70/YAR/10]

Taylor–Hall Smallpox Cemetery (1801)
located at the 13th hold of the Kings Way Golf Course, Rte. 6A, Yarmouthport

Woodside Cemetery (1753)
West Yarmouth Rd. and Rte. 28, West Yarmouth
Tel: (508)-362-3746
+ George E. Bowman, *Gravestone record in the Ancient cemetery and the Woodside cemetery*, Yarmouth. (Boston, Mass., Thomas Todd, 1906)
[F74/Y2/B68/1906/also Loan]
+ NEHGS [MS70/YAR/10]
+ NSDAR [G.R.C./S1/v. 403]

Yarmouth Indian Memorial Stone
Indian Memorial Dr.

CORRIGENDA

AGAWAM (1855)
Massachusetts Veterans' Memorial Cemetery (2001)
1390 Main Street, Agawam, Mass.
Tel: (413)-821-9500

Index

A

Index

Index

Index

Index

Index

Index

Index

D

Daddy Frye's Cemetery, 122
Daggett Family Cemetery, 201
Dalton, 51
Damon Cemetery, 45, 145
Damon Family Cemetery, 218
Dana, 51
Dana Center Cemetery Site, 51
Danforth Cemetery Site, 150
Daniel Bliss Cemetery, 109
Daniel Devol Family Cemetery, 221
Daniel Wood Cemetery, 205
Daniel Woodward Family Cemetery Site, 37
Daniels Cemetery, 122, 205
Daniels Court Cemetery, 3
Danvers, 51
Danvers State Hospital Cemetery, 51
Dark Corner Cemetery, 14
Darling Cemetery, 89
Darling Repose Cemetery, 206
Dartmouth, 53
Davenport Cemetery, 122
David Anthony Cemetery, 182
David Lynde Cemetery, 107
David Pearson Family Gravesite, 107
David Sanford Family Cemetery, 223
David Sisson Family Cemetery, 223
David Southwick Cemetery, 207
David Vicur Cholim Cemetery, 24
Davis Family Cemetery, 221
Davis Family Cemetery (1787), 221
Davis-Luther Riley Cemetery, 192
Davisville Cemetery, 75
Dawes Cemetery, 50
Day Cemetery, 129
Day Street Cemetery Site, 107
Day's Cemetery, 220
Deacon Silas Parmalee Gravesite, 168
Dean Cemetery, 16
Dean-Dillingham Cemetery, 16
Deane Hill Cemetery, 76
Deardon-Perry Cemetery, 182
Dedham, 60
Deer Island Cemetery, 24
Deerfield, 60
Deerfield Village Old Burying Ground, 61

Delano Family Cemetery, 74
Dell Park Cemetery, 133
Deming Family Burial Ground, 175
Deming Family Cemetery, 187
DeMoranville Family Cemetery, 55
Dennis, 61
Dennis Village Cemetery, 62
DeWolfe Cemetery, 206
Dexter B. Bates Cemetery, 175
Dickson Cemetery, 84
Dighton, 63
Dighton Center Burial Ground, 63
Dighton Rock Cemetery Site, 16
Dillingham Cemetery, 32
Dingley Cemetery, 67
Dingley Family Cemetery, 118
Doane Cemetery, 93
Dodge Cemetery, 190
Dodge Island Cemetery, 8
Dodges Row Cemetery, 18
Doe Valley Cemetery, 190
Dolliver Memorial Cemetery, 82
Dorchester Hebrew Helping Hand, 73
Dorchester North Cemetery, 24
Dorchester South Cemetery, 24
Douglas, 64
Douglas Burying Ground, 157
Douglas Center Cemetery, 65
Douglass Yard Cemetery, 102
Douty-Newhall Cemetery, 150
Dover, 65
Dr. Bradford Braley Cemetery, 79
Dr. Edward Dean Cemetery, 70
Dr. Joseph Jacobs Cemetery, 145
Dr. Josiah Burnham Graveyard, 2
Dr. Thomas Ware-Church Cemetery, 64
Dracut, 65
Drake Cemetery, 123, 188
Drake Family Cemetery Site, 187
Drake-Tyng Cemetery, 203
Draper Family Cemetery, 212
Dresser Hill Public Cemetery, 40
Drew Family Plot, 87
Dry Hill Cemetery, 130
Dry Pond Cemetery, 188
Dubois Family Cemetery Site, 173
Duck Creek Cemetery, 213

Index

Index

Index

H

Index

Index

Index

Index

Index

Index

Index

Index

Index

Index

Index

Index

Index

Index

Index

Index

Index

T

Index

Index

Index

Index

Index